THE
ANCESTRAL
QUEST

THE
ANCESTRAL
QUEST

LOVE, GRIEF AND HOPE, THROUGH THE CONFLICT OF
WAR AND ACROSS THE RACIAL DIVIDE

A FAMILY'S JOURNEY OF SURVIVAL FROM ANCIENT CHINA TO THE WEST

F. G. KWONG

The Book Guild Ltd

First published in Great Britain in 2021 by
The Book Guild Ltd
9 Priory Business Park
Wistow Road, Kibworth
Leicestershire, LE8 0RX
Freephone: 0800 999 2982
www.bookguild.co.uk
Email: info@bookguild.co.uk
Twitter: @bookguild

Typeset in 12pt Minion Pro

Printed and bound by CPI Group (UK) Ltd, Croydon, CR0 4YY

ISBN 978 1913208 899

British Library Cataloguing in Publication Data.
A catalogue record for this book is available from the British Library.

For Caroline, Tanya Mayling, Saskia Sui-Lan and
Alexia Mei-Ling; the four graces in my life.

In memory of my father (1898–1979) and my mother (1916-1997),
without whom, this story would have no beginning,
no middle, and no end.

CONTENTS

Part II
1936 – 1952

Part III
1953 – 1960

Part IV
1961 – 1963

Part V
1963 – 1966

Part VI
1966

Part VII
1967 – 1970

AUTHOR'S NOTE

To most outsiders, for decades, the Chinese have been known as the *invisible* people: a term ascribed to them by many observers of international repute, including pre-eminent journalists and writers such as Frena Bloomfield et al. Nothing much is known about this race, regardless of whether they had remained in China itself, or their having settled overseas. Today, they have outstripped in numbers every single being on this planet. Furthermore, they are also the most widely scattered ethnic group on earth settling all over the globe. And yet despite this, they have remained the least-known and least-understood people in the world. Why is this?

Traditionally this community had kept themselves much to themselves. Particularly the Overseas Chinese, of which there are countless millions, running into several generations of descendants. Clandestine and fiercely private, they have remained as an isolated group within a foreign host country. And typical of their forebears, withdrawing largely from the Caucasian society in which they lived, and at the same time, trying their utmost to maintain their unique ethnic identity. They are plagued by legends and superstition, having been immersed in the belief and worship of the ancient spirits of the dead – much of which was controversial. Paradoxically, most members of this community combined these ancient beliefs with integrating modern technology, such as computers in their pursuit of worldly success.

Governed by ancient ritual, filial respect, and piety, along with a strict adherence to their social role in the family and in their wider community, ceremony and ancestral worship played a dominant part in their behaviour which had been ingrained indelibly in their psyche. This pattern of behaviour had been passed on to them from their parents and grandparents – who were arguably once influenced by the teaching of Confucian philosophy along with Taoism. Most classes of Chinese practised this to a greater or lesser extent; whether they came from the upper echelon of society, or from the mass of peasants who for centuries were the dominant group in the indigenous population of China.

It is widely recognised that the Chinese peasantry and their descendants represent one of the largest migrant groups overseas. However, they have remained bound by the thread of their ancestors so that they could continue to be connected to their motherland by duty and obligation, which includes sending money back to their families in perpetuity. This has been laid down by the protocols of clan that had governed family behaviour. However, almost without exception, most parents encouraged their children to study religiously at every stage in their education to achieve goals set by their Western counterparts. But this came at a tragic cost to family harmony, when Eastern and Western culture clashed head-on, as the new generation of the young tried to break away from the diktats and traditions of their parents, with many eloping and marrying non-Chinese against their parents' wishes.

Born in 1898, in Taishan, China, the author's late father, Kwong Chun Ji as the eldest son and head of the family clan, hitherto irrevocably imbued in family duty, became an overseas migrant – like thousands of others, which was typical of that era. And this account in all its revelatory rawness will describe what happened to ordinary Chinese families such as his, when at the age of twenty-two, he was forced to flee semi-feudal China, and, when in 1921, he came to Britain in order to earn money to save his family from starvation and the ramifications of war. And furthermore, what subsequently happened, when he tried to impose his traditional Chinese will on to his children. Rebellion, tragic deaths and recriminations within the family, as well as vendettas by his enemies were commonplace.

The following real-life, human saga is one of obedience, disobedience, and survival; and their resultant effect on the families, both here in the West, and in China because of the seismic fall-out when these two worlds collided. It is a quest for identity, a quest for a homeland and a search for peace and reconciliation.

KWONG (GONG) ANCESTORS

1. Ging Sun Doo, 1679-1739 m (?) (or unmarried with concubine)
2. Ming Jid Doo, 1709–1781, m. Moy Sei, 1712–1791
3. Yip Gee Doo, 1745–1814, m. Chan Sei, 1795–1821 (wife no. 1)
    Yuen Sei, 1775–1843 (wife no. 2)
4. Ying Gwui Doo, 1793–1866, m. Mmn Sei, 1793–1870
5. Wah Oi, 1821–1878, m. Yau Sei, 1821–1857 (wife no. 1)
    Chan Sei, 1825–1908 (wife no. 2)

Offspring

6. Wah Sum, 1841–1901 (unmarried with concubine)
7. Biu Shu, 1843–1906, m. Chan Sei, 1851–1903
8. Kwong Loong Cheung Ham, 1875–1923, m. Fung Ting Sei, 1878–1947
9. Kwong Chun Ji, 1898–1979, m. Chow Mou Lan (Chow Choi Lin), 1916–1997

Descendants

Francis G. Kwong, 1940– (one of ten siblings) m. Caroline Morag
   Stuart, 1940–
Tanya Mayling Charlotte Ying, 1972– m. Simon Andrew Young, 1971–
Saskia Jessie Sui-Lan Young, 2014–
Alexia Sasha Mei-Ling Young, 2014–

NB: *Sei* = wife.

CHOW ANCESTORS

a)   Cao Long Gun (Cao = Chow). Dates of the following: 1600 to 1800?

b)   Cao Long Chu (Spouses?)

c)   Cao Fu Yao

d)   Cao Fu Zhou

e)   Cao Jun Yan, circa 1840 – died? Wife's name not recorded.

f)   Cao Fu Ji, circa 1860 – died? m. Moy Sei

g)   Chow Yuk Yiu, 1882–1923, m. Moy Gwut Kwai, 1883–1981. (Married 1896)

Offspring

1.   Daughter: no name. Sold at birth, but then drowned. 1897.

2.   Daughter: Chow Choi Ching, 1898–1989.

3.   Son: Chow Kit Ngwun,. Sent to Singapore aged twelve to earn a living. Died from illness through exhaustion, 1904-1920.

4.   Son: Chow Kit Kwai. Starvation. Died – walked into the sea. 1907-1937.

5.   Daughter: no name. Given away after birth. Died within a year.

6.   Daughter: Chow Choi Ping, 1912–1999.

7.   Daughter: no name. Given away at birth. Died within a year.

8.   Daughter: Chow Mou Lan (Chow Choi Lin): 1916–1997.

9.   Son: Chow Kit Siang; 1922–2004

(Chow Mou Lan survived by ten children: five sons and five daughters.)

PROLOGUE

"A S ORDINARY MORTALS, WE are not merely the product of the present to be able to say who we are, but a product of the past to enable us to recognise who we once were. And without which, we cannot progress to be the product of the future to determine whom we hope to be."

That is a saying that was once filtered down through the ancestral line via one of my earliest ancestors – my great-great-great-great-great-great-paternal-grandfather, Ming Jid Doo.[1]

Ming Jid Doo was born on the sixth day of the tenth month of 1709 in the Year of the Ox, under the reign of Emperor Hong Hee. He died on the seventeenth day of the third month of 1781 in the Year of the Ox under the reign of Emperor Qin Long. Both Emperors ruled under the Ch'ing Dynasty (also known as Qing), a tumultuous period of change in China from 1644 to 1912.

---

1   Ming Jid Doo (son of Ging Sun Doo 1679-1739) born in 1709, inherited the clan name from his father, born during the 1600s, and in turn from his father before him in the Dynasty of the Ming Emperors. The Ming Dynasty ran from 1368 to 1643, and possibly the clan name of Ming continued back for some time in his ancestors who lived during this period. 'Doo' means 'ancestor'.

In 1921, when my father Kwong Chun[2] Ji left China for the West, there existed four hundred million people in China. Only twenty-five million of them were literate. Ninety-five per cent of the total population were peasants. Both my father and my mother came from that mass of people. Historically, in feudal China they were regarded as the underclass.

China at that time was lurching from one conflict to another, and these decimated the country. Military incursions, sudden population overgrowth, overdependence on a fragile agrarian economy, and natural disasters such as gargantuan floods, led to a catastrophic famine of unprecedented proportions which raged throughout the land and claimed the lives of six million of its peasant population. Following the death in 1916 of President Yuan Shih-K'ai of China's very first republic, tribal factions of warlords,[3] having grabbed power, impotently stood by, and watched the disaster unfold. Not only that, but, having been at the mercy of unscrupulous landowners[4] for the last three centuries (who promised land reforms that never came, and burdened them with heavy taxes collected by provincial mandarins desperate to please the Manchu rulers[5] who held absolute power under the much-despised, much-feared Ch'ing Dynasty), the peasants in the countryside constantly faced starvation.

---

2   'Chun' (meaning 'rare' or 'precious') was the generation name of the children of Kwong Loong Cheung Ham (Kwong Chun Ji's father); e.g. Kwong Chun Ji's first brother was known as Kwong Chun Tin, etc. Clan name of Kwong interchangeable generically with Gong or Kong.

3   Former military cliques of President Yuan Shih-K'ai's army, as well as various renegade factions, grabbed power in different regions in China on the death of Yuan in 1916. More than six million Chinese peasants starved to death during the upheaval of the Warlord Period of 1916–27. Another eight million perished during the Nationalist (Kuomintang) Period of 1927–40, with civil war between the Nationalists and the Communists. During World War II, China was partitioned between these two factions, and formed an uneasy alliance in the war against Japan. In 1946, civil war resumed between them, lasting until 1950. In October 1949, when Mao declared the People's Republic of China, Chiang Kai-shek and his Nationalist supporters were banished to Formosa.

4   For centuries, powerful landowners also owned the peasants on their land during their lifetime, regarding them as chattels. Peasant tenants failing to pay the rent commonly resulted in the landowners taking their wives and daughters in exchange and selling them into slavery.

5   Manchu Emperors ruled on the Imperial Throne from 1644–1912 in the Ch'ing (Qing) Dynasty. (In the South, salt was often used in the form of taxes)

Uprisings and protests by the peasants were quickly and savagely put down by the government militia. The dire situation Chun Ji's family found themselves in at the beginning of the 1920s during the militant grip of the warlords was little different to the years under the previous Manchu Emperors of the Ch'ing Dynasty.

Then, in February 1912, Imperial Rule, which had lasted for over two thousand years, collapsed. The last Emperor of China, Hsian-T'ung – the Boy Emperor P'u-i – was forced to abdicate, giving way to the first Republic of China under the revolutionary Dr Sun Yat-sen, with Yuan Shih-K'ai as President.

As well as dying from disease or being killed during conflicts, thousands died through lack of food, or walked into the sea or the swollen rivers to drown so that their relatives might live. Others were forced to sell or give away their baby daughters to reduce the number of mouths they had to feed. Some, if not all, of these events happened at one time or another to my parents' families.

My father, whom I never really got to know, and much of whose background remained a mystery to me until the last few months of his life, seldom spoke of his life in China. Recently my daughter, Tanya Mayling pressed me about what happened to the family and the clan in old China, and what brought them to the West. I have now tried to piece together the jumble of notes, letters and fading recollections that were left behind by my late mother and father, as well as by the remaining relatives in China and those dotted around the globe.

It is a common fact that we as humans are never curious about our background until we face the autumn of our years. Where did we come from? What shaped our lives? What influenced our character, our attitude, and the way in which we relate to others around us? Nevertheless, one cannot dispute that the influences around us when we are growing up are extremely powerful in moulding and modifying the way we think and behave.

I was born in Liverpool in 1940 and brought up in the West. My thinking, my speech and my dreams are all in the English tongue. For all intents and purposes, I am fully and happily integrated into

Western society, with the natural ease of one of the first generation of descendants from the early Chinese immigrants who settled here. On the face of it, I should be happy and satisfied with the hand of cards that life has dealt me.

But then, why do the questions about certain aspects of my upbringing keep recurring – particularly the unanswered questions about what made my father and my mother tick. And regarding their remote manner – often quite alien to us, it seemed always contradictory in the way they treated us, their children.

And why did my father treat *me* with strange ambivalence, and with extreme diffidence – often bordering on hostility – for most of his life, despite my being the eldest son?

Somehow, as a direct legacy of the tumultuous events that took place in China over the centuries, could the resulting troubles influencing our ancestral thread have in some way rubbed off on the generations through time, and perhaps even affected their offspring living today? For instance, could this rear its ugly head from time to time between father and son, or for that matter between siblings?

This is something I have tried to find out through tracing my ancestors. But, due to the wholesale upheaval and the wanton destruction of many of the genealogical records and ancestral tombs during the Cultural Revolution in 1966, I could only trace one of my earliest paternal, ancestor as far back as 1679; this being Ging Sun Doo, who died in 1739. It has not been shown that he was married, or that he was living with a concubine, but nevertheless, his son, Ming Jid Doo was born in 1709 – the Year of the Ox. Not unnaturally, I am curious to find out what happened to my ancestors before that date during the previous Ming Dynasty (1368–1644)[6] and the dynasties beyond. It is known that many generations were slaughtered, their clans completely wiped out following a misdemeanour by a single member. Could such a tragedy have happened at this point in our history?

---

6   The last of the ruling Ming Emperors was defeated by the Manchus in 1644, subsequently committing suicide. The Manchus then invaded China from the north, thereby sweeping in the beginning of the Ch'ing (Qing) Imperial Dynasty, which lasted until 1912.

Notwithstanding this, let us now just suppose that, if some records, however sparse, still exist, all Chinese could, as their starting point, trace back their ancestry to a forebear living at the time of the First Emperor – the Emperor Qin Shi Huang-di.[7] He established the Qin Dynasty from 221 BC to 227 BC, when he unified the Seven Warring States of China to form the first Imperial Dynasty. He also built the Great Wall to repel the barbarians of the north. During his reign, he strode the Middle Kingdom of China like a colossus. His fame in history became global with the discovery in 1974 of the magnificent and vast army of terracotta soldiers and horse-drawn chariots found guarding his grave near the ancient capital of Xi'an.

Curiously, the First Emperor's own surname was Ying; quite a common name at that time. He was born Ying Zheng. Previously, as the King of Qin, he had declared himself the First Emperor of China and created for himself the title Qin Shi Huang. But, after the dynasty collapsed, with wholesale recriminations, his family all changed their names to Qin to avoid persecution. In old China, the practice of changing one's name was quite common. It was done for different reasons; occasionally on a whim, or to honour a ruling Emperor, or due to a government census. After Qin Shi Huang-di's death in 210 BC, the mighty Han Dynasty (206 BC–220 AD) swept in with a flourish – remarkable for its celebrated expansion of its arts, culture, and military dominance.

Some historians have argued that the First Emperor (also known as the Yellow or Golden Emperor) could legitimately claim to be the father of the Chinese nation. Arguably, as China's first illustrious

---

7 The vast mausoleum of Emperor Qin Shi Huang-di (aka Ying Zheng) located in Xian has not been excavated due to the dangers posed by the vast rivers of mercury set inside the tomb, which was constructed to imitate and to contain a map of the world with the great Yangtze and Yellow Rivers flowing to the sea. Magnificent palaces and scenic towers were erected within to house his entourage of hundreds of officials, servants, scholars etc., together with his vast priceless treasures and artefacts. Scores of concubines were sealed into his tomb alive to provide for him in the afterlife. Immediately following the ceremonial burial of the embalmed body of the Emperor, on his son's instructions his loyal soldiers suddenly and without warning lowered the gate and slammed shut the heavy, leaden door to the tomb, thereby sealing it off from the outside world with the architects and craftsmen still trapped alive within its passageways.

ancestor, he and his generation are thought to have started a vast ethnic group, known as the Han Chinese people who represent over ninety-two per cent of the indigenous population of China: this would include, the family clan of my late father, the Kwongs and that of my late mother, the Chows.

Forty years ago, a wise old man by the name of Master Ho Lung Deng impressed upon me, when I made a brief study of kung fu under his tutelage, that Chinese people, regardless of where in the world we are born, can only claim to have a birth history of real provenance (*Wang Bien*)[8] if, firstly, we can say, when asked by strangers, which family clan we come from. Mine is the **Kwong** or **Gong**,[9] from Taishan, Guangdung,[10] China, despite the fact that I happened to be born in the West.

And, secondly, if we can trace the thread that runs through, and which continues to weave through our lives, and the line of our ancestors. For our progeny to survive through the centuries, the thread must be unbreakable. It is this sustainability and enduring

---

8   The most scathing insult one Chinese can give to another is that they have forgotten their origins – their *Wang Bien*.

9   'Kwong' is interchangeable with 'Gong' or 'Kong' depending on dialect or pronunciation. The Clan name 'Gong' was derived from 'Kwong' when Kwong Chun Ji's father, Kwong Loong Cheung Ham, was born in 1875 during the reign of Emperor Kwong Shui. Commonly, a family name is influenced by the name of the Emperor ruling at that time. When Chun Ji was born in 1898, the Clan name reverted to the ancestral name 'Kwong'.

    The earliest reference to the origin of the surname dates to the time of the First Emperor, Huang-di. There was a court adviser named Gonggong – a fusion of two surnames meaning 'water' and 'dragon'. 'Gong' is the ninety-ninth most prevalent Chinese surname listed in the ancient Song Dynasty text – *Hundred Family Surnames* (960–1279 AD). Gonggong had two sons. One of them settled in the Pearl River Delta in Guangdung Province and reportedly begat the Gong (Kwong) ancestral line, whereas the other and his descendants continued to serve the Royal Throne throughout the dynasties.

    Nonetheless, the ancestral thread still managed to run intact through the line of their forebears and their progeny, regardless of whether it was called 'Ming' in the seventeenth century or 'Kwong', 'Kong' or 'Gong' in the nineteenth century. It is also possible that the clan Kong/Kwong was a strand from an ancient clan known as 'Kuang', who migrated in 220 AD from Central China (modern-day Hunan Province) to the south to settle in Guangdung Province, where they remain today.

10   This province was known as Canton in the old colonial period, in the province of the same name. Its capital city is now known as Guangzhou. Taishan was and still is a sub-province of the province of Canton, with its capital city of Taishan.

strength which has held millions of Chinese together by utilising the power of filial duty by their family clans in modern China; and, arguably, has over the decades driven the Chinese nation to where it is today. Having emerged like a slumbering, ancient mammoth from years of hibernation, China is now starting to exert its economic and political clout as a powerful international force with implications for the rest of the world.

Like it or not, I must admit that the power of the bloodline (like the other family clans of China) is part of the continuum of the tapestry of the past. Its influence, good, bad, or indifferent, which we have inherited in our lives today, cannot be denied. This influence we must recognise is a powerful legacy handed down to us via the ancestral thread, and we would be naive or foolish to ignore it.

There are large gaps in my father's history. For much of our time together he failed to tell me, or perhaps did not want to reveal, certain chapters of it. Perhaps there was a dark family secret: a vital part hidden, for reasons known only to my father when he was alive. But the burning question of why he treated me – his eldest son – with such cold disdain for most of his life, and yet never dared to cut the cord that bound us, is one that I must answer before the end of my own life. I am convinced the reason is hidden somewhere in the annals of my father's past. To find the elusive missing piece of that jigsaw, and to find out *who I am,* what I am, and *what he was* and *why,* I have to go back and search for that link, and for what Master Ho called, in those days long ago, *'a quest for that ancestral thread'.* And this, the following true story, is my father's story.

Francis Gong Shui[11] *Lun Kwong,*
London, England, 2011

---

11 'Shui' (meaning 'favourable' or 'lucky') was the generation forename of the children of Kwong Chun Ji, e.g. Kwong Shui Lun (i.e. Francis Kwong), his sister Eileen (Kwong Shui Dee) et al.

Part I

1921 – 1936

Chapter 1

THE PILGRIMAGE

Dai Dune Chun (Deep Waters Village) Taishan, China, 10ᵗʰ January 2011

I SHALL NEVER FORGET the date. It was the 10ᵗʰ January 2011. I was standing at the foot of a small mountain, several miles east from an obscure rural village called Dai Dune Chun, south of Taishan City in Guangdong Province, China. I had never been to China before. Accompanied by my brother Alan, I had recently travelled there from England. Facing me, enshrouded in patchy mist, was the peak of a mountain where for the past three hundred years my father's ancestors had been buried. Ten miles away in Dai Dune Chun was where my father, Kwong Chun Ji, was born. Similarly, it was where his forebears were born, lived and died. How the villagers, all descendants of the Kwong (Gong) family clan, clad in the traditional white of mourning, managed to walk that distance while bearing their dead aloft, the bodies wrapped in a white shroud[12] covered in white chrysanthemums on bamboo cradles, I shall never know. And that was not all; because then, the burial party had to climb the tortuous path to the pinnacle of the mountain. In keeping with

---

12   Traditionally, some descendants would carry the remains of their deceased in ceremonial jars, or in boxes made of willow or bamboo, after exhuming the bones from a temporary grave; this would be less arduous to transport. Some clans even carried the bones of their ancestors with them from place to place where they settled.

3

Chinese tradition, the dead had to be buried with their heads at the highest point to heaven and their feet pointing downwards to earth to facilitate easier access to the afterlife.

My journey was the fulfilment of a promise I had made to my Aunt Chun Rei (affectionately called 'Joy'), my father's younger sister before she died in 1975; namely that I would visit the ancestral home and resting place of her and my father's ancestors in China. As I stood there in the cool winter breeze, sobered by the solemnity of it, one of the overriding, sad reasons I had embarked upon this pilgrimage came flooding back to me.

My Aunt Chun Rei and I were particularly close, as she was the first and only one of my parents' generation, I could confide in. For instance, in 1970, she was the first member of that generation I told that I had eloped and secretly married a non-Chinese – a wonderful European girl – three years earlier, against my father's wishes. Fearing my father's wrath, she interceded on my behalf.

The tragic last days of my aunt's life were played out in Birkenhead, Merseyside. She was a tiny slip of a woman, only four feet ten inches tall, skinny as a grasshopper, and spoke and crept about as quietly as a dormouse. She had been widowed many years before whilst living in China; indeed, she had returned to the same village as my father and their ancestors, as expected of her, when she was widowed. Her husband was killed in the civil wars that had gripped the country in the mid '30s during the fighting between the Kuomintang Nationalists led by Chiang Kai-shek and Mao Tse-tung's Communists. Thirty years later, she was brought to England to live with my father's family. Tragically, her only child died at birth, and so she doted on her nephews and nieces. At the not-so-ancient age of sixty-one, she felt that, as the children grew up, she felt somewhat lost. On one of the last sunny weeks in September 1975, she went to stay with my father's youngest brother, Chun Tileng and his family on Merseyside. (She has stayed with them before, many years ago when Uncle's children were younger). Aunt Chun Rei loved the sea, and one morning she took herself off to visit

New Brighton, ostensibly to paddle in the water as she had done many times before – not only here, but also back home in China. By dusk as she did not return to Uncle's, the authorities were alerted. Sea and air search with rescue teams were immediately scrambled; but it was too late. A fatal tragedy had taken place. Two days later her tiny body was found off the coast of New Brighton.

The coroner pronounced a verdict of misadventure: Mrs Lum (her married name) had accidentally drowned as this coastline was notorious with the tides coming in fast to unsuspecting visitors and they could easily be cut off. It was particularly treacherous for non-swimmers such as in Aunt's sad and tragic case. Within the confines of my wife and my family, I knew deep down that the coroner's verdict was not completely accurate. I think that Aunt had made a calculated decision to end her earthly life to enable her to join her husband, her father, and his forefathers. In her old-fashioned Chinese mind, this was common at the time and not dishonourable and was a way to avoid being a burden on the rest of the family as she faced old age alone. It had happened many times before in our family over the past two hundred years, and perhaps this tragic death will not be the last.

At my father's deathbed in June 1979 in Staffordshire, England, I had made a silent vow to myself that I would one day, before it was too late, visit his homeland, his ancestral home, the place of his birth – the place of his father and his father before him. Logistics and red tape prevented the traditional ritual of taking his body back to China. In ancient China, you could exhume the bones and take them with you to be reburied in the ancestral graves, or wherever you eventually settled. But this would not be permitted in England.

The date of arriving at my father's house was portentous. It was precisely *ninety years* to that day, on the *10th January 1921,* that my father, as a young man of twenty-two, had left China to seek his fortune in the West. In fact, as the firstborn and the oldest son, he was forced to leave home so that he could save his parents and siblings from starvation. His simple farm dwelling, which had stood for over three hundred years, had been empty for years. The original village of over a thousand inhabitants was now in decline and had been decimated to barely ninety. Only the elderly remained. The young had left in droves for the cities or abroad, many moons ago. Two elderly neighbours (indirect kinsmen, but bearing the same clan name as ours) opened the house for us to visit. This was where my father was born.

As the shutters were drawn, sunlight flooded the simple dwelling. Wafting motes of dust that had just been disturbed danced in the sunbeams like ghosts from the past. A strong smell of old, burnt charcoal from years of wood-burning inside the house pervaded the fabric of the building and clung to our clothes. Standing on the cold stone balcony which opened out via shutters from the front room on the first floor, I took in a deep breath. A deep river, swollen with the winter's rain, swirled in front of the house. The waters meandered through fields of swamp-filled marshlands, before making their way eventually to the sea some twenty miles away to the south. In the distance, to the east and west, a mountain range could be seen in the mist, sheltering the village of Dai Dune Chun. Made up of various hamlets of simple rural dwellings that had been strung together over the years it lay in the bowl of a fertile valley of unbroken swathes of paddy fields which were interwoven with rich green carpets of watercress that flourished in the river dykes.

Glancing up from the ground floor, in the main living area of bare stone walls blackened over the years from the burning of wood in the kitchen stoves and atop the blood-red flagstones that were set in the raw earth, our eyes were drawn to an enormous ancestral shrine. Carved in wood, with large Chinese calligraphy etched into the board, it reminded us of our ancestral lineage. In keeping with Confucian philosophy, it complied with the essential aspect of filial piety (i.e., reverence and respect for one's parents) – the earlier influences of Tao and Buddhism, with its effigies, had long since gone. The shrine measured eight feet tall by two feet wide and was set back on the farthest wall at the mezzanine level. It bore carvings of ornate symbols as a eulogy to the ancient ancestors. Although in the main burnt by fire in black characters, the whole was edged in gold and red which had dulled over the centuries.

With the aid of a precarious ladder, my brother and I took it in turns to climb up to reach it and ceremoniously place food and wine, which had been brought on the advice of our young relatives, Jiang and his sister Li. They had met us off the coach from Taishan, and were the grandchildren of my father's first brother, Chun Tin. Alan and I placed joss sticks at the foot of the shrine and lit them. Bowing from the waist three times, with the palms of our hands pressed together and our arms outstretched in front of us, we paid our respects to our father's ancestors. As soon as we descended the ladder, the neighbours advised us to set fire to the ghost paper money which we had also brought with us to offer to the small statue of the Land God, who sat staring impassively at us from the corner of the flagstones in the back room. I overheard the elderly neighbours whispering to our young relatives in the local dialect. They were asking if we were Christians, or of another religion. Tactfully, I chose to ignore the question, as I felt I could reconcile my Western religious beliefs with ancestral worship as a form of paying respect on behalf of my aunt and my father, which I had promised I would do.

On that day, the January sun of 2011, I remember, was weak and watery. But as it approached noon, the clouds which had followed us all the way from our hotel in Taishan some thirty-odd miles away to the north, suddenly peeled back to reveal a gap of blue. A shaft of sunlight felt incredibly hot as it landed on the back of my neck. Pulling back the collar of my thick anorak, which I had brought from the cold winter of England, there was a sharp frisson of anticipation as I took in my surroundings. It seemed impossible that we had left London Heathrow just three days ago and had reached China by taking a train to Canton (Guangdung) from Hong Kong. A distant cousin had met us, and then, after spending a night in a modern luxury hotel, we were put on a coach which took us seventy miles south to Taishan City, where we also stayed.

On leaving our father's house, our two young relatives, Jiang and Li, agreed to take us up to the tombs where the Kwong descendants were buried. 'It's quite a long walk, and quite steep,' warned Jiang when they collected us from our hotel. The cautionary remark made our grey hair greyer and our stiff knees creakier than ever.

We decided to leave our driver with the minibus at the foot of the mountain in a side clearing next to an old, derelict factory, which, according to the sign on its forbidding gates, had been built in 1959, ten years after the Communist Revolution, to manufacture electric cables. There was not a soul in sight and the site was clearly deserted, which made our arrival there that more evocative. Jiang and Li led the way. Clearly, they had been there before, though they confessed they had not been for some two years. Leaving the clearing, we quickly came across a large, stagnant pond whose water lilies were strangled by weeds, discarded litter and rusty tin cans. *Not a good sign*, I thought as I hitched up my heavy rucksack on my back. I had brought offerings of food and wine to place at our ancestors' graves, together with joss sticks to burn at the burial ground.

The youngsters beckoned us to follow as they scrambled up the first path they came to. They pointed to the top of the mountain, which was now bathed in limp sunshine, almost like a halo. 'It will take half an hour or so,' said Jiang breathlessly, as he negotiated the steep path, which twisted and turned with increasing sharpness. What struck us was the eerie silence all around us, save for the echoing rustle of our footsteps on the beds of the undergrowth as we climbed. There was not even a sound of a bird cawing or a cicada chirping.

After ten minutes, we stopped by a gnarled tree to gather our breath. Excitedly, I pointed to the side of the mountain, where a freshly dug grave faced us. Sticking out from the orange earth were bamboo canes, about two feet high. Attached to them, white paper banners fluttered in the shallow breeze. Inscribed on these, in Chinese calligraphy in black dye, was the name of the deceased and a eulogy to him. Instinctively, I began to bow towards the grave out of respect. Jiang immediately called out for me to stop. *'That's not your direct relative. Yours are at the top of the peak!* You'll bring us bad luck,' he added. I felt suitably chastened, if not visibly embarrassed.

We tried to carry on, but the path grew steeper and steeper, and became dangerously slippery underfoot. The rich undergrowth had taken over and cascaded over every bit of exposed soil. Lichen, moss, and bare tree roots weaved an impervious rug in front of us. Dense bushes and thick branches from overhanging trees made an impenetrable wall, snapping at our ankles and cutting into our faces.

Li shouted that we had to try to get through via another route. She led us sideways, attempting an access towards the right; but again, the rudimentary path was blocked by a barrier of overgrowth from thick bamboo. Jiang tried to chop the branches and the roots of the saplings with his knife but failed to make any meaningful impression. He said that to climb further in the present circumstances would be dangerous, and muttered that he would hate to allow the mountain to claim another of us before our time arrived. I intended to ask him what he meant, but I never got around to it.

After a while, we all sat down on a grassy knoll to catch our breath. Defeat stared into our young relatives' faces. They explained that we may have to abandon the idea of reaching the graves. Nature's rampant vegetation had taken over. Jiang explained that, with the number of villagers dwindling rapidly over the years, they no longer chopped wood from the undergrowth to fire their stoves. And what is more, those who were left were now able to use modern gas and electric stoves to enable them to cook. Our hearts sank at the news that we would not reach the tombs of our ancestors. We were so near and yet so far. My brother and I had made many sacrifices in order to get here, and had travelled such a long way to seek our grandparents and great-grandparents, and to trace our other ancestors… *but what now?*

'Look,' offered Jiang, trying to encourage us, 'the best time to return would be Ancestors' Day[13] in April after the New Year, when hordes of Overseas Chinese return to pay homage to their ancestors' graves. And by then, the paths in the undergrowth will have been cleared by others, such as hired coolies using axes and machetes.'

---

13 On Ancestors' Day (Quing Ming Festival) on the 5th April, hundreds, if not thousands, including overseas Chinese, return to their ancestral home and their ancestors' graves with offerings of food and wine, and to clean (sweep) the gravestones.

Meanwhile, we were advised to find a quiet clearing nearby so that my brother and I could look up to the summit of the mountain towards our family tombs. From that spot, we were told, we could kowtow towards the graves. It was a poor consolation, but we reluctantly did it. From the safety of a nearby copse where the ground had grown level, burning joss sticks with our arms outstretched, we bowed three times in the traditional Chinese manner with our eyes locked upon the top of the mountain. But deep down, we felt cheated.

Longingly, I looked towards the peak; for in my hand, I clutched a phial of soil from my father's grave which I had brought from Staffordshire. It was part of a promise that I had made to my father on his deathbed; that, when I visited the ancestral tombs, I would scatter on the side of the mountain a sample of the earth that would have been hopefully, in contact with his remains. In the light breeze, I unclenched my hand, and threw the soil high into the air towards the mountainside. Then, solemnly, in the shade of the copse, I also planted a cherry stone that I had plucked from the tree overlooking his grave in Stafford, hoping that one day it would eventually grow.

As we climbed down towards the safety of our minibus, I said there and then that I would never be able to return as time was against us. But as we drove away, giving the burial ground a last sad look, I muttered, 'Perhaps I should never say *never*; ever again.' For, as it happened, back home in England, my daughter Tanya Mayling who, hitherto when growing up, had never shown much interest in her Chinese heritage, was now starting to ask questions. Perhaps it was to do with the progeny yet unborn, and the ancestral thread yet to be sewn into the generations to come, long after my siblings and I have departed this earth to meet our ancestors.

Chapter 2

DUTY

Dai Dune Chun, Taishan, China, 10th January 1921

A T THE CUSP OF the main road which separated the cluster of houses and smallholdings making up Dai Dune Chun, the whole village had turned up to say goodbye to the young man, Kwong Chun Ji. The unmade road was rough, a dust bowl of swirling, burnt-orange soil that snaked through the enormous arch; the sole entrance and exit of the village. Even today, the name of the village could still be deciphered in the large, ancient Chinese characters etched into the decorative tiles that were cemented into the face of the arch high above them, although the glaze on the letters had worn badly over the centuries.

The village inhabitants – the numerous and distant descendants of the Kwong Clan – stood impassively outside the doors of their dwellings, watching with interest. The womenfolk stood back at a respectful distance. Word had got round that Kwong Chun Ji was leaving. It was a momentous occasion. Meanwhile, the immediate members of Chun Ji's family gathered solemnly under the ornate arch, before waving him off on his journey. It was four hours by foot along that road, which would take him north to the nearest town, Taishan – thirty-odd miles along the belly of the valley which twisted tortuously along the basin of the Pearl River Delta. Hugging the side of the mountain ranges to the left and right of him, he would have to negotiate the paddy fields of rice where the water buffalo struggled, heavy-footed, in the squelching mud. Facing him on that journey would be many dykes and rivers swollen from the winter's rain, straggling across his path to slow him down. He was also warned that roaming bandits and poisonous snakes posed constant danger.

From Taishan City as the crow flies, it would be a further seventy or so miles to the north to reach Canton, the provincial capital at the neck of the Pearl River,[14] which, on winding south-eastwards, would eventually take him to the open sea. He hated to think how long it would take him to continue, on foot. If luck was with him, he might be able to bribe a ride or two in a farmer's ox-drawn cart. Once he had reached the seaport at the mouth of the estuary of the mighty Pearl, he could seek a passage on a cargo boat that would take him to the West. The rudimentary map, hand-drawn by his Uncle Kwong Cheung Hai, with directions crudely scribbled all over it, was in topographical terms wildly inaccurate, because no one from the present generation had made this journey before. Those intrepid travellers who might have done so in the past had long since died.

Chun Ji stared at his father, Kwong[15] Loong Cheung[16] Ham, searching for what to say. In deference to the older man, because of their relationship, and in particular because of their imminent parting, the son did not dare to look directly into his father's eyes. It was awkward for them both. Deep down, he wanted to ask why he alone had been chosen to leave the ancestral village. In the months leading up to this fateful day, it had felt as if he was about to be exiled from his family home and the homeland that he had known all his life.

Kwong Loong Cheung Ham, a prominent member of the Kwong (Gong) Clan, was born on the twenty-fifth day of the seventh month in 1875, when the Emperor Kwong Shui held power. True to his

---

14 So, called because of the pearl-like translucency of the shells lying on the riverbed.
15 Generically, 'Kwong' is interchangeable with 'Gong' or 'Kong'.
16 'Cheung' denotes the generation name of the offspring of Biu Shu; e.g. Kwong Loong Cheung Ham and Kwong Cheung Hai.

upbringing from that time, Cheung Ham tried vigorously to retain the strict way of Chinese tradition as head of the family clan. He was just forty-six years old, though he looked much older than those years written on his birth chart. After a lifetime of labouring in the fields in the unforgiving sun and struggling with the storms that swept across from the south coast, he looked wizened and wrinkled as an aged walnut, his hair bleached white as new-milled flour. However, to keep face with his family and neighbours he always presented himself as straight-backed and sufficiently austere, so that his eye level was higher than those of the rest of his family, and particularly his wife, Fung Ting. She was three years his junior, and, in accordance with tradition from Confucian principles (The Three Codes)[17] always remained three steps behind him.

It was still on the tip of Chun Ji's tongue, but the question remained unasked. And yet, as if he knew what his son was thinking, his father insisted, '*You have to go, my son!* It has been your duty from the day you were born. *You are the eldest son.* Be strong! We are of Cantonese stock. But first and foremost, remember, we are Taishanese. You have a duty to save the family from starvation. You have three brothers and two sisters to feed, and one more on the way.'

Chun Ji's mother shuffled uncomfortably from foot to foot and stared vacantly into mid-air.

'It is an obligation of loyalty you must not question. China is being carved up by many foreign powers. Once again, I fear that war cannot be far away...

Go now! Save us all from being wiped out. If not, then at least save yourself, so that one day the ancestral line will live on with you!'

Swallowing hard, Chun Ji hesitated. He had been told that on the other side of the world was the New World overflowing with wealth and opportunities. Europe could be reached via the Indian and

---

17 Confucian principles on obedience: (a) A wife is subjugated to her husband. (b) Likewise, a son must be obedient to his father. (c) All three subjects are subjugated to the Emperor.

Atlantic Oceans, whereas America was accessible by crossing the Pacific. Indeed, stories had been told of his grandfather, Biu Shu, and his father Wah Oi before him, having brought back gold from the gold rush seventy years earlier in America. Word had it that much of that gold had been swallowed, to be passed out later through the body and smuggled out from under the eyes of the harsh mine-owners. Many Chinese labourers were flogged to an agonising death if caught. This was the kind of cruel new world Chun Ji was about to face.

Biu Shu was born on the sixteenth day of the ninth month in 1843, the Year of the Hare, and died from illness aged sixty-three on the twenty-ninth day of the fifth month in 1906, the Year of the Horse. The impacts this formidable ancestor had already made on young Chun Ji's formative years – he was just eight years old at the time of his grandfather's death – were indelible. Biu Shu had revealed on his deathbed that his father, Wah Oi, and hundreds of other Chinese peasants had in 1848 been press-ganged[18] – abducted by criminal gangmasters in the pay of European slave owners who were forging the railroad from California in the west across America to the Atlantic in the east during the gold rush. It appeared that Wah Oi had eventually managed to escape after killing two of the camp guards with a meat cleaver (which he had obtained as one of the camp cooks), throwing off his chains, and obtaining a passage back home to China by bribing his way across the Pacific.

Chun Ji looked around him for the last time. He tried to catch his mother's eye for a flicker of acknowledgement. But her deep-set

---

18　Press gangs comprised of criminals and renegade militia would lure unsuspecting peasants to the cities and ports with promises of work, then throw a sack over their victims' heads after beating them unconscious. They were then shipped in slave ships across the Pacific and forced to work in the gold mines (as in the gold rush of 1848) and the building of the transcontinental railroad, using their bare hands. Wah Oi and others were kidnapped in the port of Canton. In the same way, vast numbers of Irish labourers were enslaved for similar manual labour. They were kept in chains, like the Negroes in adjacent camps. Stanford, one of the founders of San Francisco in the mid 1800s, shipped in thousands of Chinese labourers (coolies) from across the Pacific to build the city. Afterwards, instead of returning back to China, many of them escaped into hiding and eventually established the vast Chinatown which still exists in modern San Francisco. In the 1800s many became cooks and worked their way across the Wild West in the covered wagon trains.

eyes remained still, as if she had been frozen to the ground. Only his nineteen-year-old sister Chun Ho managed a hint of emotion, as tears welled up in her eyes. But she kept herself occupied by hanging on to their youngest sibling, their four-year-old brother Chun Tui, who clutched at the hem of her Chinese tunic and hid his face, thinking it was a game. Their youngest sister, Chun Rei, aged just seven, realised what was happening. She appeared agitated, as if she wanted to run towards him for the last time but did not dare to. Standing silently just a half-step in front of her, their brothers, Chun Tin, now seventeen, and twelve-year-old Chun Yee, both stared into the distance. Their father kept order with a solemn glare. Stiffly, he kept his hands firmly together inside the wide sleeves of his long black tunic to avoid any physical contact between father and son, or with any member of his family, for that matter. There was little room to spare for sentiment in old China, where there were greater priorities in life, such as food for survival.

Uncle Cheung Hai, although ten years younger than Chun Ji's father, looked the older of the two due to his hunched spine and haunted look, as if he bore the weight of the world on his shoulders. Ten years earlier, fired with nationalistic fervour, he had joined the peasant uprising in Canton with the revolutionary Nationalists, the Kuomintang, led by Dr Sun Yat-sen and General Chiang Kai-shek,[19] to overthrow the last of the Manchu Emperors. Betrayed by a hostile neighbour, he was captured and tortured by government spies loyal to the Imperial Throne, which nearly killed him. He had been rescued by his brother, Cheung Ham, who was also attacked and left for dead by government troops, leaving him scarred for life.

The uncle shuffled forwards in his well-worn sandals. Slowly picking up a battered leather suitcase near his feet, he handed it to Chun Ji with a stiff nod of the head. The well-travelled suitcase, much

---

19   Dr Sun Yat-sen and General Chiang Kai-shek were instrumental in the formation of the First Republic of China on the 12th February 1912, following the collapse of the last of the royal dynasties under Emperor Hsuan-t'ung – the Boy P'u-i – who had been placed on the Imperial Throne under the control of his aunt, the old Empress Dowager Tz'u-hsi (Cixi).

scuffed at the metal corners, had seen better days. Chun Ji had been told that it had previously belonged to a distant great-uncle, who in the 1800s had crossed the Pacific to California in search for gold. But, like many Chinese at that time, due to impoverished circumstances he was forced to work as a cook, travelling with cowhands, drifters and pioneering settlers in a covered wagon train crossing the frontiers and plains of the Wild West. Stories abounded of fierce battles with the Cherokee, in which he was nearly scalped alive. However, his pigtail and the copper-yellow colour of his skin managed to save him, with timely intervention by an old Indian Chief who warned that it would be taboo to kill a foreigner whom he considered a possible blood brother,[20] thinking that they had much in common. And so the uncle had survived.

Inside the case were simple items of clothing the family thought Chun Ji would need for his journey. Rudimentary medicines obtained locally from the rural barefoot doctor,[21] in the form of powders for fever, and balls of herbs for cuts and mosquito bites, sealed in waxed paper, were wrapped within the clothes. There was also a small pewter rice bowl, a sharp iron knife for skinning rabbits and snakes for food, and a pair of bone chopsticks, sharply tipped with silver – essential to detect hidden poison as the silver would turn black. Not only were these implements used for eating, but they could double as a useful weapon against potential attackers. In the right hands, you could kill assailants by piercing them through the eardrums, eyes or belly button. He had been told that, some time ago, when bandits rode down from the mountains to attack the village, his grandfather, Biu Shu, although somewhat aged by then, had managed to save his niece from being raped. Using the sharp silver tip of a chopstick, he deftly skewered the attacker through the scrotum and perineum, causing him to bleed to death.

---

20 Also, both the North American Red Indians and the Ancient Chinese commonly practised the worship of the bones of their ancestors.
21 'Barefoot doctor' was the term given to the rural medicine men who were often self-taught or used rudimentary traditional Chinese medical knowledge handed down from generation to generation.

Reaching behind him, Uncle Cheung Hai thrust a canvas bag tied with rope towards his nephew. Tightly rolled up within the bag was a newly washed, flock-filled quilt (*min-whwoi*) – a Chinese custom for the traveller leaving home.

According to tradition, there would be no show of familiarity, so Chun Ji gave a short bow to his family as a final gesture, lowering his head to his father to bid him farewell. Staring resolutely at the open road in front of him, and with an abrupt turn of the heels, he turned his back on his family and started on his journey. The weak wintry sky started to cloud over rapidly. There was a long walk ahead to reach the next resting place before sunset, when the cold winter's night would close in mercilessly on him.

Chapter 3

JOURNEY INTO THE UNKNOWN

Canton, China, 11ᵗʰ January 1921

T HE CITY OF TAISHAN was almost four hours away by foot. A much-welcomed lift from a sympathetic farmer in an ox-drawn cart eased part of the journey, but there was still quite a long way to go. Eventually, Chun Ji reached the rambling outskirts of the city. He stopped briefly to gather his wits and to take a sip of water from his tunic flask whilst taking in his new and strange surroundings. Densely packed buildings appeared to sprawl forever in front of him. He had never seen electric lighting before; back in the village, all they had were oil lamps and candles made from pig fat. Bunches of old cables in their hundreds for street lighting, and an assortment of wires for the odd telegraph, straddled the roofs of the buildings like washing lines. They hung down mournfully at the sides of the walls, sparking intermittently at the exposed live terminals due to the sheeting rain that had suddenly fallen after a clap of thunder that had rapidly rolled by.

It was dark by the time he made his way to the centre of the town. Above a dingy old teahouse at the edge of a narrow, dilapidated alleyway – a hutong²² – he found a room, and then bought a bowl of

---

22 Hutong: narrow, criss-crossing alleyways, often densely crammed with families living in semi-dilapidated and tiny rooms with primitive facilities.

cheap noodles from a street vendor just outside. He had already spent half of one precious yuan from the money his family had saved to give him. He made a mental note to eke out the rest of it more carefully, as it had to last for the whole of his journey, which had barely begun.

Pushing aside the dirty net curtain that was hanging by a piece of string across the dusty windowpane, he looked up and down the street before deciding to test the uninviting mattress that covered the frame of the old cast-iron bed. He had been about to sleep on the floor, but hurriedly changed his mind when a large, bulbous cockroach, bloated with bloody mucus, scurried across his foot. The room reeked of old cooking smells and stale human sweat, so he eased the window up a fraction – although not overly wide, fearing thieves. He felt around his waist. Under his shirt, a money pouch made from pigskin had been securely tied around his stomach. He hitched it up. A length of linen his mother had given him had been wound firmly around the pouch, so that it appeared less obvious when he was standing. Sleeping with this tied around his body would be no hardship, he decided, as he had become used to sleeping rough in the countryside. He had been warned to be wary of whom he spoke to, as thieves and villains would slit his throat just for the sheer hell of it after stripping the clothes off his back.

Once in his room, he jammed the back of an old wooden chair against the doorknob for safety. He did not trust anyone, including the shifty-looking man at the desk at the foot of the stairs, who had asked him repeatedly in Cantonese if he had just come from the country. It may have been a perfectly innocent question, but Chun Ji couldn't be sure. Instinctively, he kept feeling the lumpy band on the middle finger of his left hand for reassurance. For security, before he left home, he had squashed the family ring of solid gold, on which was carved the ancestral name of Kwong, onto his middle finger – it being the fattest. He was told that no one would be able to slip it off easily without resorting to chopping off his finger. A reasonable price to pay, he thought, to safeguard this family heirloom which was the only remaining reminder of his family name left on his body. But again, for extra safety, he was advised by his mother to wrap a piece of muslin around it to hide it from view of greedy eyes, so as not to attract unnecessary attention.

When he unrolled the flock quilt his uncle had given him, something solid fell to the floor, making him jump. He picked it up. A knowing smile crossed his face when he realised that his younger brother, Chun Tin, must have surreptitiously hidden a pair of rice flails inside the quilt when no one was looking. For the last seven seasons, Chun Ji had used the flails in the fields for cropping the harvest. As a result, his upper body became increasingly sinewy, lean, and strong. Like a familiar glove, one of the handles, carved from solid, polished bamboo, and joined by a short hemp rope to the other, fitted snugly into his right fist, whereas, the other handle could spin freely at a murderous speed, forming a vicious circle to whirl in front of him. The centrifugal force thereby unleashed was powerful enough to shatter branches, fences, as well as any obstacle standing in the way – or even smash the bones of an adversary, for that matter. Many peasant workers, including Chun Ji, were adept at using flails to fight off attackers, which they did from time to time when bandits rode down from the mountains to raid their village. For good luck, he slipped the rice flails – or nunchaku, as they later came to be known – into the inside pocket of his jacket, hoping that he would never have to use them again for whatever reason.

For a few hours, Chun Ji slept fitfully as his mind was still in a spin. He was awoken by the sound of the first cock crowing and the gabbling of geese from the gaggle in the teahouse yard down below. The hazy light of dawn started to creep over the tiles of the rooftops outside his window, announcing a new day. As he looked out to the narrow streets, he heard the bustle of traders pushing their ancient carts filled with vegetables, fruit, and livestock as they made their way to market. When they scraped along the uneven cobbles, the wheels made a peculiar rattling noise; a sound alien to him as he was used to the friendly crunch of ox-drawn carts churning the rich, hungry soil, or the squelch of the water buffalo toiling in the paddy fields where he was brought up.

As he splashed water onto his face from a bowl on a stand in the corner of his room, his thoughts flew back to the days when he had tended the cattle, pigs and chickens on the farmlands around Dai Dune Chun for a neighbour. The local farmer, although a kinsman and part of the clan, was a distant relative by marriage on Chun Ji's uncle's side and gave him some money from time to time when he was in a generous mood. Chun Ji was not one to complain of his lot. At least he had been given a large-brimmed coolie hat to keep off the sun, and a fresh set of clothes on Chinese New Year. As he grew up, he was taught to read and write by the village elders, though, like most peasant families, his parents simply couldn't afford formal tuition for him to take the exams set by the government that would allow him to better himself by securing a government position or going on to further study. Calligraphy and the art of the abacus were essential, even for the humblest of families; the eldest and the firstborn son taking priority. In keeping with most families, these skills were successfully handed down from father to son. In his spare time in the cool of the evenings, Chun Ji mastered the rudiments of the callisthenics of the Ten Patterns, taught by his elders as a way of maintaining good health, and for self-defence.

He shook his head to dispel his daydream, and cursed under his breath. Moreover, he just could not afford to waste time on nostalgia, which might, if indulged too much, weaken his resolve to continue his journey. There were important chores to carry out before he left the city. Firstly, he had to collect his papers from the Taishan office of the Bureau of Public Safety for Canton. His father had told him that it had all been arranged ten weeks ago, through an intermediary – a paid agent – who was versed in the matters of foreign travel documents and would secure the necessary Certificate of Identity and other papers to enable Chun Ji to travel to the West.

Forsaking a breakfast of watery grey gruel made from broken rice, he quickly bundled up his belongings and hurried into the street.

Taishan was a rabbit warren of streets and alleyways criss-crossing one another. Dwellings – most of them dilapidated and blackened with soot from open fires – rambling stalls, tired-looking shops, makeshift offices, and ancient temples sat cheek by jowl, like unhappy neighbours forced to live together. Neglect and wars from centuries past had written their history all over the fabric of their bricks and mortar, and yet this very neglect appeared to bind them together in the impoverished circumstances of the present day. In the centre, around a large square, were some pristine lawns surrounded by mature palm trees and a series of austere-looking government buildings around the perimeter.

The morning rush was well under way. As he dodged the traffic, a cacophony of noise spread from the streets in a rising swell. Bicycles in their scores – many with live chickens and ducks tied by their feet to the handlebars – wobbled in and out between the handcarts and old motorbikes overflowing with goods for market. Drivers shouted and cursed at Chun Ji as he weaved dangerously between the creaky rickshaws and the jumble of assorted motor vehicles, whose battered old exhausts continued to belch out choking black fumes to add to the deepening smog.

He asked a coolie who was brushing the leaves off the street where the Bureau of Public Safety was situated. Glad of the chance to take a break from his task, the coolie willingly pointed with the end of his broom to the grandest building, whose entrance was flanked by tall, Palladian-style pillars. Hurriedly, Chun Ji ran up the broad steps to the entrance and walked self-consciously into the lobby. The porter at the desk informed him that the department for travel documents was on the first floor.

There were two other men, both older than him, waiting in the passage outside the office with bored resignation etched on their faces, so he sat down on the nearest chair and waited patiently. When his turn came, he knocked on the door, entered and gave his name at the counter. A miserable-looking man behind the desk stared at him coldly and asked him to repeat his name. After what seemed like an eternity, the man returned from the back office with a package secured with a piece of ribbon and pushed it with a sullen growl, into Chun Ji's grateful hands. He was then asked to apply a thumbprint from his right hand to a document to acknowledge the safe receipt of his papers. Then, without further delay, he hungrily tore open the package and examined the documents, spreading them carefully over the top of the mahogany counter. As far as he could tell, his Chinese passport with its grainy photograph was inside, along with his Certificate of Identity, and permission to travel from Guangdung Province, with the official red-wax seal of approval from the authorities in Canton.

On leaving the building, at the bottom of the steps, he noticed that one of the men who had been waiting before him was also examining his papers. He stood out, being the taller and heftier of the two, with a hairline that appeared to be greying prematurely at the temples. Chun Ji asked him if he was going towards Canton. The man introduced himself as Lo Wu, and replied that he was, and that he had motor transport, and if the young man would contribute towards the cost of fuel, he would give him a lift. Gratefully, Chun Ji accepted and they nodded in agreement, bowing at the same time. But his face fell when he saw that Mr Lo's vehicle was an ancient three-wheeled van with corrugated-iron side panels that appeared to be held together by rust and wire. He suspected that it had probably been converted using an old motorbike engine – common at the time. But he thought anything would be better than walking, so bit his tongue and swallowed his opinion.

It was getting on for midday by the time they had gathered their possessions, and the weak wintry sun started to disappear swiftly behind thickening clouds. They soon left the perimeter of the city and headed north. Mr Lo told Chun Ji that it would take most of the day to cover the seventy or so miles to reach the city of Canton. He revealed that he had to find his brother-in-law, as it was for his benefit that he had collected the documents. As the roads were largely unmade and poorly signposted, Mr Lo wanted to get there before it grew dark.

He admitted that he had only travelled that route once before, and that he had been warned that there may be hazards along the way. 'Rumour has it,' he said, 'that from the beginning of this year, Dr Sun Yat-sen's revolutionary party – the Kuomintang – have been in the throes of trying to form a government in Canton, with General Chiang Kai-shek as head of the Army. Unrest in Guangdung Province, from where the core of Sun's revolutionaries originate, was still rife. Furthermore, from time immemorial, peasant uprisings have been common, and Dr Sun is now feverishly gathering support amongst them. The different factions of the warlords have failed to quell the unrest, and so the Army has yet to get a grip on the anarchy posed by splinter groups of renegades and opposition forces that roam the countryside, fighting, looting and raping unchallenged in the towns and cities!'

Chun Ji hardly took in what he said and leant back in the passenger seat. The sway and rhythmic rocking of the tiny old van along the long, rough road soon made him close his eyes, although the fumes from the soot-black exhaust and the smell of crude fuel leaking alarmingly from under the engine almost asphyxiated him.

Four hours later, the van suddenly screeched to a halt, flinging its occupants abruptly forwards. Chun Ji woke up with a sudden jolt. In the middle of the road, a body was lying across their path. Mr Lo cursed loudly and slammed on his brakes, stalling the engine.

'*What the blazes is tha…?!*'

He had started to open the driver's door when two figures sprang from the undergrowth at the side of the road. Grabbing hold of his door, they smashed the window with an iron bar. At the same time, the figure lying in the road suddenly leapt up, wrenched open the passenger door and sprang at Chun Ji's throat.

'*Damn bandits!*' yelled Mr Lo with a screech. From beneath his seat, he grabbed a well-oiled machete and, with a blood-curdling cry, swung it in front of him. With a swift downward chop, he severed one of the outstretched hands that gripped the open door. A horrific scream filled the air as the man fell into the road, clutching the blood-soaked stump on his wrist.

Chun Ji managed to kick his attacker away, forcing him out of the van by whipping the rice flails across his face, smashing the bridge of his nose. *'Quick. Let's get the hell out of here before others come!'* he shouted breathlessly to Mr Lo.

Adrenaline quickly drowned their fear. It all happened so quickly. The van shot away, with Mr Lo's foot flat on the accelerator pedal.

They did not stop again until they reached the safety of the outer walls of the ancient city of Canton. Dusk was falling fast, like a blanket shrouding the remnants of pink in the sky, and soon they felt a little bit safer, melting amongst the city's many buildings and its anonymous mass of people.

'Where did you get the machete from?'

'Oh, it's a favourite tool of mine for chopping up melons and skinning livestock… and for other kinds of dangerous pigs I come across,' replied Mr Lo tonelessly. He wiped the congealed blood off the blade with a soiled piece of rag and stared straight ahead without elaborating further. Then, nonchalantly, he scooped the remains of the blood-soaked flesh off the floor of his van into the road. *It suddenly dawned on Chun Ji that this man had killed before.*

Time was disappearing fast, and so they took a direct route through one of the ancient gates of the city. Soon they skirted the boundary walls of a cluster of opulent buildings belonging to the British Consulate and other foreign legations. The bulk of the overseas concessions – the settlements for foreigners – were housed outside the walls, but within striking distance of the waterfront. Chun Ji had never seen anything like it in his life, with its grand, marbled mansions containing elegant courtyards surrounding manicured lawns which were fed constantly with fresh, clean water. Such opulence was enhanced by the Romanesque statues and fountains which contrasted starkly with the simple, local design of pagoda-sloped roofs of green tiles and red-brick buildings belonging to the indigenous population.

'Is it like this anywhere else?' he asked, his eyes agog with astonishment.

'I'm told it's even bigger and grander in the international settlement in Shanghai. And, what's more, I've heard that we, the Chinese, are forbidden to go anywhere near for fear of being beaten to death by the bearded Sikh police who patrol there,' replied Mr Lo. 'And did you know that notices are stuck outside the gates of all the public parks there, warning,

Dogs and Chinese are strictly forbidden!'

Heaving a murderous shrug, he spat out of the window in disgust.

On hearing that, Chun Ji went deathly quiet and decided not to risk any more questions.

At the jetty near the quay, where a group of old cargo boats, sampans and sailing junks were moored at the neck of the mighty Pearl, they bade each other farewell.

'Safe journey, my naive young friend,' said Mr Lo with a nod. *'And watch your back!* You're a green sapling just starting to sprout. You'll soon learn about life, having been thrown to the winds!'

The young man bowed and thanked him profusely, and then walked away swiftly, not daring to look back.

It was already pitch black by the time the cargo junk was loaded. A large throng of passengers crowded onto the deck, talking and yelling excitedly in a mixture of dialects. Some of them struggled on with crates and cases that seemed bigger and bulkier than their owners. Others carried bicycles, or hauled aboard bamboo cages full of live chickens, geese, or piglets. Men and women, young and old, many with wooden yokes balanced across their backs laden with goods, fought their way on board, pushing and jostling.

Bricks of tea, battered casks of opium and bales of tobacco were strapped to iron rings fixed to the middle of the deck, for safety and to prevent pilfering. Then suddenly, as the mooring ropes were released, people elbowed their way towards the boat rails as the ancient sampans with their flimsy bamboo awnings were flung aside by the violent wash of the junk, like giant moths swatted away from the beam of a light. Shouting and spitting indiscriminately into the deep, blackened waters, they watched the lights of the old city fade as a tug pulled the junk slowly along the river until it reached a wider and deeper channel. It made its way gradually towards the estuary as it gathered some wind in its sails.

The hours gradually melted away during the long, tortuous river journey which slowly wound its way southwards through the narrow and twisting, treacherous gorges that made up the natural plains of the Pearl River Delta. Eventually, the river widened. To most unseasoned travellers, like Chun Ji, this arduous journey of nearly one hundred miles or so from Canton to the open sea felt like an eternity. Constantly, he suppressed the urge to be sick.

As the early hours of the morning approached, the mouth of the open ocean was in sight. Light was just breaking through a thick sea mist that hung tenaciously over the cold water. To the east, the port and docks of the British colony of Hong Kong loomed up from the edge of the horizon. He had been told by his uncle that he would recognise it as most of its buildings were heavily influenced by the grand contemporary architecture of the West – something that he had no prior concept of, and so he did not know what to expect, or what to compare it with.

Having fought for a tiny corner next to the gangway to get away from the amorphous mass of jostling humanity, he had dozed fitfully on the journey, for he felt increasingly nauseous, having never been on a boat journey before. But nothing that he had experienced before in his life would prepare him for the final stage of his journey by ship that would take him across many oceans to the West and the New World. It would be a journey that would take him eleven long weeks across some eleven thousand miles – and what seemed to him, when looking back, a lifetime of hell on hostile high seas.

By the time he disembarked, dawn had broken from the east, casting early shadows that grew and evolved over the grey shabbiness of the port buildings. At the docks, following instructions from his uncle, he found a cargo steamship that he could afford. It was called the SS *Liberty*, a name that would eventually stick in his mind. The captain looked miserable and grim, just like the vessel he commanded, Chun Ji thought, somewhat anxiously. Still, with half of his money remaining, he parted reluctantly with the fare for a passage to the West. But now, there was no turning back.

The living quarters below deck were filthy, cramped and airless, but he felt he had no choice. What he did not anticipate was that, when the ship set sail, the captain and crew had packed nearly seven hundred passengers into the stinking, black hole, which was already full of cargo. Little did he realise that, by whatever kind of crude maritime law existed in 1921 for safeguarding passengers, the ship was originally intended for barely a fraction of the numbers it now carried.

When he later described the journey, he refused to go into detail as it was too traumatic for words. Packed like animals in a suffocating, fetid heat of choking oil fumes and open furnaces, the crew (and some of the passengers, who were forced to work as they owed money for their passage) shovelled in coal continuously to power the steam for the engines. Passengers constantly succumbed to illness. Apart from the seasickness, cholera, typhoid, tuberculosis, dysentery and malnutrition were rampant. Dangerously ill and feverishly contagious, many became too weak to climb out of the cargo hole and, covered in their own excrement and vomit, had to be hosed down by the crew. Many fell into the treacherous, shark-filled waters as they squatted desperately over a hole in a plank placed over the edge of the ship to empty their bowels. Fights, rape, and murder were commonplace. Nearly three hundred passengers died on that journey as the steamship made its way through the South China Seas, the Indian Ocean and around the Cape of Good Hope[23] to reach the Bay of Biscay. The space in the cramped, rat-infested area below deck was eased when those who had died, or were near to death, were promptly buried at sea. If the truth be known, they were callously and unceremoniously thrown overboard.

---

23 The shorter passage of ten thousand miles through the Suez Canal and the Mediterranean would have cost considerably more (which many simply could not afford) than the longer (approximately two thousand miles) and more dangerous journey around the Cape of Good Hope.

Chun Ji had never felt so wretched in his life as he did on that journey. Disorientated and light-headed from dehydration and hunger, he could only watch in vain as starving, salivating fellow travellers fought over a dead rat, their daggers drawn. To sustain his sanity, he dreamed of riches and an infinite amount of palatable fresh food that one day might be his if he managed to survive this journey from hell. And hope spurred him on. He befriended one passenger, a Mr Wong Sing, with whom he shared precious fresh water and food, which they hid from the others in order to survive. They took it in turns to sleep whilst the other kept watch to keep them from being attacked. These cargo vessels that crossed the oceans from China would later be referred to as 'floating hell ships' by the survivors.

On the 2nd April 1921, Kwong Chun Ji landed in Liverpool, England, after a long, harrowing journey since leaving his ancestral home in China on the 10th January that year. It was an experience that would change him forever.

Chapter 4

A DOOR TO THE NEW WORLD

Liverpool, England, 2nd April 1921

THE HEAVY IRON DOOR of the police cell slammed shut behind him with a deafening bang. It echoed with an eerie finality; a terrifying sound, like he imagined a door to a tomb would sound as he was buried alive. The young man stared around him, trying to adjust his eyes to the semi-darkness. With his right hand he gripped his chest, willing his heart not to thump loudly in case the police guard outside sensed that he was afraid. Kwong Chun Ji[24] stood proud and erect, feigning defiance. As a stranger, and a foreign one at that, landing suddenly and without warning in this strange land, he did not want his jailer, especially one the Chinese would call a gweilo,[25] to see that his courage was just a front. It was imprinted in his head; the first rule of survival: *'Never, ever allow them or any other mortal to smell your fear!'* It had been drummed into him by the village elders before he left. 'And, apart from your father and the bones of your ancestors, you must never kowtow to anyone. Remember, you have five thousand years of illustrious history behind you!'

---

24 Chun Ji is the forename; Kwong the surname.
25 'Gweilo' is a derogatory term aimed by the Chinese at Europeans, describing them as 'white ghosts'; i.e., implying that their faces are like those of corpses, having a deathly white pallor.

The cell was dimly lit from a tiny window high above his head, airless, stuffy, and cold. Two short, stout bars were welded vertically against the window frame, rusted with age. A single tiny light bulb, yellowed by stale cigarette smoke, swayed precariously from a short brown flex high up on the ceiling. The room measured ten paces in one direction and five in the other. Each wall was painted a dirty grey, over bare plaster peeling off at the edges. In the corner stood an old metal bucket full of dents; it smelled strongly of bleach in a futile attempt to mask the pervading stench of stale urine. A concrete bunk ran across the width of the cell, with a meagre horsehair mattress which was well worn and stained. It had been squashed thin in an effort to flatten the irregular lumps over the years, witness to the hundreds of incumbents who, like Chun Ji, had previously stood there, feeling stunned and desolate. He had never felt *so* alone, *so* abandoned as he did at that moment.

As soon as he heard the dull thud of the jailer's boots drifting away down the passage, Chun Ji sat down on the edge of the mattress and slumped forwards, holding his head in his hands. He pulled the collar of his quilted Chinese jacket over his throat for some warmth and shivered. Savagely, he pressed his eyelids with the backs of his hands, hoping to block out the nightmare that had just overtaken him. His mind flew back to twelve weeks ago at the start of his journey, when he saw his family for the last time on the other side of the world. The adventure had started off so well. There had been a bit of optimism, although tinged with some sadness. It now seemed a lifetime away. From his trouser pocket he pulled out a small, battered calendar. The date was the 2nd April 1921.

Weariness started to get the better of him, so reluctantly he closed his eyes. He tried to lie down, but his mind refused to let go as he fell into a fitful sleep.

After a while, he stirred with a jolt. He thought he must have dropped off without realising it. His arms felt numb with pins and needles. Thinking that he must have slept awkwardly on them, he shook his hands vigorously and stretched like a cat. He was still only half awake, but however hard he tried to stop it happening, memories from the distant past, and more recently, flashed in front of him as though his whole life suddenly unfolded in an all-consuming nightmare which he tried in vain to shake off…

…For Kwong Chun Ji was twenty-two years of age[26] when left his ancestral home – a rural village called Dai Dune Chun in Taishan, Guangdung, China. For the rest of his life, he would never forget that date. It was a cold, wintry day, the 10th January 1921, and the chilled winds had blown in from the north from across the mountains. He had never travelled out of his village, let alone to the other side of the world. He was born on the twenty-seventh day of the tenth month of 1898, the year described in the old Chinese calendar as Mow Soot Nin, under the reign of Emperor Kwong Shui. (Also known as Emperor Kuang-hsu)…

Then, staring up at the ceiling, Chun Ji tried hard to keep awake – but the haunting images kept recurring…

"…In 1898 when he was born, it had been a tumultuous year in Chinese history. In the Forbidden City within the walls of Peking, known as the Imperial City, the old Dowager Empress Tz'u-hsi (Cixi), the daughter of a Manchu nobleman under the Ch'ing Dynasty, and now in her sixties, had without warning regained her grip on the Dragon Throne. She had stripped the Puppet Emperor Kuang-hsu, of his power, placing him under house arrest because of his increasing leanings towards ideas of reform from what was considered the barbaric West.

Prior to this – in the south, at the southernmost tip of the province of Guangdung, Hong Kong's New Territories had

---

26 Kwong Chun Ji was born on the 27th October 1898. According to Chinese tradition, he was considered to be already *one* year old when he was born due to the 'womb time' following a gestation period of nine months within his mother's womb. In 1921, therefore, he was considered to be twenty-two years old.

been ceded to Britain for ninety-nine years by a weakened and demoralised Ch'ing government still reeling from the carving up of China by the colonial powers from Europe. With this loss of face (extremely important in the Chinese psyche), the rest of Hong Kong, together with Kowloon, had similarly been forfeited following the disastrous Opium Wars of 1839 and 1856.[27]

In that same year of 1898, the mighty Yellow River had burst its banks, flooding hundreds of villages. This was followed by a devastating drought. Widespread famine rapidly spread as the rice crops and the wheat harvest failed. Hundreds of thousands died. The countryside was in chaos. Revolution was simmering.

North of the Yangtze, the powerful Boxer Movement in the uprising of the 'Righteous Fist', with its martial arts militancy, had gathered momentum. The increasing turmoil had been blamed on the foreigners, especially those from the West. For decades, Japan, Russia, Holland, Portugal, France, Germany and Britain had established – often by force – legations and consulates in the major cities of China, namely Peking, Nanking, Shanghai and Canton, to protect their valuable trade interests.

Although it had been three years following the end of the first Sino-Japanese War of 1894–5, Japan once again mobilised its military incursion into China from the north-east, with designs on Manchuria clashing with Russia's interests. Immediately, Russia extracted from the defeated Ch'ing rulers a twenty-five-year lease on the Liaodong Peninsula and had established a naval base at Port Arthur. France, Germany, and Britain lost no time in wringing concessions in trade and port access, as well as land, from the weakened and hapless Ch'ing government.

---

27 The First Opium War of 1839 had been provoked by Britain invading China to protect its valuable tea and opium trades. In 1842, under the Treaty of Nanking, Hong Kong Island was ceded to the British. During the Second Opium War (beginning in 1856), under the Treaty of Peking, in 1860, China ceded the Southern End of the Kowloon Peninsula and the surrounding territory to Britain. In 1898 China was forced to sign the Convention for the Extension of Hong Kong Territory, granting a ninety-nine-year lease to Britain for the remainder of the Kowloon Peninsula, along with its adjacent two hundred islands known as the New Territories.

America waited with interest on the sidelines. At the same time, missionaries from Europe had spread across the provinces in a zealous attempt to convert the so-called indigenous heathens. The buzzards of multi-imperialism were hovering as the vulnerable underbelly of China was now ripe for plucking.

Two years later in 1900, the Empress Dowager sought an alliance with the Boxers[28] in a futile attempt to rid China of the colonial powers. On the 21st June that year, war had been declared. In a frenzy of nationalistic fervour, the Boxers having burst into Peking, burnt down the homes and churches of foreigners, and killed and mutilated Chinese Christian converts. Firstly, the Chancellor of the Japanese legation having been assassinated, was followed by the German Minister. Bands of Boxers in their thousands, now heavily armed, laid siege to the capital's foreign legations. Decapitated heads rolling around the legation grounds were not an uncommon sight. Animals had been slaughtered at random, their carcasses left to rot in the stifling heat."

Then suddenly without warning, a scream shattered the deathly silence. The desk sergeant and his colleague rushed to the holding block at the rear of the station, and in a panic slid open the viewing hatch of the cell that held Chun Ji. On the bunk, the young man was thrashing about in his sleep, his face ashen, groaning and with spittle around his lips.

'What the… blazes?! Look, Sarge!' gasped one officer to the other, pointing anxiously. 'It's that young Chinese fella having a blinkin' turn! Do we need to call the doc?'

'Nah. Don't think it's necessary! He'll live! He looks strong as an ox… not like the last poor sod who topped himself the other day!'

---

28 A Chinese secret society immersed in martial arts, and who believed in magical powers, consuming potions in order to be immune to bullets and swords. They rose up in the Boxer Rebellion of 1899–1901, initially to support the Peasant Revolt to bring down the Imperial Throne. Later they were reluctantly supported by the Empress Dowager Cixi to rid the country of all foreigners, colonial powers and missionaries, in the Righteous and Harmonious Fist Uprising.

With a contemptuous shrug, and exchanging reassuring pats on each other's shoulders, they spun on their heels and promptly returned to the front desk, leaving the young inmate writhing about in a terrifying nightmare of headless corpses, during which, he saw his father and uncle being slaughtered in cold blood...

... The horrific images continued, as the young inmate Chun Ji saw before his sleep-filled eyes...

"...Situated close to the Gate of Heavenly Peace in the Imperial City was the largest legation; that of the British. Nearby were the others – Russian, American, Spanish, Japanese, French, German, Austrian, Italian and Belgian – housing diplomats, missionaries and their families. A coalition force of twenty thousand troops from these countries, led by the British, had been despatched to the Chinese coast at Taku to the east. By August, the allies had scored several decisive victories over the Chinese and marched triumphantly into Peking, which was now in ruins. Soon after, the Empress Dowager, with her protesting Puppet Emperor, fled to the ancient capital city of Xi'an, which had now become the seat-in-exile of the court.

In September 1901, articles signed by China, in the collective note known as the Boxer Protocols, then brought an end to hostilities. Draconian measures were taken against the Chinese. Over one hundred Boxer leaders, sympathisers, ministers and officials had been executed or imprisoned for life. China faced a gargantuan indemnity of sixty-seven million pounds to be paid over thirty-nine years at a penal rate of interest, imposed by a heavy levy on custom duties and tariffs. The valuable British trade interests in tea and opium had thus been protected. China had also been forced to agree to a ban on all arms imports, and to the stationing of foreign troops from Peking to the sea. At the same time, two hundred thousand Russian troops had occupied Manchuria on the pretext of restoring order. Three years later, Japan went to war with Russia to regain the region.

In 1902, the following year, in a hollow show of ostentation, the Empress Dowager having returned to Peking, was carried shoulder high on a sedan chair trimmed with peacock feathers. Reluctantly, she had thereby conceded a raft of reforms to her people. A revision of the ancient, brutal penal code having been decreed, which promised to end the punishments of death by slow-slicing by sword in 'a thousand cuts' (known as 'Ling-chi'), beheading, flogging alive by bamboo and other indescribable acts of torture – one of the vilest being for the condemned to be shackled and crucified alive on a wooden cage to die in the insufferable heat of the sun."

It was against this background of volatility and cruelty that the young Chun Ji had grown up in. One might have thought that, living deep in the countryside, he and his family would have been shielded from such scenes of violence and turmoil, but this was not always so. Like a windborne disease, news of the turbulent events had spread rapidly, sparing no one. His father, Kwong Loong Cheung Ham, and his Uncle Cheung Hai, whilst hiding from government spies, had on many occasions witnessed beheadings in the street, summarily carried out by the police and government soldiers who roamed around the city of Canton, and sometimes even nearer in the town of Taishan, just thirty miles away. They had often described the streets running with blood...

Floundering in this awful nightmare - his ordeal rumbled inexorably on...

"...In 1898, as it happened, a young Chinese Christian doctor named Sun Yat-sen, the son of a poor Cantonese peasant farmer emerged from Guangzhou. Preaching revolution, he had formed

the League of Common Alliance, espousing the Three Principles for reform – nationalism, democracy and socialism.

Three years earlier however, an uprising in Canton had disastrously failed, whereupon Dr Sun fled to Europe. In 1900, fired by a renewed revolutionary zeal, he tried once again in Canton. He drew support not only from the lower classes, including Guangdung's local peasants,[29] but from the gentry and merchants in an attempt to restore China's prosperity. This had fared no better. And so, five years later, he subsequently set up the Revolutionary Alliance, drawing together other revolutionary groups, mostly from students scattered across the country, all dedicated to driving out the hated Manchu rulers and establishing a republic. Irrevocably, the seeds of revolution had now been sown. The days of the Celestial Kingdom heralding the new century under the Ch'ing Dynasty were numbered.

In 1907, the Empress Dowager Tz'u-hsi suffered a stroke, but she nevertheless continued to make the Emperor Kuang-hsu effectively a prisoner. After a decade of illness, aggravated by her abusive treatment, he took to what proved to be his deathbed. It was said that, in his final throes, he had scribbled a curse on Tz'u-hsi. He died on the 14th November 1908, and immediately the old Empress Dowager nominated his nephew P'u-i as the new Emperor Hsuan-t'ung. As the child was barely three, his father, a weak man, was made Regent, and the late Emperor's widow became the new Dowager Empress.

The very next day, with great irony, the Empress Dowager Tz'u-hsi herself died. Her stranglehold on the Dragon Throne, which she had kept a firm grip on for nearly half a century, had now been extinguished at a stroke.

---

29 Hundreds of peasants from Guangdung and Taishan, including Chun Ji's father and his Uncle Cheung Hai went to hear Dr Sun speak of revolution in the city of Canton (nowadays called Guangzhou), the capital city of Guangdung (Canton) Province. Inspired by revolutionary fervour, the uncle had joined the Kuomintang Nationalists. Historically, Canton could be considered the cradle of China's first revolution following the end of its two-thousand-year Imperial Dynasty period.

The weakened Ch'ing court, with its rudderless government drawn largely from the hapless Manchu officials, and with only the corrupt Chinese eunuchs to attend to the Boy Emperor's menial needs, was now in disarray. The Provincial Governors of the regions began to flex their muscle, each in turn flirting with independence. In 1910, the Revolutionary Alliance under Dr Sun Yat-sen drove a fateful dagger into the country, which was already bleeding badly. From Szechwan in the west, unrest had spread across the land. From the north, a powerful and cunning general by the name of Yuan Shih-k'ai, who controlled China's only modern army, met Sun Yat-sen's representatives in Shanghai, hoping to seek an alliance."

Then, there was a sudden and massive crash in Chun Ji's cell. Owing to his violent tossing and turning, he had rolled out of the bunk onto the cold stone floor, narrowly missing the bucket of urine. Blearily, he half-opened his left eye, only to look up and see the yellowed bulb swaying on its short and dirty flex from the ceiling with its peeling grey paint. For a split second or so, he thought that he was at home in his village. He wondered where his sisters and brothers were. Half-concussed, he curled up instinctively into a foetal position at the foot of the bed for some warmth, and fell into a hazy sleep but the disturbing images carried on...

"...Later that year, as the unrest grew, the revolutionary touchpaper had been well and truly lit. And so when the Governor General of the Szechwan Assembly, who was loyal to the throne, arrested the leaders of a militant protest, the Revolutionary Alliance, together with various other revolutionary groups, retaliated with extreme violence. Angry peasants, members of secret societies and even bandits having joined in, caused unremitting mayhem. Police and tax offices having been burnt down, jails were broken into, warehouses were looted, and telegraph wires and railway lines were

sabotaged. Already weakened by multiple defections to the revolutionary cause, the government troops were overwhelmed by over a hundred thousand militant citizens.

The revolution had spread like fire. During the night of the 10th October 1911, after intense fighting, rebel soldiers and their revolutionary comrades broke the back of the Ch'ing authority in the city of Wuchang. A military government of Hupei having been formed, declared a republic. In the weeks that followed, all government officials in the greater part of the Manchu garrisons in fifteen provinces had been murdered, and under the leadership of the Army and the Revolutionary Alliance, these provinces immediately declared their independence. Nervously, the foreign powers watched the turn of events with bated breath.

Soon after the Wuchang Uprising, the court, fearful for its survival, had turned to its general, Yuan Shih-k'ai, and appointed him as Prime Minister to negotiate with the revolutionaries. But this did not stem the haemorrhaging in the country, as cities and counties across the land proclaimed their autonomy. By now, most of the provinces in China had set up a regime headed by a military governor. Old China had been swept away.

By the end of 1911, Dr Sun, with the support of the revolutionaries of Nanking, had set up a provisional government of the first **Republic of China**, *with him acting as its first President, on the understanding that, on the demise of the Ch'ing Dynasty, he would step aside for Yuan Shih-k'ai.*

Negotiations between the factions ended with a pronouncement from the Ch'ing court on the 12th February 1912 that, 'Due to the will of the people, and by the will of divine intervention', the monarchy having been renounced and a republic decreed. And so, after almost three centuries of the Ch'ing Dynasty, with its Manchu Emperors who had ruled from 1644, the Dragon

*Throne with its so-called 'heavenly mandate' swiftly died. And
together with it, an unbroken period of over two thousand years
of omnipotent rule by Emperors throughout the dynasties had
come to a sudden end."*

*The news at that time had flashed like lightning through to the
countryside. Chun Ji's family having heard it from a traveller
returning from the city. In the village, celebrations had begun
in earnest. Suckling pig was roasted on open spits. Firecrackers
exploded, filling the air with the pungent smell of gunpowder
smoke. Kites flew high into the sky. Immediately, there was a
mass ceremonial lopping-off, of the much-hated pigtails from all
the males in the village. Chun Ji remembered it well. He was just
thirteen years old when it happened. With unrestrained glee, the
men, youths and even children cut off each other's pigtails,[30] the
wearing of which had been the symbol of enforced subjugation by
the Manchus, who had used it to control the native Chinese over
the centuries when they ruled China during the Ch'ing Dynasty.
Symbolically, the villagers then burnt the plaited braids in a huge
bonfire in the square and threw the ashes into the nearby river
to float downwards to the sea. Like millions of other peasants in
the land, the Kwong Clan, along with their friends and relatives,
felt for the first time in their humble lives that they had now been
set free.*

*But was that euphoria to last? The Chinese people, you
would have thought, deserved a period of peace and stability
after that momentous year in 1912 when the last line of the
royal dynasties had been swept away, bringing with it the birth
of the new republic with General Yuan Shih-k'ai as its de facto
President.*

---

30 Pigtails (or plaited braids) known as 'trailing queues' had been enforced by the ruling
Manchus with the surrounding skull shaved to distinguish the indigenous Han Chinese
males, who hitherto used to wear their hair tied up in a knot until the Manchus came to
power. By Manchu decree, the Han Chinese could not fraternise with or marry Manchus
– a crime punishable by death.

However, Yuan Shih-k'ai's election had not been without opposition. There were constant uprisings, and his armies had to quell Canton's efforts to break away from the Empire. The Cantonese, including Chun Ji's family, had feared for their lives as marauding troops spilled over from Canton into the province of Guangdung. Even nearby Taishan hadn't been immune to the troubles. Bandits on horseback from the mountains and renegade pirates from the sea, a constant threat for decades, had run amok in the rural areas of Guangdung unopposed...

Like a rumbling drain Chun Ji's sudden snoring escalated as the terrifying dreams persisted...

"...Tibet, supported by Britain, having meanwhile, rebelled against its status as a Chinese dependency. Outer Mongolia was then ceded to Russia. Japan having increased its incursion into Manchuria, and when the First World War broke out in 1914, the Japanese occupied the province of Shantung.

Yuan's government had been fast collapsing. Provinces continued to break away. The Western Allies had forced Peking to declare war on Germany. A clandestine attempt to restore the last Ch'ing Emperor had been foiled by Army generals sending a plane to bomb Peking. Warlords, recruited from dissident generals bent on gaining power, roamed Northern China, whilst in the south, Sun Yat-Sen's followers again set up an opposition government. Meanwhile, Japan had increased their grip by financing many of the warlords and rebels. In June 1916, Yuan died.

*In Russia the following year, the Bolshevik Revolution overthrew Czar Nicholas. Soon, Russia's Communist Revolution of 1917 would have far-reaching consequences for the whole world. In 1918, the hostilities of the **First World War came to an end**, with over fifty million military and civilian casualties. But then,* a pandemic – "Spanish Flu" (Influenza) gripped the world until Spring 1920 with up to fifty million dead.

In 1919 the following year, a World Peace Conference was convened in Paris. On the heels of that, The League of Nations was established. Furthermore, the map of the world, and particularly the face of Europe, having been redrawn. The conference debated the Chinese situation. When the decision had been taken to confirm the rights given in secret by the Allies, and by Yuan five years earlier to the Japanese over Shantung, three thousand students immediately gathered to protest at the Gate of Heavenly Peace. Violence followed as pro-Japanese officials had been savagely beaten up and a government minister's house having been burnt down. The government had rounded up hundreds of students for imprisonment. This had then led to wholesale protests and marches, with the support of factory workers and the merchants of Shanghai in a massive strike of unity.

In 1921, Sun Yat-sen, as leader of the south, changed the name of his revolutionary party to the Kuomintang – the Citizens' Party; often referred to as the KMT or the Nationalists.

Then, on the 1st July that year, with the encouragement of Soviet Russia, several Chinese met with Bolshevik agents in Shanghai to form the Communist Party. In Peking, Mao Zedong[31] emerged as a young student revolutionary and immediately joined the fledgling Communist Party.

At the time, the KMT thereby accepted cooperation with the Communists, since the Russian Communists having advised Sun on framing his party's constitution, had also helped to reorganise the armies of Southern China, now led by Sun's ambitious military aide and brother-in-law, General Chiang Kai-shek.

---

31 'Mao Zedong' written in Pinyin – a more common spelling based on China's own simplified, Romanization system as opposed to 'Mao Tse-tung', based on the older spelling devised by the Europeans called 'Wade-Giles'.

Under Sun, the first Republic of China, with its government based in Canton, fought for foreign recognition of its universal legitimacy, with a rival government of warlords – allied to the old regime having remained in Peking".

It was against this backcloth of unrest and imminent civil war that would eventually split China in two that the young Kwong Chun Ji in January 1921 had embarked on his eleven-thousand-mile journey[32] to the West to save his family…

The young man was still groggy from his fitful dozing, reeling from the disturbing images which he assumed had been nightmares of China being torn to pieces over the years, when he thought he heard a short grinding sound. It was as if a key was being turned slowly in the lock on the cell door. He cocked an ear towards it, but there was no further noise. Cautiously, his teeth rattling with cold, he pushed himself up off the floor, using the edge of the mattress for leverage, and crept barefoot towards the door. Holding his breath, he pulled the handle to open the door just a crack. Warily, he peered around it. Outside, it was quiet as a grave. And so, quickly and silently, he slipped on his sandals and tried again. This time opening the door wider, he crept stealthily along the stone passage that led to the entrance of the police station. As he reached the front desk, he suddenly shrank back in alarm, for standing with his back to him was the officer who had thrown him into the cell the night before.

The officer spun around as though he were half-expecting him. 'Oi, son!' he barked. 'You'd better hop it before I change my mind! By the way, there's a visitor waiting for you outside!'

Chun Ji's suitcase and his canvas bag were thrust brusquely in front of him, with some of his papers slipped inside the rope that was tied around the case. The officer spat out the end of a cigarette butt that he had been chewing from the corner of his mouth and jerked his

---

32   Hong Kong to Liverpool by boat in 1921 took over eleven weeks to cover the thirteen thousand or so miles on the slow journey around the Cape of Good Hope, having to stop to refuel and for fresh supplies en route.

head towards the entrance, then swiftly he added, *'And don't let me see the likes of you here again!'*

Quickly gathering up his possessions, Chun Ji hurried through the open door. The cool, fresh air made him gasp as he filled his lungs with a deep breath. Dawn was just breaking, though the light remained hazy. Silhouettes hung starkly over the tall buildings in front of him as his eyes tried to get used to being set free. Warily, he glanced all around him, expecting a trap. To his surprise, suddenly a tall Chinese stranger with a narrow face, wearing a Western trilby and a dark jacket, stepped out of the shadows of the building next door.

'Kwong Chun Ji?' The stranger approached with his hand outstretched in a friendly welcome. 'I'm your mother's relative, Fung Nam. You must call me Uncle Fung!'

He grabbed hold of the young man's case, and protectively ushered him away from the police station. Once Chun Ji had got over the shock, curiosity quickly replaced it, for there was a barrage of questions bursting to be asked.

As they hurried down towards the tram that would take them to his home and laundry business across the River Mersey in Rock Ferry, the uncle told him that he had been alerted by the Kwong family back in Taishan to look out for a nephew who would arrive in England about this time. And, luckily for Chun Ji, it was just in time, for he was down on his luck, and down to his last penny (yuan) with only the clothes (now filthy and threadbare) he stood in.

'Bu... But I thought I was on the way to America!' he protested. 'But as soon as the boat docked, it was too late. And then when I looked round, the boat had set sail again. Then suddenly the police arrested me!'

The older man nodded sympathetically. 'Your papers, I was told by the British authorities, were not in order. Your travel document, passport and certificate issued in Canton were forged. And so when you disembarked at the docks your landing pass and passport were confiscated, hence you were arrested. I'd wager my life that the intermediary agent your family entrusted to go to the office of the Bureau of Public Safety in Taishan was crooked. I bet he pocketed most of the money your father paid, and fiddled the bribes, so that you were sold false papers. That's happened before and it will happen again! It is more than likely that the agent was in the pay of the Triads[33] who control many of the officials back home, and most of them are corrupt anyway. The Triad gangmasters, and there are many who are affiliated to different criminal groups, such as the secret Snake Head tongs, do this so that they can keep track of you wherever you go, so that you are always in their debt.' Chun Ji's uncle heaved a grim sigh, spreading his hands helplessly.

'What?! Even as far away as the West?'

'Yes, young man, their tentacles of evil spread right across the world. So welcome to Liverpool and to Great Britain. And welcome to this, the new and free, New World!' he added, with a huge dose of irony.

It was at that moment that Chun Ji felt a pang of homesickness. He suddenly wished that he could turn the clock back to the beginning of the year; to his old life – well before the 10th January, the day he left Dai Dune Chun for the last time.

Leaving the tram, they hurriedly made their way towards the Pier Head to catch the ferry to cross the Mersey. The uncle and his nephew, whom he had met only once as a child in Taishan, continued in silence towards Chun Ji's new home so that he could start a new life. Somewhere in the distance, a young blackbird started to sing. And then Chun Ji noticed for the first time that the blossom on the trees lining the road had started to bloom. Spring was around the corner, together, perhaps, with a glimmer of hope...

---

33 Criminal gangs (tongs) originating from secret sects that go back decades. Sworn to secrecy, members enforced to life allegiance to their society by rituals and the threat of deadly recriminations. Notorious today for protection rackets, drug trafficking and prostitution.

Chapter 5

FROM THE FURNACE INTO THE FIRE

Merseyside, England, 1921–1923

URBAN LIFE ON MERSEYSIDE soon settled into a boring and laborious routine for Chun Ji, but he did not complain as he was fed and watered and had a roof over his head. His uncle proved a kind and generous guardian to his young nephew, whom he regarded as a naive innocent abroad who needed protecting. Being a widower with no children, Fung Nam was glad of the company of a young relative to remind him of the clan village back in China. And furthermore, as one of the elders, he regarded it as a family obligation.

Chun Ji was given a small room in the attic at the back of the shop. Previously, it had been used as a storeroom, and it reeked of toxic chemical detergents which had soaked into the fabric of the floor and the walls. The only other spare bedroom was used by one of the Chinese workers his uncle had employed in the laundry business. In Britain at that time and for many years to come, the Chinese were restricted to menial jobs. They did not dare to compete with the indigenous workers in the factories, shops or transport, for fear of causing trouble and racial resentment in the towns and cities with accusations of stealing local jobs. And so, the migrant Chinese (who did not constitute a big immigrant population in the country, remaining mainly in Liverpool and London near the seaports where they had landed) kept themselves to themselves. And those who were resourceful, opened hand-laundry businesses at which the Chinese excelled. Fung Nam said it meant long, hard hours of labour for little return. But it was a small, honest living, nevertheless.

To earn his keep, Chun Ji was put to work immediately. At five o'clock each morning, he had to get up to stoke the fire in the boiler and carry in the sacks of coal that were stored in the rear yard. It was back-breaking work, but he did not complain. There was little time to think about anything else, but work. Starting each day from the back of the premises, using buckets of industrial bleach, he had to scrub out the large wooden tubs where the linen would be soaked overnight. The following morning, he then had to wash the linen by hand, pummelling it against a large zinc washboard. No sooner had he finished that task, than he would have to hose down and scrub the floors, including the outside lavatory at the back of the yard before he could have a break and some food. The day would be long and exhausting, filled with a continuous round of washing and boiling the endless piles of sheets, pillowcases and towels in the copper boiler. Rinsing them and then wringing them out by hand, and eventually hanging them up to dry in the boiler room, was never-ending. Ironing was done using heavy hand irons that weighed over eight pounds and were heated on a cast-iron stove whose chimney stack was crudely vented through an open window. The solid stove, hexagonal in shape, against which the irons were propped up vertically like magnets, was fired by smokeless coke fuel which needed topping up every hour or so. The daily tasks, all of which involved standing on his increasingly aching feet, never appeared to stop. Poisoning from carbon monoxide was a constant hazard. Continually exposed to the fumes, but unaware of their potentially fatal consequences, Chun Ji fortuitously survived, but developed a chronic cough, having suffered some irreparable damage to his lungs.

As a novice, Chun Ji wasn't yet allowed to touch the shirts, starched collars and smaller items such as cotton handkerchiefs – work that would have been less arduous. He rarely got to bed before midnight. The choking smell from the caustic washing soda, the acidic bleach, and the dense, pungent steam from the drying and washing soon infiltrated his nose, ears and eyes, which rapidly became raw and inflamed. With their skin drawn back from the constant soaking in the bleach and the soapy water, his hands soon shrivelled like those of a corpse, and the blood vessels swelled up like purple worms which crawled at the backs of his hands. The worst part of the labour was when he had to drag the sacks of raw washing powder up from the cellar on his back, and then up to the ground floor to the rear of the shop. That was not all. In between all this, he had to heave up the heavy bars of industrial soap which were packed in wooden crates. The soap came in dense, two-foot blocks which he had to cut up by hand using a knife, which soon became blunt. Quite rapidly his skin cracked open and bled. Soon he developed contact dermatitis and chronic hay fever.

Hardly a day would go by when he longed to see and smell the open skies again; the mountains, the rivers; and to hear the friendly squelching sounds of the villagers back home tramping systematically through the paddy fields of rice, the women singing happily to themselves as they worked.

The other worker lodging at the laundry was another young man about Chun Ji's age, named Chang. Surly and moody, he was supposed to help Chun Ji by sharing the work after showing him the ropes. Craftily, Chang would stay in bed until six o'clock in the morning and only leap out a few minutes before Fung Nam started to stir. Chang told the boss that it was *he* who had done most of the work long before five, claiming that the nephew, being a country yokel, was lazy and stupid and hadn't a clue what to do. To avoid an argument, Chun Ji kept quiet and tried his best to get along with Chang. Similarly, not wanting to upset his uncle, he did not make an issue out of it.

On Sundays, the business was closed for the day. Once a month, Uncle Fung would take his young nephew to Liverpool, to the Chinatown that had grown around Nelson Street. To make him feel at home, he would take him to a small Chinese restaurant for dim sum, after shopping for Chinese groceries – rice, tinned goods, dried fish, wind-dried sausages and bean curd. However, mixing with the Chinese community made Chun Ji miss his family and his ancestral home even more.

At the Chinese Overseas Club next to the old church at the bottom of Nelson Street, his uncle would play Mah-jong with his friends. Whilst waiting for him, Chun Ji would sit with the families and the younger boys and girls to watch old films in the hall in the basement. The films were usually from America. They were either gangster movies or Westerns; all in black and white, badly streaked and with a grainy quality as the reel of film often broke down in the projector. His uncle said that it was a good way to learn English. However, silent movies, such as those featuring Charlie Chaplin or Buster Keaton, proved a futile way to learn!

After three months, his uncle decided that Chun Ji had better try to become more English; if not in his mannerisms, then at least in his appearance. He thought that his nephew ought to try to blend in with the local population. Two things happened as a result. Firstly, one of Fung's loyal customers, a retired clergyman, offered to teach Chun Ji some English on Sunday afternoons, when they were both free. In exchange, his uncle did not charge for this gentleman's laundry, which comprised shirts, household linen and even curtains from time to time. *'It's a fair exchange!'* exclaimed Fung Nam, clapping his hands gratefully.

Chun Ji was a fast learner and within six months had grasped the basics of conversation. Soon he was able to order goods from the local English shops, and he even managed to travel on trains, trams and buses on his own, informing the conductor of his destination. Similarly, at other times, he was able to enquire confidently about directions. Gradually, he acquired basic writing skills, so that he could fill in forms. He was soon able to sign his name as **'Kong Ji'** (an alternative pronunciation, by which increasingly he became known to the authorities) with a flourish using a fountain pen and Quink ink.

He was once teased that he might be distantly related to an obscure descendant of Confucius, born Kong Zi, who became head of the Kong Clan based in Qufu in 551 BC. Uncle Fung dismissed this as extremely unlikely, and what is more, virtually impossible to prove. 'And moreover,' he claimed, 'although the Confucian line of Kongs fell into extreme poverty at the turn of the century, they would have never ended up doing this type of menial labour – in a pauper's hand laundry, for heaven's sake – even if their very lives depended on it!'

Secondly, Fung thought it important that his nephew change his look from that of an obvious country peasant, and a foreign one at that, to that of a typical English worker. 'You must blend in with the wallpaper,' commented Uncle, gesticulating wildly. And so, one Saturday afternoon, he arranged for Chun Ji to go shopping in Liverpool and bought him a set of clothes from the high street. However, being sensible and thrifty, and bearing in mind the economic state of the country since the horrific Great War had ended just three years ago, during which over seventeen million died, with thirty-seven million casualties, they managed to secure a hardly-worn three-piece suit that fitted him perfectly from a pawnbroker's shop. *As long as it didn't belong to a corpse!'* insisted his uncle to the pawnbroker. He was reassured that the previous owner had left the city in a hurry to return to Ireland due to the recent partitioning of the north from the south,[34] and wouldn't be returning to claim the suit, which had been pledged as security.

After a good English haircut from the barber, Mr Breen, who had the shop next door to his uncle's, Chun Ji looked the part. His jet-black hair was parted down the middle with a fashionable short back and sides and slicked down with Brylcreem which made it glow like newly-hewn coal. A foaming wet shave with the traditional cut-throat razor added the final touch of refinement.

---

34 The Government of Ireland Act 1920, which came into force on the 3rd May 1921, provided self-governing parliaments for Northern Ireland (predominantly Protestant) and Southern Ireland (predominantly Catholic). This partition inadvertently sowed the seeds of unrest between the two countries, with riots in Belfast and Londonderry over the next seven decades, starting in the '30s, '40s and '50s, and latterly with a guerrilla bombing campaign by the Provisional Irish Republican Army (IRA) which spread to the mainland of Britain.

An appointment was made with the nearby photographer's studio in Rock Ferry. Sepia and black-and-white photos were taken of Chun Ji wearing a winged, starched collar and tie, a pinstripe three-piece suit and polished black city shoes that completely transformed his appearance. When these pictures were sent back to his parents and siblings in Taishan with an accompanying letter, his father replied that he did not recognise him. His mother felt that the change was far too radical, but still, they were grateful for the small amounts of money Chun Ji had managed to save to send back home each month. He didn't receive much in wages, as board and lodgings had to be paid to his uncle. Indeed, Fung Nam, although philanthropic, was also realistic, for bit by bit he deducted the cost of Chun Ji's new clothing from his weekly wages. In those days it was ten shillings (*fifty pence in today's sterling*), rising in ten months to one pound.

To get used to his striking new image, on Sundays Chun Ji would put on his best clothes and walk down the road to catch a tram. On more than one occasion, he would pass a European girl in the street, and, from habit, remembering what he had been taught in old China about life in the cities under Western control, he would step wide to the outside of the pavement to allow the person to pass. Similarly, when opening a door, he would allow the person to enter first. In China this was in deference to the Westerners who had colonised parts of the country, including Canton, since the early 1800s. But when Chun Ji did this on Merseyside, as often as not, the girl would give him a half-friendly smile in acknowledgement. At first, he would avert his eyes in embarrassment, not knowing how to interpret what to him were confusing signals. Either he thought that he was still being recognised as a blatant foreigner – an oddity sticking out like a sore thumb, an object of curiosity, or, at worst, a figure of derision – or did he detect in that coy half-smile an encouragement of sorts?

When he delicately brought up the subject one evening with his uncle, the latter was shocked and appalled. 'Look, nephew, I have to remind you that your great-grandfather Wah Oi would be turning in his grave if you consorted with the foreign devils after what he went through! Your ancestor was born exactly one hundred years ago in 1821, the Year of the Snake, near Canton. His family was there when, shortly afterwards, the British sent gunboats and warships up the Pearl River to take control of Canton. Although it was done under the pretext of trading for tea exports, making out it was all in China's favour, it was the rotten trade in imported opium[35] grown in India which was thrust onto the local population. Armed British coastal clippers sold the drug into many outlets along the south-eastern coast. Gangsters, Triads and smugglers all joined in this illegal free-for-all, knowing how easily the addiction would spread and eventually weaken the resistance of the native population. This would make them much easier to control. *So, you can see why we, the Chinese, historically distrust these foreign white devils – these gweilos!'*

Chun Ji didn't know quite what to say to this salutary piece of history, so he lamely asked when and how his great-grandfather Wah Oi had died. Apparently, he had died in 1878 in appalling circumstances. In 1848, along with others, he had been abducted by criminal gangs in the pay of European slave owners to work in California on the transatlantic railroad, before escaping by killing his guards and then making his way back home to China.

And although this was decades before Chun Ji was born, by then, opium, promulgated by the British, had spread like wildfire across the country, with opium dens and opium offices selling the drug in the open. From his uncle's helpless expression, he suspected that Wah Oi must have died of opium poisoning. But the terrible Opium Wars of 1839–60 between China and Britain over the sale of the drug by the British failed to stop the trade. 'Fortunately,' added Uncle, 'your own father's immediate family were too poor to buy opium, and so they escaped that evil. To them, the more pressing evil was poverty. This, more than anything dominated their everyday lives with the daily

---

35 Opium was used by the British to pay for silk, tea etc., as they had run out of silver as currency.

task of simply finding enough food in order to survive from one day to the next!'

Snippets of news from Chun Ji's parents back home came via letters which took weeks to arrive by sea. By then the news was often out of date. It was rarely good news. The family was near starvation, and sometimes there had been yet another peasant uprising in Guangdung, which had been quickly and savagely put down by government forces. Conscience-stricken, he would send as much money as he could back home using postal orders mailed from the General Post Office in Liverpool. Sometimes, he would use the services provided by the Bank of China. By the time he had finished work late at night, he was often too exhausted to write much in his letters. Besides, at night it was extremely difficult to read and write as the rooms above the laundry were mainly lit by the dim flicker of gaslights fixed high on the walls. He would set aside Sundays to write a bit more when he could concentrate. He used a set of calligraphy brushes borrowed from his uncle. They were sharply tipped with rabbit hair, which he moistened between his lips before dipping in the ink he made by grinding an ink stick and adding water to the resulting powder.

He was reminded by his uncle not to mention to the family back in China that he worked in a laundry. Poor and humble though they were, he said, they would be horrified to learn that their eldest son had to handle foreigners' dirty washing, as some unfortunates once did in the overseas legations in Canton. And, like many migrant Chinese, because of that shame, they had to pretend that they worked in a shop, without elaborating further.

The next year dragged as laboriously as the first one. Work's tedious routine was the same and dominated his life. Chang became more resentful as the months rolled by, for he noticed that Chun Ji appeared to grow in confidence and become more self-reliant. He was particularly jealous of the ease with which his co-worker became, on the face of it, more 'at home', and looking more 'English' as time went on and had heard with increasing resentment that he had received various compliments and admiring glances. But to Chun Ji, this was far from the truth. He remained intrinsically Chinese inside and out, no matter where or when, or how often he wore Western dress or spoke English. These paradoxes remained until his dying day. In every cell of his body, he remained Chinese, both in outlook and in attitude honed by tradition and shaped by his upbringing. Reporting every month to the British authorities only reinforced the view that he remained, irrevocably, an alien. And moreover, he had to be registered as such with the police and was often forced to comply with the restrictions under the Home Office's Aliens Order of 1920 in specific circumstances of heightened security and curfew. That brought home the reality of his life with resounding clarity.

Towards the autumn of 1923, two major events happened that shattered his steady routine. Early one morning, Uncle Fung rushed into Chun Ji's room, out of breath and looking agitated. He shook his nephew to wake him up. 'You have to leave immediately! Two horrific things have happened! Chang told me last night that some shifty-sounding characters have been making enquiries about you – the young Kwong who has been living on Merseyside after arriving on the *Liberty* two years ago.'

Chun Ji looked puzzled as he dressed quickly. '*What does it mean, Uncle?*'

'I really don't know. But I don't like it one bit, especially coming from Chang. Perhaps he's been shooting his mouth off in Chinatown about your missing papers when you docked at Liverpool, and how well you have made some money since then. And what's even more sickening is that he must have taken a bribe and betrayed you!'

'Could it be something to do with the Chinese gangster network you warned me about?'

'Possibly,' replied his uncle as he hurriedly helped Chun Ji to get his suitcase. 'If it is, then they will never let you out of their clutches, if they find you here! You had better go into hiding and lie low for a while.'

As he threw his possessions into his case, Chun Ji asked anxiously, 'And what was the next terrible thing you were about to tell me?', though he feared that nothing could be worse than the first.

Uncle Fung leant wearily against the open door. 'I've just received a letter brought over by a Merchant seaman... it must be weeks out of date now.' His voice tailed off hoarsely. 'It's bad news I'm afraid, nephew. Your father has died suddenly.'

Abruptly, Chun Ji stopped what he was doing and slumped heavily onto the bed, his face ashen with shock. 'Wh... *what do you mean... di... died?* Was he ill?'

His uncle shook his head, either because he did not know the answer or because he was as stunned as Chun Ji was. 'Look, nephew, there's no time to lose. You've got to get out of here before it's too late! Hurry! I have an old friend who has a business like mine in Cardiff. If we hurry, you can catch the first train out of Liverpool. I've made all the arrangements.'

Chun Ji hardly had enough time or the heart to ask where this strange place called Cardiff was. He had just about adjusted to living on Merseyside with a part of his Chinese family, the nearest in England he could call his own, and now he had to start all over again. He was being forced to leave the comfort of a home, yet again – the second time in two years.

As they hurried from the shop with Chun Ji's meagre possessions crammed into his well-used old suitcase, and his uncle carrying his rolled-up quilt that had been brought from China, a curtain twitched above the shop. Chang peeped out over the street, grinning slyly to himself as he watched them leave.

Chun Ji clambered onto the train with a heavy heart. With a deep bow of gratitude, he said goodbye to his uncle. He choked back words that he wanted to say; nothing came out. He leant out of the window of the carriage door, which had just snapped shut with a brutal thud. He did not notice the clouds of steam mixed with grimy engine oil which swirled in swathes around him.

As the steam train started to pull away, his uncle ran along the platform, and shouted through the open window, 'Remember, you have to mourn your father for at least three months. You must wear white and fast as much as you can! Tradition decrees that you must not wash your hair for four weeks. I remind you, nephew, that you, as the eldest son, are now the head of the family clan!

'And the last thing: keep away from the foreign devils – especially those pale-faced Welsh women!'

His voice was drowned out by the loud hooting from the engine's siren. But by then his warning had fallen on deaf ears.

The chugging locomotive clanked and squealed slowly out of Liverpool's Lime Street Station, carrying Chun Ji away on yet another journey into the unknown. Cursing his luck, he felt he had been banished yet again. He wondered if some past misdemeanours by his ancestors had put a curse on him. Or was it a punishment in advance for something he might do to incur their wrath sometime in the future? Just then, it suddenly struck him that he would never see his father again. Kwong Loong Cheung Ham had died of a mysterious illness aged just forty-eight. The date was the 16th December 1923; inauspiciously, the Year of the Pig. He could not help it, but suddenly, a terrible thought flew across his mind. Perhaps his father had known that he had only two years to live when he said goodbye to Chun Ji as he left Dai Dune Chun. Of course, his father wouldn't have dared tell him, otherwise he would never have left. Tears welled up inside of him, but his emotions by now were still raw, so he choked them back as he had before when he left China. He couldn't decide whether the tears were for his dead father, whom he would never see again; or for himself. This was not the time for self-pity, he scolded himself. He had to start his life again somehow – a new life in new surroundings, in another town somewhere else, because of Chang's treachery.

But he would never forget what happened on this date in England. It would be carved forever in his memory. The weather was dull, grey, the sky covered in a thick blanket of cloud with the threat of rain hovering in the distance. Like a bad omen, it clung heavily, accompanying him all the way to another new place. For the second time in his life, he was heading into the unknown, and this time he would be forced to go on the run and into hiding. Barely two years had passed since he had landed in England, and so much had already happened to him since then.

Chapter 6

THE MISSING YEARS

1924–1935

For eleven years, Chun Ji moved like a fugitive from place to place – Cardiff, Swansea, Stoke-on-Trent, Hanley, Burton-on-Trent, Crewe, Newcastle upon Tyne and Scarborough – seeking work via the Chinese network whenever he could. It appeared that he was desperately and constantly on the run. Always keeping one step ahead of the Snake Head gangs[36] that controlled the protection rackets to extort money from Overseas Chinese workers who had family back home, he managed to avoid direct confrontation, for that might have led to his being badly maimed or even killed.

In 1926, a general strike brought Britain virtually to its knees, after one million coal miners were locked out over a dispute with the mine owners – the National Coal Board (NCB) – who wanted to pay them less for longer hours. The Trades Union Congress (TUC) called out workers from the buses, rail, docks, printing, gas, electricity, building, iron, steel and the chemical industries in support. From 1929 to 1933 the Great Depression had gripped the West. In Wall Street in the States the stock market collapsed, with reverberations in Britain

---

36 Snake Head gangmasters were connected to the Triads and other criminal elements (e.g. Tong gangs), who were commonly involved in blackmail, drug trafficking and prostitution.

and Europe. Unemployment had reached record levels of over three million in Britain alone. In protest, hundreds of men – miners and shipbuilders, desperate for work to feed their families, had marched two hundred miles down from the north to Parliament in the famous Jarrow March.

Although work was sparse, somehow Chun Ji managed to scrape together what little money he had to send it back home to his family in China, who were teetering on starvation owing to continuing military incursions and civil unrest. In 1924 in the south, Dr Sun Yat-sen's fledgling Nationalist government (the Kuomintang), propped up by General Chiang Kai-shek and his armies, still struggled to establish themselves as the first Republic of China based in Canton. But the rival government of warlords allied to the old regime remaining in Peking in the north was still a major threat. Following the death of Sun Yat-sen in March 1925, Chiang increased his grip on China. Meanwhile, Mao Tse-tung's Communists were growing in strength and influence day by day. By 1934, after the Long March north to Yan'an, Mao's peasant armies were regrouping, and continued their fight against Chiang Kai-shek's forces for the control of China.

Both factions were fully aware that the old (and now, common) enemy, Japan, had been in occupation of Manchuria in the north since 1931. A Japanese state was established, with the return of the last of the previous ruling Manchus – P'u-i,[37] who in 1934 was installed as puppet ruler and Emperor of Manchukuo.[38] From there as a springboard, Japan's historical designs on China continued unabashed. Chomping at the bit, Japan was mobilising once again to engage in a full-blown conflict as the fighting between Mao and Chiang Kai-shek escalated. They did not have long to wait for a chance to exploit the infighting,

---

37 Formerly known as Hsuan-t'ung, the Boy Emperor (P'u-i). He had been forced to abdicate on the 12th February 1912 following Sun Yat-sen's Republican Revolution. He remained in the Imperial Palace in the Forbidden City in Peking until 1924, when he was forced into exile. He then went to live in Japanese-occupied Tianjin.

38 A puppet state created in Manchuria by the Japanese in 1932. P'u-i was enthroned as K'ang Te in 1934. Despite guerrilla resistance against his puppet regime, he held on until 1945 when he was captured by Soviet troops.

and in 1937 invaded deep into China, whereupon the Kuomintang and the Communists formed an alliance – albeit an uneasy one – to engage the Japanese forces.

In the face of the disturbing news and everything else, family obligation took priority as Chun Ji, the eldest son, had to continue to help his mother and siblings regardless of his own needs or circumstances. These unbreakable ties of blood to the family clan could never be forgotten, even for one minute. The word **'duty'** still resonated in his consciousness. For the rest of his life, it dictated what he did and the reasons for it.

Years later, it was revealed that he had escaped deportation by the skin of his teeth, when the authorities raided premises in the seaports of the cities, particularly Liverpool, where he was working at the time. Sympathetic English neighbours hid him in their cellars whenever immigration enforcement officers swept through. At one time, the local butcher hid him amongst the freshly slaughtered animal carcasses hanging in the cold room. How he managed to avoid death by hypothermia, we shall never know. At another time, a Jewish neighbour rolled him up amongst the bales of cloth in his tailoring workshop. Chun Ji, seemingly with little fear for his own safety, had previously helped his neighbour to fight off anti-Semitic thugs (stirred up by Sir Oswald Mosley, a former Member of Parliament who in 1932 formed the British Union of Fascists with his band of Blackshirts) who were attacking the tailor's shop and threatening his family.

But very little was recorded of what he did or who he was living with in those missing years from 1924 to 1935. Being the alfa-type of man he was, and largely testosterone-driven with an innate sense of survival, as well as some necessary companionship, it was inconceivable that he would choose to live on his own for any length of time. Either he was too ashamed to admit that he was living with someone, or the fact that he was constantly fearful for his life from criminal gangs, and forever looking over his shoulder. But one way or another, in those years, it is certain that he lived out of a suitcase which was always packed, ready for him to flee at any moment.

Chapter 7

THE LETTER

September 1935

CHUN JI WAS WOKEN early by the clatter of the letter box as it sprung back on its hinges. He crept downstairs on tiptoes, not daring to disturb his girlfriend, Ruby, or her young son, who were sleeping soundly. Lying on the doormat of his laundry was a letter from China. He opened it with trepidation, expecting a plea for more money, or fresh bad news such as a tragedy in the family or further military insurgency around his old home. The letter was curt and to the point:

> *Dai Dune Chun,*
> *Taishan,*
> *Guangdung,*
> *China,*
> *1ˢᵗ September 1935*

Dear Chun Ji,
   It has been decided by the elders of the family that, since you are now approaching thirty-eight, it is time that you took a wife. As you know, your younger brother Chun Tin is already

married, thanks to your money. It has been arranged that you will be married to one of the daughters of the late Chow Yuk Yiu, from the Chow village of Shek Tsui Chun over the mountains in the next valley. For some reason she has not been given a proper name by her family but is called Mo Nui – 'Little Girl'. We have been told by the marriage broker that she is young, healthy and just eighteen. Though we have not seen her face to face – in fact, we do not know what she even looks like – we will be able to examine her properly to ensure that she is chaste once she arrives. She will join the family in fifteen days, delivered here by her uncle and the intermediary.

She will stay here for six months on trial and to be instructed by the womenfolk of the family in how to be a dutiful wife and mother. During that time, her papers will be arranged via the British Consulate in Canton to allow her to travel to the West to join you. A dowry has been accepted – though it is far less than what the family normally requires for the eldest son doing well in the West. We have assured the Chow clan that you are self-sufficient, but still dedicated to your obligations to China and to your ancestral home. And furthermore, that you are well established in the West, clean-living and celibate.

Please arrange a photograph for the ceremony, so that we can then also insert it into the family portrait once you are married. It has been decreed that you will be married by proxy here in the village. The clan elders have made all the arrangements.

There is no time to lose. We do not know what is beyond the horizon. China is again in turmoil. News from the cities reports that Chiang Kai-shek and his Nationalists continue to fight for power against the Communists. Mao Tse-tung has emerged as a powerful leader and, bolstered by the overwhelming support of a massive peasant army after the Long March of last year, they have moved northwards, we are told, through the western part of China, and are now biding their time in Shensi Province, waiting to seize power.

Although the two factions continue to fight each other, it is reported that they are both bracing themselves for the imminent threat posed by the Japanese, who are mobilising their forces once more to invade our beloved country. Lawlessness and starvation again threaten to destroy our family. Bandits run amok and continue to ride down from the mountains and rape our neighbouring villages. Since your father died some twelve years ago, we look to you as head of the family to save us from destruction.

Finally, it is urgent that you send some more money as your second brother, Chun Yee, is getting married and needs to build a new house.

The letter was signed by his first brother, Chun Tin – the next oldest on behalf of their mother, Fung Ting.

Stunned by what he had just read, Chun Ji grabbed a chair and sat down. Beads of sweat broke out over his forehead. The news from China could not have come at a worse moment. How could he tell Ruby, his live-in mistress of two years? He had better get rid of her, because if news got back home about his foreign *Gwoi-paw*,[39] the shame would not only ruin his family, but also devastate the Chow family. Any other prospective brides would regard him as tainted goods. And furthermore, he would never be able to return home. Up until now, he had by some means managed to conceal his secret life from the Kwong family. For Chun Ji, like for all Chinese, 'saving face' was a priority.

He decided to tell Ruby the news without delay before a stab of conscience caught up with him. He dared not succumb to sentiment, or show a slither of gratitude to her for her help in building up his business, or for the time she had looked after him when he was ill. To admit these things would be a sign of weakness.

Duty to his family in China must be obeyed above all else.

---

39 A derogatory term for a European (Occidental) woman consorting with a foreigner, especially an Oriental man.

She was barely awake when he told her. He expected tears and tantrums after their years together. Instead, he was met with a cold, ashen look that he had never seen from her before. He would have preferred it if she had attacked him physically. But instead – sheltering her young son in her arms she started to pack in deathly silence.

Shortly before noon, as she swept through the door, she turned abruptly and snatched his letter from his hand. She crumpled it underfoot and spat, '**Duty? Obligation?** You'll *never* be free of those damn chains! *They will be the death of you one day.* Just mark my words. They'll put a curse on you!'

The door slammed, rattling the windows in the frames.

His face in his hands, Chun Ji slumped against the back of the door, deflated. He felt that a trap was closing in on him again. Sudden memories of being thrown into prison on that fateful day fourteen years ago when he'd first landed in the West came bursting back. Whichever way he turned, he felt cornered: not only here in England, but also eleven thousand miles away in China. The tentacles of family obligation were far-reaching.

At this moment, dare he tell his family that the future was not all that safe and certain in Europe either? It was not a propitious time to take on a new young wife. Dare he tell them that fascism had reared its ugly head not that far away in Germany with its emerging xenophobic Nazi Party, and that racism and extremism were gathering pace and spreading? Germany's new Chancellor, a certain Adolf Hitler, was growing in power and strength. The German military machine was flexing its muscle. News coming from across the Channel day by day was not encouraging.

Chun Ji's dismay and objections did not last long. There was no room for introspection or for feeling sorry for himself. Duty to the family must come first. Shrugging his shoulders, he was forced to accept the inevitable. He started planning to have that photograph taken to send back to China to enable him to be married by proxy in his ancestral home.

Chapter 8

THE ARRANGEMENT

Shek Tsui Chun (Beak Slate Village) Taishan, China, 15th September 1935

'WAKE UP! WAKE UP, Mo Nui!' Choi Ping seized her sister roughly by the shoulders and shook her vigorously.

Mo Nui groaned, rolled onto her front and pulled the blanket over her head.

'You have to wake up, big sister. They have arrived – they're waiting for you outside!' Choi Ping screamed into Mo Nui's ear.

Slowly and reluctantly, Mo Nui climbed out of bed. She rubbed her eyes. Fear and apprehension had fixed her gaze. 'I don't want to go!' she wailed. 'I don't want to leave you, Choi Ping, or our little brother! It's so unfair.' Her eyes were blood red and swollen from crying all night.

'But you *have* to. Mother will be furious and will beat us with the bamboo to punish us for failing to rouse you!'

Chow Choi Ping was just fifteen, three years younger than Mo Nui. She and their younger brother, Chow Kit Siang, would now be the only siblings left in the family home in the village of Shek Tsui Chun. Shek Tsui Chun was a sprawling village of smallholdings thirty-five miles south of Taishan City, which in turn was over sixty miles west of Guangdung in Southern China. It had been the ancestral home of the Chow Clan for the last three hundred years.

A much older sister, Chow Choi Ching, born in 1898, had married and left the village many moons ago to live with her husband Yung in his village to the south. The remainder of Mo Nui's siblings had either died tragically or been given away at birth. The family records made depressing reading: another older sister had died; no name was ever recorded for her. Chow Kit Ngwun, the oldest brother, had been sent away at the age of twelve to Singapore to earn a living. He died aged twenty, suffering from exhaustion. Another brother, Chow Kit Kwai, a few years older than Mo Nui, had died by walking into the sea after suffering starvation in the wars that had swept through the province ten years earlier. Two baby sisters were given away at birth but died within a year. Another was sold as a baby when her mother was just fifteen.

Mo Nui quickly thought about what had happened to her tragic and decimated family as she splashed cold water onto her face from a bowl near the window. As she glanced out across the paddy fields, the water buffalo were already at work. It was past six in the morning, and dawn was just skimming over the mountains to the east of the valley casting an early glow. Condensation hung on the ledges of her window like stubborn limpets. Autumn had crept in early with a sharp bite in the air, though it was still only mid September. She shivered, and quickly dressed for the journey. She wrapped a quilted jacket over her cotton dress and long, baggy trousers, and, pulling on her sandals, made her way down the rickety stairs.

At the foot of the stairs, her mother, Moy Gwut Kwai, was waiting impatiently with hands on hips, ready to explode like a simmering volcano.

'And *what* took you so long?' she demanded, blind fury etched over her face. 'And don't you dare answer back, you, sullen, worthless girl! *Just look at you!* Your cheongsam looks as if you slept in it all night! Looking at the state of you, I won't be at all surprised if the Kwong family cancel the arrangement. And where would that leave us, you ungrateful girl?! You'd better hurry before they change their minds. The marriage broker and your Uncle Sei Nging are waiting outside to take you!'

Choi Ping and Kit Siang hid behind Mo Nui, shaking with fear. Their mother had been born on the seventh day of the seventh month in 1883 and had ruled the family with an iron fist ever since the children's father, Chow Yuk Yiu, died of cancer early in 1923, aged forty-one. Behind her back, Moy Gwut Kwai was known as Loong Nar – the Dragon Woman – because of her explosive temper. Mo Nui had never been her favourite. Indeed, 'Mo Nui' meant 'Little Girl' (or simply 'Girl'), because her mother had refused to give her a name from the day she was born. In fact, she had wanted to give her away, as she had done to two other newborn daughters. But this time, Mo Nui's father had refused, having taken pity on her.

For the past eleven years, Mo Nui had never forgotten her last haunting images of her father. Following his death, her mother had forced Mo Nui, at the tender age of seven, to ceremonially kowtow to his decaying corpse every morning for four months as a penance for being saved, telling her that it was a Chinese tradition. Six months after he died, his body had been exhumed from the grave,[40] and placed next to the ancestral shrine in a windowless room at the back of the house. Remembering the horrific sight and smell of the rotting flesh of her once-beloved father, Mo Nui continued to have nightmares for many years to come.

Their father, Chow Yuk Yiu, had been born in 1882 in the same village of Shek Tsui Chun. Hundreds of the Chow Clan had migrated from the north-west of the province and established the village in the mid 1600s at the time of Ming Dynasty. Like most of the millions of Chinese at that time, they came from peasant stock, and had spent centuries tilling the land and rearing livestock. At the tender age of just thirteen, Yuk Yiu was married by arrangement to Gwut Kwai from a nearby village. She was a year older than he was, but seemed older still,[41] having survived hiding in the mountains as a child with her mother to avoid having her feet forcibly broken and bound in

---

40 Exhuming the bodies of the deceased was previously common practice in order to carry the ancestral remains from place to place when moving home.

41 Often wives, if they were older than their husbands, were more mature and advanced; especially in sexual matters.

accordance with the fashion that had started centuries ago at the Imperial Court, when small feet were deemed delicate and desirable.[42]

Chow Yuk Yiu was a professional gambler by trade and entertained the guests by playing the tables of Mah-jong at weddings and funerals throughout the region. When times were good, he was able to feed his family with spit-roasted goose and suckling pig, and expand his smallholding, whilst at the same time enlarging his fields of rice. On the surrounding borders, lush watercress grew abundant and flourished in the autumn rains which filled the banks of the river dykes in front of his house. The ancestral house grew larger than their neighbours' and occupied the best position in front of the village, facing the open paddy fields directly in front of them.

To the east, a small mountain range meandered gently away from the valley, hugging the horizon. Twenty-five miles south, following the course of the river, flanked by weeping willow and bamboo groves, was the open sea. The house, though simple, was plain and flat-fronted. It was built from dull grey stone with rounded terracotta tiles on the roof. The gable ends of the roof curled upwards, scrolled to mimic a classical pagoda style. When times were bad, and that happened often, Mo Nui's parents had to sell the lead from the gutters and strip the decorative tiles, some of which were glazed in silver leaf, from the front of the house, perched high above the shutters and windows.

Outside, a small crowd had gathered. Although they were all called Chow in this village, they were not all direct descendants of Chow Yuk Yiu's ancestral line, but they were curious, nevertheless, having heard that the daughter with no name belonging the village gambler was being escorted across the mountains to the Kwong village of Dai

---

42   Foot binding was an ancient Chinese custom carried out at the Imperial Court of Emperor Li Yu since the tenth century (in the Southern Tang Dynasty) to ensure delicate feet (called 'lotus feet') amongst their womenfolk, particularly their concubines. Clan elders often copied this fashion in a ritualistic ceremony amongst their community, hoping to improve the marriage prospects of their daughters. Not only was it considered dainty, but, some say, it became a surreptitious method to ensure that women remained faithful and were unable to run away. The forefoot and toes were broken and forcibly bent over at an early age (often from the age of two), and continuously bound with strips of cotton or silk. The practice was outlawed in 1912 at the start of the Nationalist government of the first Republic of China.

Dune Chun to marry one of the eldest sons of the clan, who happened to live thousands of miles away in the West.

As Mo Nui gathered her meagre possessions together to leave, she was still reeling with the shock. Only seven weeks ago she had been told by her mother, the Dragon Woman, that the decision had been made with the consent of the village elders for her to marry. '*I don't want to marry, I'm too young!*' Mo Nui had cried. 'And particularly to a dreadful stranger… and one who lives on the other side of the world!' And when she had heard that the chosen husband, arranged by the Chow and Kwong families via the marriage broker, happened to be nearly twenty years older than her, she was overcome with panic, teetering on terror.

'Stop your foolish protests, girl!' her mother had demanded, twisting Mo Nui's ear violently. 'I was just fourteen when I got married to your father. I had *no* choice in the matter. *I even gave birth to your older sister when I was barely fifteen!* Anyhow, I need to be rid of you, so there will be one less mouth to feed. You've been nothing but trouble since that fool of a father of yours stopped me from selling you when you were a baby! And what's more, the dowry – something we can ill afford – has already been paid.'

Although the Kwong family had demanded much more than the two young hens, a fat piglet, a roll of cotton and a single piece of raw silk that was on offer, they had to be satisfied with the fact that at least the Chow girl came with a valuable provenance. This was a letter of proof from the local barefoot doctor that she was unmarried, a virgin and had no formal name attached to her – making it easier to rename her, once married.

Mo Nui gritted her teeth and made her way through the open door, carrying a rolled-up quilt containing a comb, a facecloth, a coarse linen nightdress, pyjama trousers, a tiny piece of unpolished jade her father had given her, which she had kept from the beady eyes of her mother, and a tiny bamboo cricket cage containing her pet cricket; seemingly the only friend she had left. Choi Ping and Kit Siang wanted to rush to her side for the last time, but they did not dare, fearing their mother's wrath. The neighbour's two Chow dogs, pale cream in colour, lean in body and thin in fur because of the hot summers, gently nuzzled up to her ankles fondly, as if they sensed that she was going away. She gave them a cursory stroke on their heads for the last time.

The marriage broker, a wizened, dour-faced old spinster, and Mo Nui's old Uncle Sei, threw her possessions into a bamboo handcart and started to walk solemnly towards the end of the village, with Mo Nui reluctantly shuffling two steps behind them. *'Hurry, girl!'* they urged; 'we have a long day ahead of us to reach the mountain pass, which you can just see in the distance. It's another two hours from there to reach the village before the light fails.' Like all travellers, they were wary of the bandits who still hid in the mountains.

As they dragged the cart behind them, its rough wheels kicking up a dust storm, the crowd quickly scattered. Within minutes the clouds began to shut out the morning sun which had risen weakly from over the mountains to the east. Mo Nui refused to look back for fear of bursting into tears. Pulling her jacket tightly around her shoulders, she stared resolutely ahead. Her heart was leaden and at bursting point. Passing the stone well at the end of the village, as if in defiance of her mother, she vowed to revert to calling herself Mou Lan ('The Girl Who Fetched the Water' – a sobriquet). It was a name that she had secretly adopted during a spell at school, where she had been given three years of basic education by the teacher in exchange for fetching water from the well. But the sight of the well made her shudder with the memories of tales she had heard of unwanted babies thrown down there to drown by their families, despite their wailing and their screams.

The onlookers had drifted away by the time she and her escorts reached the tall watchtower that had been built two centuries ago at the exit from the village. It was here that the villagers, armed latterly with guns, took it in turns to climb up to watch for bandits from the hills or marauding pirates from the sea, who over the years had raided their village on a number of occasions. The story had it that, twenty years ago, bandits had one night kidnapped a baby girl from the village who subsequently grew into a beautiful savage. On becoming leader of the bandits, she returned with them to the village on horseback to rob and pillage. Until one day she was betrayed by one of her gang, who laid a trap because she had spurned him. She was captured by the local militia, raped, disembowelled, and then beheaded for refusing to become a concubine to the one of the generals. The severed head was spiked on the tip of a spear and left to rot on top of the watchtower as a warning to others. The skull remained there to that day, in a state of decay, and untouched by human hands due to local superstition.

As she left the village through the ornate archway at the end of the road, Mou Lan, as she was now to become, bewildered and stunned, sneaked a quick glance backwards at her home for the very last time.

Weep no more for me, you sheltering willows,
For no tell tale signs have been left of childhood there.
As if I had never been home in this friendless place.
No footprint stark upon the banks of grass,
No fields of rice to feed me more.
For I have been plucked and cast aside,
As corn chaff scattered in the conspiring breeze.
Though now the cold witness of the autumn winds
Would blow a chill through my dead father's soul.
Cry not for me, you restless rivers and rich bamboo,
For I will return, and return I must,
To be recalled by fresh seasons when born again.

It would be sixty long years before she was able to return to her ancestral village of Shek Tsui Chun.

Chapter 9

THE CEREMONY

Dai Dune Chun, 9th February 1936

T HE DAY HAD STARTED badly for young Mou Lan. She had been woken up early by Kwong Fung Ting, her future mother-in-law, screaming that she had to get up immediately to feed the geese and chickens at the back of the house. It would be an hour before the light of dawn rose over the roofs of the houses that formed the village of Dai Dune Chun. She had been living at the Kwongs' for nearly six months now, and she still felt like a stranger – a commodity that had been traded, unwanted by her own mother who wanted to get rid of her.

From the day she arrived at their ancestral home, Kwong Fung Ting had treated her with cold indifference. Although formally agreed through a marriage broker to be the future wife of the Kwong oldest son, Chun Ji, now living in the West, young Mou Lan was made to feel that she was a burden on the family and was there on sufferance. Since the death of her husband, Loong Cheung Ham, thirteen years ago, like most matriarchs in China who were forced to be the head of the family, Fung Ting ruled with a rod of iron.

Six months had dragged by interminably. And although the next phase of her life seemed frightening, Mou Lan felt nothing could be any worse than what she was dealing with at present. She shared a tiny room on the mezzanine level, next to the ancestral shrine with nineteen-year-old Chun Rei, the youngest of the Kwong sisters. A ladder propped next to the platform was the only means of getting up and down from there. The stairs at the corner of the house were for the sole use of her future mother-in-law and the remaining males of the family.

'*Are you getting ready for the ceremony?*' shouted Chun Ho. Already married, and being the eldest of her future sisters-in-law, she was delegated to act as young Mou Lan's chaperone for her wedding, which was today. 'Hurry, the chicken has been prepared!' added Chun Ho pointedly. 'The village elders are waiting and getting impatient.'

Mou Lan made the final touches to her cheongsam using her reflection in the nearest window. It was the only dress she had brought with her. Her heart raced. It was not for joy, but resigned inevitability; she had been forced to accept that the marriage had been irrevocably arranged by the families according to Chinese tradition. She had no say in the matter. For if she did object, it would be dismissed out of hand, and she would be severely punished for protesting. Unmarried women had no status in old China, and even less of a voice.

Covered in a red veil, Mou Lan was escorted in a procession to the eastern corner of the village and the ancestral community hall where all the oldest members of the village were assembled. Scattered amongst the sprawling bamboo groves surrounding the building, the inhabitants of the village had turned out in their hundreds to see this young woman – a girl with no name, to be married by proxy to the eldest son of the late Kwong Loong Cheung Ham and his widow, Kwong Fung Ting. It was to be a unique occasion, for it was not often that the groom happened to be ten thousand miles away, living in the West. Their wholesale curiosity was one thing but sharing in the village feast afterwards was an added incentive, for suckling pig and barbecued goose were rumoured to be freely on offer.

Let's get it over and done with, thought Mou Lan wearily as she was ushered through the door of the hall by Chun Ho, and Chun Tin, the next oldest brother.

Nothing had prepared her for what happened next, during the marriage ceremony. At the earlier mention of a chicken, she naturally assumed that it would be part of the meal. But in fact it turned out to be the proxy to which she was to be married. A photograph of her future husband was balanced above the seat of a chair, where a *live* chicken – *a young cockerel*; one of those she had fed earlier that morning – was tethered to the chair leg by a length of red ribbon.

'You cannot be married by proxy using another human being,' declared a village elder, with exaggerated sagacity, on seeing her discomfort. *'It would be bigamy!'* he added, stroking his white goatee beard. 'But it has been decreed that another two-legged creature, as long it's not a person, can legally represent your future husband by proxy. He will be told by letter in due course.'

Mou Lan was in a state of shock. Hysterics and tears almost took over. But the savage looks on her in-laws' faces, particularly her mother-in-law's, immediately wiped out any facial expression. Forced to sit on an adjacent chair to the proxy, she shuddered with fear. Just then, a gruesome thought flashed through her mind. Would the elders slit the throat of the hapless bird at the end of the ceremony and offer to mix its blood with hers? Or would it be allowed to live? She never did discover its fate.

Years later, when she tried to recall the events of that day, it did not matter how hard she tried; the details were erased from her memory. Words that she had chanted on instruction from the elders vanished into thin air. All she would say, when asked, was that she had been married by proxy to a chicken. She remembered very little of the setting off of firecrackers, or the village feast in the ensuing aftermath. But, not surprisingly, she lost her taste for poultry for many years to come.

Six weeks passed and her simple possessions were packed. She was now ready to leave the Kwong family. But before she did, she released the lid of the tiny cage to allow the last of her pet crickets to escape out of an open window. 'At least one of us will be free!' she murmured, as the cricket spread its wings gratefully and flew away into the fresh country breeze.

On two successive occasions her brother-in-law had escorted her to Canton to get her passport and travel documents from the British Consulate. The first visit was to attend an interview to explain her reasons for joining her new husband in England. In front of a stony-faced deputy consul, she signed her papers with a thumbprint, for she had never been taught to write her name in English.

In the middle of March, as the winter snows started to thaw from the tops of the mountain ranges that cupped the valleys of Guangdung Province, an ancient bus took her northwards from the village to Canton. The early rain of spring had just begun when she boarded a ferry which was towed south by tug, down the Pearl River.

It had been twenty hours since she had left the Kwongs' village. It was an arduous journey for someone who had never travelled by boat before, let alone, someone, who had only just left the safety and the familiarity of her home village a few months ago. On reaching the port of Hong Kong at the mouth of the South China Sea, she boarded a steamship that was destined for England.

As with most of the passengers crammed into the ship, seasickness, dehydration and disease were a constant curse. The trip on the rough seas took forty-eight days. A decade earlier it would have taken at least twice that time, as it might have been forced by cost to navigate the treacherous waters around the Cape of Good Hope, but Mou Lan's ship reached England via the safety of the Suez Canal. She was accompanied on the journey by one of her mother-in-law's cousins, Sher Yik Fung and his wife.

Hidden in her suitcase was a sepia photograph of her new husband. It was the same photograph that had been used at the ceremony. Kwong Chun Ji was twenty years older than Mou Lan, and in his Western-cut suit, winged collar and waistcoat, he looked terrifyingly like a typical Western foreigner, except for the slant of his oriental eyes which gave him away.

She would have to get used to this new world; a place which would be far removed from what she was familiar with. How would she get on with the stranger she had been forced to marry from the other side of the world?

Would he treat her better than his family back in the Chinese village had? How would she cope in this new life she was about to be thrust into?

She thought then that it could not be any worse than the treatment she had suffered in China following the death of her father all those years ago. But there again, now duty-bound, only time would tell.

On the 8th May 1936, her ship, the SS *Western Hope*, docked at Liverpool.

Part II

1936 – 1952

Chapter 10

LIVERPOOL, ENGLAND

8th May 1936

THAT MORNING, WITH THE sea mist still stubbornly hanging over the Mersey like an impenetrable curtain, Chun Ji had got up earlier than usual. Clutching a tiny passport-size photograph of his new bride, he caught a tram and hurried down to the docks. He didn't have long to wait before hundreds of passengers began to disembark from the cargo steamer that has just arrived from the Far East. Almost immediately, the cargo was offloaded by winch amidst the deafening blast from the ship's horn and the clanking of heavy chains from its grinding machinery. A pungent smell of diesel choked with steam swirled around the crew and greeted the dockhands waiting to reload goods for the return journey.

Screwing up his eyes against the midday glare, Chun Ji waited impatiently at the quayside. Amongst the last group of passengers to leave, he managed to recognise his mother's cousin, Sher Yik Fung and his wife from old family photographs that had been sent to him from China, though of course they looked so much older now. Walking behind them, struggling with a suitcase and a large, cumbersome wicker trunk tied with rope, was a young woman dressed in a Chinese tunic under an oversized man's greatcoat. Her flimsy sandals, which looked more suitable for Eastern shores, shuffled along with her tiny steps. She seemed out of place.

Greeting his distant cousin warmly, Chun Ji gave Mou Lan a cursory glance. In return, she gave him a blank, tired look. She raised her head briefly after staring at the ground. Giving a grunt, he barely acknowledged her and grabbed her suitcase perfunctorily. If he sensed that the situation was awkward, he disguised it well. In accordance with Chinese tradition, there would be no display of emotion in public between husband and wife.

Mou Lan tried desperately to adjust to her new surroundings. But seeing this older man – her new husband; this stranger who, although he spoke in her local dialect of Cantonese, seemed to her much more of an alien, a typical gweilo, than Chinese – made the task much harder. Dressed from top to toe in Western clothes, Chun Ji wore a trilby to match his overcoat, which he draped over a pinstriped suit, complete with waistcoat. At first glance, despite his oriental features, he appeared to blend in with the mass of Westerners milling around the quayside.

A further blast from the ship's siren shook her out of her trance-like state. Finally arriving in the New World which she had heard so much about, with its strange sights and smells, she knew that it would take a monumental effort to acclimatise. Leaving the gangway from the foot of the quay, Sher Yik and his wife said goodbye with a brief nod as they left to join a Chinese family who had been sent to collect them.

With a deliberate jerk of the head, Chun Ji gestured to Mou Lan to follow him to the tram. It would take them to his home, soon to be her new home, which was above his laundry business in an impoverished part of Liverpool in Rocky Lane. She dutifully followed her husband, remaining three paces behind. And, in keeping with Chinese tradition, she was not allowed to speak until he spoke first. This had been drilled into her back in China at the Kwong family home.

Obedience to her husband in all matters was paramount. It was a duty expected of a wife that would last until death.

Early on, Chun Ji had decided that he must get rid of his new wife's Chinese hairstyle at the earliest opportunity. Her long, unruly fringe of jet-black hair, rigidly straight at the sides, would look out of place in England. Jettisoning the names Mo Nui and Mou Lan, Chun Ji *renamed* her **Choi Lin**,[43] as befitting a sibling of her sisters, who had already been given the nomenclature of 'Choi', such as *Choi* Ping and *Choi* Ching back in China.

Mo Nui – the girl with no name through the spite of her mother
– had now at last been given a name!

On the 9th March 1937, Choi Lin gave birth to their first child, a daughter. She was given the name Shui Dee, together with an English name, Eileen, as suggested by an English neighbour. Boiled eggs were dyed red using cochineal and eaten by way of a celebration. The baby was delivered at home by the local midwife, who cycled everywhere in spite of the distances. Chun Ji brewed a potion from a concoction of Chinese herbs that he had bought from a herbalist in the growing Chinatown which had sprung up around Nelson Street. The foul-smelling tea mystified their doctor and appalled the midwife. He claimed that the brew had restorative powers and was commonly used postnatally in China. Choi Lin was back on her feet within two days. Hitching the baby onto her back in a sling, wrapped in swaddling, she returned to work. The doctor and the midwife just couldn't agree on whether her seemingly rapid recovery was because of the herbs, or due to the pressure of her being self-employed which had forced this young mother to return to work earlier than usual. They were told that, as there were just two of them in the laundry, her husband was reliant on her helping him with the business.

True to his upbringing, Chun Ji had little to do with his newborn daughter. Changing her nappies and feeding her, he believed, were women's duties. Furthermore, he felt that to reveal sentiment or emotion to the newborn, never mind to his spouse, would be a sign

---

43   'Lin or Ling' means 'delicate' or 'daring'.

of weakness. But at the end of the day's work, just before midnight, using candlelight to save electricity, he pulled out a long sheet of paper to use as a scroll. Dipping into a small jar which he had filled with water mixed with the shavings from a black ink stick, he started to write, slowly and deliberately, in classical calligraphy which had been taught to him by his father. Using a bamboo brush tipped with fine rabbit hair, he inscribed, starting from the right-hand side of the paper, the name of his firstborn – Kwong Shui Dee – and the time and date of her birth. He had decided that the *generation name* for all his children would be **Shui** – meaning *'lucky'* – and this would run as *an unbreakable thread* throughout that generation. This was expected of him in typical Chinese family tradition. For posterity, this scroll would be the family chart of his children; for those who had been born and for those yet to come.

Not long afterwards, out of the blue, a letter came, addressed to Choi Lin, thinking at first that it came from her mother. However, it had been written by her younger brother, Kit Siang. It was stark and to the point.

Shek Tsui Chun
Taishan
Guangdung
China
6th May 1937

Dear sister,

It has been decided that Uncle Sei, our late father's brother (you will remember him, as he escorted you to the Kwong family home when you were eighteen to be married), will soon leave China and take your mother and me to Borneo to start a new life. Choi Ping has now married and she will remain in the family house. There is an uncertain future here in China, with the continuing civil war between the Communists and the

Nationalists. And with the Japanese preparing to invade our country, we feel that we must make a fresh start before it is too late.

Uncle is a capable builder and says there are opportunities in the wood and oil industries of Borneo, where the Cantonese community is growing. He doubts that Japan will be interested in such a place, with its uninhabited islands and jungles. They are more likely to have designs on Singapore due to its thriving economy and strategic port. And what's more, Mother says that I can find a young bride with a good dowry not far from where some distant cousins have settled.

Uncle Sei, now a widower, we are sure will look after us like his own immediate family, since his son, our cousin Kit Chong, was tragically killed last year when his boat exploded in battle in the South China Sea. Mother says we have not heard from you since you left to join the Kwong family. We heard from them that you are now settled in a place called Liverpool with your new husband and making a good living.

Your brother,

Kit Siang

Choi Lin was tempted to screw up the letter and throw it in the fire, remembering full well how her mother, 'Loong Nar', the old dragon, had treated her from childhood. But, since it had been written by her brother, she decided to put it aside.

In May 1939, she gave birth to a second daughter, named Shui Mein. She was given the English name of Rose, indicative of the month of her arrival in the spring. Chun Ji added her name, and the date and time of her birth, to the family scroll next to her sister's.

Since arriving in England, Choi Lin had had little time for anything else, as looking after her two young daughters, cooking, cleaning and working in the laundry took up every minute of the day. It was a difficult time in which to scrape a living; not only for their family, but for countless others around them. And yet, in response to his family's pleading letters, Chun Ji managed to send half his money back to China as the conflict between Japan and China escalated. His wife thought that he should consider their immediate family needs first, but she did not dare to raise the subject for fear of her husband's short temper. At least, she conceded, he had proved a hard and clever worker as well as a good provider and would protect his family with his life.

As the clouds of war gathered in Europe, Chun Ji grew fearful for his family. Day by day, Nazi Germany, having rearmed in contravention of the Versailles Treaty,[44] grew in military might as Hitler, demonstrating his expansionist ambitions, reoccupied the Rhineland in 1936. Not long afterwards, he was poised to annexe the Sudetenland, which stood on the border between Germany and Czechoslovakia. Meanwhile, the rest of the European powers stood impotently by.

The Fascists under Mussolini in Italy, together with Japan on the other side of the world, became allied to the German cause. Neville Chamberlain, the Prime Minister of Britain, tried to avoid another major conflict in Europe by attempting appeasement. In September 1938, he returned from Munich in triumph, proclaiming that, by ceding the Sudetenland to Germany, hostilities between Britain and Germany had been averted. Waving the agreement in the air, he had declared, '**Peace in our time!**'

He spoke too soon. The following year, Hitler invaded Czechoslovakia. When German tanks rolled into Poland in September 1939, Britain declared war on Germany. Eight months later, Winston Churchill replaced the hapless Chamberlain. It was the beginning of the terrible Second World War – a European conflict that would soon envelop the whole world.

As it happened, in that same year, Ruby, Chun Ji's scorned mistress, opened a rival laundry business opposite his in Rocky Lane. Whether

---

44 Signed on 28th June 1919 following the defeat of Germany in 1918 after the First World War ended

it was coincidence or deliberate, he could never prove. He had his theories, which he kept close to his chest. His business, already struggling to pay the rent, meet the doctor's bills, and feed his wife and family, was suddenly and savagely cut in two, for the area could barely sustain one, such laundry, never mind another one. As soon as the shop had closed for the day, Ruby, with her young son on her lap, would glare out of the front window overlooking the street, and try to catch the eye of Chun Ji's wife. It was disconcerting to say the least.

'*Why is that English woman keep staring at us?*' Choi Lin would ask, puzzled.

Not daring to tell her the truth, Chun Ji would only shrug his shoulders and reply that he did not know, dismissing it as the behaviour of a deranged woman – a mad *Gwoi-paw*.

Since he had turned Ruby out into the street four years earlier, a terrible curse had threatened to materialise. It began with a desperate and unnerving war of nerves.

Chapter 11

THE BLITZ

28th August 1940

ON THE 5TH MARCH 1940, Choi Lin bore a son, whom they called Shui Lun, with an English name of Francis. Soon after the birth, Chun Ji displayed some obvious disappointment. Choi Lin could not understand it, thinking that he would be pleased to have a son. But there was something her husband was holding back. She wondered what it was. He muttered something about being the runt of the litter. Nevertheless, he still added the boy's name to the family chart – after being reminded to do so. With other pressing matters on her mind, such as survival from day to day, she dismissed it as typical of her husband's austere nature. Tactile affection towards the children, never mind to her, was not in his nature; nor indeed his upbringing. Not being demonstrative towards his family was ingrained in him, and to outside observers could be construed as callous. In stark contrast, she noticed how affectionate her English neighbours were with their families and each other. Perhaps it was to do with the way Chun Ji had been brought up by his father, and even his father before him, she thought to herself.

Chinese tradition, duty and obligation came at a price.

No sooner had the bitter winter disappeared, when spring brought in the start of a very dark time in the history of Europe. With the invasion of Denmark and Norway, the war on the Continent escalated. *The gathering storm was about to break.* Rationing had already begun. Gas masks had been distributed and air-raid shelters[45] were quickly built in the major cities and around the strategic ports of Britain. Finland capitulated under the Russian invasion. At the beginning of the war, the Soviets had allied with Germany. On the 10th May – the same day that Winston Churchill replaced Chamberlain – Germany invaded France, Belgium and Holland. By June, France had capitulated with the occupation of Paris. A vast expeditionary force of British and French troops was forced to retreat humiliatingly from mainland France and had to be rescued from the channel port of Dunkirk by a ragged fleet of pleasure craft, Merchant trawlers and Navy destroyers. But in the close-fought Battle of Britain, the Royal Airforce squadrons managed to defeat the German Luftwaffe for control of the skies over Britain.

On the 28th August, the bombing Blitz[46] on Britain by the deadly Luftwaffe intensified with a vengeance, starting on Liverpool. In September, the docks of London, situated in the East End, took the brunt of the next wave of the bombing. The devastation spread to the centre of the city. Even Buckingham Palace was damaged. The King and Queen refused to be evacuated contrary to the advice from the government. They had decided to stand firm with the British people. Airfields, rail links and factories in Birmingham and Coventry that were involved in the production of aircraft and vehicle engines and munitions were targeted. The ports of Southampton, Bristol and Plymouth, and shipping in the English Channel were heavily bombed.

In the major cities throughout Britain, including Liverpool, children were being prepared to be evacuated to the countryside for

---

45 Communal air-raid shelters were built of reinforced concrete. Some were located in schoolyards and hospitals. Anderson shelters, made out of corrugated iron sheets, were issued to the population to be half-buried in their back gardens.

46 'Blitzkrieg' in German means a lightning war employing fast-moving tanks and military vehicles in tandem with dive-bombers. In Britain it came to mean rapid but massive air assaults.

safety. Chun JI refused to let his family leave. *'We live as a family, so we will die as a family!'* he declared defiantly.

In May 1941, massive air raids concentrated on Liverpool to cut off Britain's main artery for supplies and its main conduit across the Atlantic to the United States. The latter remained neutral, though continued to supply Britain with arms and supplies. Over two and a half thousand people died on Merseyside, and the same number were injured. Tens of thousands of homes were destroyed as Liverpool was ravaged. Although blackout blinds on all buildings were mandatory, this did not stop the relentless bombing attacks at night.

Having covered up his windows, Chun Ji decided to modify the cellar in the basement of his shop for shelter against the sustained bombing as the air-raid shelters were situated some streets away. If he tried running there in the dead of night with his young family in tow, he felt that they would never make it in time. The trapdoor, hinged at one end, was reinforced with an extra layer of wood and metal bars, though if a direct strike hit their building, his family who were hiding down there with basic food supplies including live pigeons and chickens (which he had reared from eggs), would be buried alive.

Together with his neighbours, he had been recruited to help in the local fire-watch duties and to work the crocodile lines, carrying buckets of water to put out the fires from the incendiaries and bombs that had landed in the neighbourhood.

In those eight nights of the May Blitz, 1,746 people lost their lives and over one thousand were seriously injured. Night after night, any glimmer of light from the moon and the stars was totally obliterated by the swarms of German bombers which blackened the sky, dropping their bombs with apparent impunity. Relentlessly, they dived low repeatedly like a thick cloud of deadly locusts. Their warplanes appeared to be impervious to the network of floating barrage balloons,[47] or to the anti-aircraft guns trying to pick them off between the lonely beams of searchlights that oscillated upwards in

---

47 Gigantic balloons acting as barriers or deterrents, filled with hydrogen which would
    explode and ignite on contact.

desperation from the ground. The terrifying sound of their *rat-a-tat-rat-a-tat* crackle, together with the thunder of explosives, continued to split the smoke-filled air at a devastating pace. The sight and smell of burning and destruction was like hell on earth.

At the end of the eighth night, even before the wailing of the air-raid sirens had subsided, with the dive-bombers wheeling away, Chun Ji's neighbour, who was a fire warden, raised the alarm that the row of shops opposite had been hit. In rising panic, Chun Ji immediately rushed out to help; but the fire was too intense, so they were forced to wait for a fire crew to arrive. Desperately, he hurled buckets of water onto the flames. But to no avail. The shop where Ruby had been living had taken a direct hit. The building was burning like a cauldron, the flames leaping higher and higher into the night sky. The fire warden hastily pulled him back from the inferno, and, after much persuasion, made him return home to keep an eye on his family.

'Did anyone get out?' Chun Ji asked, with a tremor in his voice.

'No one stood a chance!' replied the warden, shaking his soot-covered head.

Choi Lin asked the same question as soon as her husband wearily closed the front door. He just stared into space his eyes glazed over as if in shock. She didn't press further regarding the reason for the tears that streaked down his blackened face, for fear of a reply which she largely suspected. Banishing it to the back of her mind, she told herself that his tears were shed for the terrible week of bombing which had just ripped the heart out of Liverpool. This proud city – the heartbeat of Merseyside – had been her home for the last five years, where she had sought refuge from China, and which had given her protection, solace and comfort. This new home and newly adopted country of hers were now in danger of being destroyed.

They did not speak of it again.

Chapter 12

RAVAGES OF WAR

1941–1945

I T WAS FOLLOWING THE defeat of Mussolini's armies in Greece and Tobruk in early 1941, that the German forces arrived in North Africa. Greece and Yugoslavia soon capitulated. By June, Hitler turned against the Russians, and by the end of the year Moscow came under attack. On the 7th December, the Japanese mounted a surprise attack on the US naval base in Pearl Harbor, Hawaii, and invaded the Philippines, Burma and Hong Kong. This brought the United States into the conflict, and Germany declared war on the US. *The bitter conflagration now encompassed the whole world.*

On the 24th December 1941, Choi Lin gave birth to another son, Shui Ming, or Alan. Christmas Day that year was not an auspicious time for the Kwong family. However, Chun Ji seemed pleased with his second son, as young Shui Ming, unlike Francis, his older son, was more akin to what he perceived as close in likeness to others of the Kwong Clan. This time with an undisguised flourish of pride, he added Shui Ming's name to the Kwong-Gong family scroll. With seemingly prescient irony, he felt that having only four children was unlucky, as phonetically, 'four' ('*see*') means 'death' in Chinese, which caused him some concern.

Food was extremely scarce and their business was barely functioning. Imported Chinese provisions were still obtainable at a premium from one or two of the shops in Chinatown. These were not sought after by the indigenous population and somehow escaped the scrutiny of official rationing. But certain other commodities, such as rice, were exchanged for potatoes, lard, sugar and so on. Such was achieved by skilful bartering with neighbours in exchange for the relevant food stamps from ration books.

German nationals were being rounded up and interned in camps for the security of the country.[48] In America, Japanese citizens were also being rounded up. The hounding of anyone thought to be Japanese was spreading in some quarters, even in Britain. Unruly youths, having cunningly avoided the war effort, would prowl the streets of Liverpool, spoiling for a fight. On several occasions, thugs tried to smash the windows of Chun Ji's shop. The last time it happened was the night of the 5th November – Bonfire Night – when two gangly youths aimed a kick at the shop window and yelled abuse at the 'Yellow Peril Japs!', having thrown burning fireworks through the letter box. Chun Ji's temper snapped. From inside the front door, he grabbed a wooden pole that was used for pulling down the window blinds and chased after them. Hauling one of them back by the scruff of the neck, he handed the thug over to the local bobby,[49] who had run down the street to intervene. *'Leave the cowardly yob to me, Mr Ji!'*[50] urged the constable, dragging the youth away in a strong armlock.

Afterwards, Fred Brownsell, the neighbouring butcher, advised Chun Ji to hang out a Chinese flag from an upstairs window. The fire warden, who had got to know him quite well over the past year, suggested it would be prudent to hang a Union Jack flag beside it to also show his loyalty to Britain.

---

48   German nationals were interned on the Isle of Man and were interrogated by military intelligence from 1940 to 1945. One of the German-speaking officers was one Major Charles Stuart, who in 1967 happened to become Francis Kwong's father-in-law.

49   Bobby (or peeler) was slang for a police constable, after Sir Robert Peel (1788–1850), who was twice Prime Minister and who created the Metropolitan Police Force.

50   Due to Chinese forenames coming last, Kwong Ji, sometimes became known to the authorities as Mr Ji, as they believed that Ji was his surname.

Added to this, Chun Ji pasted a large black-and-white photograph of Chiang Kai-shek in the shop window. Whether that would have any meaning for people who were not conversant with the politics back in China, he didn't really know. His brothers in Taishan had thought the photograph might help, and had sent it to him that summer. Together with it came another plea for money as the next-oldest brother, Chun Tin, wanted to train as a schoolteacher. Another English neighbour suggested writing under the photograph that this family happen to be Chinese, *not* Japanese. Regardless of these efforts, several Chinese businesses in Liverpool were attacked by mistake as news of the Japanese victories in the War of the Pacific was broadcast on the BBC via the wireless.[51] Racial tension bubbled to the surface.

The Chinese, although they kept a low profile, were randomly subjected to insults from groups of lawless thugs ('Chinks go home!'), as Japanese residents were few and far between to attack. Another neighbour, Mr Manny Silverman, the local tailor, told Chun Ji that his relatives in Germany were suffering similar racial persecution by the Nazi mobs. He said that Jewish businesses had been firebombed, and that there were stories of atrocities meted out to the Jewish population, with the rounding up of Jews into concentration camps. Later, details of the horrors of the camps also filtered through. Jewish property was not immune to sporadic attacks in London and Liverpool by thugs inspired by Oswald Mosley and his Blackshirts who had held fascist rallies in the cities a few years earlier. But in the main, the majority of British people proved tolerant and sympathetic to the plight of the migrants, whichever country they came from. The hand of friendship and kindness was evident in the way the Liverpudlians treated Chun Ji and his family, and other foreigners seeking refuge.

In 1942 the Americans set up airbases in England, from which they would launch their attack on Germany and their Axis allies. The Blitz continued in England with the bombing of the cathedral cities, and in retaliation the RAF intensified their aerial bombardment on the

---

51 Later known as the radio.

German cities. In the Pacific, the Japanese continued their expansion into Borneo, Java, Sumatra and Singapore.

Following the Japanese invasion of Malaya, Choi Lin heard that her mother and brother had fled with Uncle Sei to take refuge in the jungles of Borneo. With China having eventually succumbed to Japan, and now with Malaya being overrun, it appeared that the Chows, having fled from a simmering pot, had fallen into a blazing fire.

But by the second half of that year, the British 8th Army, under Montgomery, gained the initiative in North Africa against Rommel's elite German troops. Meanwhile, Russian forces counter-attacked at Stalingrad. The beginning of 1943 saw the humiliation of the German surrender at Stalingrad. Hitler had foolishly underestimated the ferocity of the Russian fightback in the sub-zero conditions of ice and snow, having previously dismissed the Russian forces as an ineffectual army of peasants. The Battle of the Atlantic intensified, with the German U-boats sinking twenty-seven Merchant vessels in an attempt cut off supplies from across the Atlantic. Then with the vital help from the codebreakers at Bletchley Park[52] and the long-range aircraft of the RAF, heavy losses were inflicted on the U-boats.

Chun Ji's neighbours told him that perhaps at last the tide of the war was beginning to turn. He wrote to his family in Taishan that 'Churchy Herald' (as the Chinese in Britain affectionately called Churchill) would save Britain from Hitler. The Kwong Chun Ji family, like many others, tried to continue their lives with a modicum of normality. But this was of course nigh impossible under the dreadful circumstances of war.

Shui Fei (Milly) was born in November of that year. She was the last to be born at Rocky Lane.

'Another young mouth to feed!' Chun Ji groaned, adding her name to the family chart. He looked increasingly worried as he surveyed his ever-expanding brood of five children.

---

52 A secret estate in Buckinghamshire whose covert code breakers managed to break the German Enigma Code, which swung the sea battle of the Atlantic in the Allies' favour.

Francis (Shui Lun) recalls:

Somehow, under the critical eye of my father, I thought I must have been a badly behaved child; certainly, at an early age a degree of rebellion crept in. Perhaps it was to get some attention, as he made it plain that I was not his favourite son. Once, by mistake, I gave my younger brother Alan a boiled sweet which I had been given by a neighbour's boy I used to play with in the air-raid shelter at the end of the road. I think the sweet was an acid drop. Unfortunately, my brother began to choke, and so when I raised the alarm, Father hurried us both to Mr Brownsell, our neighbour the butcher, and between them they turned Alan upside down and slapped him on the back. Fortunately for him and for me, the offending sweet popped out.

That misdemeanour – however unintentional – was punished disproportionately, I felt. Forced to miss supper of the wonderful, steamed buns my father used to make from barbecued pork leftovers wrapped in bread dough, I decided to retaliate. I tried to jam the wooden lid my father had made to enable the children to sit on the 'throne' (the lavatory in the outhouse) without falling in over my neighbour's son's head. Further punishment ensued, with my father tying me up in the attic with a piece of strong cord to the banister. One hour passed. Only after I cried out that I wanted to go to the lavatory before I wet my grey flannel shorts did help arrive from my sister, Eileen – Shui Dee – who took pity on me. She tried to untie me, without success. Mother was helpless to intervene, as she didn't dare cross my father. Rescue ultimately came, with the air-raid sirens suddenly starting to wail above the city. Immediately, Father rushed up to untie me so that we could all run and hide in the cellar until the bombing raid had eased. It was just as well, as the chimney stack in the corner of the roof was blown off by the impact from a stray bomb.

Although I was rather frightened of my father, I have to say that we were all also slightly in awe of him. In difficult circumstances, he still managed to scrape a living and feed the family through the war years. The butcher next door gave him a salted pig carcass that he had managed to get from a farm in Cheshire. From the trotters, belly, ribs, cheeks and snout, Father would make wind-dried sausages, leaving the bones for stock. He managed to grow mushrooms and lettuces in boxes of soil in the cellar. Who taught him to sew, I do not know, but he managed to make shirts and clothes for the children and mend our shoes, as well as making a few pieces of furniture, such as a wooden bench and stools using classic mortise-and-tenon joints.

Regardless of his relatively poor command of English, he managed to get on well with our English neighbours. They called him Stanley. Even the local bobby who would check on all the neighbours by calling late at night to test if our doors and windows were securely locked called him Stanley after a while. Initially, it was formally 'Mr Kwong or Mr Ji', until Father gave him a cup of China tea and a cigarette. It was the bobby's and our neighbours' suggestion that we children should be baptised at St Luke's, the local church, and attend the local school to learn English. 'It would be better for your children in the long run, being brought up in England,' remarked our neighbours, trying to be helpful. Father reluctantly agreed, but was adamant that the speaking of English was still forbidden at home.

In contrast to this, my mother was never allowed to mix with the locals or learn the language. This caused quite a bit of strife within the family, as Mother increasingly noticed the relative freedom and equality that the English women enjoyed with their husbands. This would later lead to a crescendo of a showdown with my father.

By mid May that year, the German and Italian forces in North Africa were defeated. Mussolini had fallen, and by September the Italians surrendered to the Allies, prompting a German invasion of Italy to engage the Allied forces. In the Pacific, US forces drove back the Japanese from New Guinea and the Solomon Islands, whereas British and Indian troops began their guerrilla campaign in Burma. On the Eastern Front, the Russians recaptured Kharkov and Kiev from Germany.

Nineteen forty-four began with Japanese advances in Burma, New Guinea and Guam. Japan, who had occupied territory in Central and Northern China since their invasion in 1938, began their last offensive in the country by capturing further territory in the south, thereby moving closer to Canton and Guangdung Province, but meeting resistance from Chiang Kai-shek's Nationalists and Mao Tse-tung's troops. The Kwong family wrote to Chun Ji that they feared the worst as the Japanese edged closer to Taishan.

Chun Ji's business finally gave up the ghost after five long years of trying to struggle throughout the war. The rent far exceeded the income. He started to have stomach pains which the doctor diagnosed as ulcers that had erupted due to stress and working with toxic chemicals and detergents. The doctor suggested rest and Milk of Magnesia. Chun Ji wrote to his family in China that he would be unable to send money back for a little while. For the first time in his life, he was forced to shut up shop, and so he took the family to live in a small, terraced house in Leopold Road, in another part of Liverpool where the rent was much cheaper. The bombing was less intense in that part of the city. The two girls and his eldest son managed to attend the local school in between air raids.

Rome was liberated by the Allies in June that year, the day before the mounting of the D-Day landings to liberate Europe by the Allied forces of US, Britain, Canada, Australia, Belgium, France together with Czechoslovakia, The Netherlands, Greece, New Zealand, Norway, Poland and Rhodesia. Spearheaded by the US and Britain, (under the command of General Eisenhower and Field-Marshall Montgomery), 5,000 ships, amphibious craft and aircraft managed to land more than 150,000 troops, by land, sea and air on the Normandy beaches on the 6th June 1944 – codenamed Operation Overlord – was truly staggering. The liberation of France and the march on Germany were slow and arduous with heavy casualties. Cherbourg was recaptured by the end of June, and Paris followed two months later. Meanwhile, on the Eastern Front, the Russians pushed west to Warsaw, taking Bucharest, Estonia and eventually Budapest.

In 1945, the notorious Auschwitz concentration camp was liberated by Soviet troops. The extent of the horrors of the Holocaust was revealed, and other death camps, such as Belsen, were discovered as Allied forces swept through Europe. In April, the British, the Americans and the Russians reached Berlin in a pincer movement. Hitler committed suicide and Germany surrendered on the 7th May. Mussolini was executed by Italian partisans.

The following day, the 8th May 1945, was celebrated as Victory in Europe (VE) Day.

Clem Atlee replaced Churchill as British Prime Minister, and Harry Truman became President of the US on the death of Roosevelt in April. With the Americans making progress in the Pacific, and British forces advancing further into Burma, Japanese forces began to withdraw from China. Soon afterwards, civil war resumed between Chiang's Nationalists and Mao's Communists.

Postal communication between Chun Ji and his family in Taishan returned to normal, with his mother pleading for some money as one of his brothers had another addition to the family.

*After atomic bombs were dropped by the US on Hiroshima and Nagasaki, Japan finally surrendered on the 14th August 1945. **At long last, the end of the war was finally over.***

Celebrations took place in Britain and across the free world, although the joy was muted after six long years of war in which over sixty million people had perished.

In September that year, another son was born to Chun Ji and Choi Lin. He was named Shui Kai – known as Tom. This made Chun Ji even more worried as to how they would survive.

Now, as it happened, living not far away were Francis's and Milly's godparents, Ong Hing Bak and his wife, who were relatively well off.

Having no children of their own, they had visited the Kwong family on several occasions, and made it known that they would like to take the toddler Milly – who looked like a doll, with her pale ivory skin and big brown eyes off their hands and adopt her as their own. When they offered Choi Lin a purse full of Chinese jewellery in twenty-four-carat gold, she was outraged. Although she was bedridden, having just given birth to Tom, Choi Lin blatantly refused and chased them out of the house, remembering only too well how many of her own younger sisters had been given away in China, as well as the threat to herself as a child about to be sold by her own mother.

'*What can we do?*' muttered Chun Ji, holding his head in his hands. '*We are down to our last penny!* We shall all die of starvation.'

Francis recalls:

Even as a child, I remember the day vividly. It was the day the unwelcome visitors, Ong Hing Bak and his wife, skulked out of the front door. My sister Rose said that we needn't see him again, with his blatant showing off with his mouth full of gold fillings, or his wife with her fingers rattling ostentatiously with heavy gold rings. My teacher had that day given me a wooden box of Windsor & Newton watercolours, as apparently, I had shown talent at painting. When I proudly showed my mother my prize, and a copy of a watercolour I had painted of the Battle of Britain – a Spitfire engaged in a dogfight with a German Messerschmitt – she snatched the paintbox out of my hands and threw it into the fire.

Distraught, I howled like a scalded cat. I was inconsolable, until my sister Eileen told me that we needed wood for the fire to keep Mother warm as she had just given birth to Tom, my baby brother. And, as Father was ill and out of work, she said that we all had to make sacrifices. For an eight-year-old she was wise beyond her years. Duly contrite, I offered to throw my wooden boats into the fire as well. I had made these at school out of bits of packing cases. I used to float them down the street

*gutters in the torrential rain with a pal named Lenny Prossler,
who lived four doors away. In one rash moment, I was about to
throw the children's lavatory seat into the fire, but I had a rapid
change of heart fearing my father's murderous temper.*

*I remember the events well. In fact, we all did; as next door
to the Prosslers lived a family called the Sourbutts, who kept
themselves to themselves. One evening, Mr and Mrs Sourbutts
had gone out and left their thirteen-year-old son alone at home.
Apparently, a thief cut the cable to the wireless, which came into
the house via the backyard. Mrs Sourbutts used to leave the
lower sash window ajar; it overlooked the back entry[53] to the
terrace of houses, from which she used to sell halfpenny toffee
apples from time to time. However, that evening, the son left the
door open when he went to investigate the sudden cutting-off, of
sound to the wireless. Just then, the thief must have slipped into
the house, and after the boy closed the door, he was callously
strangled with a loose piece of cable. Everything of value was
stolen from the Sourbutts' house. That same night, hordes of
police descended on Leopold Road to investigate the horrific
murder. Cold-blooded murder was rare in those days. But we
never did hear the outcome of that terrible crime.*

*Father, when he heard of it, said immediately, 'That's it. We
can't possibly stay here. It's far too dangerous!' Pushing himself
out of his chair near the window, he paced around the room,
hovering in a trance around the fireplace, his chin gripped by
finger and thumb in deep thought.*

*But Mother questioned how we could possibly leave, as we
had no money and all these children to feed. I remember very
clearly, Father scratching his head and announcing suddenly
that he thought he had a way. By the end of the war, at the age
of forty-seven, he, like a lot of people around him, had suddenly
and visibly aged, even though they had managed to survive...*

---

53 Edwardian terraced houses, originally built for artisans, usually had a passage running
the whole length of the terrace where the back door of each house exited onto a rear
yard. This was called an 'entry'.

It was revealed much later that Chun Ji was lucky to have survived by the seat of his pants, having previously just escaped deportation as sympathetic locals and friendly neighbours hid him in their attics and cupboards whenever the authorities combed through immigrant communities, looking for those whose papers were not in order.

Kwong Chun Ji and many like him were made stateless after the fall of the last of the Emperors in old China and the setting up of a new Republic of China in 1912, and therefore had no access to China's consular facilities. It appeared that perhaps a list of names had fallen into the authorities' hands, which had once been held by one of the criminal Snake Head gangs. Such lists had hitherto been used for blackmailing purposes.

He had also heard that many other Chinese migrants had not been so fortunate as to have got away with it. It happened that, following a recent law regarding the repatriation of aliens (the British Nationality Act)[54] they had been rounded up and shipped back to Hong Kong. What was shocking was that hundreds of them had been hired specifically from the colony of Hong Kong by the British government during the war to man the Merchant ships to help the war effort, as many of the British Merchant seamen had been recruited into the Royal Navy or the Army. It was known amongst the Chinese community that many Chinese were torn from their English wives and partners and forced to sail to the Far East, leaving behind their families, whom they never saw again.

Giving an abrupt sigh of relief, Chun Ji slumped back into his chair and stared at his wife with the urgency of a man who had suddenly found a way out of their present dilemma. With the threat of starvation and homelessness looming, he had decided to radically chance his luck, so that he and his family could have a chance to survive.

His wife looked on expectantly, but nevertheless held her breath, fearing the worst.

---

54 The repatriation of aliens/non-British nationals following the end of the Second World War. Thousands of migrant seamen who had been recruited to man the Merchant Fleet during the war were sent back to the colonies from whence they came, e.g., Jamaica, India, Ceylon, Hong Kong etc. Likewise, foreign workers who had been working in the factories or on the railways for the war effort were repatriated after the war. This was done to make way for members of the armed forces returning to get jobs on 'Civvy Street'.

Chapter 13

A GAMBLE WITH LIFE AND DEATH

1945–1946

CHUN JI WAS STUCK. His back was against the wall. He felt that there was now no alternative, so from under the bed he pulled out a dented old biscuit tin and counted what money they had left: the paltry sum of four pounds and ten shillings.[55] It was all that remained of their life savings from the now-defunct business, apart from the keys to the old shop in Rocky Lane. Carefully folding the banknotes into his back pocket, he crept downstairs as soon as the family was sound asleep. It was barely ten at night when he caught the tram to Nelson Street at the bottom of Chinatown.

Skirting past a pile of rubble surrounding a bomb site that was still smouldering from a recent fire, he hurried towards a gambling den in the basement of an old Chinese Seaman's Club next to a disused church. The night air was decidedly chilly, and the moon was hidden by dense, scudding clouds, which he was pleased about as he did not want to be recognised. He pulled up the collar of his jacket to shield his face. Quickly descending the dirty stone steps, he pushed open the door.

---

55 Ten shillings would be equal to fifty pence sterling. Twenty shillings to one pound sterling.

A dense fug of cigarette smoke and a sweet smell of opium greeted him as he struggled to see in the dim light of the dingy cellar.

'Hey. Look what the cat's brought in!' shouted an old Chinese seaman by the door. The old man spat out the remains of a cigarette butt through his missing front teeth and doffed his flat cap in a facetious greeting. *'Haven't seen you in years, Mr Kwong, sir – been too busy for the likes of us, then?!'*

Chun Ji ignored him and, brushing past several gamblers, made his way to the central table. Looking around the room, not much had changed since the last time he had come here. It was to play Mahjong in celebration with a fellow laundry owner shortly after his eldest daughter was born. The den was grubbier than ever, being airless, and the walls brown with smoke and peeling paint. The floor was covered in cigarette ends that formed a loose layer over the holes in the lino. Five tables of Mah-jong were in progress, along with three games of Fan Tan, Mah-Pai (Chinese Lottery) and Chinese roulette.

Suddenly, there was shouting across the room as a runner carried in trays of tea and noodles ordered from a café across the street. The place was bustling with at least fifty men; all Chinese, most of them professional gamblers or out-of-work drifters. Chun Ji suddenly remembered the advice he had been given by his old Uncle Fung, after landing in Liverpool in 1921; that he must keep himself to himself, as criminal elements hung about in Chinese gambling dens, on the lookout for rich pickings.

At the central table, under a dim bulb protruding from a bowl-shaped shade, yellowed with age, a local variation on Fan Tan and Chinese Dice was taking place. Tactfully, Chun Ji edged his way to the perimeter of the table, where ten other gamblers stood casually in a circle. Their eyes were focused on the round metal dish, about the size of a dustbin lid, fixed to the middle of the table. There were numbers and symbols painted on the inside of the dish, zero to six in different colours. The higher numbers were in the middle and the lower towards the outer rim, which was raised to prevent the dice and money from rolling out.

He kept his hands firmly in his pockets and spent the first ten minutes carefully studying the game in play. He noticed the croupier – a tall, thin man with a badly trimmed moustache – leaning over to the right-hand side of him, shouting the odds. The jackpot in the middle would increase exponentially with each round played, in tandem with the number of gamblers joining in. Once a person had placed a bet on a chosen number on the rim of the dish, he would then roll a pair of Chinese dice, one after the other, towards a stack of silver coins, made up of florins, crowns and half-crowns,[56] in its centre.

For instance, if someone placed a bet of ten shillings on the number *three,* and if each dice he rolled managed to reveal *a* matching three on their uppermost faces, then he would win not only the money in the centre of the bowl, but would also recover his initial stake *threefold.*

Similarly, if pinning a bet on the number *two,* he would have to match that number on both dice in order to win, and to recover his stake, having thereby *doubled* it.

The number *four* – marked by the symbol of *a black skull* – was to be avoided at all costs, as the number four – 'see' in Cantonese – means 'death', and therefore no one in his right mind would place his bet on it.

However, if a successful bet was made on the number *six,* then the person could walk away with six times his original wager, plus the *jackpot* in the middle – the croupier making up the amount from the house, if necessary.

Chun Ji licked his lips, which had suddenly gone dry. On the third round he decided to join in. With shaking hands, he proffered a tentative ten shillings.

Several of the gamblers glared at him, sensing that he was a relative newcomer. One of those to his left, a mean-looking, sallow-faced man with tobacco-smelling breath, growled, *'Heh! Bet he's a joker, only come to piss against the wall!'*

---

56   Half a crown = two shillings and six (old) pence; eight half-crowns to a pound. Four crown pieces to a pound. Florins = the name for two-shilling coins; ten florins to a pound.

Suddenly, Chun Ji thought that he recognised him. It was Chang, his former co-worker at his uncle's old laundry business in Rock Ferry twenty-odd years ago. He had never forgotten the day that this surly, spiteful man had betrayed him to the authorities, or possibly to the gangmasters, forcing him to go on the run. Whether or not the recognition was mutual, Chang didn't let on.

Chun Ji bit his lip and said nothing. Then, deliberately making eye contact, but not daring to linger, he stared at each gambler in turn to show that he wasn't going to be put off. Little did they know that the bravado was all false, for inside he was shaking like a leaf. He tried not to show it. But so much was at stake.

After three more rounds without a win, his money, like his luck, was beginning to run out.

Feeling inside his pocket, he realised that all he had left was one pound ten shillings. Sweat beaded on his forehead. Three of the gamblers had walked away, cursing that they were cleaned out, although others joined in the game. As the stakes multiplied the prize increased substantially to what looked like over one hundred pounds in the middle of the dish.

Deserting the other games, a crowd gathered around the centre table with increasing interest due to the high stakes and, therefore, greater prize money. Early on, Chun Ji's keen eye had noticed that two of the gamblers, one on each side of the croupier, rubbed a ring on their finger before each throw of the dice. And each time, they were able to recover their stake, and either walk away or try again. Whether they were signalling surreptitiously in order to cheat, or the gesture was simply an innocuous superstition for luck, it was impossible to tell. It was known in gambling circles that cheats often worked in pairs to beat the system. Some would chew on a toothpick and point it about in pre-agreed directions.

He knew that it was now or never. It would be his last throw of the dice.

Raising the next stake, the croupier demanded five pounds or more for a chance at the jackpot. This time, the house would accept the highest matching numbers achieved, if not six, on the pair of dice thrown for the round. But, as before, the numbers had to match the number where the bet was placed in the first place.

There was a slight tremor of his hand when Chun Ji offered his remaining one pound and ten shillings. It was waved away dismissively. *'A minimum of five pounds, my friend, or leave the table!'*

Undeterred, Chun Ji reached into his pocket with his clammy fingers, grabbed the keys to his business in Rocky Lane, and he threw them onto the table on top of the crumpled remains of his money. *'That's worth twenty times my stake!'* he croaked boldly.

An undertone of muttering flew around the room like wildfire as more people jostled strategically around the centre table.

Choosing a new set of dice with his right hand, Chun Ji turned them over carefully, as if to warm them up; though the clamminess of his hand made them stick somewhat to the pads of his fingers. He knew that it now would-be life or death with this final throw.

Using an extravagant gesture, he purposefully placed his bet on the number four, over the symbol of the black skull.

There was a horrified gasp all around the gambling den. 'The imbecile is raving mad… *It's sheer suicide… a damn death wish!'*

Scratching the top of his head with one hand, Chun Ji nervously tapped his front teeth with the other, as though for luck. He held his breath. Gripping the dice between finger and thumb so that the figures of four would face upwards and the undersides of three stuck to the sweat on the pads of his fingers, he threw them carefully, one at a time, towards the pile of money stacked high in the centre of the large metal dish.

The air froze. Around the table, everyone leant forwards in expectation, their eyes focused on the dice rolling under the glare of the overhead light. The first dice rolled onto its side and suddenly stopped to reveal the figure of four. Cries of *'Oh, hell, it can't be!'* broke the silence, together with much swearing.

The second dice kept spinning as if bewitched. Sweat poured from Chun Ji's face. At first, the dice began to settle on the figure of two. His heart sank. Then, slowly and miraculously, it turned over as it hit the bunch of keys, flipping to the figure of four to match the other one.

There was a stunned silence. Then a gasp of incredulity flew around the dingy cellar. Derisive calls of *'Can't believe it... You filthy cheat!'* filled the smoky air. Suddenly, two of the seasoned gamblers moved menacingly towards him, but one of the burly onlookers he recognised as a fellow laundry owner, from Penny Lane nearby, together with his old adversary Chang, held them back.

The croupier shook his head, his jaw agape in disbelief. Chun Ji quickly nodded in Chang's direction in polite acknowledgement. Then he stretched across to scoop up the piles of banknotes, silver florins and half-crowns, together with his bunch of keys, and jammed them into his pockets. After tossing a few coins to the astonished croupier, he walked purposefully towards the door without a second glance. Closing it firmly behind him, he leapt up the stone steps two at a time and rushed out into the welcoming cold night air.

Checking that he was not being followed, he strode swiftly towards the tram station and hurried home as quickly as his legs could carry him, hoping that his heart wouldn't burst out of his chest with the adrenaline and the euphoria. For one fleeting moment there was a tiny flash of guilt. He felt that he had just beaten the system by some fluke, or luck or whatever, and probably (and luckily for him in this instance) managed to cheat the dice of death.

Choi Lin woke up immediately when she heard the front door slam. Chun Ji ran upstairs and pulled out the battered old tin, then crammed in the banknotes and silver coins, much to his wife's astonishment. Breathlessly, he explained what had happened and his reasons for reinforcing the front door and the downstairs window by pushing a chest of drawers and a table against them.

'We must leave Liverpool as soon as possible!' he said. It's not safe here. Not after tonight. They may try to follow! '

It was five long, anxious weeks before the Kwong family managed to move out of Merseyside. Chun Ji remembered that, during the Blitz, an old friend by the name of Wong Sing had moved with his family to North Wales. Chun Ji had met him on that fateful boat journey from Hong Kong in 1921. Through this contact, with his winnings Chun Ji had quickly bought another laundry business in Wrexham, which was just over the border in Denbighshire, North Wales, forty miles away. The retiring owner wanted to return to China as soon as possible and therefore wanted a quick sale of the going concern.

And so, at the start of 1946, with the sharp frosts of winter rapidly turning to snow, the Kwongs and their six children found themselves at Number 29 Pen-y-Bryn ('On Top of the Hill') on the outskirts of Wrexham. Graphically, this sprawling industrial town was described by some as being like a spider's web within a string of suburbs, of which Wrexham was the central hub. Gratefully perceived as a refuge, however, it was right in the middle of an obscure Welsh community, surrounded by rural and coal-mining villages that generously welcomed this family of foreigners as needy refugees following the air raids on Liverpool.

It would be some time before the family was able to relax and settle in. Some extra beds, a table and chairs were obtained from a second-hand warehouse nearby to furnish the five sparse rooms which were their living quarters above the business. In the yard, next to the outbuilding which housed the industrial washing machines, was a tiny brick shed for the outside lavatory, something that the family had got used to in Liverpool. Baths had to be taken in the copper boiler at the end of the evening, using the remnants of the water that was still warm after the day's boiling and washing of customers' linen and the embers of the furnace underneath had died down. On the ground floor, dim lights powered by an old electric meter struggled to serve the shop and business. Upstairs, the cold, bleak bedrooms were made seemingly gloomier by the ancient brown wallpaper that had peeled and bubbled, scorched over time by the single gas lamp that hung mournfully over the small cast-iron fireplace which appeared in each room, with the exception of the attic and cellar. But for the Kwong family, this seemed like paradise – a welcome refuge from the exhausting war years with the constant threat of being killed during the bombing of Liverpool.

Chun Ji celebrated by roasting a chicken and barbecuing a pork loin obtained from the neighbourly butcher next door. To toast his winnings, he even bought his wife a modest fur coat, which he simply left in brown wrapping paper on the counter of the shop, remarking gruffly that it was colder, living in Wales. The children could share a bag of sweets from the sweet shop over the road. It was run by two kind old ladies, who invited them to pick up windfall apples from the tree in their back garden in the autumn.

The new neighbours were puzzled as to why Chun Ji and his family had remained in the city throughout the darkest days of the air raids, and only now decided to escape to the relative safety of the countryside, after all hostilities had ended. Chun Ji tried to explain, but his English faltered, as the neighbours conversed mainly in Welsh, so he just shrugged it off with an animated but pleasant gesture.

He did not dare tell his wife, but for the first time in years he hoped that he would now be able to stop looking over his shoulder. Putting the fear of the extortion gangs and the inquisitive authorities behind him, he could perhaps let go a little. In making a clean start by coming to Wales, he secretly hoped that the move would not prove to be a dreadful false dawn.

Chapter 14

A CLEAN START

Wrexham, North Wales, 1946–1947

T HERE WAS NO TIME to waste. Chun Ji had to make some money again to feed his family – both here and in China – so he quickly set about getting established in the new business. The former owner's name was stripped from the front of the shop and amended to **Kong Chun**.[57] The business rapidly improved because of his fresh input and dedicated hard work. He became known for turning out immaculately starched collars and shirts, which started with the officers of the British Army. From a radius of twenty miles, members of the armed forces stationed at Denbigh, and the Royal Welch Fusiliers who were in barracks nearby, sent him their laundry by mail. It was dealt with efficiently and returned promptly, also by post. Eileen and Rose readdressed the labels, adding a polite note with an invoice, then took the parcels to the small post office at the end of Pen-y-Bryn. Invariably, by return the customers would send their payments by postal order, which would include the cost of postage.

Chun Ji's reputation for service grew. With his acute business acumen, he quickly realised that if he diverted any *dry cleaning* across

---

57 He decided to use this as a trading name Kong Chun instead of Kwong Chun Ji. Not only was it more appropriate in its English pronunciation, but he probably hoped that it would throw unwanted visitors from his past life off the scent.

the road to the dry-cleaning business run by his neighbour Mr Gareth Young, he would reciprocate and send work that required actual *laundering* across to "Kong Chun".

Because of the nature of the business, hard manual work couldn't really be avoided. However, to improve efficiency and lessen the physical burden, Chun Ji decided he would try his hand at automation. He searched out and gradually brought in large machinery (though much was second-hand or altered from spare parts) that could wash in volume and spin-dry. Befriending the garage owner in Pen-y-Bryn, he adapted a workbench motor and fan belt to drive these previously manually operated machines. Similarly, he motorised a large ironing machine called a 'Callendirone' to deal with wide and cumbersome items such as sheets and linen.

Apart from the sweet shop, post office, dry cleaners and butchers running side by side, Pen-y-Bryn also had a bakery, a barber's shop, a fish-and-chip shop and a general provisions store. There was a pub at one end of the street and a garage at the other.

The two eldest girls went to the local school, Victoria Juniors, which was within walking distance, whereas the two boys went to the Infants, leaving the two youngest to stay at home. Chun Ji did not object when it was suggested that the children attend Sunday school at the nearby church, as it was just three streets away. But he still insisted on keeping up strict Chinese traditions at home: for instance, the family could not start their meal until he did; and could not speak until he did. These rules applied not only to his children, but also to his wife. Disobedience was threatened with a narrow stick made of willow, which he kept on the mantelpiece above the fireplace. Furthermore, the speaking of English (or Welsh) at home was strictly forbidden.

In 1946, with the hardships still imposed by shortages and rationing, and with servicemen returning to seek employment, it was fortunate that Chun Ji and his countrymen did not look for work in the industries traditionally occupied by the indigenous population, such as transport, factories, offices or shops, as this might have led to racial strife.

In the aftermath of war, large swathes of the population were displaced; many had found that their family homes had been destroyed, or that their loved ones had moved away or been killed.

The Atlee government had launched their much-heralded welfare state with free and urgently-needed healthcare for all with the passing of The National Health Act. But it would be another two years before it was implemented.

The wounded servicemen returning from the war, and those who had suffered untold deprivation, having been prisoners of war in Europe or the Far East, did not now have to worry about how to provide for their treatment.

Three other Chinese families had sought refuge from the war much earlier and settled on the other side of the town and outlying villages, such as Rhos. Wong Sing, his wife and young son lived in a small house on the outskirts of Wrexham. Wong, being much older than Chun JI, had retired early after suffering bouts of chronic ill health, which his wife blamed on the disease-ridden conditions on the boat from Hong Kong when he first came to England.

When business was closed on Sundays, some of the families would meet to share news of their kin back in China. Whilst the women gossiped over tea, for nostalgia's sake the men would play Mah-jong whilst sipping brandy. News would be disseminated about the power struggle and the continuing civil war between Chiang's Nationalists and Mao's Communists, and how it impacted on their families in Taishan and Guangdung.

Towards the end of the summer that year, Chun Ji received a young caller at his shop. It was a tall, fair-headed Irish girl with a well-scrubbed, angelic face, void of make-up, by the name of Pat McCarthy. Pat had been working temporarily as a land girl[58] in the countryside around Wrexham and was looking for more permanent work. She said that she was strong and had worked in a laundry in Ireland. It transpired that she wanted to stay around Denbighshire because

---

58 Women who did manual work on the farms during the war. Also, due to the men being called up to serve in the armed forces, women replaced them in factories and transport.

her boyfriend, Heinryk, was being treated in the Polish Hospital at Penley,[59] next to the Polish resettlement camp on the border between England and Wales in an area known as Maelor.

It appeared that Heinryk had fought with the Polish troops alongside the British Army when they journeyed with the Polish migration across the Middle East towards Italy, and then to England in the latter years of the war. This massive exodus began at the start of the war in September 1939 when Germany invaded Poland. Stalin's Russia then invaded from the east and thousands of Polish citizens, men, women and children, were deported by the Soviets to gulags and labour camps in the depths of Siberia. Two years later, Germany turned on Russia. But by then it was too late for many of the Poles, who had already been displaced or had perished.

How Pat had met her Polish soldier, she didn't say. However, Chun Ji listened sympathetically and said that, as it happened, he and his wife could do with some extra help, not only in the business, but also with the children.

Pat proved a keen and able worker. With her cheerful demeanour she was a considerable asset when dealing with some of the more awkward customers, as well as fitting in with the family's Chinese way of life. The children thought the world of her. Their schoolwork improved with her help, though the pronunciation of certain English words was complicated by her Irish lilt, together with their Welsh and Chinese translation. Christmas time became an increasing joy, as Pat taught the children how to make cards, decorations, and simple presents out of cardboard, pieces of string and coloured wrapping paper. Christmas stockings included a few simple gifts, such as a tangerine, an apple, and the rare luxury of a piece of chocolate wrapped in glittering foil. Letters to Santa Claus were written and sent in flames up the chimney, to the delight of the younger ones, though Tom, as a toddler, just chortled at the bright flames.

---

59 The hospital had previously been occupied by the Americans during the war in readiness for the D-Day landings to liberate Europe.

Although she was lodging with a local miner's family, Pat spent Christmas and Boxing Day with her soldier at the Polish Hospital and resettlement camp. She had been invited to spend it with Mr and Mrs Kwong, who cooked a special Chinese meal, which in other circumstances she would have relished.

The winter came quickly with the rapid change of seasons. At the first fall of snow in late 1946, Pat taught the children how to make a snowman in the patch of garden at the back of the shop yard, using lumps of coal for his eyes and pieces of broken twig for his nose and mouth. The snow was still hard on the ground late in March following one of the harshest winters on record, when a letter came from China. Chun Ji opened it with trepidation, assuming that it was either a request for more money or more bad news. It was written by Chun Tin, his first brother.

Dai Dune Chun
Taishan
Guangdung
China
20th February 1947

Dear Chun Ji,

I am writing on behalf of the family. Kwong Fung Ting, our dear mother, died on the 27th January at the start of the New Year after a short and terrible illness. She was just sixty-nine years old, but sadly seemed increasingly older than her years in the past twenty-four years since our father died.

She had been hoping to see you for one last time before she joined our ancestors. It seems a lifetime since you left home twenty-six years ago. Your younger brothers and sisters have difficulty remembering you but remain grateful for the money you continue to send to us. Thanks to you I was fortunate to train as a teacher, and your younger brothers also hope to improve their prospects with your help.

You are now the head of the family, even though you live in the West. The civil war continues in China and we still fear for the future.

I attach a letter to you from our dear mother. It was written on her deathbed with my help. After a period of mourning, she will be buried in a traditional family ceremony beside our ancestors.

Your brother,

Chun Tin

Chun Ji was speechless, and the blood drained from his face. He grabbed the nearest chair and slumped down heavily, his head in his hands. Choi Lin and Pat quickly ushered the children away to the next room, not wanting them to see their father – whom they had always thought of as fearless and unemotional – dissolving in tears.

Chun Ji tore opened his mother's letter. His eyes, though wet and swollen, carefully scanned the page. It read:

To my eldest son, Chun Ji,

I have grown weak over the days, so I fear that there is not much time left. A quarter of a century has passed since you left your home in Taishan. Each year we waited patiently for news that you would return to visit us, before I grew too old. Now I fear it will be too late. Your brothers, Chun Tin, Chun Yee and Chun Tui, keep asking for your return. They, and your sisters Chun Ho and Chun Rei, have all got married. There are several nephews and nieces that you have not seen, but I hope that one day, before it is too late, you will meet them. Regrettably, Chun Ho had to sell her one and only daughter after she was widowed in tragic circumstances. Sadly, we heard that the little girl died aged just seven. Also, I need to tell you that Chun Rei's only child died at birth, and that her husband was killed in the fighting between the Nationalists and the Communists. I have often wondered if there is a curse on the Kwongs due to some past misdemeanour by one of our ancestors resulting in an act of unspeakable evil.

Since your father died, two years after you left, times in Taishan have been extremely difficult. With the never-ending conflict in our country, there has been constant turmoil and hardship, which war inevitably brings.

I ask from you, my son, these last requests. When you do return, please attend your father's and my grave at the ancestral burial ground on the mountain, light joss sticks and pay your respects to us and to your ancestors, in the hope that you will meet us again one day.

Finally, you will have heard that, in that fateful year of 1921 when you left, I was carrying your fourth brother. Chun Tileng was born later that year, but tragically your father became ill and died two years later, so they never got to know one another. As head of the Kwong family, it will be your duty to take care of Chun Tileng until he is suitably married, as he is the youngest of the family. I remind you of your family obligations, not only to him, but to the rest of your siblings.

Your mother,

Kwong Fung Ting

For the next four weeks Chun Ji remained silent as a ghost. He hardly ate. He continued work perfunctorily. He just barked out orders using the minimum of words. The family thought that he was seriously ill. His wife explained to Pat that he was in mourning, so they left him well alone. The children tiptoed around him and were on their best behaviour.

Spring soon came with the first flush of daffodils sprouting up in their thousands in the countryside around Pen-y-Bryn. The bright yellow blooms carpeted the banks of flower beds surrounding the oval ponds in the recreation park behind the garage in Pen-y-Bryn. A new season was on the way as Chun Ji's period of enforced mourning came to an end.

In April, Choi Lin gave birth to another son, who was named Shui Mun, or Sam. Their GP, Dr Leigh, and his able midwife delivered the baby at home. It was just as well that Pat was on hand to help. Gently, and as tactfully as possible, she tried to explain to Mr and Mrs Kwong that it must be exhausting for Mrs Kwong to go through the trauma of childbirth again, and that there were now ways to prevent this medically. Chun Ji explained, with a wry look, that in China only half the family would survive due to war, childbirth, disease and starvation. Pat nodded, with some understanding, as she said that she herself came from a large family of eleven; and, as it happened, her parents had also suffered the heartache of a high degree of infant mortality, as well as enduring famine and ill health back home in Ireland.

It wasn't long afterwards when the peaceful routine at 29 Pen-y-Bryn was shattered. Early one morning, no sooner had the shop opened than two tall, officious-looking men dressed in long trench coats and trilbies pulled down over their faces came looking for Pat. (Neighbours later told Chun Ji that it was rumoured that they were from the Secret Intelligence Service). They wanted to question her about her Polish boyfriend, Heinryk. It appeared that, with war records gradually filtering through, doubts had been raised about his true background. Although he was fluent in German, as indeed were quite a lot of Poles who had lived on the border between Germany and Poland before the war, his story didn't quite tally with the military records of the Polish 2nd Corps when he said that he had fought with them alongside the British 8th Army.

Francis recalls:

I remember clearly when, two days after that incident, Pat, extremely agitated and tearful, returned to work to pick up her things. We were distraught. She gave all the children a hug and looked as if she had been crying all night.

'Please, please remember, young Francis,' she said haltingly, 'you and your brothers, when you grow up, must fight for your country. It is not Germany you need to fear. It will be Russia – the Soviet Union. They will have terrible and dangerous weapons like the bombs dropped on Japan, and much worse than those!'

Being so young at the time, I didn't quite understand what she meant, but it scared us somewhat. All I knew instinctively was that fighting for my country would not mean fighting for China – a country so far away, and which seemed totally foreign to me. Born and bred in England, with school friends who were predominantly English, and now Welsh, I felt that my loyalties would lie with Britain.

A few days later, Pat's landlady told us that, during the night, Pat had packed her bags and left without a word. Apparently, her boyfriend had been taken away by the Military Police on suspicion of once being a German agent. We were in deep mourning. We never heard from her again or heard what had happened to her boyfriend.

Chapter 15

FRANCIS CONTINUES THE NARRATIVE...

The Old Opium Man (Yin See Bak) – 1948

T HE WINTER OF 1948 will be imprinted in my memory forever, because of two significant things:

Firstly; even though I was quite young at the time, I remember vividly that it had been just as bitter a winter as that of the previous year, when the whole country became snowbound and was brought to a standstill. The rail and road networks became impassable as snow fell continuously for months on end. At school, I was told that Britain was wholly dependent on coal for its heating and power. Soon, supplies began to run out as mining dwindled to virtually zero, as without coal to fuel the power stations, all industry, including mining, ground to a halt. According to the wireless, eventually, the nation would run out of supplies to heat their homes or even to cook. Inhabitants far and wide burnt everything they could lay their hands on. Wallpaper was peeled off the walls in desperation and thrown onto the fire, together with cardboard, old rags, garden fences and even vegetable peelings and old shoes: in fact, anything that was vaguely combustible. Thousands died due to hypothermia. Our friends and neighbours in Wrexham suffered like the rest of the country.

Secondly: shortly afterwards, on the tailcoats of the Spring thaw, I was lucky enough to win the prize for writing (plus drawings) about my childhood memories and so on, in what was the county's Chap Book competition for which I was presented with a coveted copy of the Pears Children's Encyclopaedia at the local library. At the *"grand old age"* of eight, I was encouraged, by the organisers (the success having rather gone to my head!) to diligently write down from then onwards, my family's story (warts and all) for what was grandly called – 'for possible, posterity'. But sadly, nothing more was heard from the library or the competition organisers. Despite this, undaunted, it just spurred me on in my scribbling endeavours. But, as I grew up, I soon realised that it was a popular misconception that people write for others, when in fact, they write for themselves. Well so be it…

When I look back at my diaries from that time, I found that I had recorded with pride that a good neighbourhood friend, called Colin Sturgess had saved the day during that savage winter. Colin was two years older than me and seemed quite inventive. Naturally intrepid, he often bordered on the reckless. His widowed mother sold soft drinks wholesale, such as Vimto, dandelion and burdock, and sarsaparilla delivered in large wooden crates. He managed to hide the crates in his mother's now-empty coal shed, and returned the empty bottles loose to the suppliers, swearing that the crates had been stolen by thieves scaling the wall of the warehouse yard in the dead of night. Throughout the winter, he managed to keep the fire alive in the cast-iron range at his house by using the chopped-up crates.

As soon as he heard that that my father was struggling to maintain the copper boiler in our laundry, he took me by sledge (which he had made out of packing cases) to Erdigg, which was the land around the Yorkes' country estate not far from Pen-y-Bryn.[60] Sheltered by the failing light of dusk, on most evenings, and by carefully dodging Squire Yorke who patrolled the estate with a shotgun on the lookout

---

60   A vast estate of rural beauty surrounding a large, historic stately home. It was bequeathed to the National Trust in 1973 by the last of the Yorke family.

for poachers, we managed to scrape together enough firewood from the surrounding woods.

But, we didn't dare to return to Erdigg Woods again, because on the last occasion, whilst fleeing in the dead of night from Squire Yorke's clutches, he mistook us for poachers and fired his shotgun over our heads. Clambering over a perimeter fence to escape, I slipped and managed to gash the top of my head open. Not stopping to stem the bleeding, we managed to get home in one piece after running all the way. Father was absolutely, furious. However, it was too late to call a doctor, so he immediately applied his knowledge of first aid that he had picked up as a young man in China from the barefoot doctors. Quickly shaving off the hair from my crown, he bathed the wound in a white powder mixed with hot water as a poultice. Then he melted a ball of antiseptic herbs encased in wax to clot the blood, and stuck it over the gash, pulling the edges of the wound sharply together. The waxen ball solidified. I had to keep the seal on the wound for ten days. Colin teased me, saying it was like a small rat glued to the top of my skull. After the wax was removed, Dr Leigh, our GP, examined me and stated that he was simply astounded by how the wound had healed cleanly, without the need for stitches or antiseptic. Colin told our friends that it was Chinese witchcraft.

Undeterred by the inevitable mishaps and having narrowly escaped being killed, our desperate quest for fuel for our homes continued unabated. At least twice a week, we would make our way to the nearest slag heap, which was at Bersham Colliery near Rhostyllen, to scavenge for lumps of discarded coal and coke from under the snow. Triumphantly, we would wheel the 'black gold' (as it was euphemistically called) home in a handmade cart which was fashioned from an old pram. Inevitably, news of this illicit discovery soon spread. Our neighbours heard of our desperate initiative and followed in our tracks like a swarm of ants scurrying over a mountain of sugar. This clandestine activity continued for several weeks, until we were all chased away by an irate pit manager from the NCB who threatened to call the police or, at worst, set the guard dogs on us if we returned.

By the end of the spring of 1948, the welcome thaw came, bringing with it some world news which rarely seeped through to a small, sleepy backwater like Wrexham. Before she left, young Pat McCarthy had warned us about the dangers posed to world peace by the Russians. Presciently, she had suggested that the threat would come from Soviet Russia rather than defeated Germany, and, in her humble wisdom, she was starting to be proved right. For instance, post-war Germany had been divided by the Allies – the United States, Britain, France, and the Soviet Union – into four zones of military occupation. The capital, Berlin, was likewise divided into four occupied zones. Provocatively, in June 1948 the Soviets forced the other Allied powers out of Berlin by cutting off access to the Western sectors, effectively creating a blockade to which the West responded with a massive airlift of supplies. This battle was considered to be the opening salvo of the Cold War. Teachers at my school worried us to death by speculating about the consequences of such if it ever got out of hand.

Then earlier in May that year, a Jewish state of Israel, headed by David Ben-Gurion, was finally established in their ancestral land by the partitioning of Palestine. It had taken decades to implement, with bitter resistance from neighbouring Arab countries, particularly Palestine, as well as some Western powers, ever since the 1917 declaration by Lord Balfour which recognised the right of the Jews to a national home. My father often wondered how his former Jewish friends and neighbours in Liverpool would react to the news.

However, nearer to home, despite events over which we had no control regarding what was happening around us, my parents were grateful for the fact that the family was just managing to keep its head above water as well as other small mercies. For instance, Eileen, now a polite and sensible eleven-year-old, was doing extremely well in arithmetic, English, Welsh, and domestic science at the Secondary Modern School for Girls, where she proved popular with the teachers and pupils due to her sunny and helpful nature. Rose, just a year younger, had the opportunity to sit for the Grammar School Scholarship. When the news came through that she had won a place, Father was pleased, though he showed it in his typically restrained manner, not daring to congratulate her or give her a hug. However, he bought her a school desk from the local auctioneers to enable her to do her homework, and a bicycle so that come the autumn, she could cycle to her new school – Grove Park Grammar for Girls. Mother was given some money so that a uniform and a leather satchel could be bought. Although the girls did their homework straight after school, they were still expected to help around the shop, dealing with customers and folding and parcelling up the laundry to be collected, as well as helping our mother.

In June, another sister was born, and was named Shui Wen, or Brenda. The two eldest girls took it in turns to help to nurse the new baby as Mother soon had to return to work.

Now that Pat had disappeared, it became apparent that the business needed an extra hand. Through the Chinese community, an old man of an indeterminate age named Tsang Soo Fat was introduced. At first, my father wasn't too sure whether to employ him. The old man had been out of work for some months and was desperate to work for his keep and lodgings. His only remaining relatives lived in Liverpool – although, as distant cousins, they felt that they couldn't continue to keep him without him earning his way. Having offered to work for little money, old Tsang moved into one of the attics on the top floor of the shop. Although he ambled slowly around the place like a tortoise fresh from hibernation, he was quite conscientious in his work, rising each morning at 5.30 to light the furnace to the boiler. Furthermore, he didn't appear to intrude on the Kwong family way of life. After work he would retreat to his room, lie down on his bed and snore like a drain.

But the children had noticed that on his bedside table he kept a mysterious lump of what seemed like a rectangular cake of wax on a saucer, about four inches by three and wrapped in greaseproof paper.

Eileen and Rose used to do an occasional errand for him by running across to the sweet shop for a packet of his favourite tobacco, for which they were rewarded with a penny. I was never asked to run the errand as the old man thought that I would be too inquisitive. One day, naturally intrigued, I peeped through the crack of the attic door and observed old Tsang cutting through the end of this lump of wax with a small penknife. He placed a slither of the substance on top of his tobacco, which he stuffed into a long-stemmed pipe that was clamped between his jagged yellow teeth, and then lit it as he slumped back onto his bed. The smoke had a pungent, sickly smell which wafted out onto the landing and made me retch. After I had stumbled downstairs, feeling nauseous and rather off colour, my father grabbed hold of me and shook the story out of me. The word *'Opium!'* flew out of his mouth in horror. When my mother heard about this, she said that we must get rid of the old man.

The next day, Father had words with old Tsang, who pleaded for his job and promised that he would only smoke outside the premises. It was decided to give him another chance. Completely undeterred, I noticed that two weeks later, 'Yin See Bak'[61] – the Old Opium Man, as the children called him behind his back – was back to his old habit. But this time, he would lock his bedroom door, stuff an old towel against the bottom of the door and fling open the skylight as far as it would go. Later, it was discovered that, to conceal his tracks, he would use a water pipe to smoke whilst draping a wet tea towel over his head. Defeated, Father would shrug, resigned, and tell his friends that at least the mice in the attic would be asphyxiated, which would not be a bad thing, for they had been attacking the sacks of rice kept in the attic room opposite old Yin See Bak's.

Towards the end of the summer, which had been one of the hottest on record, the old man failed to return from a visit to his relatives in Liverpool after the bank holiday. Word came back that he had been found dead in his bed with a pipe jammed in his mouth, having

---

61 Literally means 'Opium Uncle'. *Bak* means 'uncle' – all older Chinese men were addressed as such as a mark of respectful seniority, whether related by blood or not.

swallowed a lump of opium and choked. Three weeks later, without warning, the relatives swarmed like flies to Pen-y-Bryn, wanting to gather up the old man's sparse belongings. It appeared that old Tsang was a former soldier who had fought alongside General Chiang Kai-shek's Nationalist army against Mao Tse-tung's Communist troops in the late '20s. As a mercenary, having seen many campaigns, he had been paid handsomely. He later changed sides and threw in his lot with the mass of peasants who supported Mao. There were rumours at the time that he was a paid government spy, and that his slide into an opium stupor was the only way he could blank out the horrors of warfare, especially when he was sometimes forced to betray his comrades.

Old Tsang's trunk and suitcase were duly brought up from the cellar. Like hungry vultures, the relatives smashed open the locked trunk. Greedy anticipation soon turned to crushing disappointment, for all they found was a large collection of opium pipes, a rusty old Army revolver and a pile of musty old Chinese currency, now obsolete, which dated back to the end of the last century, when one of the last Emperors, Emperor Kwong Shui, ruled China. *'Bah! Worthless!'* they spat as they threw the old banknotes into the fire. My father could hardly suppress a self-satisfied grin on seeing their downcast faces and ushered them brusquely out of the door.

The following day, the neighbours advised him that, in the interests of safety, he'd better call in at the local police station in the middle of the town and hand in the revolver with the remains of the contents of the suitcase. The officer at the desk didn't seem all that interested (for many service weapons were handed in after the war) as he issued a receipt for the firearm.

'Not much use now, sir. Appears this was an old Army issue from some foreign source; it couldn't possibly hurt a fly!'

Dismissing it out of hand, he said that it appeared rusted up and useless. Calmly springing back, the cocked trigger, he took aim at the party political bulletins on the noticeboard behind him. The revolver exploded and almost blew his hand off. 'Cor blimey, sir, you didn't tell me it was loaded!' the officer gasped breathlessly.

Making a rapid exit, my father luckily was halfway down the street, gratefully clutching the receipt in his hands.

Then, something very strange happened at the laundry after the old man had died. For the next few weeks, on the dot of 5.30 in the morning, when Father, bleary-eyed, shuffled downstairs to light the furnace at the back of the shop, he found that it was already well and truly lit with the embers glowing away merrily. Scratching his head, he asked Mother if she knew anything about it, in case it was she who had got up earlier, in secret, to do it to save him this early chore.

'Of course not! It must be the old man's ghost returning to help out!' she replied in jest.

He shook his head. Even though he and my mother, like a lot of old-fashioned Chinese, believed in ghosts, he could not believe that this could happen to him in a small Welsh town, in a foreign country which was thousands of miles from his homeland. That scepticism was reluctantly overturned when one morning he swore that he could detect a whiff of the familiar sweet smell of opium lingering in the air when he went to inspect the already-lit furnace on getting out of bed in the early hours.

'At least we don't need to pay him or even feed him!' Father remarked with immense relief.

At the beginning of the autumn, a letter from China informed Father that his youngest brother, Chun Tileng, had made his way to Hong Kong and was working as a tailor, and would arrive in Southampton in October on the SS *Carthage*. Chun Tileng was born eight months after his brother Chun Ji had left the ancestral home in January 1921. Father quickly worked out that, at the age of fifty, he was nearly twenty-three years older than this youngest brother whom he had never met, and whom he was now expected to look after at the request of his brothers and late mother.

'We could do with extra help in the business, with the old man gone,' he stated to my mother firmly, without allowing her a chance to reply.

And so, with just a small photograph to recognise him by, my father caught a train to Southampton Docks to meet his brother. We were quite excited about having an uncle from China coming to live with us. We called him *'Tieng Sook'*, which literally means *'Long Tall Uncle'*. The Chinese often play on sounds phonetically, as *'Tileng'* sounds like *'Tieng'*, which translates to 'long' in English.

However, our uncle was immediately taken away to the sanatorium near the Minera Mountains, west of Wrexham. He had contracted tuberculosis due to the disease-ridden and crowded conditions on his boat journey and was plainly quite ill. Like other TB patients, he spent several months recuperating, sleeping in the open air for most of the time, even in the depths of winter, surrounded by snow and ice which gathered around the foot of their beds. This treatment of isolation in the fresh air was considered a 'kill or cure', commonly employed for this type of disease.

From the playground of Victoria School, I would point out to friends with an outstretched arm the Minera Mountains in the distance, and boast that my long, tall uncle was sleeping outside, covered in snow. They quickly dismissed this as another of my wild stories. And when I recounted that a benign, drugged ghost visited my father's shop each morning to light the furnace, they really thought that I had finally lost my marbles.

Chapter 16

THE DRAGONFLY KITE

1949

BY THE SPRING OF 1949, Uncle Chun Tileng had recovered sufficiently to be brought home. As he gradually regained his strength, he threw himself into work like a dervish as though to make up for lost time and to also repay his debt to my father – his older brother. After work, they reminisced about their ancestral home in China, and little by little got to know one another. When time allowed, they would take it in turns to practise the *Zhu* – an ancient string instrument, rather like a zither – Uncle had brought from China, which used to belong to their late father. By striking the wired strings (which were strung over the belly of the hollow rectangular body made of polished rosewood) with a pair of bamboo flails, one could produce a high-pitched sound from its short range. The alien sound, which sounded like a strangled top C to a non-oriental ear, unfortunately made Nero, the family's pet black cat, bolt out of the house in fright. Such musical evenings reminded the brothers of old China, when families had time to play and sing together after a hard day's toil in the fields around their home in Taishan.

From time to time, a pastor from the Chinese Church based in Liverpool would visit to help the children learn Chinese. Uncle continued the lessons in his absence using simple texts from the religious books the pastor would leave. My father, not having been brought up in the Christian faith, found it conflicted with the beliefs of Buddhism and ancestral worship with which he had been raised, although now lapsed. Therefore, with extreme difficulty, he tried to come to terms with the fact that his children were leaning towards Western religious beliefs, especially when the four oldest started to attend the local Sunday school in the centre of town. This conflict was compounded by the fact that earlier he had agreed for all his children to be christened in the Church of England.

'At least the children are still being immersed in the Chinese language, regardless of the contents of the texts,' said Uncle to pacify him.

Father was still determined to prevent the family from being radically changed by the Western way of life. But, day by day, a wedge was driven into his futile attempts to keep his children imbued in the ways of ancient Chinese culture. It was an impossible task, thought Uncle, bearing in mind that the children had been born and bred in Britain. But he didn't dare offer his opinion to his older brother, especially one who was also head of the family clan.

Although the immediate neighbours in Pen-y-Bryn were perfectly at ease with having a Chinese family in their midst, there were rumblings within the wider community around Wrexham who feared that a floodgate would be opened if too many foreign migrants came to settle in the locality. At present, the total Chinese population consisted of no more than six families in the whole of the area. Irrational though it may seem, fears of the unfamiliar – particularly with regards to foreigners, who did not speak their language and physically stuck out like a sore thumb, and who had different customs – inevitably caused some disquiet in certain pockets of the community. Resentment and ignorant gossip about 'an invasion of foreigners' had already started to fester because of the establishment of the Polish Hospital nearby, which led to a rapid increase in the number of Polish families settling in the area after the war.

Now, as it happened, by midsummer a kite competition was scheduled to take place at the Wrexham Recreation Ground across the road from Pen-y-Bryn. The organisers had retrieved some wreckage of a German warplane which had been brought down during the air raids over Merseyside, and the local community planned to have a bonfire with it, together with a firework display and kite-flying.

Not surprisingly, that day stuck indelibly in my mind. Although I was somewhat afraid of my father's reaction to my speaking to him without his specific permission, I decided to tell him that my school friend Colin had told me about the kite competition. Father just grunted, as if to ignore me. But, to our surprise and secret delight, my brothers and sisters noticed that, in the evenings at the end of the working day, he and Uncle started to put together a Chinese kite. It was the biggest kite we had ever seen. Shaped like a gigantic dragonfly, its wingspan was at least four feet, with a long, tapering body and tail. The skeleton was made from thin strips of bamboo cane, which Father had bent into shape by soaking it in water. Using twine, the bamboo was skilfully bound into a three-dimensional shape whilst still submerged. After seven days, the twine was removed and the whole left to dry in the open air. Stretched over the frame, he glued stiff greaseproof paper, which he had soaked in turpentine and varnish.

Enormous black-and-red dragon eyes were painted on the head, with two thin wires protruding as antennae. We noticed that he had secured a roll of string which measured over one hundred feet to pinpoint attachments on the kite; one on the underside of each wing and one under the belly of the body.

The day came for its inaugural flight, which would either be the real test of my father's ingenuity or end with him red-faced in embarrassment. I told Colin to bring his family, including his older brother Arthur, who had just returned from serving in the forces in Aden. It was the last day in July. A hot and balmy evening welcomed the local population. They arrived in their hundreds, with their children and pet dogs in tow. Fathers clutched their precious kites, all home-made, and everyone was desperate to show off their skills and workmanship. By 9pm the bonfire was roaring away in the sultry summer's evening. It was a clear black night, with a carpet of crystal stars so sharply in evidence it was as if they had been painted in silver on a giant canvas. The organisers welcomed everyone to the sound of fireworks exploding in the night sky. Luckily, a sharp breeze was whipping up as the competitors unfurled and launched their beautifully painted kites into the air. Most of them were the traditional diamond shape. Some were box-shaped, and flew haphazardly around the park, some reaching fifty feet or more.

I remember the strange look of hostility my father received from the locals as he placed his kite on the grass verge next to the roaring bonfire; though our neighbours – particularly Mr Gareth Young from the dry-cleaning shop across the road, and Mr Willy Jones, the baker who had lent Father his industrial bread oven to cook our large turkey last Christmas – gave us a smile of encouragement.

'That foreign monstrosity won't even get off the ground!' snorted a large, rotund man wearing a string vest that was a bit small for him. Derisively, he poked the tail of Father's kite with his foot as soon as he and Uncle started to unpack the rest of it.

'Wrong shape! Too ugly! And too blinkin' heavy!' catcalled another man, whose tiny kite had just fluttered limply and crashed to the ground after a lull in the breeze.

Hundreds of heads turned to stare at us. Disapproving silence greeted Father and Uncle, who did not say anything, but took deliberate and measured steps away from each other. Uncle carried the belly of the Chinese kite across his body and Father simultaneously began to unravel the coil of string.

Just then, the cooperative breeze that had been blowing all evening suddenly stopped dead in its tracks. My brothers and sisters and I crossed our fingers and said a silent prayer for a hurricane to whip up and save our family's face.

'I'd pack up if were you, mate!' sneered another onlooker, to guffaws of support from his pals.

No sooner had those words been uttered than the breeze picked up. Encouragingly, Father felt a sharp tug as the faint breeze gave some lift from under the belly of the kite. Keeping the line taut, Father nodded a signal to Uncle to throw the Dragonfly Kite into the wind, which thankfully was now increasing to a welcoming swell. At ten feet parallel to the ground, the kite started to fly. The crowd held its breath.

But suddenly, our hearts sank as the kite began to struggle. It appeared to be nosediving into the ground, straight into the dying embers of the bonfire. Then all at once, the wind whipped up as if a storm was in the offing. Father quickly fed out the string and the kite started to soar, giving a noisy flap of its wings as the wind propelled it upwards, as though it were heading for the stars. Higher and higher it went, as the string was fed out to its maximum. The locals had never seen anything like it before.

Oohs and aahs greeted the spectacle as the kite dipped and zigzagged majestically in the summer night sky, illuminated by the stars in the background and the glow of the bonfire below, which had found a new lease of life due to the fresh wind.

Later, Mother told me that Father hadn't flown a kite since he was a boy of thirteen, at the ceremony of the cutting off of the much-hated pigtails, when his village back in China celebrated the end of the Ch'ing Dynasty in 1912.

After thirty minutes or so, Father and Uncle brought the kite down to the ground. They were immediately surrounded by scores of locals, who clapped spontaneously at the display.

'Well done!' shouted Mr Young from the dry-cleaning shop.

'That was brilliant, Mr Kwong!' said Willy Jones, the baker.

Many kite-fliers gathered around to examine Father's kite. They wanted to know how to build one like it. Father explained, in his broken English and with much gesticulation, how it had been built.

'It is to do with the bowed shape of the wings being buoyed by the air, like in an aeroplane. The weight of the kite is supported in the air as air streams move above and below the wings, giving it a sandwich effect, which buffets it,' he said, quite matter-of-factly.

The success of the Chinese kite, which had reached record heights never achieved previously in Wrexham, had won the cynics over. My friend Colin said that most of the locals would never look at our Chinese family in the same suspicious manner again. In that moment, I felt a sudden burst of pride in being Chinese and ethnically different, when hitherto I had often craved to be like one of the indigenous locals, so that I could melt anonymously into the background.

After the display, Father, Uncle, and the girls left promptly to return home. Colin, my brother Alan and I, together with another boy called Johnnie Lewis who knew Colin, dragged our feet because we wanted to see the end of the fireworks. When we left the park via the exit at the end of Pen-y-Bryn, which was beside the side entrance of the local garage, we were in high spirits and did not want the night to end. Colin and Johnnie Lewis gave us some fireworks they had produced out of their pockets and, cock-a-hoop, we lit them and threw them into the air. Unfortunately, one of the fireworks, known as a volcanic banger, ended up over the wall of the garage yard and landed in a pile of old rubber tyres.

Within minutes they caught fire. A tiny spark rapidly became a raging bonfire. As the rancid black smoke plumed into the air, we were stunned at the ferocity of the blaze. Naturally frightened, we all ran home as fast as our legs could carry us.

Remarkably quickly, two fire engines rushed up the hill from the town centre and got the blaze under control. Scared out of our wits, my brother and I hid under our blankets in our bunk beds, not daring to tell our parents what had happened.

Shortly after midnight, a policeman and a member of the fire crew knocked on our parents' shop door. Shame-faced, we were dragged out of bed by my irate father, who yelled at me because I was the older brother, and he blamed me for leading young Alan astray and for bringing shame on the family. My father threatened to punish me, and punish me he did, with three strokes of the willow cane across my backside. The police officer said that was enough punishment, and added to my father that, by the way, everyone had enjoyed his amazing kite display.

The following morning, Father went to see the garage owner and offered to pay for the damage. To his surprise, the owner said that he wasn't overly worried as only old, worn tyres had been destroyed, and that fortunately the blaze hadn't spread to the petrol pumps. He said that he had wanted to dispose of the tyres for months as they were blocking up his yard! What is more, he said he would make a claim for the loss of new tyres from the insurance. To make amends, Father did not charge him for his laundry for many weeks. I was put on gruel and plain steamed rice, soaked in dripping. I accepted the punishment like a man, for I didn't not want to reveal the name of the boy who had actually thrown the offending firework that almost burnt down our local garage. It seemed that, at the age of nine, I preferred to be called a Chinese pyromaniac rather than be labelled a treacherous snitch!

Chapter 17

THE FINAL STRAW

1949–1952

N INETEEN FORTY-NINE HAD BARELY come to an end when news
from China reported that, after three years of civil war, Chiang
Kai-shek and his forces had been driven from the mainland by Mao
Tse-tung and the People's Liberation Army. Chiang, together with his
family and supporters, had fled to Formosa[62] to set up a Nationalist
Chinese state.

**On the 1st October 1949, a triumphant Mao Tse-tung proclaimed
the People's Republic of China.**

An amnesty was declared, inviting all Chinese émigrés sympathetic
to the socialist cause to return to China to help with the establishment
of the new republic. It was announced that, from now on, all Chinese
not living on the mainland were to be classed as stateless.

In early December, my father received a letter from Chun Yee, his
second brother:

---

62   Later renamed Taiwan.

> *Dai Dune Chun*
> *Taishan*
> *Guangdung*
> *The People's Republic of China*
> *5th December 1949*

Dear Chun Ji,

You may have heard that Mao Tse-tung has finally driven out Chiang Kai-shek. Although everyone we know is nervous of what will happen with the new rulers, very few will grieve for Chiang Kai-shek and his family, who taxed our people mercilessly to fill their own coffers. The Red Army has occupied Canton since mid October and we are all frightened in case they march on Taishan. We do not know what will happen to the villages and our peaceful way of life if that happens.

We would appreciate some help with a dowry as our eldest daughter is soon to be married. We understand that our youngest brother, Chun Tileng has recovered well from his illness, and in his last letter he managed to send us some money for which we thank him. Chun Tin also sends his regards.

> *Your brother,*
> *Chun Yee*

Nineteen fifty arrived with the birth of a new decade full of hope. It heralded momentous changes in Britain. Winston Churchill, who had saved Britain and Europe from Nazi Germany ten years earlier, was returned to power in April. A feeling of optimism swept the country as it recalled his morale-boosting speeches during his iron leadership in the darkest days of the war.

The following month, a fifth daughter, Shui Ning or Ester, was delivered safely at the General Hospital. For the first time in our lives, it was noticeable that my father displayed some real emotion towards this doll-like child. Affectionately, he bounced her on his lap, something he had never done with his other children. At the start of the autumn, when a travelling fair came to the market square on the other side of town, he returned clutching a large toy horse on wheels which he had won on a rifle range, and which he proudly gave to his new young daughter.

In June, fighting broke out on the Korean Peninsula as troops from North Korea, supported by Russia and China, crossed the 38th Parallel into South Korea. The bitter conflict lasted three bloody years, with troops from the USA fighting alongside their Western Allies in the south in an effort to stem the spread of Communism. The world feared that World War III was imminent. But fortunately, in the peaceful backwaters of Pen-y-Bryn, Wrexham, the Kwong family weren't troubled by being mistaken for Koreans. Father gave a shudder, for he had never forgotten the hostility he had endured in Liverpool when mistaken for Japanese during the last war, until he was advised by his English neighbours to hang out a Chinese flag from his window next to the Union Jack.

In the spring of 1951, I managed to pass the scholarship exams for the local grammar school, joining Rose, who attended the girls' school. Father barely acknowledged my achievement, which led to another exchange of words between him and my mother.

'You should be proud of what your son has achieved!' she remarked pointedly.

'Bah! He's been nothing but trouble since the day he was born,' growled my father dismissively. He then turned abruptly away.

Britain was in a festive mood. The end of the war receded into distant memory as the months rolled by. Around the country, celebrations were taking place to commemorate the Festival of Britain, as it was the centenary of the Great Exhibition that took place in the Victorian era. In London, on the South Bank of the Thames, an enormous festival park with exhibitions, a fairground and other attractions had been built, which brought visitors from all corners of the country and around the world. Iconic structures such as the Festival Hall, the Dome of Discovery and the Skylon – a huge, UFO-shaped structure had been constructed, altering the river skyline.

Not uncommonly, tragedy can quickly follow triumph like a bad penny. The following year, the country's palpable joy was suddenly deflated by sadness. News of King George VI's death was announced on the wireless. Britain was in mourning. Young Princess Elizabeth had heard the sad news whilst she was on tour with her husband Prince Philip in Africa. An announcement from the government declared that she was now Queen of Great Britain and the Commonwealth. Her coronation was to follow.

On the international stage, Britain sought to maintain its position alongside the USA as a major nuclear power, competing with the Soviet Union by testing its first atomic bomb in 1952.

During that year, Alan followed me by winning his scholarship for Grove Park Grammar School, achieving a distinction. This time, my father was overtly proud.

In August, a fifth son was born: he was christened Shui Fah, or Walter. After initially taking interest in his young son, Father gradually found that looking after a brood of ten children was beginning to take a toll upon him. The responsibility of bringing them up and ensuring that they were all fed and clothed began to weigh heavily. Traditionally, that was a duty which in the beginning he did not shrink from, but the added financial burden as head of the Kwong clan back in China became increasingly intolerable. When my mother reminded him that their own children must come first, it led to the first of many rows. She began to express an opinion, which to his way of thinking was strictly forbidden. Differences of opinion began to emerge into the open, though in fact they had been smouldering quietly over the years.

My father tried to put in extra hours hoping to earn more money, but he was getting increasingly tired and irritable. He felt that time was running out on him. *There must be more to life*, he thought, than working like a slave in a business he had grown to detest. Stoically, my uncle carried on the work. And, with my mother caring for the younger children and unable to put in the hours in the laundry, a friend of Uncle's by the name of Pak Sang came to help in the business.

It was a typical hot summer's day in July, and noticeably airless, when out of the blue my mother received a letter from Borneo. With trepidation she opened it, and was forced to ask my father to help her to read it. It was from her brother Kit Siang, and got straight to the point:

Borneo
14ᵗʰ June 1952

Dear sister,

I trust you are well. I do not know if you have heard of the increasingly difficult times, we, the Chinese, have endured in Malaya. For years we have been trying to live peacefully with the indigenous Malays.[63] *But historically, they resent and despise us for our single-mindedness and hard graft in setting up businesses, and our dedication in helping our families to achieve material success. Over the years we had hoped that the two peoples would learn to get on. I must tell you that more racial trouble has flared up following the rape and killing of a local girl. Mass riots have erupted, and this time, Uncle's timber business and our furniture factory which we have built up over the years were burnt to the ground by a rampaging mob. We constantly fear for our lives, as north of the island many Chinese have been killed in the looting, attacks and arson.*

I beg you to help us to start again by sending some money as a matter of urgency. Our mother reminds you on your conscience that the Chow family has never asked for your help before. Please help us now before it is too late.

Your brother,
Kit Siang

---

63 Historically, tensions between the Muslim population of Indonesia and the non-Muslim migrant population had been simmering since the eighteenth century, when Chinese immigrants took the brunt of the ethnic unrest. For example, massacres took place in 1946. The racial tension spilled over from Indonesia to Malaya (later known as Malaysia) where resentment and anger festered constantly because the Chinese immigrants controlled most of the banking, finance, trade, businesses etc. In South-East Asia, the overseas Chinese, particularly the Hakka peoples, have historically been known as 'the Jews of the East' because of this.

Father exploded with rage, shouting, '*That's impossible!* There's *nothing* left!' and threw the letter on the floor and banged his fist on the table. Frustration and anger boiled over.

Ashen-faced, Mother was lost for words and stared disconsolately at the floor. She shooed the children into another room and slammed the door shut so that we wouldn't have to see what was going on between our parents.

'We *have* to help,' she pleaded, crying at the top of her voice. 'The Kwongs in China have always had our help in the past. So now it's my family's turn!'

Another blazing row followed, which raged for several days. But, despite this, Mother scraped together some money from their meagre savings and mailed it via the post office across the road.

To inflame matters, not long afterwards, at the start of autumn, another letter came from abroad. This time it was from China, again asking for more money. This was the last straw. The resentment that Mother had swallowed over the years about their hard-earned money going back to China to help the Kwong Clan suddenly erupted. Angry words flew between her and Father.

Fearing that the volatile situation was getting out of hand, the next day Uncle persuaded me to try to pacify my parents on behalf of the children, who were becoming increasingly frightened by their squabbling. The atmosphere was getting more fractious by the minute.

Immediately after breakfast, I plucked up the courage to try to say something in my broken Cantonese. Haltingly, I pleaded in a subdued and nervous voice, 'Please. Please… the children are getting scared and—'

But before I could finish, my father cut me short with a furious wagging of his finger. 'How *dare* you speak to me? Look! Let me tell you something. From the start, you have never behaved like a true member of the Kwong family. And furthermore, you've always favoured your mother's side. Obedience and loyalty to a father? Bah! You don't know the meaning of it! And another thing; you have never looked like one of my sons – never mind the eldest! You are *not* one of mine!'

Abruptly, he turned his back on me and stared vacantly through the window, as if preoccupied with something else.

The final insult struck home. At that moment, it began to dawn on my mother why my father had resented me – their eldest son – from the outset. Without a word, protectively she pushed me, red-faced, out of the room. As she turned to confront my father, he exploded.

'I can't cope with this anymore! Family duty! Children to feed. A marriage that was forced upon me. Work that is killing me. Ancestral obligations for the last thirty years! It's relentless. It will be the death of me!'

My father gripped his throat and spat out, 'I've had enough… right up to here!' His face black as thunder, he turned on his heels and stormed out.

He sought lodgings at Mrs Wong Sing's house at the other end of town. Her late husband had travelled with him to England all those years ago. With cold, calculated calmness, he decided to go on hunger strike in order to die. It was a simple act of defiance to finally cut the chains of blood that had hung around his neck like a poisonous curse.

At that moment, it struck him that perhaps Ruby, his scorned ex-mistress, had been right after all, when, seventeen years ago, having been turned out with her young son, she had cursed him, predicting, **'Duty and family obligation will be the death of you in the end!'**

Chapter 18

A RADICAL CHANGE

1952

Fıve weeks passed, and seemed like a lifetime. The atmosphere at Number 29 Pen-y-Bryn was strained to breaking point. Uncle Chun Tileng and my mother did not dare to bring up the subject of my father's absence, as though it was taboo. The younger children, especially Ester and Walter, fretted for their father. The older girls, Eileen and Rose, stayed silent, not daring to mention it when asked by the rest of the children what had happened to him. Everyone appeared to be walking about on eggshells, as if in a state of mourning.

At the onset of winter, the dark, dank nights arrived with a vengeance. It started to close in rapidly as the daylight shrank. Early one Sunday morning, shortly before sunrise, there was a loud knock on the door and an impatient rattling of the letter box.

'*Please let me in. It's important!*' yelled a voice through the letter box.

Uncle was the first to wake up. Rushing downstairs, he unbolted the door to let in Simon, Mrs Wong Sing's teenage son. He was panting like a horse, having cycled through town in a panic.

'Your... your *brother*, Mr Kwong is seriously ill! He's at death's door!' He continued to garble hoarsely in a torrent of words. 'He refuses to eat. Mother has called the doctor, but he refuses to see him. He only sips water when we force him to!'

The older girls and I had got dressed and called our mother down to hear what Simon had to say.

'Someone has to speak to him before it's too late,' he gasped.

Thwarted, Uncle shook his head, knowing that he was held back by Chinese protocol. As the youngest sibling, he could not possibly approach his eldest brother, the head of the family. Nor did my mother dare to make a move, even if she had been allowed to.

All eyes suddenly turned to me in earnest.

'I'm afraid it's your job as the eldest son to speak to your father,' whispered Simon with a look of desperation.

'*But... but I'm... I'm just a kid!*' I stammered. '*Besides, Father hates me!*'

Uncle placed a consoling hand on my shoulder, as though to confer the transfer of family responsibility. 'You've got to face up to him one day, son. After all, you are nearly thirteen and nearly grown up. In old China, you would be betrothed by now – just like your mother's father, Chow Yuk Yiu, when he was your age!'

I shrank into my collar, suddenly feeling hot. Conflicting emotions rushed up and engulfed me. There was little time to argue.

Simon tugged at my sleeve with a vice-like grip. 'Come on, you idiot, before it's too late!'

Reluctantly, I followed him out into the street. Chewing over what to say to my father, I hurried along to Mrs Wong Sing's like a zombie. '*I have to pretend to be extremely brave when I face him, even if he screams at me,*' I muttered to myself. 'He can't possibly raise his hand to me if he's so weakened,' I shouted, bolstering my courage as I got nearer to the house even though the knot in my stomach screwed tighter.

Simon's mother opened the door to the small, terraced house, alarm etched upon her face. 'Your father's in the parlour, resting.' Looking increasingly worried, she pointed the way.

I tapped nervously on the door, which was already ajar. I hovered on the threshold, my sweaty hand gripping the doorknob like a prop. It was a shock to see my father sprawled, apparently lifeless, in an old armchair in the corner of the front room, which was in virtual darkness, and airless due to the curtains being tightly closed. Noticeably drawn, his skin was pale and dry as parchment.

Sunken eyes greeted me suspiciously. *'Wha... what the devil brings you here?'* he croaked.

'I-I am to tell you that your children are worried about you, Fa-Father. Young Ester and Walter are fretting. Uncle says the business needs you, and that you must come home so that you can get well again.' Stammering, I spat out the speech that I had rehearsed in my head on the way there.

'Ha! It's going to be *too* late! I've had enough of the damn laundry business over the last thirty-odd years. I've had it up to here!' He gestured with the edge of his hand, fluttering under his throat. *'I've had my fill of family eating away at me, constantly, all this time!'*

Mrs Wong Sing crept into the room with a glass of water and forced it into my father's hand. 'You'll not die here. What will the neighbours think?! And think of the shame you will bring on your family.'

'So, what bright suggestion have you got for me to earn a living and feed the family?' he challenged cynically.

'Well, you can always run a restaurant. You've always been a good cook!' she retorted.

'What?! You must be joking! How can I switch from one life to another? It's a pipe dream.' He snapped his fingers derisively in the air.

'Not if I can help you, Father,' I ventured, saying the first thing that came into my head. 'I can search the newspapers for a business for sale; say, back in Liverpool. I can help at the solicitors, with the documents and so on. I can be your interpreter in all the transactions!' Emboldened, my ideas began to run away with me.

It was one of those seismic moments when, on the spur of the moment, I offered to do something out of the ordinary for Father. But to be honest, I hadn't quite worked out how to go about it. Seeing him vulnerable and weakened, I felt I could say almost anything to him. In that moment, he did not scare me as he used to. I suppose, in retrospect, it could be said that I took advantage of him while he was down. And from that time onwards, the dynamics of our hitherto fraught relationship changed beyond all recognition.

Silence followed. But somehow, the seeds of my suggestion began to slowly sink in. My father's face, despite being gaunt and depressed from lack of food over the last few weeks, began to light up.

Mrs Wong Sing and her son shooed me out of the room. 'Come back in five days' time. I'm sure I can get him to start eating again. We've made a breakthrough,' she said quietly. 'And remember what you promised your father.' An admonishing finger waved in front of my nose emphasised the point.

A week later, I accompanied Father back home. Every night after doing my homework, I ploughed through the adverts in the Liverpool newspapers. I became an expert at reading about café and restaurant leases for sale, going concerns, goodwill, licences and so on. Father put 29 Pen-y-Bryn up for sale as a going concern via the Chinese network.

An uneasy truce was established between my father and me, for he began to depend on my dedicated efforts in contacting estate agents and people selling catering businesses in Liverpool. Uncle and my mother didn't speak of what had happened over the last few months, and which had led to the family row. A modicum of peace returned to the family. The children were content again. Having a father figure around once more, albeit one who was sometimes grumpy, was better, they thought, than having no father at all.

I crossed my fingers in a desperate hope that I really could find that all-important business for Father that would radically change his life. How could I possibly forget that rash moment when I confronted him as he was almost at death's door at Mrs Wong Sing's, and glibly promised that I would help him to change his working life forever? It was a promise I hoped that I would not live to regret.

Part III

1953 – 1960

Chapter 19

A LEAP INTO THE DARK

Liverpool, England, 1953–1955

I N THE EARLY SPRING of 1953, with the first scent of blossom in the air, I found something that my father and mother could start off with. It was a large English café in West Derby Road, Liverpool that needed a new lease of life and a radical change of direction. Taking a chance, I stuck a pin into a list of solicitors obtained via the agents. I then took my father by train to Liverpool. We found an established firm called Allsop's, which was based in an old-fashioned office in the centre of Liverpool, on the first floor of a large, soot-covered building next to the entrance to the Mersey Tunnel.

The senior partner, Mr Peter Allsop, was a tall, imposing figure of a man, balding and bespectacled; dressed immaculately in a well-worn tweed suit with a silver pocket watch spilling out of his waistcoat. Because of his considerable height, he had to stoop to talk to my father, in a patrician but kindly way, deliberately avoiding patronising language when addressing foreigners. His small, dusty, dimly lit office with its narrow stained-glass window added to the Dickensian appearance. Jostling for every spare inch of space were a large oak desk crowned with dark brown leather, and two bulky antique armchairs facing it. From floor to ceiling it was piled high with books and folders, and there was just enough room left for a large grandfather clock, which chimed sonorously at each quarter-hour.

We immediately felt at home with the quiet but professional manner in which Mr Allsop dealt with our affairs. My father asked if it was financially safe to buy, when possible, a small property in Liverpool to house the family. The old gentleman-lawyer peered over his half-moon glasses and nodded his head confidently.

'Of course, Mr Kwong, our proud city will *soon* rise out of the ashes like an irrepressible phoenix, despite the terrible damage it suffered during the war. Buying property in England will be perfectly secure… unless of course there happens to be a revolution and the country becomes a Communist state, as happened in your old country!'

Feeling reassured, my father nodded wryly. And so, he signed the lease and took on the business in West Derby Road, and not long afterwards bought a small house in Sandringham Road, Tuebrook, with the help of a mortgage of three hundred pounds from a local building society. Then he swore on his ancestors' name, hoping he wouldn't live to regret taking his family back to the city whence they had fled after the war.

It was with some anticipation and hope, tempered by fear of the unknown, that my father made rapid arrangements for us to leave Wrexham and the life that went with it. Events moved quickly. The business at Pen-y-Bryn had already been sold to a relative of one of the Chinese families who lived in Rhos, not far away. Uncle Tileng found a new job in Liverpool, and Pak Sang left immediately, rather under a cloud. Nero the cat had gone missing, and the children suspected that Pak Sang had shot him dead with his air pistol, as he had previously threatened to do after the cat had accidentally scratched him once on the leg. The children were inconsolable.

On the 2nd June 1953, the coronation of Queen Elizabeth II took place, and it seemed that the whole country came to a celebratory standstill. The family had been invited to watch the ceremony at Westminster Abbey on the tiny television set owned by the Youngs across the road in Pen-y-Bryn. To mark the coronation, models made by Dinky Toys Ltd of the coronation coach, pulled by a team of horses from the Royal Household Cavalry, were offered as exclusive prizes in a national painting competition mounted by the *Daily Mail*. Being a budding artist, I was encouraged to enter by my school art master as six such prized models were on offer.

I was thrilled to receive one of these prizes in the post. With trembling hands, I ripped open the cardboard box, which was at least fifteen inches long. Sparkling inside was the most beautiful thing I had ever seen. The coach was crowned in scintillating gold, with the Queen and the Duke of Edinburgh inside. Escorted by the mounted Household Cavalry in their shining full regalia alongside a team of magnificent white horses, it was almost lifelike. When I proudly showed it off to my mother, she just nodded approvingly. My siblings thought it was the most wonderful toy that had ever graced our home. But my father grumbled under his breath that art couldn't possibly lead to a meaningful job in the future. Conscious that our delicate truce was still holding, I held my tongue as I didn't want to get into any arguments. I had to remember that it wasn't that long ago that the family had nearly lost our father when he almost took his own life; so, I just swallowed my pride and grimaced.

Not long afterwards, the family moved back to Liverpool. Although it was the end of June, Father had simply forgotten how grey and bleak the city looked, as though a pall of smoke hung permanently over it like a veil, despite the tiny pockets of dappled sunshine. Large swathes of bombsites with the remnants of crumbling brick walls pockmarked many of the streets after the devastation of the war. Patches of grass and weeds grew forlornly amongst once-proud buildings. Shaking his head, he was alarmed to see gangs of young children – some barefooted and seemingly without their parents – playing around the sad and arid wasteland. They were kicking a ball aimlessly between freshly hung lines of washing, fluttering in the breeze like rows of bunting, which were strung neatly from poles that sprouted from the backs of houses that bordered the waste ground. How different Liverpool looked to when he had first landed there in 1921 as a young man forced to leave China and seek his fortune in the New World.

As his eyes scanned West Derby Road, which was a major thoroughfare going north-east from the city centre, he saw a bank of shops on either side. Some of them were recently occupied and newly renovated. There was a variety of new businesses. It looked promising. But equally, interspersed with these were several units that were boarded up, empty or offered with *To Let* signs, looking dejected.

Immediately opposite the café premises, which was situated between a general provisions store and a newsagents, both of whose exteriors could have done with a lick of paint, stood two prominent stone buildings with large, flashing neon signs. One was the Grafton Rooms, and the other was the Locarno Ballroom.[64] Both places were major dance halls, with visitors coming from all over Merseyside. When negotiating the sale of the lease and business, Father was told by the retiring owner of the café that, *'You'll get a lot of business from these at the weekends, if you stay open late. Hamburgers, cola and tea will simply fly from your premises like there's no tomorrow!'*

At the end of the block, in a side street just behind the café, stood the mammoth building and substantial warehouse of the Ogden's Tobacco factory, which employed a large workforce. Father decided that, overall, the Feng Shui[65] was suitable to take a chance and make a living in this place by running an English café and Chinese restaurant in tandem. He did not dare to admit to my mother that inwardly he was quite terrified, for it was a gargantuan leap into the unknown. Wisely, he kept his worries to himself.

There was a large room above the café, and the family managed to squash into it as temporary accommodation. Shortly afterwards, the

---

64 The Locarno Ballroom was a dance hall owned by the Mecca Leisure Group. Originally built in the '20s as a massive indoor circus.

65 A Chinese philosophical system dedicated to harmonising one's surrounding environment. Commonly used to assess (often using astrological signs) the luck and future well-being of a building, e.g.,. the potential prosperity of business premises.

older children moved to Sandringham Road, two miles away. It was a small, bow-fronted Edwardian terraced house with three bedrooms and a box room overlooking a large green (which the locals called affectionately, the Boulevards) from where the tramcars juddered northwards along their lines which weaved between rows of tall ash on one side and lime trees on the other like guardian sentinels.

On one leisurely Sunday morning at the beginning of August, as the summer heat began stall, the rest of the family had barely settled into the house when a knock came at the front door. Milly, now a serious and beautiful nine-year-old, rushed to open it. A middle-aged Chinese couple stood outside the porch, shuffling from foot to foot. The woman was dressed smartly in a bright red suit with a thick Chinese gold chain supporting a large jade pendant around her neck. Smelling strongly of perfume of Lily of the Valley, she smiled coyly at Milly. The man opened his mouth to reveal a row of gold fillings.

'*Doh sun, dai lieng nui. Nee low moo, um waj jek low dew ho yuk kee mah?*' ('Good morning, my big, pretty girl. Is your mother, or perhaps your father, at home?')

Startled, and not quite understanding what the man meant, Milly shouted upstairs for our mother, who, with some of the older children, was still trying to unpack the rest of the crates that had been shipped from Wrexham. Irritated at being disturbed, Mother grumbled and started to come down the stairs. On seeing the couple framed against the sunlight, she gave a gasp of horror and, without a single word, ran down the remaining steps, pushed Milly aside, and quickly slammed the door in their faces without giving them a chance to explain. Leaning heavily with her back to the door, she slid to the floor, her face pale with shock.

'Who's that, Mama?' asked my sister, puzzled.

After a while, Mother went into the kitchen to take a sip of water before sitting down. 'That was that pushy old godfather of yours, Ong Hing Bak, and his dreadful wife. I thought we had seen the last of them eight years ago. You were too little to remember, but they wanted to buy you in exchange for jewellery, as if we were pawnbrokers or something!'

On hearing this, but not quite realising the implications, Milly burst into tears, thinking that they had returned to take her away, having heard that the family had just moved back to Liverpool.

Our mother did her best to reassure her. She sat her down in the nearest chair. 'In September 1945, at the end of the war, I had just given birth to your baby brother at our old house in Leopold Road, where we were last living in Liverpool. Your father was ill. The business in Rocky Lane had shut down. Even though we were near to starvation, there was never ever in a million years that I would sell you or any of the children! And so, I chased Ong Hing Bak and his wife out of the house.'

Arching her eyebrows with a roll of the eyes, she continued hesitantly, 'You see, when I was little in China, my parents gave away two of my baby sisters rather than drown them in the well at the end of the village, as others did. Another was sold. All died within a year. My mother was a tyrant and wanted to sell me too, but my father intervened and stopped her...'

Long before Mother had finished, Milly burst into tears again.

By September, Alan and I were transferred to the grammar school in Shaw Street; the Collegiate near to the city. The rest of the children, apart from of the two youngest, went to the local primary school in Tuebrook. Eileen had left school and was able to help our parents in the café. Rose had stayed on in Wrexham to enable her to sit her GCE exams. She lodged with a neighbour of Mrs Wong Sing, named Mrs Tallow, in a similar flat-fronted terraced house in Birch Street, whose occupants scrubbed their windowsills and thresholds until they gleamed. Rose said she couldn't wait to leave as she felt the bedroom, she slept in was haunted. Apparently, it was a shrine, filled with photographs of the landlady's only daughter, who had mysteriously disappeared during the war. Rose recounted that, when she returned from school each day, the framed photographs on the mantelpiece and shelves would all be lying face down. She didn't dare to mention it to Mrs Tallow, because when she commented, shortly after she moved in, that her own belongings had been flung off the bed and chairs, the landlady just gave her a strange, dismissive stare, saying that she must have been mistaken due to the stress of her studies and being away from her family.

In July, when Rose had finished her exams, she joined the family and worked at the café with Eileen and with two local girls, Mary and Nancy who had worked there under the previous owner. They were able to provide some continuity and help the Kwongs familiarise themselves with the new business following the complete redecoration of the premises inside and out. The double-fronted shop, with its expanse of windows on either side was renovated to admit more day light, so that potential customers could see from outside the fresh new look that would welcome them.

'Oh,' remarked Mother, 'the window cleaning will be quite costly.' Not unusually, my father ignored her opinion.

A new neon sign went up: *"The Kwong-Wah"* – literally translated, this means 'the language of Kwong'. The metal sandwich board, propped outside the door courtesy of Coca-Cola, was likewise amended.

In the first few months the business grew briskly, and it augured well. Alongside the staple English fare of roast beef, fish and chips, and hamburgers, the new menu of simple Chinese dishes, such as curry, sweet and sour, chop suey and chow mein, proved a success. This was an unusual choice for a café, and for what was once a basic English snack bar and tearoom; but the news of it spread. Not only did the workers from Ogden's come to eat during lunchtime and in the afternoons, but in the evenings the musicians from the Locarno and the Grafton came in their numbers to be fed before they went on stage. Well-known swing bands, such as the Joe Loss Orchestra, and Duke Ellington, as well as ballroom dance musicians such as Victor Silvester, came to eat. Chinese cooking was popular with the visiting American bands as many of them had served in the US Armed

Forces in the last war and were already quite familiar with Chinese food, which was prominent in America's Chinatowns. Within a year, Kwong-Wah's Chinese cooking became quite famous locally.

The nearest Chinese eating place was nearly five miles away, in the Chinatown around Nelson Street near the city centre. But that was a place for the adventurous, for Chinatown's cafés and restaurants catered mainly for the Chinese population, offering more complex and obscure regional Cantonese cuisine, such as steamed duck's feet, and shark fin and bird's nest soup.

'Never in a lifetime would the locals be ready to face that sort of menu!' declared my father knowingly.

The growing popularity of his café was no doubt a lot to do with my pretty sisters, Eileen and Rose who served at the tables. They had a natural charm mixed with innate tact in dealing with customers and had an advantage over the Chinese eateries in Chinatown, for they spoke excellent English. My father soon realised that many customers came to eat not only for the good cooking, but also to be served by the two girls. Early on, he decided that he would have to keep a stern and tight rein on his daughters. On most weekends, I was able to help in the evenings for pocket money, as one of the English girls, Nancy, had left to get married. Mary, the remaining one, worked part time on Saturday and Sunday nights.

Business grew at a steady pace. It was greatly helped when rationing came to an end in 1954 the following year. Imports of foreign goods became easier, not only for us, but for many others in the country. Liverpool, like many other cities in Britain having endured the full impact of the war, questioned why this had taken so long, since the war had ended nine years ago. It appeared that Britain was still struggling to pay back a hefty war debt of billions to America and did not have sufficient foreign exchange to end rationing much earlier. Despite everything, Father took a gamble and brought in some extra help in the kitchen to take the pressure off my mother. And so, an old cook by the name of Yiu-han Bak was hired. After much hard work and with considerable relief, Father was able to pay back the loan he had obtained from the local bank and keep up the mortgage payments on the house in Sandringham Road. So, after all the struggles he had faced and the hardships he had endured, now, he was quietly quite pleased with himself.

Chapter 20

NEVER HAD IT SO GOOD?

1956–1957

O N ONE SHARP AND sunny morning in October 1956, with the leaves of autumn beginning to turn, just as the café was getting ready for lunch, a neighbour from the newsagents rushed through the door.

'Mr Kwong… *Mr Kwong!* Have you heard on the wireless that Soviet tanks are rolling into Budapest to halt the Hungarian Revolution and stop their new leader breaking away from the Soviet Bloc? My wife is scared that Europe is going to war again!'

The neighbour flopped onto the nearest chair to catch his breath. 'And you won't believe this, but just as terrifying, fighting has just broken out in the Middle East as well! Colonel Nasser of Egypt has just seized and nationalised the Suez Canal and kicked out the French and British.'

'*Oh no, not another damn war!*' cried my father, fearing the worst. It also came to him that, some thirty-five years ago on his journey to the West, he had heard of the vital importance of the Canal as it was a strategic shortcut to the Mediterranean. At that time, he simply couldn't afford that short way round, and so had been forced to travel the extremely long and more dangerous way around via the Cape of

Good Hope. Shaking all over, he said that the hellish long journey from China haunted him still.

'Hopefully, it won't spread this time,' replied our neighbour. 'But according to the news, the British and French Armies, supported by the Israelis, have gone in and there is bitter fighting with the Egyptians.'

As the Canal was closed, the fighting lasted until March 1957. Harold Macmillan had taken over from Anthony Eden as Prime Minister earlier that year due to the latter's ill health. In July, as things gradually returned to normal in Britain, Macmillan, with great fanfare, declared on the wireless that *'People have never had it so good in the history of this country!'*

Whether this optimistic feeling of prosperity had spread to everyone up and down the country, it was hard to say. But as far as immigrants such as our family were concerned, things were looking up. With the help of hire purchase, we managed to buy our first television set; a Ferguson model set in a walnut cabinet with a twelve-inch screen. Also, the girls were thrilled to have saved up enough to buy a radiogram from the local Curry's, so that they could play their precious '78 records from their favourite singers, Mario Lanza and Doris Day, having seen their films at the nearby Odeon cinema.

However, I became smitten with the new sound in music: rock 'n' roll. It was revolutionary. For most teenagers, Elvis Presley's hit record 'Heartbreak Hotel' the previous year had changed the face of popular music forever. As did Lonnie Donegan's skiffle group's 'Rock Island Line', which dominated the pop charts on both sides of the Atlantic.

In common with my school friends, 1957 was a turning point in my teenage life. GCE exams were over, and we had entered the sixth form, with my opting to study science. Life seemed liberating, like the beginning of a new chapter. Not one for standing still, I was inspired to help launch a weekly social gathering of boys and girls at the school to meet, play and hear the latest types of music, as well as dance. Like most boys of my age, I was painfully aware of the segregation of the sexes in the all-boys' and all-girls' schools in and around Liverpool.

As a member of the second XV school rugby team, our previous club socials had been limited to tea and biscuits after a match, with only a few hardy girls daring to turn up. They were mainly girlfriends or sisters of the team.

Together with a classmate who played in the first team, I plucked up the courage to persuade our headmaster, Mr Craft – who was a humourless and extremely reserved Quaker – that our social committee would like to hire the large canteen building located in the schoolyard for one night a week, preferably Friday, as a fundraising venture. Once we submitted a programme of respectable ballroom dance music – largely selected from Victor Silvester, the doyen of ballroom – he reluctantly consented. However, we surreptitiously inserted two slots for auditions for local bands, and to play the latest beat and rock music under the guise of jazz.

We were encouraged when Mr Craft said that he was tone-deaf, and that he didn't really understand any form of modern dance music and preferred not to attend; but he agreed on the condition that we wouldn't corrupt the young people attending by playing that 'dreadful and sinful' (his words, not ours) rock music from America, and that our rugby master would look in regularly to supervise the goings-on. But luckily for us, he never did pop in. And so, our venture into a social dance club was launched later that year at the start of the new autumn term. Threatened with six strokes of the cane by the Head, alcohol was strictly forbidden. Though we couldn't prevent many of the boys sneaking out to smoke in the bike sheds which were adjacent to the toilets at the other end of the schoolyard.

Like wildflowers seeding in fallow fields, amateur skiffle groups[66] and bands were sprouting up all over the country. They were irrepressible. Liverpool became a fertile ground for many local bands with blossoming talent, whose music started with skiffle based on

---

66 In the mid '50s, amateur groups sprang up in the UK with acoustic guitars, drums, washboards and often a home-made bass using a tea chest and a strung broom handle to pluck on. Originally playing American blues and folk music, skiffle was popularised by Lonnie Donegan, who led a professional group, having broken away from Chris Barber's Jazz Band.

American folk music. The neighbouring Quarry Bank School gave birth to John Lennon's Quarrymen.[67] whereas the Collegiate launched the Barmen with Chas Newby as lead.

Sending out invitations to the girls' high schools and grammar schools in Liverpool, and also to boys from rival schools, such as the Liverpool Institute and Quarry Bank, our Friday nights became a roaring success. And giving groups their chance to play at our dances proved a powerful magnet for boys and girls from all over Liverpool, who also brought their latest records for us to play.

The girls sat awkwardly in a row on the bank of seats on one side of the hall, and the boys self-consciously on the other side, until the music got under way. A heavy curtain was draped across one end of the dining hall, which became a stage, where the microphones and amplifiers were installed next to the record players and boxes of records. I became one of the Masters of Ceremonies (MCs) and DJs, as I enjoyed public speaking, or being brash or 'hard-faced' enough, as one of my classmates said witheringly. The Collegiate also had the core of a very accomplished jazz band, and one evening, whilst we were clearing up after a late session, I happened to notice Fred Ebshaw, who was a drummer in the jazz band, drumming with a young Pete Best[68] (both were members of the rugby first XV) by beating a rhythm up and down the rungs of a ladder parked behind the stage!

Friendships were born and friendships died that winter; but at least our school pioneered what was to most of us the normal and healthy getting together of the sexes.

One night, after spinning the record of the 'Last Waltz', which always signalled the end of the evening, I happened to end up with a young, pretty girl who had a mane of dark hair flopping over her

---

67 In 1957, whilst at Quarry Bank School, John Lennon formed a skiffle group which branched out into rock music. Later he was joined by Paul McCartney and George Harrison from the Liverpool Institute. Together, they later formed the legendary Beatles. (Chas Newby years later, played bass guitar with the group for two weeks after they returned from Hamburg).

68 Pete Best later joined the Beatles to tour Hamburg (along with Stuart Sutcliffe, who met John Lennon at the Liverpool College of Art), having previously drummed with the group at Mona Best's club The Casbah.

forehead. Encouraged by her friends, I escorted her home. Nervously, we caught the bus, then walked the last part of the way to her family house somewhere in Anfield. Noticing that the lights were still on in the front parlour, I delivered her to her front door. Giving me an awkward peck on the face, she said that her name was Dorothy and that she hoped she would see me next week at the dance, and perhaps arrange for us to visit the newly opened club called The Cavern in Mathew Street.[69]

The next week arrived, and, just as I was adjusting the mic in front of the stage to make the announcements, I happened to put on my glasses, being extremely myopic. At the same moment, I noticed that Dorothy was also wearing glasses. After the last time, when we had met, she said that her parents were thrilled that she had met someone, but had asked her why she didn't invite me in to say hello? It struck me there and then that ours was probably her first date, and that they wanted to give me the once-over.

Well, after that I must confess, I avoided her like the plague. To be fair, she did the same to me. On reflection, it was the glasses that did it: both of us realised that being short-sighted had skewed our first impressions of each other, especially in the dim lights, which probably made us look more attractive than we were. Spectacles, I soon discovered, were a considerable leveller, and gave Dorothy and me a truer picture of each other that probably killed off any closer friendship or romantic potential. I made the rapid excuse to her best friend that my father didn't really allow me to go out with English girls. Because if I did, he would kill me, I added, if he ever found out. Moreover, I exaggerated a little, claiming that he would track down the hapless girlfriend's family to complain and put an end to it. I think that there was a sobering lesson in there somewhere.

Eventually, skiffle gave way and morphed into raw rock music, heavily influenced from across the Atlantic by the Everly Brothers, Little Richard, Bill Haley, Buddy Holly and Chuck Berry to name

---

69   The Cavern's original location in 1957 was Mathew Street. It was a popular venue for many Merseyside music acts, including the Beatles and Cilla Black.

but a few. New clubs and coffee bars had begun to spring up around the country, providing opportunities for many embryonic bands. Breaking new ground, The Cavern in Liverpool had well and truly been placed on the map for posterity. And that was only the start. Music would never be the same again on Merseyside.

When my father asked my sisters why I was out so often on Friday nights, they covered for me and said that it was to do with my obligations in fundraising for the school sports socials. He would have had a fit if he'd known that I went dancing with English girls and listened to that so-called decadent pop music from America, (according to my father). It would have been just as disastrous if he'd discovered that I sneaked out to practise ballroom dancing with my sister Eileen. In exchange for this conspiracy, there was nothing I wouldn't do for my dear sister in return.

Eileen, as it happened, had for some months been secretly writing to a penfriend: a young, handsome English sailor, who served in the Royal Navy. She had met Kenneth when he happened to call in at the café as a customer with his shipmates after visiting his widowed mother, who lived locally. Rose and I agreed to keep this a deadly secret from Father, for we knew that he would blow his top, and, even worse, turn our dear sister out of the house, as for years he had made it plain that one day arranged marriages to Chinese – indeed, only to fellow Cantonese – would be made by him for the daughters (and sons) of the family. Nevertheless, we continued to conspire in silence for our sister's sake, for on many occasions I acted as the messenger to deliver and receive letters securely to and from Kenneth via his mother's house.

Our younger siblings were doing well at school, having made new friends. Our unremarkable and contented lives, both individually and as a family, seemed to march along quite happily with little interruption. And with the family business continuing to flourish, the Prime Minister's declaration in July that we had *'Never had it so good!'* seemed, as far as we as a family were concerned, apt and prophetic, rather than the wishful political propaganda dressed in spin that was often thrust upon the population.

And so, it seemed that, for the first time in as long as my father could remember, he suddenly felt quite relaxed, appearing content with life. It was a dry, sunny day at the height of summer with hardly a cloud in sight when he came out of the kitchen and stood outside the front door of his business to casually pass the time away. Folding his arms, and feeling at ease with the world, he looked up and down the street with some self-satisfaction. His debts were all paid. The family savings were slowly growing again. There was food on the table every day, and there was little time for cross words with my mother as the children were quite well behaved; especially me.

Father also managed to send money back home to China, as a dutiful son should. His brother Chun Tileng had just got married to a wonderful Cantonese girl named Fong, introduced through their sister Chun Rei in Hong Kong. Through hard work, Uncle had established a new business in Wavertree, not far away, and had promised to repay the loan my father had given him. But Father waived that aside in return for all the help his loyal brother had given him through thick and thin over the last few years. And so, with everything in the garden seemingly rosy, he was tempted for the first time in his life to afford himself a modest, self-congratulatory pat on the back.

Chapter 21

BACK TO EARTH

September 1957

THEN, ONE GREY AND cloud-filled morning in late September, as the first of the autumn rain began to fall, something out of the ordinary happened.

It was a typical quiet Sunday morning, much quieter than weekdays as the usual customers from Ogden's and the nearby offices did not, as a rule, turn up to dine due to businesses being closed for the weekend. The Sunday silence was only broken by the faint sound of bells ringing in the distance, calling the faithful to church. Then two strangers – Chinese men – quietly let themselves into the café just as the front door was being opened. My father was surprised to say the least, as it wasn't often he got Chinese customers travelling from as far away as Chinatown.

Politely, he nodded a greeting. '*Doh Sun. Nee ho mah?*' ('Good morning. How are you?')

The taller of the two visitors, aged about fifty, gaunt and balding with a pockmarked face, merely grunted, kicked the legs of the nearest chair with his foot, and pointed to his companion to sit down at the table next to the serving counter. The other man, somewhat younger, was thickset and had greasy hair, greying at the temples to match the stubble on his chin, which bore a faint scar. He stood at about five foot seven, just an inch or so shorter than my father, and, with an acrobatic sweep of his arm, threw his raincoat over the coat stand near the front door.

As Chinese custom dictates, Father called for a pot of China tea from the kitchen, which Eileen brought up and nervously placed on their table. Hoping that they did not notice the cups rattling against each other, with great effort she poured the tea.

With their legs splayed akimbo, the visitors quickly appeared to make themselves at home. Slurping their boiling-hot tea, they raised their cups in traditional acknowledgement, and one of them, the stouter one, started to pick his teeth with a toothpick. Lighting a cigarette, the taller one half-grinned, revealing a couple of missing front teeth. Gesticulating with an extravagant sweep of his arm, he wafted smoke across the room and said, '*Ho sang yee mah… biu hing?*' ('Good business, eh… my fellow countryman?')

At the same time, his companion deliberately rubbed his thumb against his forefinger in full view of my father's face.

Warily, Father stood, leaning with his back against the service counter, and nodded politely. '*Mah mah dee. Fun a sik!*' ('Not bad. Just about making a living!')

He shrugged his shoulders in a helpless gesture.

After an awkward silence of some minutes, he mumbled his apologies and said that he had to get back to the kitchen to prepare for the day's business. Summarily dismissed, the two men got up abruptly. Pushing back their chairs, which made the legs squeal against the linoleum floor, they slowly walked towards the front entrance before collecting their coats on the way out. Just then, as they made their way into the street, they happened to brush past old man Yiu-han, who was just coming in to work. They gave each other a hostile stare when the strangers slammed the front door. The Perspex open/closed sign rattled noisily on the glass pane in their wake.

Father told old Yiu-han what had happened. The cook warned him to be careful, as he was sure that they were part of the criminal gangs that were snooping around new Chinese businesses, looking for easy pickings. He added that he had heard through the Chinese grapevine that splinter groups from the ancient Triads, and who were just as dangerous, were blackmailing Overseas Chinese who were living in Britain with false papers. And as most of these migrants were stateless (just like old Yiu-han and my father), they were therefore increasingly vulnerable to organised extortion.

'Well, they won't find anything here!' Father growled determinedly. *I managed to keep one step ahead of those filthy vermin shortly after I arrived in Liverpool, and after the war,* he thought grimly to himself. 'They don't scare me that easily!' he added, though his attempts at seeming unconcerned didn't quite ring true.

His situation was so different to the old days, because now he had a family, with young ones to feed and to bring up. Murderously, he gripped his meat cleaver and started to chop up the chickens for that day. He slammed the carcasses down hard on the chopping board in blind fury, his mind churning furiously on how best to protect his family in case there was trouble.

My sisters told me what happened that day, and naturally made us all extremely nervous and on tenterhooks.

I was normally extremely scrupulous in acting as a go-between for my sister Eileen and her sailor friend, Kenneth. Having collected a recent letter for Eileen, mailed from his ship in Gibraltar, from his mother's house, it had fallen out of my pocket one Thursday evening when, preoccupied, I was getting changed in order to help out in the café.

Then disaster struck.

Father managed to find it under the washbasin in the toilet next to the litter bin. In front of my mother, he confronted me with the letter, which he had displayed accusingly on the kitchen table. His face looked stunned with shock and anger. He demanded to know what was going on behind his back. I was forced to translate the essence of the letter, which he had already worked out. And furthermore, I had to admit that this clandestine friendship had been going on for months, right under his nose. It transpired that Kenneth had asked Eileen to meet him one morning at ten, two weeks from the date of the letter, at Lime Street Station, from where they planned to elope to Gretna Green[70] to be married.

Rose and Eileen, meanwhile, were already behind the service counter, ready for the evening's work, and couldn't help but overhear through the kitchen hatch as my father screamed at me, incandescent with rage, his blood pressure at boiling point. I knew there and then that he wouldn't directly confront and castigate his beloved daughters – particularly Eileen. As in the past, his wrath would be vented upon me – his favourite whipping boy! The look in his eyes, followed by deathly silence, was worse than if he had struck me physically. That, and so much more, I could have taken, feeling as I did that through my carelessness and a moment of weakness, I had betrayed my sister. I could, in fact, have lied about the letter, but I felt trapped in the middle. I wanted my dear sister to be happy, but at the same time, I did not want to suddenly lose her forever if she ran away to be married to someone she hardly knew.

Reluctantly, I agreed to place the letter back into the envelope and reseal it, with a note written across the back:

'Eileen has been forbidden to see you anymore, so please do not contact her again.'

I looked at Mother for help, but she just stared blankly at the stone floor, her arms folded tightly across her chest.

Sheepishly, not daring to face Eileen, I skulked out of the door to deliver the letter back to Kenneth's mother. For two whole weeks both my sisters did not speak to me. I felt I fully deserved punishment with hellfire and ash for what had happened. Soon afterwards, full of remorse and guilty as sin, I tried to make amends. But it was too late. The damage was done.

---

70 A small village just north of the border in Scotland, where any couple over the age of sixteen could get married at short notice, often without much scrutiny.

The routine resumed at the café and the episode was never mentioned again, either by my parents or by my sisters. It would have been better if it had all come out into the open and we, as a family, had had a blazing row to clear the air. But that was not the Chinese way. The continuing awful silence and the pretence of normality were even worse to live with. Eileen carried on with a brave face. At night, in her room, we knew that she sobbed uncontrollably.

Four weeks later, one of Kenneth's shipmates called in to say that Kenneth had been found dead on board his ship whilst in the harbour at Malta. Tragically, he had hanged himself with a leather belt, in one of the storerooms after coming off duty that night.

Eileen was inconsolable.

Chapter 22

AT BOILING POINT

October 1957

BECAUSE OF THE DRAMA of the family crisis, my father had largely forgotten the visit by the two sinister Chinese men the previous month, until, three weeks later, they turned up again. This time it was a Saturday lunchtime, and they brought with them two youths: one was English and the other half-caste[71] – part oriental, part occidental. Dressed fashionably as Teddy Boys,[72] they wore long, Edwardian-type jackets with velvet collars, and extremely narrow drainpipe trousers over winkle-picker shoes.[73]

Tilting his head, Father asked, '*Doh Sun! Nee sik mut yeh ah?*' ('Morning! What would you like to eat?')

The tall Chinese man prodded the English youth on his left, who appeared to be studying the menu.

'Curry chicken off the bone, pal. And it better be good!' came the reply. 'And me mate will have that chow mein. Make it chop-

---

71 An unflattering term for a mixed-race person.
72 A fashion in the '50s of youths dressing up in long jackets with velvet collars mimicking the Edwardian era, but with 'drainpipe' narrow trousers and skinny ties. The hairstyle copied the '50s film stars, such as Tony Curtis and James Dean, and was swept back with a quiff flopping over the forehead.
73 Narrow pointed shoes.

chop!' With a sullen curl of the lip, he took out a comb and swept it ostentatiously through his grease-plastered hair, which emphasised his long, sharp sideburns.

The Chinese indicated that they were not going to eat and continued to sip at their China tea which Rose had brought up from the kitchen.

'Oi!' said one of the youths. 'None of that cat's pee for us, love. Give us a good ole English brew fit for the Queen!' he added facetiously.

Blushing, Rose quickly retreated to make a pot of strong Typhoo.

'*Biu hing…*[74] *Ho sang yee mah? Dai bah tin?*' ('Fellow countryman… good business, eh? Making plenty of money?') enquired the stouter Chinese, addressing my father.

Giving a sly grin, he rubbed his hands together, then draped his coat across the service counter with one of the pockets purposely pulled inside out – it was clearly empty. He deliberately nodded towards it.

Father chose to ignore it, and returned to the kitchen to help old man Yiu-han as another table of customers had come in for lunch. Meanwhile, Eileen served up the food that the two youths had ordered. They wolfed it down, wiping the plates clean. Smacking their lips, they wiped their mouths with the backs of their hands.

'Good, eh?' chortled the taller Chinese.

The half-caste youth just offered a loud burp and patted his stomach facetiously.

But, when Eileen presented the bill for the meals at the table, one of the youths slowly picked it up, and deliberately crumpled it in his fingers and threw it to the floor, grinding it underfoot. On hearing the racket and the heated exchange of words, Father ran up from the kitchen.

'*Not paying for that rubbish! Neither will me mate. Not a bleedin' patch on the stuff like you get in Chinatown!*' snarled the youth.

My father's patience finally snapped. '*Get out! The damn lot of you!*' he demanded, as he pulled the table away from them.

---

74 A patronising expression used by Chinese addressing their countrymen in an attempt to ingratiate themselves.

Menacingly, the stouter Chinese got up slowly, sneering in a mocking, sing-song voice, 'You'll soon regret that, *Mis-ter Kwong-Wah*, or whatever your family name is. A curse on your filthy ancestors! And may your sons be barren, and you all roast in Hell! *'Neeg wang bien ho fie see!'* ('Death to your ancestral clan!')

His face twisted in blind fury. He spat on the floor, then snatched at his coat after quickly fumbling in vain inside the pocket in which Father had refused to place extortion money.[75]

'Don't you *dare* come back here and show your damn rotten faces, or I'll call the police!' shouted Father, his voice in a quiver. *'You're all banned from here!'*

Old man Yiu-han had come up from the kitchen behind him, gripping a meat cleaver.

'You'll be sorry, pal! Just you wait and see!' they snarled under their breath. Defeated, they sauntered out into the street, their faces contorted with hate. Swearing out loud, they kicked the front door shut behind them.

Shortly after the family had started to clear up for the night, having locked the front door after a busy Saturday, as soon as we had placed the chairs on the tables to sweep the floor, a horrendous crash was heard. Eileen and Rose screamed.

A massive brick had been hurled through one of the main windows. Shards of glass exploded into millions of splinters which showered everywhere and spread like a snowstorm, covering the floor.

Father and I ran outside and scoured the road in the darkness, but all we could see were a few latecomers emerging from the dance halls opposite. The police soon came to investigate and quickly arranged for an emergency company to nail wooden boards across the gaping window for the night, so that the insurance company could replace the plate glass as soon as possible.

---

75 Pockets pulled out and exposed as empty invite the payment of money. Often used as a Chinese method to elicit the surreptitious payment of a bribe when the recipient leaves the premises with the said pocket now filled with money. A similar method was used for extorting money in protection rackets.

Two weeks later, at the end of another busy Saturday night shortly before closing time, it happened again. This time, a huge piece of concrete was thrown through one of the windows and the metal sandwich board hurtled through the other, smashing the plate glass to smithereens. A filthy paraffin-soaked rag, its limp flame fortunately failed to ignite, soon followed.

There were a couple of late diners in the café at the time, including our good neighbour, the newsagent. They screamed in horror and ran to shield the girls, then hid behind the serving counter for safety. Without a second thought, my father rushed out with a meat cleaver hidden under his chef's overalls. I ran after him. Our eyes swept the road.

Across from the café, near the alleyway just behind the Locarno dance hall, we saw, standing partly hidden in the shadows, the stout Chinese and the half-caste youth. In that split second, they casually lit a cigarette which illuminated the scar under the Chinese man's chin. They stood for a minute or so, as if surveying the scene of their dirty work, then flicked their half-smoked cigarettes into the road in our direction, as if to taunt us. We were stunned for a minute or two; then Father leapt across the road in pursuit. Seeing him charging towards them wielding a meat cleaver, the two started to run down the alley. They then fled through the backstreets in two different directions. We couldn't catch them.

Doubled up and breathless, I pleaded with Father, who was gulping for air. *'Please... let's go back! It's too late. There may be a gang of them waiting... It could be a trap! We'd better leave it to the police.'*

Halfway across the road, our neighbour came out to meet us and ushered us back to the safety of the café. 'This is not the way, Mr Kwong,' he said firmly as he gently prised the cleaver from my father's hand.

Sweat poured from my father's tortured face in frustration. His family name had been smeared and threatened. Family safety had been severely compromised, and we were now in real danger. He felt so impotent. And what is more, justice and retribution had just slipped from his grasp. The failure of his revenge had punctured his confidence. He continued to rage. My mother, fearful for my father's life as well as for the family, agreed that this was not old China, where scores would be settled summarily in such a manner – gouging out an eye for an eye and lopping off a limb for a limb.

The police told my father that we were lucky, for they had heard that other businesses in the city had been firebombed, with fatal consequences. But try as they might, they could not break into the Chinese criminal network because potential informants had been scared off.

'That's it!' my father decided. 'It's *too dangerous* to stay on here. That scum of evil pigs has destroyed everything I've worked for. I daren't risk our family's lives. We'll have to go far away from Liverpool, to a place where there is no Chinese community to speak of.'

The following week, after the windows had been replaced, he shut up shop for the safety of his family. He immediately put the café up for sale at a knock-down price for the lease. The whole family returned to live in Tuebrook, hoping that the criminal gang could not trace them.

Towards the end of the year, just before Christmas, a rapid sale was concluded. Harold Macmillan's mantra now appeared hollow and utterly misplaced as far as our family was concerned. What had started off as an exciting new venture, which had begun with such optimism, had turned into the darkest nightmare imaginable. It was a bitter irony that it took a small gang of evil Chinese criminals just a matter of weeks to drive Kwong Chun Ji out of Liverpool, when the whole of the German Luftwaffe had failed to do so in all the years of the war.

Although Father was approaching sixty, when others would be contemplating retirement, because of what had happened, he had to start from the beginning again. There was no alternative. His family in China, as well as us in England, depended on him in order to survive. He told me to look for businesses in the Midlands immediately – particularly Birmingham, where he had heard that the motor industry was expanding at a phenomenal rate.

Since the Industrial Revolution, Birmingham had been renowned throughout the world for engineering and every type of manufacturing, from jewellery, tools, knives and machinery, to motor vehicles and firearms. Indeed, it had been known as 'the workshop of the world', giving birth to one of the highest number of inventions in the world. In 1774, for instance, James Watt launched a business in Birmingham with Matthew Boulton to develop the world-famous Rotary Engine and Steam locomotive.

Consequently, after London and Liverpool, the city had been heavily targeted during the war by the Luftwaffe, together with nearby Coventry, which housed factories for aircraft components, engines and munitions. When the war ended, rebuilding the city was prioritised as Birmingham, being the second largest city in England, was strategically important, as the central hub of the country interfacing the north and south with its vital road and rail networks. In the same way, its vast canal network had in the past provided an invaluable gateway from the Midlands to reach the doors of Europe, the Americas, Asia, and Africa.

And so, deep within this large and sprawling industrial city, this time, my father was going to open – in his words – *'a real restaurant – a proper, up-market restaurant!'*; and on a much larger scale, serving only authentic Chinese cuisine aimed at a discerning band of customers. At his late age, he feared that this was probably his very last chance to make a success of it.

Chapter 23

BIRMINGHAM, ENGLAND, PHOENIX RISING

1958–1960

A S THE OLD YEAR marched inexorably towards the next, a heavy flurry of snow suddenly fell. The following morning, to the delight of our younger siblings at Sandringham Road, the snow soon turned to a stiff hoar frost. From their bedroom windows, through shimmering lace-like patterns hanging from their windowpanes, they watched with fascination as the trams struggled northwards, weaving their way along the Boulevards in front of the house. Like most children at that tender age, they were largely immune to the money worries and struggles of our parents, as fun and laughter naturally preoccupied their young lives.

However, Father was restless as a caged tiger. Desperate to get back to work to provide for the family, he became extremely agitated as his savings were shrinking alarmingly. His increasingly foul mood wasn't helped by the arctic winds that blew in from the north and settled as black ice. As he was solely dependent on public transport, it hampered his travels when trying to visit towns and cities around the Midlands in his hunt for the ideal place to open a new business. I had been poring over the advertisements in the

Birmingham newspapers during my school holidays. Time was running out.

It was only a matter of days before the new school term was due to start, and I thought that I had totally failed in this endeavour – especially after the visit from Uncle Chun Tileng and his wife at Christmas, when he reminded me of my responsibilities as the eldest son. Then, fortuitously, I managed to spot an advert that showed promise. Excitedly, I showed it to Father.

'*Sale of the remaining leasehold interest of prominent restaurant premises in Central Birmingham, near to the main railway station, theatres, hotels etc. The goodwill and trading name of the vendors, Mecca Leisure Ltd, would not be for sale. Please contact agents, Edwards, Rose & Co...*'

There was no time to lose, so Father and I met the agents the next day at the premises in Station Street near to the city centre and to the theatres. The restaurant had been closed for some time now, and the owners were keen to sell the lease with the equipment and furniture. Knowing that the latter goods and chattels would be useless and would have to be thrown out, Father struck a deal. In this instance, he did not need to rely on Feng Shui to determine the restaurant's prospects, as instinct, together with the premises' favourable location, spoke for itself.

However, there was the problem of funding for the whole venture. Father confided that he had the capital for the purchase (which would exhaust most of his savings), and a contribution towards the major building work that would be necessary to convert the empty premises. To equip the kitchen, furnish the restaurant floor and provide start-up capital to fund staff wages and utilities for the first six months would need an injection of cash equal to his capital of 3,800 pounds. He decided to offer a partnership to an old contact from Liverpool, a businessman named Yeong Tan, and an old friend, Leung Wo. This would leave him with just less than half of the equity. Furthermore, it was agreed to offer a small share to the new head chef, a Mr Tau Sung, as an incentive for his loyalty.

I took Father back to see Mr Peter Allsop, the solicitor who had acted for him previously in the dealings with the café in Liverpool and the property in Sandringham Road. In the same badly lit and dusty office which still seemed to be stuck in the past, Mr Allsop advised my father that, as the active partner and founder of the new Birmingham business, he would be advised to retain the majority share of the new partnership, if only by one vote. And so, my father retained forty-two shares to Mr Yeong's forty, Mr Leung's nine and Mr Tau's nine. We did not reflect on the implications of this arrangement, but events would prove in hindsight that the old gentleman lawyer was right. Agreements on a handshake as a bond of trust made in the past soon became an anachronism when large amounts of money were at stake – for disputes and greed would soon rear their ugly heads.

Once all the legalities and agreements had been tied up, radical building refurbishments took place at Easter. I managed to take an extended holiday from school, feigning some family crisis. I engaged a local family firm of builders and shopfitters to strip out the place and install a new, fully equipped kitchen, a modern sixty-seater restaurant, and a small bar in anticipation of obtaining a liquor licence. The old-fashioned English restaurant, a relic left over from the '40s – '50s, would no longer be recognisable.

To provoke memories of Father's old home in China, it was decided that the name of the new venture would be Liang Nam, meaning 'Beautiful South' in Cantonese. By the end of July, the new restaurant was ready to open. The head chef, Mr Tau, had appointed second and third sous-chefs, two range chefs and two kitchen porters. Rose and Eileen would be on the waiting staff, together with a new head waiter and two other experienced waiters. Finally, to make up this large army of Chinese staff, two women worked behind the scenes in the still room and to man the dumb waiter – a food lift – from the basement kitchen. Apart from my two sisters, the rest of the staff were Hakka[76] Chinese from Hong Kong. Father and the partners, being Cantonese, were hopeful that they would get on with their Hakka employees, as historically and culturally the two ethnic groups had clashed for centuries and spoke different dialects. But that didn't worry me unduly. I was more concerned that the weekly wage bill would be ruinous.

On good advice, the newly appointed accountant – a local man named Samuel Pierce – suggested that the partnership should take out a bank loan to shore up the finances. Also, in an effort to reassure my father and his staff, who were worried about the reception they might receive, he added that, historically, the people of Birmingham had always welcomed foreigners from all over the world due to the city's international trade with all corners of the globe; and that, if the restaurant's formula was right, then regardless of ethnicity, they would be accepted and the business should do well.

Then quietly and tonelessly so as not to alarm them unduly, he also happened to mention that, at the end of August, London had suffered a race riot involving a white mob that included Teddy Boys, who had attacked West Indian property in an area called Notting Hill in West London.[77] The flashpoint was a domestic dispute that had got out of hand. Scores of rioters, including white youths and members of the Caribbean community, were arrested for affray, rioting, assault, and carrying offensive weapons. In the aftermath, it was now hoped that neither London nor any other inner city in Britain would have to witness such mindless violence again. It was a sobering lesson in community and race relations.

---

76 A large ethnic group of the Chinese population that, due to war and famine, had for centuries migrated south from the Yellow River (Huang River) plains to occupy land hitherto held by Cantonese-speaking peoples, including the province of Guangdung. They also migrated to Fujian and Jiangxi, and spread to Hong Kong and later Taiwan. Historically known as the 'guest' or 'gypsy peoples', resentment and clashes had occurred between them and the local indigenous population. Any women marrying into Hakka families had to learn to speak the Hakka tongue. Migrating overseas in numbers from Hong Kong, they opened restaurants in the West in the '50s and '60s.

77 The Notting Hill Riots of August and September 1958 provoked a response from the authorities, who in January 1959 held a Caribbean Carnival (the precursor to the Notting Hill Carnival) in St Pancras Town Hall in an effort to heal race relations between the two communities.

Not long afterwards, at Liang Nam's inaugural opening, a groundbreaking menu never seen before in the Midlands was launched. Innovative ideas, combined with top-class cooking and new recipes (including sesame duck, pan-fried chicken with roasted almonds, pineapple scampi, sizzling king prawns in garlic, chilli beef etc.), brought people in from all parts of the city. They poured in within the first week of opening. Newspapers wrote favourably about the new restaurant, and bookings grew at a phenomenal rate.

Within the year, the two local Chinese restaurants which had been established a couple of years before Father's, being rather small, dingy and old fashioned, closed down. Father was in his element as the new manager, and positively shone as he welcomed customers with his pleasant manner. I had to give him his due, for he could be rather charming when he wanted to be. It was no surprise that he made a good impression on most English people, for he had done for as long as I could remember. But within the four walls of his house, he was a different animal, remaining austere and diffident towards us, his family.

But as far as the business was concerned, the partners were pleased with the progress as profits gradually erased the outstanding bank loan.

Father and the girls took a flat in Moseley, where I stayed for the school holidays so that I could continue to help out. A house was rented locally to house the staff. Mother and the rest of the family stayed on in Liverpool for the time being until a new house was found. Being busy with this new chapter in our lives, there was little time for us to clash with each other. I was hoping that this would be the start of a new relationship; but again, only time would tell. At least it seemed a lifetime away from the nightmare of the café in West Derby Road and the criminal elements that drove us away from Liverpool.

The following year, I had gained a place to study pure science at King's College in Newcastle-upon-Tyne, a part of Durham University. As I had excelled in biology, chemistry and physics at A Level, the Liverpool Collegiate had hoped that I would go on to study medicine.

Not having the calling, and unable to stand the sight of blood and surgery, I opted to study bacteriology. Predictably, my father was to say the least not over the moon about his son leaving the business. And here again emerged the eternal paradox. From the outset, my father had striven to get my brothers and sisters into decent schools, and then college or university. But he felt disappointed and bereft that I, the eldest son, whom he had grown to depend upon, did not want to carry on in the family business, helping him as Chinese tradition expects.

The pull between the two diverging cultures simply would not go away. Like an open wound that would not heal, this perennial conundrum surfaced time and again. The children were being increasingly alienated from the Chinese way of life and all that our father stood for. Because of our immersion in English culture via our daily education, the problem worsened day by day. Mother once told us that Father's own education had been sacrificed because of his overriding obligations to his family in China, which put his younger brothers' education and ambitions way before his own.[78] Constantly overwhelmed by family duty and burdened by twin sets of responsibilities across two continents, it was easy to see that frustration and resentment would soon creep in.

Eventually my role in the business was taken over by Clarence Yeong, the son of one of the partners. Clarence was shy and reserved, and, unfortunately for him, at the behest of his father was suddenly thrown into the catering business, of which he had no previous experience and for which he had little aptitude, having left school early. In retrospect, it was a recipe for disaster.

Barely a year had passed when Father summoned me to return home. Mr Leung, one of the minor partners, had died and his widow had sold his share of the business to my father, who now owned fifty-one per cent of the partnership. It appeared that, behind Father's back, Mr Yeong and his son Clarence had plotted with the chef, Mr Tau, to

---

78 Money sent home to China allowed a younger brother to be educated and trained as a schoolteacher. Another sibling became a government official – a local mandarin.

take over the whole of the business. Surreptitiously, an attempt was made to remove the founder; in their words, 'the old man', Kwong Chun Ji.

I returned post-haste from Newcastle, where I had been preparing to retake my exams. I had been staying on the coast in the holidays and working in the dining rooms at the Grand Hotel, because of a young art student – a pretty, fair-headed Yorkshire girl named Tisha – whom I had met at university. It was a part of my life that I had carefully and desperately kept secret from my parents, fearing my father's hostility towards my consorting with European girls.

Having been instrumental in setting up the legalities of the partnership agreement with Allsop's, I recalled that there was a specific clause, to which all the parties had agreed, stating that, if any partner became dissatisfied with his stake in the business, he could not sell his shares to any party outside of the partnership without first offering to sell to the incumbent partner, providing he remained in situ and continued in the business. This meant that Mr Kwong Chun Ji had the first option to buy the others out as a result of any disagreement, provided that he remained the controlling shareholder. I reminded Father of this clause that would hopefully protect his interests and all his hard work which had made the restaurant a success.

Clarence suddenly returned home to Liverpool as his father became seriously ill. As it happened, Clarence's employment contract stated that, if he became absent for whatever reason for more than six months, his employment could be terminated.

(Mr Allsop had previously argued that sentiment had no part to play in a business which involved the public at large, such as catering. For example, if notice to quit was served on any member of the staff, they could out of spite cause chaos and ruin the goodwill of customers, such as by spiking the food or drink, whilst serving out that notice).

Meanwhile, there was no other option but to appoint another assistant to help. This turned out to be a mature chap by the name of Will Yuet Chen. Will Chen, being Hakka Chinese from the New Territories of Hong Kong, was able to hold the fort for the remainder of the year, and get on well with the rest of the staff as he spoke the Hakka dialect as well as Cantonese.

After a prolonged illness, Mr Yeong died. Clarence wanted to return to the restaurant and his previous post. His brother and sister had taken over their father's share of the business. The firm's solicitors enacted the terms of the partnership agreement and Father bought out Mr Yeong's shares and ultimately Mr Tau's small share, as the chef had abruptly left his job in a fit of pique without telling anyone. Clarence and Mr Tau eventually opened a rival business with others on the other side of the city.

The business in Station Street returned to normality. Home life for the Kwongs settled down. I returned to Newcastle, despite my father's plea for me to stay on in Birmingham. A large, old semi-detached house was found in Edgbaston towards the north of the city, and the family moved in early in 1960 after the sale of Sandringham Road in Liverpool. The younger brothers and sisters all found new schools, and life and the business appeared to carry on quite happily like a veritable phoenix rising.

Chapter 24

A PSYCHIC ENCOUNTER

1959

IT WAS AFTER MY first year at King's College when, one cold, bleak Saturday morning, with dark rain clouds brewing overhead, I decided to return home. My father wanted to tell me something that had been worrying him, and which he thought was important enough that it might have repercussions for the family. I just managed to catch the 11.40 train from Newcastle Central to Birmingham New Street and was lucky enough to find an empty seat in a second-class compartment with just one passenger sitting curled up near the window. It was a little old lady dressed in a crumpled navy uniform that I assumed was the attire typically worn by a district nurse. Giving me a cursory glance, she carried on tucking into a pack of sandwiches that was open on her lap. I nodded politely in her direction and took out a book from my holdall before hoisting it over my head onto the luggage rack. I put my nose into my book, which I confess did not hold my attention – *Introduction to Clinical Bacteriology* – as I was more interested in my fellow passenger. Surreptitiously, I noted that she was probably in her fifties – dark hair, with a hint of grey like salt and pepper, that was swept into a tidy bun under a tiny pillbox hat. Thin and petite, under five feet tall, in my astute opinion she looked a bit underfed.

No sooner had the train pulled away from the station than she wrapped up her remaining sandwich with a noisy rustling of greaseproof paper, got up, gave me a strange look, pulled open the sliding door to our compartment and abruptly left. Puzzled, I thought little of it. I shrugged, questioning whether it was to do with my being a foreign student. Although in other circumstances, being sensitively attuned to people, I would have picked up on vibes of offence or disapproval – which on this occasion, didn't happen. About twenty minutes later, the compartment door slid open and the little district nurse returned to her seat in the corner. By now, she had finished eating her sandwiches and started to take a sip of tea from a thermos flask. Turning deliberately towards me, she said, politely and in a gentle voice, 'Excuse me, young man. I hope you don't mind my asking, but are you Chinese?'

Uh-oh, I thought, *here we go again!* But, being quite used to that question, having been asked so many times before, I replied, simply and without rancour, 'Yes. Why do you ask?'

Guardedly, her eyes darted around us. Glancing out of the glass partition of the door in a manner that suggested she didn't wish to be seen or heard, she offered, 'Well, I don't know how to say this, but... I hope you won't be offended, but there is something about you which is disturbing me.'

I was about to be shocked and outraged when she held up her hand to pre-empt and pacify me. She leant forward conspiratorially.

'Do you believe in spirits and, um... you know... the other world?'

I must say I was taken aback. I have had many odd conversations with strangers in my life, but this must rank as one of the oddest. Meeting her concentrated gaze, I stuttered, 'I'm... I'm studying science and, really, I don't think my training would be compatible with things like that. Mind you, my parents are old-fashioned Chinese and traditionally superstitious – they believe in ghosts and ancestral spirits!'

Her reply surprised and shocked me.

I discovered that her name was Miss Vera Wilmslow, and that she was travelling to London to attend a conference on psychic studies. She explained that she'd had to leave the compartment earlier on because she had felt a strange force, which she described as an aura around me that made her agitated. Apparently, she had become a medium in later life after visiting an old man in Brighton, whose powers were passed on to her after she observed a pair of hands resting on his shoulders that came from another world. Although out-of-body, these act like tactile instruments, she said, which possessed psychic healing powers and which were eventually passed on to her after the man's death. She said that she had felt uncomfortable in my presence as one of her spirit guides was an ancient Chinese man who had lived two hundred years ago in Southern China, and that his name was Kiang. She believed that there might be a connection between the two of us, however tenuous.

She asked my family name. I told her that it was Gong or Kwong, but, thinking about it, Kiang might possibly be related to my father's clan, which goes back centuries.

Swallowing hard, Miss Wilmslow mentioned in a low voice that her other guide was an old Red Indian Chief called Running Cloud, who had led his tribe across the plains of the Wild West of America in the 1800s.

Frankly, in other circumstances, I would have guffawed and burst out laughing; but something about this little old lady stopped me in my tracks. Perhaps it was the earnest way in which she spoke, which projected the sincerity of what she told me in hushed confidence.

Old Red Indian Chiefs and ancient Chinese guides from hundreds of years ago, I must confess, I found hard to digest. The journey to Birmingham flew by in a strange but absorbing conversation with my fellow passenger. I politely declined her offer to see into the future by visiting the past, as not only did I prefer not to know – but knowing could then produce anxiety, and even alter the path that destiny had mapped out for me. Much to my relief, we soon arrived at New Street Station. I collected my bag and bid her goodbye with a polite handshake, but not before she invited me to attend one of her conferences at the College of Psychic Studies in London, so that, in her words, '*I could harness my latent healing powers to enable me to call upon them in the future*'.

That night, I couldn't sleep as the meeting with Miss Wilmslow had made a disturbing impression on me. I never did take up her offer to attend one of her meetings in London. But little did I know then that, many years later while researching my ancestors, I uncovered a connection with a relative who had ended up in America and who happened to join a covered wagon train whilst crossing the Wild West. During one of many attacks by Indian tribes he was captured, but a Red Indian Chief saved him from being scalped alive. However, in my encounter with Miss Wilmslow when she alluded to a past connection with me, I was forced to dismiss it as sheer coincidence and nothing more.

When my father returned home from work during the early evening break, he handed me a cutting from a newspaper that his brother, Chun Tileng, had sent him from Liverpool. Father was worried and wanted to know what I made of it, and if it insulted our Kwong (Gong) family clan. Apparently, Uncle had ordered a three-piece suit from a local tailor. When he went for a fitting, Uncle said that it did not fit very well and refused to pay the balance. He told the tailor that he did not want the suit, and that he could keep the deposit of ten pounds, whereupon he was taken to court.

The headline announced in bold letters:

T. GONG and the CRACKED CHINA TEA SET!

In the Courts today, a Mr Tileng Gong was being sued for damages in a dispute over a three-piece worsted suit ordered from a Mr Melvin Glassman, bespoke tailor.

The QC acting for the defendant stated in Court that Mr T. Gong, not being a member of the Church of England, could not swear an oath on the King James Bible. He requested that his client might swear using a traditional method that was accepted in the Courts of China. This involved taking an oath when throwing down a piece of china in front of the Court, with the defendant simultaneously swearing, "I will tell the truth or my soul shall be smashed like this china plate."

After consulting the plaintiff's QC, the judge subsequently agreed, albeit somewhat reluctantly.

Mr T. Gong, a distinguished citizen of Chinese heritage, on taking the stand was handed a piece of fine bone china – a plate – by the clerk to the Court.

Unfortunately, the plate hurled from the witness box just happened to bounce under a desk and remained intact. It failed to shatter into pieces as intended.

The defendant tried again. Again, the same thing happened. But on close inspection of the said plate a small hairline crack had appeared across the middle.

Whereupon the defendant's learned QC approached the bench and requested that the swearing of the oath be amended to... "I will tell the truth... or my soul shall be CRACKED like this china plate."

Permission from the Court was hurriedly granted.

There was a noticeable sigh of relief all round. Proceedings continued with due diligence and speed. The suit under dispute was shown as Exhibit A. It was demonstrated on the defendant that one of the shoulders of the jacket sloped downwards and that the waistcoat was too short at the front. Holding up the trousers, they appeared excessively voluminous. And after the end of the arguments and counterarguments, the Judge summed up by saying that this simple dispute over a piece of gentleman's apparel should never have come to court. Privately in Chambers, he expressed his surprise to the advocates that the case had not been tried at the Magistrates' Court. He was told that there were probably ethnic sensitivities at stake in view of the unusual swearing of the oath. However, the learned judge recommended

*that the case be dismissed, ordering that both sides pay their own
costs and thereby concluding the case of Glassman v Gong.*

I reassured my anxious father that the court case did not damage the
reputation of the Kwong – Gong family. The article was written, I must
admit, in rather overdramatic prose to say the least, and perhaps with
some mild satirical overtones: after all, it was published in a features
newspaper called the *Reveille*. If it poked fun at anyone, I would say
that it did so at the expense of the British judiciary. But, in the end
analysis, it didn't harm Uncle unduly, and more to the point it did
not besmirch the family name. In fact, other papers just recorded the
simple fact that the case against Uncle had been dismissed and that he
was brave enough to take a Chinese oath in an English court of law.
Later, we found out that, as a result of the publicity, he became a bit of
a minor celebrity and that his business profited from it. I managed to
telephone my uncle and reassure him. He was rather relieved, for, as
with all Chinese, saving face and avoiding an embarrassing backlash
was important to him.

I have to say that, whenever I happened to talk to Uncle, he *always*
took the opportunity to remind me of my duty as the eldest son, and
to help and protect my father. *Oh no! Not again*, I would inwardly
groan.

However, despite this, this time my ears pricked up. It seemed
that, whilst I was away, Father had clashed spectacularly with two of
his staff. I assumed that it was Father's volatile temper exploding again
through his irascibility. But it seemed that one of the waiters had been
flirting with Eileen instead of concentrating on his work. After he
had taken her to the cinema one afternoon, he was summarily sacked
without explanation. His elder brother, Man Lok, who was the head
waiter at the time, then walked out in high dudgeon, threatening blue
murder. He apparently accused my father of insulting his brother
and bringing dishonour upon his family. Heated words and threats
had followed in front of the rest of the staff, with accusations of
discriminatory treatment because they were Hakka.

'Just you wait and see, old man,' he spat. *'You haven't heard the end of this!'* Slamming the front door behind him, he put a curse on the family – then made a cut-throat gesture across his neck with a sweep of his hand.

Uncle said that all Father wanted to do was protect his daughters. But I instinctively knew that it was his method of keeping strict control over his children. Typically, though, Father had dismissed this as just another innocuous threat that did not merit concern. Having faced danger so many times in his life and got away without being maimed or killed, he carelessly shrugged it off. Confronting another vendetta would mean little to him. Unnervingly, Uncle added that many villainous Chinese would harbour a grudge in perpetuity and would return to carry it out against a member of the next generation.

Given my insouciant attitude – whether blissfully naive or with foolish bravado – for as usual, I laughed it off. Uncle warned that Father could well be a marked man and could not afford to make any more enemies in his old age. I was asked to remain vigilant, and always be on guard as far as my father and my sisters were concerned. Thinking that it was an overreaction, I put it to the back of my mind. I had other matters occupying my thoughts, such as the aftermath of meeting the strange Miss Wilmslow and her invitation to the College of Psychic Studies in London.

So when I mentioned to my sisters that I had met a psychic medium on the train home, they said that I must not mention it to our parents (who already viewed me as rebelliously difficult), as they would think that my mind had been turned by mixing with a new crowd of strangers in Newcastle, including travelling psychics.

Eventually, at the close of the day, peace and quiet descended on the Kwong family and Father's worries were placated by my explanation of the article about Uncle's court case. Crestfallen though he was at my leaving once again, I caught the first train back to college the next day before I was made to feel guilty about deserting him. This time, I made sure that I sat in a carriage full of people and avoided getting involved with any of my fellow passengers.

Chapter 25

OUT OF THE BLUE

July 1960

T HERE WAS A FRESH new season in the offing with the blossom of spring around the city now beginning to fade, and as it happened, it remained fortuitously peaceful in the Kwong household. The only festering concerns on the horizon were the perpetual letters from China which poured in like a never-ending flood, asking for financial help.

Dai Dune Chun
Taishan
Guangdung
The People's Republic of China
4ᵗʰ May 1960

Dear elder brother,
*   Your family needs your help more than ever. A terrifying famine continues to sweep the country. We cannot say much in this letter due to strict government censorship, so we are mailing this from Hong Kong via a travelling friend. He, like us, has to be extremely careful, for spies are everywhere. Even families have turned against one another.*

Since 1958 and the Great Leap Forward, millions have died of starvation. Crops have failed due to disastrous floods in the winters alternating with never-ending droughts in the long summer months. Typhoons continue to batter the nearby coast. Dwellings, people and livestock have been swept away. This is a catastrophe on an enormous scale hitherto never seen before.

We even hear that, in some parts of the provinces, some people have resorted to eating their dead rather than burying them in order to survive. Some families have had to sell their babies. Others have been forced to drown their baby daughters. Neighbours have told of relatives walking into the sea so that there are fewer mouths to feed. Even young girls have been sold into brothels. Children have had to beg on the streets for any morsels of food, however meagre or foul. Even cats and dogs have been eaten.

We are at our wits' end. Please, help us, as we are desperate and on the brink of starvation. We implore you to act quickly before it is too late.

Your desperate brothers and sisters.

Facing his obligation as the eldest, my father had continued to send money home for the past four decades in view of the circumstances that had enveloped his homeland: the bloody revolutions, the warring factions and the resultant turmoil and strife. But what about the terrible circumstances that had been inflicted on his wife and children here in England during the last war? The racial tensions they had suffered, the relentless bombing during the Blitz, the illnesses and injuries that they had endured, the rationing and food shortages, the frightening spectre of being penniless due to lack of work, the threat of homelessness that the conflict of war invariably brought, and the uncertain aftermath for the future. Although it could be argued that deprivation and suffering were all relative, even now, Britain and Western Europe were caught amid a volatile and dangerous world. The USA and the Soviet Union were involved in an escalating and explosive nuclear arms race. It was a frightening prospect.

But on this occasion, Father's siblings needed help on a scale previously unprecedented so that they could eat to survive another day. He would have to have had a heart of stone not to respond to these desperate pleas for aid in their hour of need. What would the Kwong Clan think if he turned a deaf ear to their plight, particularly if they learned that he had just bought a brand-new motor car, having just learnt to drive? Furthermore, he had also recently managed to buy a large old house with a spacious garden.

Father had heard from friends in Hong Kong that Mao's much-heralded Great Leap Forward had collapsed. The Communist agricultural policy had failed disastrously. The resultant Great Famine[79] was explained to the outside world as being:

'Due to circumstances beyond government control because of years of natural disasters, such as floods, typhoons, droughts, pestilence and disease.'

As head of the clan, he could not turn his back on his family in China. He did not need reminding that family duty and sibling obligation were sacrosanct. Almost forty years had passed since it was drummed into him by his father, the late Kwong Loong Cheung Ham, at the exit of his ancestral village in China as he departed home for the last time for the West. How could he forget that day in 1921? Further reminders of his filial duty had come by letter in 1947 from his mother, Kwong Fung Ting, on her deathbed. For as long as he lived, he could never extricate himself from that obligation even if he wanted to. Like many old-fashioned and traditional Chinese, he was made to believe that one day, not only would he have to face his father, but he would also have to confront his ancestors in

---

79   The Great Chinese Famine (during 'The Great Leap Forward') from 1958 to 1961, when more than thirty million people from the peasant population perished.

the afterlife. And thus, he did not dare to disobey his family in the present.

Conscience duly pricked, Father dug deep once again into the family coffers, turning a deaf ear to Mother's complaints that their own children must come first.

Now, as a responsible father, he thought that it was his duty to see to it that his eldest daughter Eileen, now in her early twenties, settle down and be married. Prospective suitors from the Cantonese community called on the family, introduced through family connections back in Taishan. Eileen politely ignored every one of them.

Some months passed by and the balmy breeze of early summer beckoned when, one evening after a busy day, my father noticed that Eileen had not turned up for work. He asked Rose where she was. Rose replied that she thought that it was her sister's day off work. He didn't think anything of it, until he drove home after the close of business. He had barely taken off his jacket when he was met with a strange and worried look on my mother's face as she rushed downstairs to greet him. He asked anxiously if she knew where Eileen was. Increasingly worried, they quickly climbed the stairs to the first floor and knocked on her bedroom door. There was no reply, so they pushed it open.

Nervously, their eyes searched the room from top to bottom, darting from left to right and back again, more in hope than in expectation. A terrible fear began to dawn on them, but they did not dare to speak of it, fearing the worst. Their sight was drawn to the centre of the room, where the carefully made bed had not been slept in.

A letter was found on Eileen's dressing table, tucked prominently against the left-hand corner of the mirror. With trembling fingers, Father tore at the flap of the envelope. Sliding out a single sheet of paper, he held it under the lamp over the bed.

Stunned, he could not believe what he was reading.

Portland Road
Edgbaston
Birmingham
5th July 1960

Dear Father and Mother,

I am sorry to write to you like this, but I feel that this is the only way. Despite your efforts to introduce prospective husbands to me, I have to follow my heart, and say that I must leave home now and marry Will Chen, who used to work for you last year. I know you disapprove of him as he is not Cantonese from a Taishanese family, and because, being much older than me, he has been married before. But I cannot ignore the deep, true feelings and respect we have for each other. He has started a new business in a new town and promises to support me. I hope that one day you will find it in your hearts to forgive me.

Your loving daughter,

Shui Dee (Eileen)

'Oh no! *No*... It... *It can't be!*' gasped my mother, cupping a hand to her mouth. Her face blanched a sickly colour. She collapsed onto the edge of the bed, her eyes welling up.

'I don't believe it!' screamed my father.

He rushed over to the wardrobe and flung open the doors. The rails were empty, save for some coat hangers which rattled noisily. Eileen's clothes had been removed, leaving only a single, unused, black-and-white waitress's uniform swinging eerily on its own, abandoned and alone. Furiously, he attacked the drawers under the dressing table, flinging them to the floor. Again, they had been completely emptied of his daughter's belongings.

Immediately, Rose was summoned from the next room and they demanded if she knew what had happened, and where her sister had gone, and when. Distraught and swollen-eyed, she shook her head and burst into tears. She rushed back into her room and slammed the door.

The uproar woke the rest of the family. The younger children started to cry and hid under their bedclothes, clamping their hands over their ears.

My father wailed like a wounded animal, hitting the table with his fist. 'That... that appalling man. He's not even one of us! He's not Cantonese! He is a Hakka. That... that man, Chen! He's been married twice before! The first wife killed herself because of his philandering, and the next one divorced him because of his drinking and gambling! He has even got children in Hong Kong! How *dare* he do this to us?'

Mother could no longer hold back tears. Overwrought with grief and still in shock, she turned and ran downstairs so that the rest of the children did not hear her crying.

'That's it!' he raged. *'From today onwards, I have no oldest daughter. She has brought shame on us!*

If anyone from this family ever tries to contact her, they will also be dead, as far as I and the Kwong family are concerned.'

His edict was loud, clear and final, and he made sure that the rest of the family heard him. Savagely, like a knife to his heart, he had cut his beloved daughter out from his life.

Forever.

Part IV

1961 – 1963

Chapter 26

CONFRONTATION

March 1961

I T WAS A DULL, overcast morning with a thick blanket of clouds that choked out the early morning sun that had risen gladly with the dawn. At Cullercoats Bay, a curtain of sea mist hung stubbornly over the horizon, which, like the weather, reflected my mood. I walked alone along the lower cliff footpath, ponderously contemplating the future after another row with my young and exasperated new fiancée, Tisha. Significantly, it happened to be my birthday, the 5th March; I had just turned twenty-one. Being two hundred miles away from my brothers and sisters, it was the first time I had been away from them on such an occasion, and a restless longing to see them began to fester within me.

Opening my birthday cards from my siblings, I sat on the edge of a cliff and stared at the rolling waves that fused with the swirling mist. Screeching seagulls swooped all around me, wheeling low, thinking that I had some food in my hands. My sister Rose had enclosed two letters with her birthday card. Belatedly, the first was in an old, official-looking buff envelope from the government. It, was confirmation that, from the end of 1960, citizens such as I who had been born in 1940 would be exempt from National Service, as conscription had finally ended in Britain. I wasn't particularly euphoric as I had long accepted that, along with the rest of my peer group, I would go on to military service despite being turned down for the Army Cadets at school due to my flat feet and poor eyesight.

The second letter was a short note from Rose telling me of the family fracture that had followed the news of Eileen's elopement. Reading this came as a shock as it was totally out of the blue. Swiftly, I clambered back to the upper path and sat on one of sea defence walls to hastily gather my thoughts. There was nothing for it. The next morning, I took the train back to Birmingham to confront my father.

He was in a foul and unforgiving mood. Mother said it was due to staff problems. But he warned me in no uncertain terms that if I dared to go against his wishes and visit my sister, I would be locked out of the house.

Typically, given the history of our stormy relationship, I chose to disobey him because in this matter I felt that he was fundamentally and morally wrong. I had discovered that Eileen and her husband, Will, had taken on a lease to a shop with a flat above it in a small town in Shropshire called Wetherington, and planned to try to make a new life by opening a Chinese restaurant. Like many small, parochial towns in Britain, Wetherington in the early '60s was not used to foreigners. A Chinese restaurant would be pioneering; an Indian or even an Italian restaurant would be revolutionary. I was thrilled to see Eileen, and to meet her husband again, who seemed a good and sensible man, who clearly loved her and would take care of her. Tears inevitably flowed, but we quickly put emotions aside and tried to catch up on news of the family, based on what little I knew, as I had also been away from our siblings for several months due to my clandestine life on Tyneside. When the time came to leave them, it was a savage wrench, but I promised I would visit them again as soon as I could.

It was late by the time I caught the train back to Birmingham. Father knew instinctively that I must have defied him, for when I tried to open the front door of the house using my latch key, I found that he had bolted it from the inside. It was getting cold and dark at night, with a distinct dampness in the air. Thick black clouds scudded across to smother any remaining light from overhead. I shivered. But, undeterred, I scaled the garden gate and walked along the top of the wall that separated the house from the next-door neighbours' until I reached the back garden. Clambering over the bay roof, I quietly knocked on the window of Rose's room.

Fortunately, she was still awake, and, letting me in, placed a finger across her lips to warn me not to wake up the rest of the family. The following morning, not unexpectedly, my father completely ignored me, but the censorious, black look across his face said it all. Out of his earshot, I gave news of Eileen to Mother, who gulped back tears of sadness.

Determined to remain a conduit between my sister and the rest of the family, I managed to visit her and her husband surreptitiously on three more occasions during the rest of the year.

Historically, 1961 would be fixed in my memory as a significant year for many different and personal reasons. Not least, for the rest of the population, it was memorable, given the headline news that mankind was on the brink of space exploration. In April, the Russians had successfully sent astronaut Yuri Gagarin to become the first human in space. The Americans, not to be left behind in the space race, launched Alan Shepard into space the following month. But the euphoria was dented by the escalation of the Cold War between the East and West, with the building of the Berlin Wall by the Soviet-backed German Democratic Republic (also known as the GDR or East Germany), splitting the city and the country into two. Relations between Soviet Russia and the Western Bloc deteriorated day by day. The prospect of avoiding conflict in Europe did not augur well.

In September, Eileen gave birth to a delightful baby daughter, and, after consulting my sister and me, named her Juliet, with a Chinese name of Ling Fan. But the joyous moment was marred by the news that Eileen and Will's business, having started so well at the beginning of the year, was now declining rapidly. It seemed that the inhabitants of Wetherington had initially been quite happy to support and patronise the new ethnic restaurant, but were later driven away by a group of local youths who terrorised the town centre with their drunken and thuggish behaviour. This group and a rival gang would frequent the restaurant, demanding to be served, and then after their meal, refuse to pay their bill. By the time the local police turned up the cowards had run away, only to return to threaten Eileen, her husband, and their chef with racial abuse. Any customers continuing to dine at their restaurant were also frightened off. It was a shocking and terrifying situation.

Disastrously, towards the end of the year, just before Christmas, Eileen and her husband were forced to close-up shop and file for bankruptcy. They were distraught. They had lost every penny of their hard-earned savings that they had ploughed into the business. Callously, the bailiffs for the landlords had stripped them of all their personal belongings and would only allow them to keep the few baby clothes that had been given to them at the hospital. With only the clothes that they stood in and with a newborn child, where would they go and where would they live?

Rose had urged me to return home immediately to help. Rushing back, I confronted my parents and told them of Eileen's desperate situation. Father was totally unmoved, retorting coldly, '*They have made their choice and they can live with the consequences! I can't help them.*'

My appeals to Mother fell on deaf ears as she did not dare to go against Father's ruling. But there was *no* other option. So ignoring his anger, Rose and I prepared the large attic room and we made up temporary beds on the floor. I took the train to Wetherington and brought Eileen and her family back home, even though Will protested all the way, saying that he would try to find lodgings with friends as long as his wife and daughter were safe over Christmas, for the cold, wintry weather was closing in fast. Sleet and heavy snow showers were threatening. By now it was dark and getting colder by the minute, for the chill from an icy East wind had whipped up by the time we had arrived in Portland Road. After shivering under the porch, from nerves and from the bitter night air, I opened the front door using my key. Thankfully, Father had not bolted it. I ushered my sister and her husband into the warmth of the hallway. Eileen held baby Juliet close to her, making a cradle in the inside fold of her coat. She pulled up the blanket around her daughter protectively.

Our parents were waiting up for us. Father strode into the hallway, his face dark with fury, and before he was able to launch into a tirade, I pre-empted him with a well-rehearsed speech.

'*This is your very first grandchild and your eldest daughter* – one who has helped you and the family since she was ten years old. It is right and proper that I have brought them home. No one with a shred of decency and compassion would turn a daughter and her baby out into the street – and just before Christmas, too. *And what's more, no decent human being would in the circumstances fail to forgive and forget!*'

My brother-in-law Will apologised profusely for disturbing them so late at night, and for imposing on them. Father opened his mouth, about to say something; then abruptly changed his mind. He then spun on his heels and went upstairs to his room, quietly closing the door. Mother choked back tears and possessively took Juliet into her arms, gazing gently at her with the unconditional love only a grandmother could offer. Rose came running downstairs and gave her sister an emotional hug, and both burst into tears.

Mother asked if they were hungry, fussing over them like a mother hen, but they said that they had eaten something at the railway station. Rose and I helped the three of them up to the top floor of the house, as we knew that they must be exhausted emotionally and physically, if not traumatised after what they had recently gone through. We all agreed that they needed complete rest and to catch up on sleep.

The younger children couldn't help but hear what had gone on. From the landing where they had been peeping through the banisters, they crept back to their rooms. 'Big Sis has come home at last,' said

Ester excitedly to Walter. These two, being the youngest members of the family, had been brought up largely by their big sister, and now, remarkably, she was a young mother herself. A sense of tranquillity finally descended on the Kwong household. The relief was palpable.

Chapter 27

RAPPROCHEMENT

1961–1962

F OR THE NEXT FEW days, my father kept uncharacteristically quiet; so much so that my mother thought that he was ill. She assumed that the recent events had knocked him for six and tugged at his conscience. Despite his initial intransigence, he had finally succumbed to a flush of sympathy for his daughter and her husband, for having just been driven away from their business and home by drunken thugs resonated with his own experience. How could he ever forget the day, just four years before, when thugs and criminals had in parallel circumstances driven him away from his life in Liverpool?

Christmas passed uneventfully. The Chen family tactfully kept out of the way and stayed in their room so as not to interrupt the routine more than they had to. Father, by and large, ignored their presence. Then, shortly after the start of the New Year, as a sprinkling of early snow fell from a cold, brooding sky, something remarkable happened.

Baby Juliet was sound asleep, snugly wrapped up in her Moses basket in the dining room, when Father happened to pass by. Out of curiosity, he bent down to stare at her. Just then, she stirred, opened her eyes wide and gurgled. Instinctively, he carefully reached down and lifted her – still swaddled in her blanket – out of the basket and rocked her gently in his arms. The baby let out another loud gurgle, her large brown eyes dancing back at him. To which he replied conspiratorially, a finger across his lips, 'Shh… shush, my little one.' Eileen, on hearing her baby stir, came into the room. Embarrassed, Father looked at his daughter, and then gently lowered the child back into her cot. Pretending to clear his throat, he swiftly left the room, mumbling something akin to, 'The little one must have woken up because she was hungry.'

During the next few weeks, whenever he returned home for the afternoon, he would pick up young Juliet and cradle her close to his chest at every opportunity. Eileen's husband Will, meanwhile, had found a job in a friend's restaurant in Wolverhampton. On returning home late after work and being told of the developing bond between grandfather and granddaughter, he was inwardly pleased, if not increasingly relieved. In keeping with Chinese etiquette, to save face, the Chen family did not offer payment towards their keep; instead, they brought in food shopping on a regular basis, even though our mother protested, 'Look. You don't need to. You have a young baby to clothe and feed. And in any case, you need to save for the future!'

By now, my father and I were on speaking terms again. Encouraging me to learn to drive, he bought me an old second-hand car – a Humber saloon – to practise in. Rapprochement was in the air. He urgently needed my help in applying to the Home Office for a work visa for his nephew, Kat Moon, the son of his first brother, Chun Tin, to work at the restaurant.

Six months later, my cousin Kat Moon arrived from China to start work. He started as a kitchen porter, but soon showed early talent as a cook and was able to help as a range chef. But historical ethnic prejudices between the Hakka and the Taishanese/Cantonese soon flared up like a recurring poison. The staff being predominantly Hakka (apart from Rose, my father and our cousin), Kat Moon stuck out like a sore thumb. Resentment and jealousy spread like wildfire. Amid accusations of nepotism, and that boss's nephew received higher pay than they did, the kitchen staff went on strike. In reality, Kat Moon was paid far less than the other employees as my father had paid for his passage to England, because, with a nephew now in a secure job, he felt that there was no need to send as much money back home to this part of the family in China.

Because of the walkout, the business was forced to close. This provided an opportunity to redecorate the premises, but the closure of almost four weeks took its toll financially. My father was not to be beaten, and a new set of staff was recruited with increased pay. But no sooner had they started work than they were threatened with violence by the old staff and their friends, forcing the new employees to leave en masse. My brother-in-law Will, being a prominent and respected member of the Hakka community, interceded and brokered a peace deal. In an act of solidarity with my father, the two of us stood at the entrance to the premises in case there was trouble. Forming a line in the street, the former employees came to the door one by one to receive their last pay packet from the accountant, which they had to sign for.

Sauntering in with an affected swagger, the first to turn up was the former range chef – a sour-faced, squat man with a pot belly named Wang Fieng who was the ringleader of the strike, and who, six weeks earlier, had had a fight with Kat Moon, threatening him with a large meat hook. Father was about to sack him for causing trouble, but gave him another chance, together with a final warning.

At the prospect of losing face in front of the others, Wang Fieng turned aggressively towards my father. Spitting out a gob of sodden tobacco from the corner of his mouth, he ground it into the carpet, just missing his feet. *Just watch your step, old man! A curse on your business… you and your family will pay dearly for this one day!'*

The accountant, Samuel Pierce, a mild-mannered Birmingham man who had never come across such venomous hatred within what he had hitherto thought was a predominantly peaceful ethnic community, had prewarned the police of the possibility of violence, especially after a lethal-looking butcher's knife dipped in chicken's blood had been anonymously pushed through the letter box.

Chapter 28

TEMPTING DEATH

London, England 1962–1963

THE SUMMER OF '62 would be carved upon my memory forever; not only because of what had happened to the family and the business, but because of two significant events.

Firstly, I had decided not to return to the north-east, and that I would go to London to try my luck. My brother Alan was already there and was content, doing extremely well at Imperial College. I had decided that a future in pure science, working for the rest of my life in a lonely laboratory without interaction with people, did not appeal to me. Tisha was at her wits' end with my abrupt change of plans, and so she abandoned her fine arts degree and enrolled for teacher training at a college in Roehampton in Surrey so that she could follow me down south.

Secondly, I had my first brush with death. I had passed my driving test with flying colours on my first attempt, shortly after my birthday that year. I must admit that it rather went to my head. Refusing to be seen in the old, staid Humber saloon which my father had bought for me, I sold it to a member of the restaurant staff for two hundred pounds. Against all advice from my former driving teacher, and courting my father's anger, I opted to buy an old red-and-black sports car called a Ford Falcon. It was a two-seater kit car constructed in fibreglass with a modified 105E Ford engine capable of reaching 120 miles per hour. It was sitting invitingly, all polished and gleaming, in the window of the used-car showroom of a major garage at the other end of Birmingham. It roared like a lion with a throaty exhaust. I was seduced. It was a boy racer's dream. Not unexpectedly, my father was furious at my disobeying him yet again and warned that the car would be the death of me.

The new M1 motorway had recently extended towards London and northwards from the Midlands. Early one May morning, I offered to drive my brother back to his digs in London. The weather was sunny, cloudless, and inviting. The car drove like a dream – though there was an unnerving rattle under the front suspension on reaching the speed of eighty miles per hour, and a disconcerting pull to the left passenger side on braking. On reaching London, I took it into a garage and was told that the track rod ends were worn and needed replacing.

After the weekend, I returned up the motorway on the way to visit Tisha at her family home near Sheffield, a place I had been to many times to visit her parents, but previously by train. The Ford Falcon drove smoothly in the fast lane, and after eighty miles or so I decided to open the throttle to maximum to try to experience the speed of one hundred miles per hour. The car shook as if going through the sound barrier; the long red bonnet thrashed about like a snake on a leash. It was exhilarating.

On passing the exit sign to Rugby there were major roadworks to the nearside lane, where the grass embankments were being dug out to prepare for barriers and a hard shoulder which had not yet been built. This rough terrain continued for three miles or so, then peeled away down an abrupt slope with a severe camber to the left for the whole length of the roadworks where the northern part of the motorway was being extended. To the side of the embankments, the hazards from the roadworks were clearly marked with traffic cones and concrete-filled oil drums painted horizontally in red and white. Notices on the motorway ahead warned drivers to slow down as a hidden dip followed by a sharp incline was approaching as the lanes narrowed to one due to the works on the extension. As the traffic in front of me started to slow down, it was clear that a serious accident had happened. All traffic had stopped to allow filtering one by one in single file. In the distance, a large van had overturned.

I slammed my foot on the brake. To my horror, there was no response. I tried again. The brake pedal flattened like a deflated balloon, jammed to the floor of the car. The speedometer still read eighty-five miles per hour, and instead of decelerating, the car was accelerating fast due to the downwards incline of the increasing slope of the motorway. To my horror, it was virtually going downhill without brakes! I tried to pump the foot brake again. There was a metallic squeal and a smell of smoke as the brake linings tried to grip. Yellow sparks and clouds of acrid blue smoke flew around me. It was futile. In that split second, I knew I was in real trouble, so I tried to pull up the handbrake to slow the car down. That failed, with a horrific screech. A cloud of incendiary sparks flew up from beneath me.

It is said that, when rushing towards the jaws of death, your whole life flashes in front of you. In those seconds, which seemed like a lifetime, time appeared to stand still. Stupid, isolated thoughts flashed in front of me at random…

'*How did my father cope when he was forced to leave his ancestral home in China and travel to the West all on his own, all those years ago? He would have been the same age as I am now… Did he feel indestructible at that age, as I now stupidly feel?*

But hang on – my father is going to kill me for my arrogant recklessness… then Tisha will scream at me for getting myself killed so soon after our engagement! And how am I going to break the news to my father that I'm secretly betrothed behind his back, and to a blonde foreigner, no less?

For dammit, what a lovely sunny day on which to die…'

The traffic ahead of me had slowed to a dead halt. I could see in the distance, just a couple of hundred yards straight in front of me, the rear end of a large articulated lorry. It was stationary, with its red brake lights brightly illuminated.

There was no alternative but to crash the car, otherwise I would end up piling into the back of the lorry. I jerked the steering wheel to the left to drag the car to the nearside. In that moment, I had decided to steer sharply to the left and proceed down the slope of the embankment to hit the oil drums placed one by one at the side of the roadworks. I quickly calculated that it would be the only way to get the car to slow down, and then hopefully it would come to a stop. With a horrendous judder and a crash, I slewed into them, one after another. I must have hit at least five of them.

Fortunately, on hitting the last one, the car spun to a sudden halt. It rested, semi-collapsed onto its left-hand side, with the passenger door leaning and jammed against the last oil drum at an angle of forty-five degrees. The wheels on the driver's side were upended into the air like a beached whale. The weight of the oil drum prevented the car from spinning over completely onto its roof. The bonnet and the front wings were crumpled like a large concertina that had just been crushed under a giant's foot. The bonnet lid had flown open. Steam gushed out from the burst radiator like a geyser. Black smoke billowed from the engine. Adrenaline kicked in. I quickly released the seat belt and clambered out through the driver's door window as the engine ignited and caught fire.

Rescue services were quickly on the scene as they had tracked me during the time that my car was veering out of control. The fire was tackled as I sat on the grass verge some fifty feet away, next to a tree and a parked digger. I watched my dream Ford Falcon Special go up in flames. On being asked if I was all right, I replied glumly that I was. It was remarkable: physically, I was in perfectly good shape and uninjured. But my pride had been severely punctured. Gratefully, I was put in a taxi to Rugby Station and thence headed back to Birmingham to face the wrath of my father.

(A week later I received a bill for the damage to the five oil drums from the motorway contractors Laing & Co.)

Sheepish and duly contrite, I had trudged home to face the music. Not one to be downhearted for too long, early the next morning I returned to the car showroom. Not surprisingly, the sales manager was quite cooperative when he heard that the car, they had sold me had nearly killed me. Arrangements were made for the wreck to be brought back on a trailer to the garage so that they could inspect the braking system that had patently failed. To avoid any dispute, the garage offered to refund what I had paid for the car (which was 250 pounds) as a deposit towards a new vehicle, minus the cost of transporting the wreck back from the crash site to Birmingham. The next problem was how on earth I was going to raise another 440 pounds towards a new car.

My brother-in-law Will came to the rescue. To a large extent his relationship with my father had healed. There was mutual respect; especially after his role in mediating during the staff strikes, thereby helping to avoid a dangerous situation and get the business back on track. He suggested with quiet solemnity that I could have been killed driving 'any old second-hand car', regardless of whether it was a sports car or not. Diplomatically, he slipped in that the family owed me a debt for finding and helping to set up the family businesses over the past few years, acting as interpreter and so forth. My mother nodded assiduously in the background, but pretended otherwise when my father turned around and glared at her. After much argument, my father grumpily agreed to pay for a new car; the lowest budget model available – which he deemed to be an Austin Mini saloon. Stubbornly, I turned that down. Eventually, I won the argument. I would choose a car that I could enjoy. My father capitulated and a brand-new Austin Healey Sprite sports car was reluctantly agreed upon, with Rose lending me 150 pounds. I was in seventh heaven.

But my father, aggrieved at being boxed into a corner, grumbled, *'Why is it, that you seem to spend your life arguing with me? Why don't you listen to me, just for once!?'*

I bit my lip. I wanted to blurt out that this was modern-day Britain, not old China, where fathers and their fathers before them ruled their family with an iron fist, and where sons and daughters were not allowed to offer even the hint of an opinion.

Then came a parting warning from my father: 'This final time, if you *dare* to disobey me once more, there will be no second chance. You will be thrown out on your ear into the streets – providing, of course, that you haven't got yourself killed in the meantime!'

It is well recognised that, from the beginning of time, family life has always been known to be difficult. But in the grand scheme of things, our internecine problems were trite compared to the real anxieties and danger when world events suddenly threatened the safety of nations and their people. For, on the 28th October 1962, the world was on the brink of a nuclear war. Khrushchev, the Premier of the USSR, had secretly moved nuclear missiles to his Communist ally, Cuba, within striking distance of America. From the USA, President Kennedy retaliated and set up a naval blockade around Cuba and threatened to take extreme countermeasures against Cuba and Soviet Russia. The prospect of a nuclear Armageddon was a whisker away, and it was terrifying. The world held its breath. Fortunately, Khrushchev climbed down, and the missiles were dismantled.

It was in the same month that the Beatles emerged as a soon-to-be global phenomenon, with their first record 'Love Me Do' entering the pop music charts. Some commentators wryly suggested that the present world powers could do with a massive dose of this unconditional love that the Beatles sang about. An old school colleague, Pete Best, drummed on their first record, having been with the group from its early days. Returning home to play at The Cavern after touring Germany, he was ignominiously sacked and replaced by Ringo Starr.

Meanwhile, news emerged from South Africa that, in November, Nelson Mandela had been sentenced to five years behind bars. Two years later, he was sentenced to life imprisonment for conspiring to overthrow the state. As the leader of the African National Congress

(ANC), which had led a failed anti-apartheid revolution, he was convicted as a dangerous terrorist and imprisoned on Robben Island for the next twenty-seven years.

As I tried to finish off my science course in London, and then to find a job, the bitterest winter on record blew in. In December, snow fell relentlessly, with blizzards from the east causing over twenty feet of snow in some parts of the country. Scores of communities were cut off, and many people perished. Three days before Christmas, temperatures plummeted. Rivers and lakes froze over, including sections of the Thames. Some parts of the sea in Herne Bay in Kent likewise turned to ice, not unlike the ice floes in the seas of the Arctic. The impregnable snow drifts, like my search for a fresh start in my life, lasted until March '63.

Part V

1963 – 1966

Chapter 29

A TURNING POINT

March 1963

O N THE CREST OF the welcome thaw, I managed to find work at a Mayfair-based advertising agency in the marketing and promotions department. The first step towards a radical change in my life had been taken. I must confess that my irrepressible ego was flattered by all the novel attention I was beginning to receive from some of the young, fair-headed secretaries. I soon discovered that it was all part of a game. Not unexpectedly, my secret – now dormant, engagement was starting to disintegrate.

My frosty relationship with my father drifted along like the overcast skies of winter, despite the imminent spring on the horizon. There was no escaping from the clutches of either of them.

Whichever way I turned, family obligation kept spinning its web. Like it or not, I was now indebted financially to my father. The traditional umbilical cord had begun to tighten. Uncomplaining, I just got on with it. I continued to help with legal matters, such as renewing the restaurant licence, and negotiating the rent reviews, rates and so on. Dealing with the Home Office, I managed to help my father bring a further nephew over from China to train as a cook at the restaurant. Yau Chin was the son of my father's second brother, Chun Yee. Meanwhile, Will Chen's improving relationship with the family strengthened and he was able to assist at the business as its manager. At home, the transforming effect that toddler Juliet had on her unemotional grandfather was truly a revelation. At every opportunity, as the child grew older, Father took her everywhere with him. His impatient grumbling about the stresses of life dissolved to jelly with the joyful and seemingly special bond between grandchild and grandparent.

But how was it, my siblings and I puzzled, that he remained cold and diffident in the way he treated us – his own sons and daughters?

Will tried to explain that it was to do with my father's traditional and austere upbringing in old China. 'Look,' he said, 'all of you must try to understand the profound effect your grandfather and his ancestors had upon your father, whereby any emotion shown, except in private, would be considered a sign of weakness; and any demonstration of intimate contact, particularly in public with his immediate family, would be considered taboo. It was all entrenched in family diktat, starting from the head of the family – perhaps it was for their own protection and survival during the constant conflicts, upheavals and natural disasters that ravaged the country during the last thousand years in feudal China. At the fall of the last Imperial Dynasty in 1912 with the eruption of another civil war, and with the advent of the first Republic of China, families hoped that some archaic thinking with old habits, would change for the better. But this failed to materialise.

Regardless of this, I found it extremely difficult to reconcile the circumstances that ruled the family in old China with any empathy or real understanding.

The memory of the harsh winter of ice and snow faded rapidly from the minds of Britain's people as summer blossomed with unbroken blue skies and sultry evenings that swept in with a sudden bout of high pressure that emanated from the Continent. Temperatures rose to dizzying heights; not least on the political front. The summer of

'63 brought to a climax one of the most explosive British political scandals of all time. In June, John Profumo resigned as Secretary of State for War from Harold Macmillan's government over his misleading Parliament regarding his two-year clandestine affair with Christine Keeler, a cabaret dancer and model who was a live-in friend of society osteopath Stephen Ward. It appeared that Keeler had simultaneously been having an affair with a Russian KGB officer, Yevgeny Ivanov, who was also introduced to her by Ward. It was claimed that state secrets had been leaked through subsequent pillow talk, and the Secret Services in both the UK and the USA were naturally alarmed.

Stephen Ward was tried at the Old Bailey for living off the immoral earnings of Keeler and another girl, Mandy Rice-Davies. It was alleged that he had treated many famous and high-ranking names, including royalty and the aristocracy. Reputedly, amongst others were Sir Winston Churchill, Lord Astor, Gandhi and many international stars, such as Frank Sinatra, Ava Gardner, Elizabeth Taylor and so on, whose fame and contacts he traded upon. In August, during the trial, feeling that he was being made a scapegoat by the establishment, Ward committed suicide by taking an overdose of sleeping tablets. The Conservative government was imploding at a rate of knots. Two months later, Harold Macmillan resigned to be replaced by Sir Alec Douglas-Home.

On the other side of the Atlantic, on the 28th August, the Civil Rights Movement reached a defining moment in its history as the Reverend Martin Luther King marched on Washington with two hundred thousand Americans. Standing beside the Lincoln Memorial, he delivered a most empowering speech to the people: '**I have a dream that one day, this nation will rise up and live up to its...**' It proved a seismic shift in the world's consciousness and was frequently adopted as a universal mantra.

As the leaves turned with the onset of autumn, the trees rattling overhead signalled yet another season in the offing. And, with the welcoming rain falling to nourish the thirsty soil, my mother received a letter from her brother in Borneo.

Borneo
*5*th *September 1963*

Dear sister,

It has been nearly thirty years since we last saw you, when you were taken from our family home by Uncle Sei and the marriage broker to join the Kwong family over the mountains in Dai Dune Chun.

I am now married, as you know, and our children are curious about you, the aunt they have never met. Your mother often asks about you, and so does Uncle Sei. You will remember that he is our late father's brother who managed, against all odds, to bring us here to safety in 1937, so that we could start a new life. That was a terrible time in China, with the bitter civil war between the Nationalists and the Communists, and Japan mobilising to invade our homeland.

Our sister, Choi Ping, still lives with her family in our ancestral home in Shek Tsui Chun where you were born. Due to her increasing blindness, please can you send her some more money? The Communist state under Mao has difficulty in helping every one of its people because of the massive, growing population of China. I hear it is particularly hard in the communes in the countryside, where the crops have failed yet again. Storms from the coast have battered the land, which is reeling from constant winter floods and summer droughts. For the last few years, throughout the land, there has been a famine on a gigantic scale. We are told that millions have died.

As the surviving male heir of the Chow family, I still send money back to maintain the ancestral home, even though, since the Communist Revolution in 1949, it has had to be shared with other Chows from the area. Although they are kinsmen, they are not direct descendants of our ancestors. I need not to remind you that, apart from Choi Ping and you, I have no other siblings left. Our family was tragically destroyed by wars and starvation. Our two older sisters died early. Our oldest brother, Kit Ngwun, died after being sent away to earn a living in Singapore aged twelve. Another brother, Kit Kwai, just a few years older than you, died of starvation; and two baby sisters were given away at birth, but soon perished.

Our mother has just turned eighty and is thankful that we fled here when we did. Please can you arrange to visit us before she grows too old to remember you? She was told a long time ago that when you got to England your husband Kwong Chun Ji gave you the name of Choi Lin, as our mother for some unknown reason failed to give you a proper name when you were born.

Your brother,

Kit Siang

And so, in early October as the chill of the season began to grip, Mother, accompanied by my sister Milly, was persuaded to fly to Borneo to see her aged mother. Remembering full well her treatment as a child, she took the thirteen-hour flight to Borneo with trepidation. The hurt and rawness of her mother's rejection still rankled after all these years. So how would she react to seeing her after all this time?

Father and the family took them to Birmingham Airport. I managed to see them at the BOAC terminal at Heathrow, and waved them off with mixed feelings. I was anxious for my mother's sake, but we all felt that this journey had to be made. Perhaps there would be a reconciliation between daughter and mother. At least she would see her younger brother Kit Siang again.

No sooner had they arrived safely in Borneo than I was invited to a party in a flat off the Fulham Road, held by a journalist friend of Milly's. At first, I was not that keen to go. Tisha had gone away. One of the girls from the office had invited me to her flat-warming party, miles away on the outskirts of London. So, I put on my best suit and drove from my flat in Notting Hill towards Fulham, it being the nearer of the two.

At the door, I was accosted by a delightful petite blonde, a friend of the host. She said her name was Yvonne and she was in public relations for Bodley Head, a publishing house. After a while of polite, flirtatious small talk, we exchanged numbers and promised to meet for lunch. However, in the centre of the crowded, smoke-filled room of laughter and merriment, my eyes were drawn to a slim, striking girl dressed in vivid green and black, with silver highlights in her hair. She was dancing and laughing, with flashing green eyes, surrounded by a group of people. Not to be deterred, I approached her. Perhaps it was the wine. Perhaps it was the carefree joy of the party. Or perhaps it was the feeling that I was free of all encumbrances that night. I was intrigued.

At the end of the evening, I managed to shake off a large, extroverted 'English counties' type who seemed to be commandeering her, and who glared daggers at me. I insisted that I take her home. She said that her name was Caroline, and that she was a dress designer. Her flat was only just down the road and she would be walking home with her flatmates, who were also at the party. For a moment, rightly or wrongly, I got a fleeting impression that she thought that I was a brash Johnny Foreigner – a polite nuisance at best, or at worst, something that the cat brought in. She lit a cigarette and blew a cloud of smoke over my left shoulder. I was never the type to be put off by a refusal, and so I persisted. It was partly to show off my new red sports car, but, gallingly, she was unimpressed. Little did I know at the time that, that night's chance meeting would shape and change my life forever.

Now, it is often said that everyone of a certain age can remember where they were on the 22nd November 1963. I happened to be in the office next to Park Lane, about to make a private call to fix a date with Caroline, when I heard that President Kennedy had been assassinated in Dallas, Texas, by a gunman by the name of Lee Harvey Oswald.

Chapter 30

RENAISSANCE

1964–1965

THE NEW YEAR COULD not arrive quickly enough. My various ruses to persuade Caroline to go out with me became challenging. Not only because of the situation, which meant duplicitously circumventing my arrangements with various friends of mine, but also because they meant battling, with some cunning, a particular and persistent boyfriend of hers who threatened to kill me.

Nevertheless, we enjoyed some amusing adventures, playing box and cox with various people, not unlike protagonists in a game of chess. Apart from everything else, what impressed me was that Caroline had already travelled abroad many times: France, Belgium, Germany, Italy and so on. For me, these places were distant destinations that I hoped one day I would get to. But for now, they were but theoretical countries on a map of Europe, seen only in my mind's eye, and in travel books and the cinema.

Being an accomplished dress designer, Caroline's interests took in a spell in couture at the fashion house of Nina Ricci in Paris. After visiting Rome and Florence, she illustrated, with text, a sizeable tome on Botticelli and his influence on classical Italian fashion. Reticence and modesty prevented her from approaching a publisher, which latterly I suggested that she ought to. Once, over potted shrimps and vin ordinaire at the Bistro Vino in South Kensington, Caroline recounted the tales of her childhood and being bombed out of her various homes by the Luftwaffe as she moved around the country from Colchester to Bath, to the Isle of Man. During the war, her father, Major Charles Stuart, being a skilled linguist in German and French, was amongst other clandestine assignments posted, to the Isle of Man to take part in the interrogation of German internees. In 1944 he was drafted to German-occupied Guernsey to work with the Resistance on Operation Overlord in the secret preparations for the Allies' Normandy invasion of the 6th June to liberate Europe.

It was later in 1964 when I met her parents, Charles and Mary Stuart, who had settled in a historical Elizabethan property called Hatton House,[80] teaching at the grammar school in Huntingdon. This distinguished alma mater included Oliver Cromwell and Samuel Pepys amongst its famous – or depending on your perspective, perhaps infamous – former pupils. Previously, Caroline and her family, including her brother Ian, had for some years been living in

---

80 In Post Street, Godmanchester, dating from the Tudor period and taking its name from a member of Sir Christopher Hatton's family. Hatton, MP for Higham Ferrers and a loyal subject and favourite of Elizabeth I, was made Lord Chancellor in 1587. From his residence in Ely Place, London (later called Hatton House), he would rest overnight in Godmanchester, it being a halfway staging post on his annual pilgrimage to Ely Cathedral. The cellar next to the dining room in Hatton House in Godmanchester had been sealed off for centuries. It was here that a benign female ghost visited from time to time, noted for her scent redolent of blossom from the Elizabethan period. The door to the guest bedroom upstairs was lopsided, so that it had to be pushed open against a sloping floor; but it often opened of its own accord, against gravity, according to eyewitnesses, one of whom was from the European Psychic Society.

a guest cottage in the grounds of Hinchingbrooke,[81] at the invitation of Lord Hinchingbrooke and the Earl of Sandwich, members of the Montagu family. You can imagine that, with my humble background, born in Liverpool to an immigrant Chinese family, I was naturally impressed. Given such monumental contrasts between us, it could be said that meeting the Stuarts was an important milestone of change in my life.

Certainly, that year in Britain, a remarkable renaissance was well under way. Phenomenal changes in art, culture, music, fashion, design and invention had already started to blossom out of all recognition. A subspecies of *'youth'* and their culture had evolved from the newly discovered *'teenager'* of the late '50s. Because this new class of youth was starting to have spare spending money, television, radio, newspapers, magazines, and retailers began to target their offerings at this specific group. They had tastes and needs that were completely different to those of their parents, whom they had hitherto copied and pandered to. Now they were in revolt. Commentators in history dubbed this revolutionary period *'The Swinging '60s'*.

All previous restrictions and the old-fashioned protocol regarding social behaviour and tastes were discarded virtually overnight. A new stratum of society now dictated fashion and

---

81   A vast country estate in Huntingdon consisting of hundreds of acres with farms, a stately home, a dower house, and cottages with Japanese and rose gardens, etc., with a tributary of the River Ouse at the perimeter of the estate. Originally it was built on the site of an eleventh-century Benedictine nunnery, which previously featured a Norman church. After the Reformation, it passed into the hands of the Cromwell family. It was then sold to the Earls of Sandwich; Sir Henry Montagu being the first. Samuel Pepys became secretary to the Third Earl, father of John Montagu, the Fourth Earl, who lent his name to the ubiquitous snack food. In 1564, Queen Elizabeth I stayed there. In 1603, King James I, on his way to claim the throne, also stayed overnight, later returning many times. The year 1639 marked the visit of Charles I. In 1830, it suffered a disastrous fire. One hundred and thirty years later, it survived a massive flood from a defective sprinkler system. After falling into disrepair and severe neglect, then suffering another fire, Hinchingbrooke was put up for sale in 1962. Due to the vision and drive of Mary Stuart, who was deputy head at Huntingdon Grammar School across the road from the estate she, together with the director of education, managed to persuade the local county council to buy it, so that, in 1970, it eventually became a unique comprehensive school, having absorbed Huntingdon Grammar.

all that this entailed. It was accelerated with the discovery of the contraceptive pill, and the sexual freedom that went with it. At the same time, the popularity of recreational drugs such as marijuana and LSD only exacerbated the anti-establishment rebellion of certain sections of the population. The 'Mersey Sound' of pop music was exploding like a volcano, with rapacious, far-reaching effects. It was the height of Beatlemania. Having radically changed the face of British popular music, the Beatles soon conquered America, and then, shortly afterwards, the rest of the world. Concurrently, in the south, the Rolling Stones, The Who and other bands became the new sensation at the clubs and theatres with their explosive individual sounds. The record industry expanded beyond all expectations and grossed fortunes as never before.

In the North Sea, a commercial pirate radio station calling itself Radio Caroline was launched from a ship anchored in international waters in order to break the BBC's and the record companies' virtual monopoly over popular music in the UK. It signified another break with the status quo.

From her pioneering boutique, Bazaar in the King's Road, Chelsea, Mary Quant had already started to revolutionise young women's fashion with the miniskirt. Following in her footsteps, Biba opened in Kensington. Gradually, as skirts in Britain, Europe and the States got shorter, men's hairstyles got longer, with Britain leading the way. Caroline, amongst others, had a theory that the height of the hemline was a barometer which measured the social mood and economic state of the country.

Close to the heart of Soho, an eclectic mix of shops and boutiques with *way-out* decor, some with psychedelic overtones, started to spring up en masse around Carnaby Street. They catered to the newest fashions for men; Lord John and Kleptomania were amongst them. If the King's Road was the epicentre for London's young women to strut their stuff, promenading in the latest fashion; then Carnaby Street, being synonymous with male style, was *the* place where young men preened like peacocks in their latest 'gear' – the more outrageous the

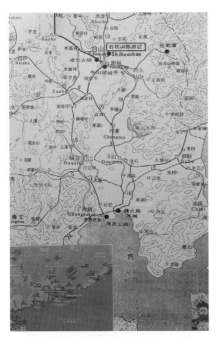

Figure 1

Figure 4

Figure 2

Figure 3

Figure 5

Figure 6

Figure 7

Figure 8

Figure 9

Figure 10

Figure 11

Figure 12

Figure 13

Figure 14

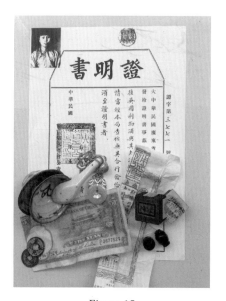

Figure 15

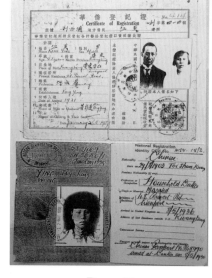

Figure 16

Figure 17

Figure 18

Figure 19

Figure 20

Figure 21

Figure 22

Figure 23

Figure 24

Figure 25

Figure 26

Figure 27

Figure 28

Figure 29

Figure 32

Figure 30

Figure 31

Figure 33

Figure 34

Figure 35

Figure 37

Figure 36

Figure 38

better. Many esoteric adjectives, like 'cool' and 'fab', soon entered the common vernacular.

A new benchmark in affordable, ultra-modern products for the home, from furniture to tableware, was designed by the forward thinking Terence Conran. These eye-catching designs from his flagship store, Habitat, were specifically aimed at the young. The new British car designs were revolutionary, breaking all stylistic and engineering boundaries with the iconic E-Type Jaguar sports car and the tiny Mini saloon with its transverse engine. Meanwhile, under wraps, a turbocharged supersonic airliner with a bullet-shaped body and a sabre-like nose was being designed and built by British and French aero engineers. This passenger jet was to be called Concorde, and would, on its inaugural flight five years later (in the same year Man would land on the moon) travel from London to New York in three and a half hours. Air travel would never be the same again.

Vidal Sassoon, a revolutionary hairdresser, launched a totally new look. Uniquely talented photographers such as Terry O'Neill and David Bailey burst on the horizon – the latter using the startling futuristic look of stunning young models such as Jean Shrimpton and Twiggy, who became the new sensations. Remarkable film epics directed by David Lean, such as *Doctor Zhivago* and *Lawrence of Arabia*, defined the early '60s. An enterprising, young cook, Prue Leith arrived on the scene and refreshingly and radically changed the face of British cooking, which hitherto, was commonly all too predictable and unimaginative. Prolific new artists, fresh groundbreaking playwrights and writers emerged, which only added further gloss to this golden decade of rediscovery.

It was amidst this maelstrom of creativity, fed by the fertile atmosphere of London, that we were swept along in the tide to see some iconic performances at the London theatres. My introduction to grand opera, at the behest of my brother who was an opera devotee, was seeing Maria Callas and Tito Gobbi at the Royal Opera House, performing in Zeffirelli's production of *Tosca* with the maestro Sir Georg Solti conducting. Mesmerised, we were smitten in more ways than one; for it soon became a life-long passion that consumed us.

Early in 1965 at Covent Garden we were lucky enough to witness a rejuvenated Dame Margot Fonteyn dance in *Romeo and Juliet* with the legendary Rudolf Nureyev. At the National Theatre – the Old Vic – we were also able to see Sir Laurence Olivier's jaw-dropping performance as Othello, with the young Maggie Smith as Desdemona. Accompanied by my 'muse', Caroline, my education in the journey of discovery in art, fashion, music, and culture had only just begun. It was a revelation.

Not long afterwards, it became apparent that, although currently working for others in the fashion trade, Caroline one day wanted to make her own mark on the industry, and under her own steam. There and then, I wondered if I could help her along the path to achieve that seemingly elusive dream.

Chapter 31

FROM RUSSIA WITH LOVE

1964–1965

I T WAS IN THE autumn of 1964, as thoughts turned to the inevitability of darker evenings closing in, that we were invited by two friends, Robert and Marcus, to a charity ball at Imperial College. These two were prominent members of an international club that promoted friendships between former students and friends from countries around the globe. A film screening took place, *From Russia with Love*, followed by a dinner dance. We were introduced to two diplomats, Major Grigor and Captain Oleg from the nearby Russian Embassy by the organiser of the event – a prominent baroness who, embarrassingly, I had to admit I had never heard of. The two officers, resplendent in the handsome uniform of the Russian military, took a polite interest in us. And, after some animated small talk with an abundance of flattery, Grigor, the taller and slimmer of the two, asked Caroline if she would teach him to dance, but not before asking my permission with a formal short bow.

Whilst Caroline was teaching the major the quickstep, the captain engaged me in conversation about my father, my family in China, what I did and my political views. The evening finished quite pleasantly and, rather to my surprise, Grigor telephoned me the next evening at my flat in Notting Hill. He said that he wanted to invite me to take tea with him at a hotel in Kensington Gore opposite to where he worked at the Russian Embassy. Politely, although naturally intrigued, I said that I was busy, but he persisted, and rang again on three further occasions. By that time I was starting to become concerned, if not rather suspicious.

On asking Robert, who at that time was working at the BBC, about them, he warned me that they were trying to recruit foreigners as agents, and that they had also approached him, and he had immediately advised them to get...! (albeit wrapped up in a polite euphemism). It appeared that over the last few years there had been a souring of Sino-Russian relations between Mao and Khrushchev, culminating in the withdrawal of the Chinese Ambassador from Moscow in July. Presently, therefore, the USSR was trying to recruit people from the Chinese community, even though I had no interest in their or anyone else's politics, especially since I had been born in Britain, and it was in this country that my loyalties lay.

Caroline, as it turned out, had a Russian family friend living in London with her husband Richard Tipping. Tamara Misernuik, as she was then, was born in St Petersburg. Some ten years after the Bolshevik Revolution, on the advice of her Uncle William (who was living in London), she was sent to England as a young girl and a newly qualified teacher, Mary Stuart, Caroline's mother, took her under her wing and taught her English. The family had a successful cotton mill and a magnificent house with land on the shores of one of the great lakes in St Petersburg, which was later taken in the revolution. Her father, Leonya, served in the Imperial Palace Guard for the last of the ruling Romanovs, Czar Nicholas II. On many an occasion, due to his anti-government views, he was purged by Stalin and imprisoned in a Siberian gulag, and latterly in a notorious labour camp where he was tortured and ultimately perished. Tamara's uncle, William Gerhardie, was a well-known writer in the '30s (*The Polyglots*; *Futility*, etc.) and a friend and contemporary of the Bloomsbury Set as well as H. G. Wells, Arnold Bennett, Katherine Mansfield and others.

When I mentioned the episode at Imperial College to the Tippings, they warned me to be on my guard and to ignore the Russian overtures, which probably came from the KGB. Richard, who was working at the BBC news desk, said that the Soviets and the Chinese were at loggerheads. It had been getting more fractious since the Korean War, in which the Communist Chinese lost up to three quarters of a million troops but the Soviets, their allies, did not commit any ground forces. After the sudden death of Joseph Stalin[82] a year later in March 1953, to be succeeded by Nikita Khrushchev, the relationship between the two former allies plumbed new depths. For example, in 1962 during the Sino-Indian Border War, the USSR supplied fighter planes to India, much to the fury of Peking. And in a long-running dispute over the contested territories near the border of the province of Xinjiang, the Chinese repeatedly claimed that these lands had been stolen from them since the time of the Czars. Eventually, as time went on the relationship between the two nations deteriorated to such an extent that their nuclear arsenals began to be manoeuvred to face each other rather than their common enemy, the USA.

Such was the Tippings' dire warning that I felt that my paranoia was justified. And so, as a precaution, my telephone, being a shared party line, was monitored by a third party, until Grigor and his colleague had been recalled to Moscow or lost interest in me.

As a footnote, however, we later heard that our friend Marcus, who was part German and fluent in several languages, had been secretly recruited. When this was discovered, we were naturally stunned and found it hard to believe, for he had stayed and holidayed with us on many occasions as part of the family. At the fall of East Germany (the GDR) years later, with the Stasi[83] records revealed to the West, Marcus was interviewed by British Intelligence; but it seemed that the

---

82　Dictator of Soviet Russia who died of a heart attack on the 5th March 1953, to the relief of many of his citizens. Although he would go down in history as the saviour of his country against Nazi Germany in World War II, during which he was an ally of Roosevelt and Churchill, he would be remembered for his rule of terror, with the murder of millions of his own people.

83　The East German/GDR Secret Service. At the fall of the Berlin Wall in November 1989, Stasi officials began to destroy their organisation's secret files, until their offices were forcibly occupied by their liberated citizens in January the following year in an attempt to expose secret personal information held on file. Many of the files were simply thrown out of the windows or half-burnt.

information he had passed on over the decades was dated and now proved worthless. It was a salutary lesson to us not to be seduced by the ineffable charms of Russian diplomats.

In October 1964, Harold Wilson became Prime Minister following the General Election, with the return of a Labour government after thirteen years of Conservative rule. The Wilson government was considered progressive and reforming; abolishing the death penalty, decriminalising homosexuality and apparently unofficially embracing the 'permissive society' which fuelled the growth of the swinging '60s. In spite of the precarious economy with its continuing balance-of-deficit woes, the British were rediscovering their confidence and sense of fun after the dark war years of the '40s and the austere gloom of the '50s.

The only blot on the landscape was the death of Sir Winston Churchill in January 1965, aged ninety. The people of Britain went into mourning, and so, it seemed, did most parts of Western Europe and the free world. In the US, against the background of Martin Luther King's Civil Rights Movement gathering pace, leading eventually to voting rights for black Americans, President Lyndon Johnson's involvement in the Vietnam War escalated amidst much protest. In March, the US *Gemini 3* space mission launched its first manned spacecraft, carrying astronauts Grissom and Young. The late President Kennedy's promise to the American people that NASA would man the first spacecraft to the moon before the decade was out appeared to be going to plan.

In Britain, the Wilson government failed in its negotiations with Rhodesian Prime Minister Ian Smith to halt the country's break away from the UK. Smith then declared unilateral independence under White Rule, renaming his country Zimbabwe. Wilson should not have been surprised; for after all, five years earlier Harold Macmillan had warned of the 'wind of change' that would blaze through Africa, signalling the end of colonial rule by European powers, as more and more colonies jostled for independence. Already in 1960 Cyprus had achieved its independence, although fighting continued to break out between the Greek and Turkish communities, forcing British and later UN troops to patrol the border between them. Macmillan's words were prescient, for the British Empire as the world knew it had already sounded its own death knell.

Chapter 32

THE YEAR OF THE SNAKE

Birmingham, England, 1ˢᵗ February 1965

A LL WAS NOT DOOM and gloom; for on the first day of February it was Chinese New Year, the Year of the Snake. This was deemed to be a year of joyful enterprise. My sister Rose and I suggested to Father that we could organise a dinner dance at the restaurant to celebrate.[84] This would be a first for a Chinese restaurant in the Midlands. Within one week, tickets were sold out and the restaurant was fully booked. Rose had a good friend named Marion, who organised a band and a PA system to be temporarily installed in a corner near the bar. My brother-in-law Will, always enterprising, had brought over from Hong Kong a vividly decorated dragon's head (which represented wisdom, power and wealth), and its trailing body to house the martial arts-dancers underneath. What was missing were experienced Dragon Dancers. Friends of one of the waiting staff suggested a team of Chinese students from the university who were adept at this traditional dance, and who were most willing to come and entertain

---

84 The restaurant in Station Street, being in a strategic position in the heart of the Birmingham theatre district, had already attracted well-known names such as Morecambe and Wise, Ronnie Barker, Lulu, Maurice Gibb, Margaret Lockwood, Anthony Steel, Ruby Murray, Eartha Kitt, Marlene Dietrich, Brian Rix (Whitehall farces), Peter Wyngarde (TV's Jason King), Albert Finney and many others.

our guests for publicity and a good, free meal. Rehearsals started at once. The head chef, Mr Yip would prepare a special festive meal of ten courses, finishing with fortune cookies.

Not one to miss an opportunity, I suggested to Caroline that it was time that she met my father to test the water. Gathering up courage, I was fully aware that the introduction would have to be under false pretences. We would be armed with a story that I would largely invent, such as that she was an important journalist – knowing full well his determined opposition to my going out with a foreigner. Furthermore, we would say that she was a friend of my sister Milly, which happened to be partially true – Caroline and I having met through Milly's former boyfriend who was working for a national daily tabloid. On the day, Caroline would travel up by train to stay at the large, modern hotel The Albany at the back of the restaurant. Rose and Marion had invited a friend, Jonathan Hill, a prominent journalist for the *Post and Mail*, and he brought along his press photographer. We let on that, out of polite respect, the Mayor of Birmingham had been invited, but we did not expect him to attend, given his busy schedule.

Collecting a nervous Caroline from the hotel, I introduced her to Father at the restaurant door where a crowd of guests was assembling. He was remarkably charming and greeted her with an enigmatic smile and shook her hand. Then, inviting Rose and Milly to guide her to the table where the reporter and Marion were seated, he turned his attention to the rest of the customers and guests. It was so far, so good.

Colourful Chinese lanterns and red roses on the tables set a happy and relaxing mood. Full of anticipation and excitement with the band striking up, dim sum starters and cocktails were served by the waiting staff, who were smartly turned out in their new high-necked Chinese jackets. My allocated job was to coordinate the music and dance programme, addressing the guests via the PA system, whose microphone was erratic to say the least. But clearly, I was in my element. It brought back vivid memories of the sixth form at the Liverpool Collegiate, when I helped to organise the dances between the boys' and girls' schools.

The evening flowed faultlessly. Sumptuous dishes followed one after another in concert with a seemingly endless flow of wine. The kitchen excelled itself beyond expectation. Between the intervals of dancing, much spontaneous laughter and merriment filled the air. It was reported later that the diners said that they had never enjoyed themselves as much as they had that night.

Midway through the evening, I announced the main attraction that everyone had been waiting for. On cue, the lights in the restaurant were dimmed.

'Ladies and gentlemen, we are delighted to give you the traditional symbol of wisdom, power and wealth. It's what you have been waiting all evening for, so let's welcome into our midst, for the very first time in the Midlands, the colourful, the vibrant, the indomitable Chinese dragon!'

To an exaggerated roll of drums and noisy applause, the Dragon Dance began. The mammoth head of the dragon, bedecked in red streamers over its bulbous eyes and ferocious teeth, peeped theatrically from behind the bar. With the serpentine segments of its body and tail articulated by poles held by three athletic, martial arts-dancers underneath, the dragon weaved its way sinuously into the dining room. Led by a man in a golden mask hypnotically beating a drum, it was followed by another striking a giant brass gong. Greeted by gasps of surprise and oohs and aahs, the dragon leapt dramatically up and down. It somersaulted off chairs and tables as it made its way around each table of diners in turn. At one point, it even poked its head around the front door, waggling its giant tongue and blowing out smoke as if to greet the cool evening. For a few tense minutes, completely unscripted, the dragon sashayed tantalisingly out of the front door to perform on the pavement. A crowd of astounded onlookers quickly gathered. The centre of Birmingham had never witnessed anything like it before. It stopped the traffic along Station Street. Taxis and buses hooted their horns in unison.

Once back in the safety of the restaurant, the dancers covered about every corner of the premises, just as the Mayor's limousine suddenly arrived at the front door. Taken by surprise, and in momentary panic, Rose and I quickly alerted Father to stand by the door to welcome the distinguished visitor. Accompanied by his driver and a security aide, the Mayor proffered his good wishes for a happy New Year. Briefly posing with the dragon over a glass of champagne, he apologised profusely for having to attend another engagement, and left immediately after the photograph was taken. As soon as the mayoral party had departed, the dragon rolled gymnastically on the floor, to be greeted by thunderous applause. The photographer had a field day with us and the laughing dragon. Two days later, I was invited, along with the Dragon Dance team, to appear live on *Midlands Today*, the local TV news programme. Like a runaway train, the publicity became unstoppable.

The loud music and the noisy spectacle soon attracted an increasing sea of people who congregated outside the front door of the restaurant. Events threatened to get out of control. Several members of the public wielding cameras then tried to barge their way in, but were held back by two friendly local beat constables, who had earlier been treated to a meal in the kitchen.

Hoping that my father would be absorbed in chatting to his accountant and his wife at their table, I took the chance to dance with Caroline, who carried it off with natural aplomb. If she was still anxious about the charade of meeting my father, she did not show it. What my father really thought about the events of the evening was difficult to say. Then it occurred to me that sweeping generalisations from outsiders about the Chinese being inscrutable were perhaps right.

At our table, Jonathan and Marion chatted amiably to us. During the conversation, it was revealed that Marion worked in sales on the fashion floor of Rackhams, a large department store that was part of the Fraser Group of stores which included Harrods in London. When she discovered that Caroline was a dress designer for the sophisticated young female market, she was intrigued. Marion said that she would mention Caroline's name to her buyer, as they were always open to new ideas and to new designers coming from London. Thinking that this was just polite conversation, Caroline didn't think any more about it.

A week later, a message was left with Rose asking Caroline to contact Rackhams' buyer, Miss Henrietta Savage. Nervously, she did, and an appointment was made for a week later at the store, on the understanding that she would sketch out new ideas for a collection of dresses for early autumn.

Matters then moved at a furious pace. After work, Caroline worked into the night to produce a series of sketches of dresses for the late-teens-to-mid-twenties age group; for the sophisticated woman who wanted something smart, affordable and a bit different. Attached to her drawings were swatches of material that would give the buyer an idea what the final designs made up would look like. Armed with this collection of ideas, full of hope and racked with nerves, I drove her up to Birmingham for the fateful appointment at this major department store.

The sky was clear and cloudless, with a hint of spring in the air as we made our way up the M1. The journey had started inauspiciously, when a van failed to brake and rammed into the rear end of my new MG sports car as we were going up a hill in Hendon! However, the meeting went better than we thought. The buyer, although impressed overall with the designs on paper, asked without obligation for five of the dresses to be made up as samples for her to look at on her next buying trip to London in mid March.

After cutting and grading the patterns, through trade contacts the samples were made up by experienced machinists in the East End. We met Miss Savage at my flat near the Portobello Road. Milly, being a perfect size twelve, had been persuaded to model the dresses. To impress the buyer, we took her out for lunch and some expensive wine, which we could ill afford. We need not have bothered. As an experienced buyer for a major store, she knew what she was looking for. She placed an order for three of the dresses across a range of sizes and colourways, each bearing the label of *Carolyne Stuart* (to save confusion in the eyes of the public, for there was already an established dress designer with a boutique in Knightsbridge called Caroline Charles).

It is often said that beginner's luck shines down on you when you least expect it, or when you aren't trying as hard. To our stunned surprise, to coincide with the new season, *Vanity Fair* magazine printed a half-page photograph of one of Caroline's dresses, with a heading saying that Carolyne Stuart was a new name to look out for. The editorial featured a scintillating black-and-gold short evening dress, called '*Sophistication*'. Within days, Rackhams sold out her collection of dresses. On the strength of this, she was interviewed on the *ATV News* programme in Birmingham, with the headline "*Is this the start of an invasion of the new young designers from Swinging London?*" Without a hint of nerves, she carried it off like a veteran.

Three months later, Harrods bought a selection of her dresses. Two of them were prominently displayed in the main window in Knightsbridge under a bright, lone spotlight. And so, in the drizzling rain as the dank, dark evenings of early autumn began to close in on us, we parked our car on the double yellow lines outside the store and stood and stared at the display. 'Pride' and 'shock' are best words I can think of to describe the feeling. But we were quickly shaken out of our daydream by an irate traffic warden who threatened to ticket the car.

The next day, Caroline resigned from her full-time job. I then joined her, and together we agreed that we would launch her own company, *Carolyne Stuart (London) Limited*. We borrowed the start-up capital of 2,500 pounds from our disbelieving parents, with a matching overdraft from a sympathetic high street bank.

All I told my father, without going into detail, was that I was going into business in clothing manufacture. Although machining clothes was something he'd once been adept at for us children during the war, I felt that he viewed my first foray into business with a large dose of scepticism, sensing that I was about to make a clean break from the family.

'So, you think it's going to be dead easy, making a living all on your own, do you?'

The cynicism in his voice was obvious.

I was taken aback. For the last decade or so, I'd thought that my relationship with my father had improved, ever since the time in Wrexham when, at Uncle's behest, I went to bring him home from Mrs Wong Sing's where he was slowly dying from self-imposed starvation after walking out on us due to the increasing burden of family and financial pressure and the manual work that he'd grown to detest. From that time onwards, I had thought that we had a truce; especially with all the help I had given him with finding the café and house in Liverpool, and then the restaurant in Birmingham, as well as all the legal and financial work that entailed. Well, how wrong could I be? For, under the surface, there remained ingrained in him a pathological mistrust left over from my childhood. It seemed that, even though I was now an adult, I was still under probation, whatever I did to try to please him.

Ill-tempered, he truculently blustered on as he threw down a thick bundle of five-pound notes on the dining-room table. It was a blatant challenge. I had little choice but to rise to the bait. I had to prove myself to him all over again. There was no mistake. He had made it plain that the family thread of obligation, with its filial obedience and subservience, would still be as binding as ever.

Undaunted, full of blind optimism and totally reliant on my ad hoc business experience, I promised Caroline's family that I would look after her in the new company and help to forge her name as one of the country's upcoming new designers.

Foolishly brave or stupidly naive, we were ready to take on the fickle and cut-throat world of fashion. Driven, like many people in their twenties, by unrealistic ambition and impossible dreams, we joined the thousands in trying to make an impact, and find fame and fortune in the swinging '60s.

We were either going to succeed or fall flat on our faces. Again, as the old, cautionary saying goes, only time would tell...

Chapter 33

1966 AND ALL THAT

A T THE BEGINNING OF 1966, the space race between the superpowers of the USSR and the USA accelerated to fever pitch. In February, the Soviets' probe, *Luna 9*, managed to land on the moon. Not to be eclipsed, on the 2nd June, NASA's own spacecraft, *Surveyor 1*, also successfully docked on the moon. Then in August, NASA's space probe entered its orbit to photograph its surface in readiness for man's first landing, anticipated to take place within the decade.

Whilst down on our perennially troublesome planet earth, anti-war protests escalated in response to US President Johnson's increasing involvement in the war in Vietnam, with the commitment of half a million troops. Protests which started off peacefully, such as that in front of the American Embassy in Grosvenor Square, Central London, like other demonstrations across the States and around the world, invariably ended in violence.

In Britain, the pioneering hovercraft launched its maiden passenger service to sail (or float) across the English Channel to France. Meanwhile, from Paris, the obdurate President of France Charles de Gaulle, still harbouring a latent resentment of Britain for its help during the last war, continued to veto the country's application to join the European Economic Community (i.e. the Common Market), repeating his well-publicised objection to UK membership; '*Non!*' Britain's Labour Prime Minister, Harold Wilson, having comprehensively won the March General Election, could do very little about it.

It was against this turbulent backdrop of fast-changing events, that the challenge from my father only spurred me on to try to make a fist of things and prove him wrong. In order that Caroline and I could make a living in the rapidly moving fashion trade, with its vast and aggressive competition, it would have to be noses to the grindstone. But with each step of the way in my new life, the cracks that had pre-existed between my father and me, had now started to widen into an increasing ravine with each passing day. I found it extremely difficult to engage in any meaningful conversation with him whenever we met. Our previously separate lives were now worlds apart.

Nevertheless, I had to focus my energies on my present path which I had chosen as the mid '60s moved at a phenomenal pace, as did world events. With the miniskirt of popular UK fashion creeping higher, Paris haute couture, with its establishment designers such as Courrèges and Yves Saint Laurent, succumbed to the short hemline in their collections. There was no going back.

Likewise, there was no time for Caroline and me to lose. On the floor, I spread a large map of Britain and drew circles in red ink around the cities and regions that were considered important to carve a name for the company. Major department stores that could stock Carolyne Stuart dresses were our primary target. Joshua Taylor in Cambridge became our first stockist in East Anglia. Again, Caroline appeared on the television features programme *Look East* to talk about her work. Her photograph appeared in the *Cambridge News*. The name started to spread.

On the South Coast in Bournemouth, the old, established family firm of Beales stocked a large collection of her designs. To promote this new name, the managing director, one of the Beale family, invited

Caroline to host and commentate at an exclusive fashion show before an invited audience of their customers. The press attended and editorials appeared in the local papers, and Caroline was invited to appear on *Look South* on television. As before, she wore one of her designs to great effect as a talking point.

Drapers Record, the fashion trade's paper, reported approvingly on Carolyne Stuart's work. Enquiries from multinational man-made textile companies, such as Courtaulds and ICI, soon flooded in. Caroline was invited to join a new group of young designers by British Celanese (a subsidiary of Courtaulds), to use and promote their new fabric Tricel in a new collection of dresses, part of which was to be displayed at the Interstoff Fair in Frankfurt to much critical acclaim. Not to be left out, ICI also invited her to design a collection of leisurewear in Crimplene. Photographic editorials soon followed in national magazines such as *She* and *Nova* to coincide with the appearance of Caroline's designs in stockists around the country.

Britain was in an optimistic mood as it readied itself for the football World Cup that would take place across the country in the major football stadiums. UK businesses boomed during that blistering summer, with millions of visitors from all over the world descending on the country, together with the world press, television and radio crews. On the 30th July, as the sun beamed down and Wembley reached sizzling temperatures, England won the World Cup by beating West Germany 4–2.

My father, Rose and brother Sam only heard about the febrile excitement from the cabin crew of their BOAC aircraft as they nervously boarded their flight to Hong Kong for a momentous journey to visit China.[85] Little did they realise that they were about to land right in the middle of the hotbed of the Cultural Revolution, recently launched by Chairman Mao to savagely purge his people of old ideas and to violently remind them of revolution. After leaving the country

---

85 The Kwongs, having never flown before, were rather apprehensive after hearing that, the previous year, a Boeing 707 on a BOAC flight had crashed into the side of Mount Fuji in Japan while en route to Hong Kong.

of his birth so many decades ago, our father Kwong Chun Ji could not have chosen a more explosive and dangerous time to return.

Only a month earlier, I had received a frantic call from Rose. The family had asked if I could return home to the Midlands so that help could be given to our brother–in–law, Will, who was going to run the family restaurant in our father's absence. To enable Father to finally see his homeland again after all this time, how could I refuse?

At the end of July, as the three of them set off on a long journey to the Far East in a large metal beast of an airliner soaring disconcertingly into a bottomless sky, China seemed light years away. And, as far as my brother and sister were concerned, that country might as well have been situated on another planet.

On the 21st October, a disaster of catastrophic proportions struck the small mining community of Merthyr Tydfil in South Wales. A gigantic mountain of a slag heap, overflowing with colliery waste and weakened by torrential rain, slid down and engulfed the local junior school in the village of Aberfan. One hundred and forty-four people perished, including 116 children. The Queen and Prince Philip, on paying a visit to the community, were visibly distressed.

Like millions of people across the country, my family was heartbroken at this tragic loss of life. As children growing up in Pen-y-Bryn, learning the Welsh language, being taught their history and embracing their national anthem, we identified with the Welsh people, who had accepted us unconditionally and without prejudice.

In November, Jim Lovell and Buzz Aldrin were launched into orbit around the earth as part of the *Gemini 12* space programme. Man took another step towards the moon.

Part VI
———
1966

Chapter 34

THE CULTURAL REVOLUTION

China, 7ᵗʰ August 1966

T HE VAST INTERVIEWING SHED constructed of old corrugated iron in which they stood was unbearably stifling and humid, having absorbed the heat of the day. It was the height of summer, even though sunrise was still some three hours away. Flies, already awake in their droves, buzzed low hungrily, sensing the sweat on the queue of foreigners patiently waiting in line to be interviewed by immigration officials and customs officers from the People's Republic of China. A state of nervous uncertainty permeated the oppressive heat.

At the head of the queue, stood a tired-looking, older man – Kwong Chun Ji, who was mopping his brow with a sodden handkerchief with weary impatience. Subconsciously, he pushed up his glasses as they slipped down the bridge of his nose due to the eruption of perspiration. Anxiously, he ran his fingers through his thinning grey hair, but he didn't dare complain, fearing a hostile reception from the group of officials sitting behind the table in front of him. His outward placidity hid the signs of his increasing frustration at the further delay of the processing of his papers. Using temporary foreign visas, and being Western Chinese, he felt that he'd better not attract special attention to him or to his family. Just

249

behind him, standing restlessly, hopping from foot to foot, was his daughter Rose, looking equally dishevelled. Petite and pretty, she nervously fiddled with her short black hair, and despite her looking normally younger than her twenty-five years, she looked now worse for wear due to the unpredictable and alien situation confronting them. Standing next to her was Sam, her teenage brother who wore a look of boredom on his otherwise young face. So as not to worry the others, he stared straight ahead at nothing in particular. Brother and sister nodded nervously to each other.

After travelling during the night – without much sleep whilst on the ferry from Hong Kong some forty-odd miles away, all three of them appeared irritable and exhausted. Having just left the ferry terminal at the port of Macao, they had followed a procession of vacant-looking passengers like dutiful sheep. Directly facing them was a tortuous, dusty road. It felt more like a well-worn track than a made-up road coated in tarmac as they tramped along it. Unavoidably kicking up the loose gravel under their feet as they passed through that section of no man's land which marked the border crossing of Portas do Cerco – the barrier gate between the Portuguese colony of Macao and mainland China – they eventually reached the old wooden bridge they had seen in the distance.

It was slow, laborious work for Chun Ji and his family as they each wheeled bicycles – heavily laden with panniers of luggage, food and other personal possessions. As soon as they crossed the rickety bridge, which was fenced heavily on each side, separating the two countries, they were met by armed soldiers and hurriedly herded into the shed for new arrivals. The modest Portuguese flag was no longer seen; instead, the enormous red flag with its five golden stars of the People's Republic of China was fluttering as they stepped foot on Zhuhai; the beginning of the mainland of China. Loudspeakers fixed high above the rusting panels on the shed roof blared out a deafening rendition of 'The East Is Red' in a deified tribute to Chairman Mao Zedong (Tse-tung). To foreign ears and eyes, the atmosphere was nothing short of electric, and equally intimidating.

The Cultural Revolution had been escalating at a furious pace since Mao had vowed, earlier that year, to stir up the youth to rise up and purge the nation of its apathy towards its **'Four Olds': old habits, old customs, old culture and old ideas.** This was to cleanse society and government of the old political ideology at the behest of its most venerated chairman. Unwittingly, the Kwong Chun Ji family had arrived in a hotbed of turmoil and revolution. Chairman Mao had mobilised the creation of a massive corps of Red Guards to punish party officials and any other persons throughout the land who showed bourgeois tendencies. This ruthless campaign was in order to stave off and purge 'Capitalist Roaders'[86] whose ideas hankered for the past – such as counter-revolutionary ideas from enemies of the state who Mao deemed had infiltrated government and society. It smacked of paranoia.

Chun Ji wiped his chin with the back of his hand, whilst his daughter Rose waved a piece of paper vigorously in front of her face to create a breeze. But it made little difference. Sam stared stoically ahead of him. He was concentrating on balancing his luggage on his bicycle, as they waited to be interrogated. His father was the first to be interviewed by a sullen-looking official who, dressed in an ill-fitting military uniform, only added to the intimidating atmosphere. Stubbing out one cigarette after another in an overflowing ashtray on the table in front of him, he asked about Chun Ji's job, his family and, in detail, his relatives living near Taishan. He had to list all his siblings living in his ancestral village and his reasons for visiting them. He explained that he had left China as a young man nearly half a century ago. Provocatively, the interrogator then asked for his reasons for emigrating to the Capitalist West.

'I had *no* choice,' he replied wearily with a shake of his head. *'It was my duty. I obeyed my father, for it was my traditional obligation as the eldest son! The family needed help. In those days, in 1921, many families in our village needed food and shelter in order to live.'*

---

86 Persons deemed to have strayed along the road to capitalism, i.e. towards the 'decadent West'.

Chun Ji tried to justify his leaving; but he avoided anything controversial, however remote, that might give rise to an argument. The interviewer was less than half his age and had not even been born then; he wouldn't have suffered the terrible economic circumstances or the famine, or the armed conflict that prevailed in China at that time. Chun Ji was longing to inform the official about old China and its family traditions and filial obligations but did not dare rile him. So he bit his tongue.

He emptied his pockets and spread his luggage out on the table in front of him, item by item, for scrutiny. An old newspaper from Hong Kong, used to wrap up some new socks and underwear, was immediately confiscated. The interviewer asked why he had brought over so many clothes, many of them new. And, moreover, why the bicycles? Not daring to say that his siblings in his village had requested them, Chun Ji said that it was the first time he had been overseas since he left China, and he didn't really know what a traveller needed or what would be their means of getting around.

The interviewer just stared at him blankly, not revealing what was really in his mind. He then seized Chun Ji's British travel document with its brown cover, waving it in the air.

'Why haven't you got a proper blue British passport like others from that country?'

'I was issued with this travel document instead,' the reply came back evenly.

'Aha!' the interviewer exclaimed triumphantly, as he examined it page by page. 'It says here that you are stateless. Why is that?'

'I had to surrender my old Chinese passport, issued in Canton in 1921, to the British Home Office as the first Republic of China no longer existed and was replaced by the new People's Republic some years later.'

'But our venerable Chairman had declared that all Chinese not living on the mainland were to be reclassified as stateless from 1949, the year our most magnificent People's Revolution came to pass! You and thousands of others wouldn't have had this problem if you had returned *when invited to reside in our noble country!'* the interviewer lectured tartly.

The official then scrutinised the visa Chun Ji had obtained via the China Travel Service in Hong Kong (the acting travel service for the Chinese government), which was stamped *'Overseas Compatriot travel permission to visit Ancestral Home'*. Giving a derisory grunt, he was questioned all over again. Then, satisfied that this old man was not an immediate threat to the Chinese state, the official waved him aside to interview Rose and Sam in turn.

Chun Ji was then given a copy of *Quotations from Chairman Mao Tse-tung* (the 'Little Red Book') in Chinese to study whilst in the country. The official then selectively extracted several Hong Kong dollars and three Chinese yuan from his wallet in payment. Reading aloud from the book would be mandatory as a way of kowtowing to Chairman Mao when the time came to exit China. When studying Mao's works and quotations, they had been warned beforehand in Hong Kong, it was advisable to do so with appropriate solemnity, otherwise there could be repercussions. It had been known at the time that some people had unwittingly taken a copy of the Little Red Book into the lavatory. This was considered blasphemous and, at best, the perpetrator was heavily penalised, or, at worst, faced imprisonment.

This made it patently clear that the regime was prohibitively strict and employed censorship in the extreme. So, he was mighty relieved that he was not subjected to a body search; for he had hidden the bulk of the Chinese currency destined for the family, and his supply of Hong Kong dollars, in a body wrap low around his waist. A shiver passed involuntarily through his body.

From the east, light was just breaking over the distant mountain range by the time Chun Ji and his son and daughter could leave. Their driver, a distant kinsman from Taishan, had been waiting patiently for them in a battered old minivan at a planned rendezvous a mile up the road beside a row of semi-rural dwellings previously occupied solely by local smallholders, but now part of a commune. He had been told that they would be easily recognisable as the trio would be in Western dress and wheeling fairly new bicycles. Gratefully, they put their bicycles and luggage into the van and drove off, with giant loudspeakers all along the route blaring Radio Peking, interspersed with 'The East is Red'. The road was rough and unmade, a veritable dust trap pockmarked with craters. To reach the city of Taishan would take four hours or so.

As soon as they reached the outskirts of the old city, memories of that day in 1921, when as a young man he had travelled there to collect his papers to enable him to travel to the West, came flooding back...

It was from here that he had managed to hitch a lift from a fellow traveller – a stranger called Mr Lo – to reach the capital city of Canton at the neck of the Pearl River. How could he possibly forget that cold winter's day at the beginning of January; that traumatic journey in Mr Lo's van, when they were attacked by bandits and nearly strangled to death before managing to fight them off? Then came the bloody memory of Mr Lo chopping off the fingers of one of the attackers with a machete when he refused to let go of the van door.

Then, of course, that stifling overnight journey down the Pearl River to reach Hong Kong in an ancient sailing junk jam-packed with travellers, livestock and cargo. And, even worse, the three months of torture on treacherous high seas in the stinking, rat-infested cargo hole of an old steamship, where almost half the passengers died before they reached the West. How he had survived that floating hell amongst the hundreds crammed into the disease-ridden bowels of the ship, with the choking, noxious fumes from the furnaces, the constant seasickness, the murderous fights for survival, the random killings, the sickening rapes and the lack of fresh food and water, he would never know. He shook his head vigorously, not quite believing all the life-changing events that he had been through, and, furthermore, those which had happened to him since.

Concerned, Rose and her brother noticed that their father had gone extremely pale and started to shake. But they were too scared to ask him why.

At that moment, it was with fresh curiosity, rather than mere nostalgia, that Chun Ji absorbed in silence the familiarity of some of the streets of Taishan and the densely packed buildings that huddled, one on top of another. Suddenly, a sheet of drizzle began to fall, making the driver curse under his breath as his van skidded over the patched-up road surface with its frequent potholes and treacherous ruts. The dampness only added to the sauna-like humidity. There was a dreary greyness to the landscape, mimicking the situation this family found themselves in.

Noticeable in the layout of the city were the sprawling new additions to the buildings, adding to the density of the urban sprawl. The crowded overdevelopment in stark, ugly concrete amplified its soullessness. But, to Chun Ji's weary eyes, certain parts of the city, particularly the ancient quarters inside the old walls, looked remarkably the same as they had all those years ago. The rambling tangle of alleyways – the hutongs, with their dilapidated mass of dwellings that sprawled amorphously across the main thoroughfares – was still the same. So, in many ways, *nothing* had changed. But there again, this time around, the smell was different. Then he put his finger on it – of course; now there was a new smell pervading the air. *It was one of tension and fear*. And it was palpable.

When he was here last, the streets at this time of the early morning would be streaming with a variety of people scurrying about along the cobbled streets on their way to market. There would be old handcarts full of goods and livestock, manned by farmers and peasant smallholders all pushing and shoving along the streets. Fighting for space amongst the rickety bicycles, run-down three-wheeled vehicles and ancient rickshaws, they would be going about their daily business. There would be shouts, screams and gossip amongst the indigenous population and country traders from out of town, as the market stalls and shops vied frenetically for business.

Today, what struck him was the lack of ordinary inhabitants on the streets. He also noticed that there were several soldiers from the People's Liberation Army mingling amongst a number of young men dressed in different uniforms – mainly greyish blue, or occasionally khaki[87] – presumably left over from their fathers' time. Noticeably, they all seemed to be brandishing Mao's Little Red Book, and they all wore peaked caps with a prominent red star at the front. There were a few women in evidence, but, like some of the men, they wore high-necked tunics with turned-down collars which Chun Ji could only describe as akin to a dark, poorly tailored boiler suit – later described as a 'Mao jacket'. The rest of the civilian population hurried along, intent on their chores, preferring to look mainly at the ground rather than stand and gossip with their neighbours on the street corners as they once had during his last visit, which now seemed a lifetime ago.

Suddenly, Sam elbowed his sister in the ribs, telling her to look across the street. Standing out from the rest, some of the buildings appeared to have thick, black graffiti scrawled across them in coarse blobs of paint. Ancient temples, places of worship, schools and libraries had been closed down and boarded up. Imperial signs had been torn down. Any monument from the past had been destroyed. The driver grunted, from the side of his mouth, that the graffiti had been daubed by the Red Guards – the young men and women in uniform whom they had seen marching about – to denote that the occupants were deemed to be 'Revisionists'[88] with bourgeois leanings. The vivid slogans were a stark warning to others.

At the end of a major road turning from a side street, the driver dropped them at a modest hotel booked for them by the China Travel Service. He promised that he would return to collect them after noon the following day. They checked into the Overseas Chinese Hotel, which was ostensibly reserved for foreigners. Unsurprisingly, due to the current political climate, the building – a throwback to the past, but now stripped of any hint of its history – was half empty. The rooms were plain and simple, but at least the showers had warm water, albeit

---

87 Khaki uniforms were a throwback to their parents' uniform from the 1949 revolution. Some original civil war uniforms were still being used as a badge of honour by the younger generation.

88 Persons wanting to revise the present order and revert to the past.

tinged with brown sediment from the rusty iron plumbing, to wash away the dust from their travels and to cleanse themselves of the day's ordeal. Frequent power cuts and shortages of basic, necessities such as soap, shampoo and other items they had taken for granted did not surprise them unduly, as they had been warned about them before they left Hong Kong. There they had stayed with Chun Rei, Chun Ji's younger sister, in a relative's apartment, and had been told of the difficulties they would face in China during the upheaval of the Cultural Revolution. But no warning could adequately prepare them for what they would encounter on this trip.

As soon as he lay down on the thin, lumpy mattress to try to get some rest, Chun Ji wondered why on earth, at the age of nearly seventy, he had agreed to this trip. Three weeks earlier, at the encouragement of his younger brother Chun Tileng in Liverpool and his nephews who were working at the family restaurant, he had been persuaded that he mustn't leave it any longer to see his homeland. Letters came from his family in Taishan, and it was pointed out that Chun Rei and his cousins would put him up. Despite it being a turbulent period in China, he decided that he had better not leave it too late. It was not the ideal time. *But when is?* he thought. Time would always be against him now that he was facing the autumn of his years. Therefore, he had little choice but to seize the moment.

He had chosen to take his second-oldest daughter Rose with him, as well as Sam, his next to youngest son. Rose had been corresponding with a prospective suitor in Hong Kong, introduced through family in Taishan. Daniel Lam was a university graduate, a couple of years older than Rose, whose family came from near Canton. He had impeccable credentials. Rose, like Eileen before her, had many suitors in England, but they were considered by the family to be totally unsuitable. Sam was on a gap year after technical college, so it was hoped that he too would meet someone suitable in Hong Kong. The teenager thought otherwise, but kept his counsel, thinking that it would be an adventure and an opportunity to see the Far East, as he and his sister had never left England before.

What finally decided the issue was when Will Chen, Chun Ji's son-in-law, offered to keep an eye on the restaurant full time, with Francis popping back at weekends. With his mind at rest, Chun Ji booked the flights for the 30th July for this momentous trip. After nearly half a century away, he hoped that he would not live to regret returning to China. As a responsible father and head of the Kwong Clan, he had a duty to fulfil. A tiring, precarious journey of over six thousand miles[89] from the opposite side of the world into the jaws of uncertainty would be a small price to pay to carry this out.

---

89 By air, as the crow flies. The distance from Hong Kong to Southampton by sea would be 10,884 nautical miles.

Chapter 35

HOMELAND

Dai Dune Chun, Taishan, China, 8ᵗʰ August 1966

NOT UNEXPECTEDLY, SHEER EXHAUSTION soon overcame the trio, so they had decided to stay put for the rest of the day. At the hotel desk, the sullen receptionist, unsmiling but eventually willing, managed to supply hot water from a thermos flask for them to make some tea. And, as biscuits and dried rice crackers were all that he could offer in the way of food, they had to delve into the rations they had brought with them which had been earmarked for the relatives.

After a restless night's sleep on old, sagging beds that had seen better days, the family rose early as shafts of light poured in through their windows with the early dawn. They were met with a bustle of noise in the street below as Taishan started to awaken. Chun Ji, now reasonably refreshed, was keen to explore the streets outside. Curious and excited, Rose and Sam quickly followed him out of the hotel lobby to be met by a cloudy sky; crisp and cold. There was a distinct bite in the air, which made their teeth chatter, as they were still dressed in the thin cotton clothes they had brought from England. Radio Peking was still broadcasting at full volume through a phalanx of loudspeakers dotted around the street.

'Let's find some breakfast at a street café!' announced their father with gusto.

Behind the hotel they found a narrow backstreet. Amid a row of stalls and shops preparing to open for the day was a simple eating place whose makeshift tables, covered in faded yellow oilcloth, spilled out into the street. Billows of steam spilled out of the kitchen from large, round pans the size of dustbins, in which was boiling a tangled mass of noodles and dumplings.

'That looks promising,' said Chun Ji, ushering his children inside.

As it was still early, only two other tables were occupied. They seemed like locals, who stared at the family with naked curiosity. Sam and Rose tactfully averted their eyes, but their father nodded in polite acknowledgement as they sat down. The proprietor came out of the kitchen, wiping the steam off his face with the edge of his apron. He was a short and bulbous man, balding, with hamster-like cheeks which failed to conceal his protruding front teeth gripping the stump of a cigarette. He ambled across to their table with a large pot of tea and, sweating profusely, asked them what they would like to eat.

'*Do Sun. Nee sik mut yeh ah?*' ('Morning. What would you like to eat?')

Chun Ji replied, '*Wun Tun mien. Tung moy Char Sui bow. Um gwoi sigh.*' ('Wonton pork dumplings with noodles and barbecued pork steamed buns, please.')

As it happened, that was all that was available; apart from the skewers of scorpions, roasted locusts and fried sow's uterus which he reluctantly turned down when his daughter pulled a horrified face on hearing of these gourmet delicacies.

Ravenous, the three of them gulped the food down. They agreed it was fresh and well cooked. More tea was served at no extra cost. Soon, with their stomachs quite full, they felt refreshed.

Well satisfied, Chun Ji gladly paid the bill, which he discovered was remarkably modest. Sam gasped in surprise as it was equivalent to one and a half English pounds sterling. The owner perfunctorily declined the tip that was proffered, as in modern China gratuities were to be discouraged. So, gratefully, they bought a box of steamed buns to take with them for the onward journey.

As they approached their hotel, they noticed a group of people stop and stare at them from across the street. They started to point and gesticulate in their direction. Suddenly, as if out of nowhere, a small crowd gathered and joined in. Immediately Chun Ji attempted to usher the children into the safety of the hotel. But they were prevented from doing so as more and more bystanders surrounded them. It was impossible to move. Various women started to prod Rose on the arm. At first it was with gentle curiosity, and then they started to giggle, pointing out that Rose was wearing a Western dress which exposed her knees and legs. Increasingly frightened, she started to redden. She clutched the box of buns closer to her, squashing the bag that they were in. Then the men started to taunt them. They demanded to know why Sam and his father were wearing bourgeois – Western – shirts and trousers. The situation, which had probably started out as good-natured banter, was getting out of hand. The atmosphere was becoming increasingly dangerous.

Just as they were being jostled by the increasing sea of people overflowing into the street, shouts rang out. A group of Red Guards had just turned the corner from a side street, and ran towards them. Alarmed, the family feared the worst, thinking that they were about to be taken away. Shouting and waving their arms angrily, the Red Guards quickly dispersed the crowd, telling them to go home or go about their business. One of the taller Guards, who appeared to be older than the rest – seemingly their leader – grabbed hold of Chun Ji firmly by the arm and pulled Rose and her brother into the safety of the hotel lobby,

'*Dai Gong Sing Bak. Gnaw do nee am gee!*' he offered breathlessly in perfect Taishanese dialect. ('Grand-Uncle Kwong, I am deeply sorry. Many apologies!')

Shocked and surprised, Chun Ji asked who he was.

Out of the sight of the others, the tall young man gave a slight bow in deference to the old man. 'You won't know me,' he said. 'I am a cousin-in-law of your nephew, the son of one of your brothers. I heard that you were going to be here before you travelled to the village. Look, I can't say any more now in front of the others, but later, maybe.'

By the time Chun Ji looked around, the young man had promptly disappeared to join the corps of Guards outside.

They heaved a massive sigh of relief. Chun Ji quickly told Rose and Sam that they must go to their rooms to pack their bags and then get some rest, as their driver would collect them sometime during the afternoon.

Shortly afterwards, the driver arrived to take them to the Kwong village of Dai Dune Chun, which was thirty miles south-east through the bowl of the valley, deep in the Pearl River Delta. It would take four hours or so due to the lack of made-up roads, and they were warned that they would have to navigate a maze of paddy fields, rivers and dykes using rudimentary dirt tracks.

Gradually, as the journey unfolded, a welcome gap in the overcast sky released a spurt of lazy sunshine that crowned the tops of the mountain range, which ran unbroken to the west as it skirted the belly of the valley as if escorting them home to the ancestral village. The countryside looked to Chun Ji's eyes, remarkably the same as it did when he had left as a young man. Heavily crowned ginkgo trees and unruly cypresses rigid with soil-caked trunks from the rich orange soil sprouted around the landscape in clumps. A lifetime ago, they were planted to protect the primitively furrowed fields for the farmers, much as they had in his younger days; though the oxen to plough the land and the water buffalo to toil knee deep in the muddy fields were now less in evidence, compared to then. Very few people were visible as they travelled through near-deserted hamlets and sparsely inhabited farmland. Groves of thickening bamboo on both sides of the track wafted in the breeze as the minivan swept by. Taking all things into account, it felt as if life here had stood still – frozen since the beginning of time.

It was early evening by the time they reached the entrance of Dai Dune Chun. A flurry of excitement rippled through Chun Ji's throat as he pointed out to his son and daughter the enormous, ancient arch looming above them. For centuries it had stood as the main entrance to and exit from the village. The ornate tiles bearing the name of the village, embedded in the face of the arch, had faded over years of blazing hot summers and freezing cold winters.

Then suddenly, with a jolt, crossing that particular spot brought back fresh memories of that fateful day in January forty-five years ago when he'd last left home, with his father saying… *'You have to go, my son. It is your duty as the eldest son. You have a duty to save the family from starvation.'*

Pressing his eyes with the backs of his knuckles, Chun Ji couldn't dislodge the vivid images he saw in front of him, as clear as yesterday. His father, stiff-backed and with receding grey at his temples, his brow furrowed as he stood unmoved, his hands hidden in the wide sleeves of his black tunic which fell to his ankles. They had not dared to reach out to each other in a show of familiarity. Chun Ji heard his father's last words ringing in his ears: *'It is an obligation of loyalty you must not question. China is being carved up by many foreign powers. Once again, I fear that war cannot be far away. Go now… so that one day the ancestral line will live on with you!'*

At that precise moment, the driver slammed on his brakes, causing the van to come to an abrupt stop. Repeatedly, he wrung his hands in a fulsome apology, saying that the family would have to walk the rest of the way as the unmade track of loose soil had turned to unforgiving mud due to the recent rain and the dykes overflowing. Chun Ji quickly shook his head to clear the picture from the past and braced himself.

Struggling with their luggage on their bicycles, the trio tramped along the track, weaving their way through fields of rice and surrounding banks of lush, vivid green watercress. Suddenly, as if materialising out of thin air like ghosts from another age, several locals sprang out of the fields to greet them, waving enthusiastically.

'Kwong Chun Ji! What took you so long to return to your homeland?' they shouted.

'*Nee ho ma, Gong Bak? Ho loi nee mang fan nee yuk kee!*' ('How are you, Uncle Kwong? It's been a long time since you returned home!')

Chun Ji returned a half-wave, slightly embarrassed, failing to recognise most of the men whom he had grown up with; although they seemed to recognise him.

As they approached the small square in the centre of the village, palls of thick woodsmoke from the houses spiralled upwards to fade into the open sky. Flocks of neurotic ducks and squawking geese fought for grains of rice and corn that had been scattered haphazardly across their path. Like high-pitched sirens, they screeched and honked from the back of their throats to warn of the approaching strangers. Apart from their being killed and eaten on special occasions, they doubled as valuable and vigilant sentries to raise the alarm. It was a practice that went back decades to protect the village from bandits on horseback from the mountains, renegade militia, and even marauding pirates from the coast. Hastily, Chun Ji explained this old tradition to his son and daughter, who immediately aimed their bicycles in a careful trajectory to avoid running over the squabbling fowl flapping dangerously in front of them.

Almost immediately, they came across a row of dwellings next to a swollen river, whose tributaries criss-crossed the dykes in the distance to irrigate the paddy fields. The surrounding marshlands glistened with dew, and there was an abundance of wildflowers in the distance. The village of Dai Dune Chun was a collection of dwellings and smallholdings that had sprung up over the centuries where the forebears of the Kwong Clan had migrated from the central plains to the south-western provinces some three centuries ago due to conflict and famine.

Most of the houses were flat-fronted and built in stone, blackened with soot from open fires over the ages. The first row was more substantial than the rest and overlooked the deep river which eventually spilled into the open sea some twenty miles away. Because of the prominent standing of the strand of the Kwongs that Chun Ji's forebears came from, and with some help from outside family funds, their terrace with its stone-built balconies occupied this coveted spot. From this, the most cherished position in the village, you could with favouring winds smell the salt air of the distant sea to the south, and wallow in the sunset that sank low over the mountains to the west.

At the water's edge, choked with banks of watercress and weeds, Chun Ji suddenly stopped in his tracks and paused for a moment or two with the frame of his bicycle resting against his hip. His son and daughter did the same. Abruptly, he spun on his heels with his back to the water and stared at the string of old houses, willing to bring the past to life. Gradually, even though the light began to fail, he started to recognise the old place; the surroundings of childhood familiarity where he had grown up. Ah, yes; how could he even *begin* to forget? It was here, amongst this collection of simple rural buildings, that Kwong Chun Ji was born a long time ago in 1898, during the reign of the Emperor Kwong Shui. And this was where his father, and his father before him, had been born, lived and died.

Apprehension and fear gripped him; it had been such a long time away. The layout of the streets and alleyways appeared to be about the same, and the vista across the river and the fields of rice remained unchanged even after all these years. The sights and smells were the same. Time did not alter that. Then he wondered whether he would recognise his family, and, more to the point, whether they would recognise him...

Chapter 36

THE ANCESTRAL HOME

L IKE A FIRE FANNED by the wind, the news of Chun Ji's homecoming spread quickly. His brothers came running out into the street in unison to welcome the return of their oldest brother.

'*Dai gwaw! Yee gar fan yuk kee!*' ('Senior brother! You have finally come home!')

You would think that, after all these years, they would greet each other with unbridled brotherly warmth – with the touch of a friendly hand, perhaps on the shoulder, or a gentle embrace of sorts. But this was not the way of Chinese families steeped in old traditions of formality. They had to remember that Chun Ji, being the eldest, was still the head of the clan, and as with their father before him, deferential distance had to be kept as a mark of respect for his seniority, and to maintain the status quo of the ancestral line.

Awkwardly, Chun Ji and his brothers stared at each other, nervously and self-consciously tugging at the cuffs of their sleeves.

'*Dai gwaw. Nee ho ma? Ho loi mo guin ah!*' exclaimed Chun Tin, the first brother. ('Senior brother, how, are you? It's been such a long time, not seeing you!')

They were about to offer a hand in greeting, but suddenly they dropped their arms to their sides in embarrassment. They felt like strangers which they were. Chun Ji offered a wry smile to Chun Tin, who would have been just seventeen when he left in 1921. His next brother, Chun Yee, had been twelve, and the youngest brother, Chun Tui, just four. It was a shock to think that even the latter, one of the youngest Kwong children, was now fifty years old. And how grey and wizened they all looked, due to years under the merciless summer sun and the harsh winter storms. Chun Ji gave them news of their youngest brother, Chun Tileng, who had now settled in England and was married with four children.

Soon, a crowd formed around them as the rest of the village spilled out of their houses. They were curious to witness the welcome return of the erstwhile prodigal son who had left as a young man and had now come back as an old man. Word had quickly got around that the oldest son of the late Kwong Loong Cheung Ham had returned. One by one, and then in their droves, the villagers had deserted their tasks in the fields or had rushed back from wherever they were to see Kwong Chun Ji – the stranger, the westernised blood relative, the head of the Kwongs who had travelled home after nearly half a century in an alien land on the other side of the world.

Rose and Sam hung back. Overwhelmed, they gripped their bicycles firmly. A few minutes later, the wives and children hurried out in front of their houses to be introduced to Kwong Chun Ji and his son and daughter whom they had never seen before.

Not long afterwards, Chun Ho, Chun Ji's sister who had been nineteen when he last saw her, came to join them. Tears of emotion welled up in her eyes, but she tried to hide them. She said that she had married not long after he had left home – just before their father had suddenly died. Her husband and their grown-up children lived in a neighbouring village, befitting of her husband's clan. She asked about their younger sister, Chun Rei, who had fled to Hong Kong some years ago, having suffered the loss of her only child and husband in the civil war.

'I must show my son and daughter my father's old house where I was born,' declared Chun Ji.

The crowd parted respectfully as he made his way to the house, which was in the middle of the first terrace. The door had been left wide open in anticipation of their visit. With trepidation, Chun Ji crossed the threshold into the cool darkness. Sam and Rose followed, not knowing what to expect. The brothers hovered near the entrance, keeping a tactful distance.

As Chun Ji stood in the bare entrance room, his eyes took a moment or two to adjust to the sudden change in light. The first thing that hit him was the cold air radiating from the rough, blood-red flagstones set in the raw soil. He gripped the open neck of his shirt around his throat. It was an ethereal feeling of déjà vu which he could not suppress. Memories suddenly came flooding back like ghosts. It seemed like only yesterday that he had left. Time has a way of cheating on you. He had come home at last to his father's home. He had come home to his childhood; the life he'd thought that he had left behind.

Looking through the gloom into the large, empty expanse of the kitchen, he stared at a blackened wok sitting nonchalantly on a soot-covered range fired by wood and shivered. It felt as if something cold had run down his spine. The blackened remnants of charcoal were still there, as though untouched by time. His mother's pots and cooking utensils, dented and stained by constant use, still stood all alone, seemingly abandoned beside the range, which was caked in cooking grease as it had always been.

Then suddenly, he could have sworn that he heard his mother, Fung Ting, calling him…

'Chun Ji, soi doi. Fie sik fan. Ho fie doong ah!' ('Chun Ji, young son. Quickly, eat! It will soon get cold!')

In the impenetrable darkness, she was standing there, next to the old wooden table on which were laid bamboo chopsticks and earthenware bowls. Her hands, gnarled from years of working in the fields, were placed impatiently on her hips. She was dressed in black from her neck to her sandals in a well-worn, high-collared tunic. Her hair was tied back in a severe bun. She looked wrinkled, tired and old before her time. She always had as far as he could remember.

He was just ten years old. He remembered the day well, for it was getting towards winter and the storms crossing the mountains had started to erupt with warning lightning. The date was the 14th November 1908. His father had come rushing into the house, breathless. He couldn't contain himself.

'I've just heard the news. A traveller from Taishan has returned and told the village elders that the old Emperor Kwong Shu has just died in the Forbidden City. The old Empress Dowager Tz'u-hsi, the power behind the Dragon Throne, has chosen his young nephew P'u-i as the new Emperor!'

'Bah! But he is just a baby. *He's barely three years old!*' retorted Fung Ting, aghast. 'Can you imagine it? Why?…Our eldest son, Chun Ji is *years* older than that boy who is now the ruler of all China!'

Standing rigidly in his deserted family home, Chun Ji hadn't yet uttered a word. He stared vacantly across the gloom, his eyes unblinking. Totally oblivious to the questioning looks from his family, he appeared rooted to where he stood.

After a prolonged silence, his brothers grew concerned, for they could have sworn that he had fallen into a trance. They thought he was suffering from exhaustion, so they gently shepherded him towards a chair in a corner of the room and brought him a sip of water. Brushing them aside, he shook his head violently to dispel the memories.

'I *must* pay my respects to our parents and our ancestors!' In the next room, again stark and empty with bare stone walls, stood a large, old wooden carving encased in red and black with gold lettering. Propped up high above them at mezzanine level, it could only be reached by climbing the ladder next to it. The carvings in black-and-gold calligraphy recorded a lengthy eulogy to the ancestors.

The brothers watched in awe as the elderly Chun Ji, like a fit young gazelle, swiftly tackled the ladder. Carefully, he placed food and wine at the foot of the shrine, then lit joss sticks in the tiny urn beside it. With his arms outstretched and his hands pressed together, he kowtowed from the waist three times in prayer to his ancestors. Following his example, his son and daughter did the same; but to them, being westernised, it didn't have the impact it had on their father.

In the corner of the room, against the flagstones, they then burnt ghost paper money in homage to the Land God, whose tiny, squat statue stood glaring at them with a cross-looking expression.

Rose whispered to her brother that they should go outside for some air whilst their father climbed the rough wooden stairs to see the bedroom where he was born. He recognised the old bed – a simple piece of furniture hewn out of dark rosewood, where three generations, including himself, as a baby had slept. Everything was exactly as he had left it forty-five years ago. Time had frozen. But, despite the protection from old linen sheets, a layer of dust had over time infiltrated the faded inlay on the camphor wood chest, and the damp had warped the bamboo cupboard with its painted rural figures. Only recently had there been glass in all the window frames, as for many years the houses in Dai Dune Chun hadn't had such a thing. Silently, he stared for a few minutes, and then nodded conspiratorially to his brothers, trying to invoke the past when they were all living there as children.

However, they would have been too young, or not even born, to remember their father's father, their grandfather, Biu Shu, who was born in 1843. Chun Ji was just eight years old when he died in 1906, but his grandfather had made a lasting impression on him, with extravagant tales of California, the gold rush and the building of the railroad across America. His grandfather had recounted the story of when his father, Wah Oi, had been lured by the promise of work in the port of Canton; then press-ganged by criminals who attacked him. Blinded by a sack thrown over his head and then knocked unconscious, Wah Oi, like many others, was sold and shipped in chains to California on a slave ship, forced to work on the railroad and in the gold mines for European slave owners, before killing his guards and making his escape.

Before he died, Biu Shu had reminded his young grandson that he had grown up during the Opium Wars between Britain and China, and had witnessed the depressing sight of gunboats sailing up the Pearl River to Canton. China had suffered an ignominious defeat, and the weakened Imperial Court, with its hapless Ch'ing Emperor, had ceded Hong Kong and its surrounding territories to Britain.

'I hope that one day you will live to see the return of our lands to China,' Chun Ji's grandfather said on his deathbed. 'I also hope that you will grow up to see the overthrow of the Ch'ing Emperors who have shackled us for centuries. And to witness an uprising by us – the peasant people – to make our motherland independent and strong as a tiger once more, and one day to take its rightful place in the world with its head held high, fearing no one!'

Suddenly, Chun Ji's reverie was broken. A noise erupted down below. Angry, raised voices could be heard. In one large stride, he stood at the top of the stairs and looked down towards the front door. The source of the disturbance was just outside in the street.

'What on earth is that?' he asked.

Chun Tin looked anxious. 'I think it's one of our local party cadres from the commune arguing with some of the strangers from the city who've been sent here by the authorities to live amongst us.'

There was a noisy attempt to barge into the house. The brothers quickly led Chun Ji out of the front entrance to be met by one of the commune leaders, who rapidly explained that the people were livid that the late Kwong Loong Cheung Ham's house had been kept virtually empty as a shrine, when habitable living space was at a premium. And, under the new Communist Party directive, all property should be shared equally by all.

'But, comrades, *wait*,' insisted Chun Tin, deliberately raising his hand, trying to placate the gathering crowd, who were becoming increasingly hostile. 'We, the permanent residents, must still be respectful to our visiting family who have travelled a long way from the other side of the world to see their ancestral home; the place where he – my brother was born!' Nervously, he added, 'And furthermore, we must be polite to those who have helped to build some of the dwellings in the village over the years, like Kwong Chun Ji here. He is head of the Kwong Clan in this part of the village, and he and his family have a *right* to stay in this house for the duration of their visit!' The effort of his speech made him sweat under his collar.

But his appeal fell on deaf ears. Angry mutterings could be heard: *'Anything associated with ancestors and the old order must be swept away!'*

From the midst of the crowd, someone shouted, 'Let's burn their wretched ancestral shrine! It has no place in the new China!'

Another voice screamed, *'They should be worshipping our venerable Chairman, not some ancient family ghost or worthless gods!'*

Helplessly, Chun Ji stared at the mob surrounding the doorway, his fists tightly clenched. His brother quietly drew him aside and tried to explain that, since the Cultural Revolution, many urban youths from privileged backgrounds had been banished to the rural villages such as theirs to be re-educated by working in the fields. It was a heady and volatile mix. City intellectuals with Western leanings and even recidivists were also sent to mend their ways, and to learn from the workers and farmers in the countryside and the mountainous regions of China. It was thought that across the country, seventeen million young men were re-educated in this manner. In various parts of the country, it was rumoured that at the start of the revolution, some who refused to change, were butchered in clashes with some of the Red Guards who had got out of hand. Others were thrown into prison. There were even ugly rumours that in some places incidents of cannibalism had taken place.

However, this did not unduly frighten Chun Ji or cut much ice with him. He had seen sights worse than these: such as people dying from starvation – their bellies bloated, (leading to some poor wretches trying in vain to chew their own flesh in their madness); street beheadings and gratuitous torture, when growing up in the chaos following of the fall of the last of the Manchu Emperors in 1912 and with the hostilities that followed.

Meanwhile, like a resurgent tidal wave, a hardy core of agitators pushed forward from the back of the crowd and again tried to force their way into the house. Forming a barricade, the brothers stood resolutely across the threshold. Then, just as the situation was getting out of control, the crowd suddenly started to disperse, almost as quickly as they had gathered.

'*What's happening?*' asked Chun Yee, startled.

When they looked across the road bridging the river dyke, a tall youth and a girl – in Red Guard uniforms – were running towards them. They had arrived in a mud-splattered old jeep driven by a soldier from the PLA who, they later discovered, happened to be off duty and was travelling back to his village nearby. Straight away, Chun Ji recognised one of the guards as the young man who had earlier saved them from the jeering crowd outside their hotel in Taishan. There was a fierce exchange of words between the commune representatives and the Guards to defuse the stand-off. A compromise was struck, whereby it was reluctantly agreed that the visitors from the West could stay at their ancestral home for the duration of their visit, but the house would be requisitioned for communal use immediately afterwards. An incriminatory mark in red paint was swiftly daubed on the outside of the front door by one of the belligerent cadres, to sardonic applause.

Chun Ji nodded gratefully towards the young Red Guard for saving them yet again. But the young man completely ignored him, as though they had never met before. Just as the jeep had arrived out of the blue like a spiritual visitation, so it quickly disappeared into the distance in a thick plume of smoke, completely covering its occupants in an impenetrable cloud of dust.

The crowd drifted away, reluctantly dragging their feet. A rumbling of discontent could still be heard. With sullen faces, they spat at the ground, scowling. A crescendo of fury began to swell.

'*Let's join your son and daughter and tell them what's happening,*' suggested Chun Tui.

Subdued and deep in thought, like an automaton, Chun Ji followed his brothers towards their homes at the end of the terrace, as a family meal had been arranged at Chun Tin's house. He mulled over what had happened to the old China he had left all those years ago, now replaced by the new, which was radical and completely alien to him. How would his father have viewed modern life in new China? Chun Ji thought that Kwong Loong Cheung Ham and his forefathers before him must surely be turning in their graves.

Amongst the young Mao's achievements, the sweeping away of the Four Olds – old habits, old customs, old culture and old ideas – during the Cultural Revolution had taken hold and had a profound effect on the Chinese way of thinking. If it had drastically altered the way of life in the obscure and humble village of Dai Dune Chun, and in Taishan, then what must it be like in the other major towns and cities throughout China?

He shook his head in sheer disbelief and tried to suppress his anger at what might have been.

I have seen through my father's eyes,
Those rampart barrels of gunpowder fire,
Beneath the Red Flag that flew higher and higher.
And all the sacred makings of a nation once noble,
Swallowed up in days what took centuries to build.
They scattered the ashes of a thousand years.

I have heard through my father's eyes,
A witness seen as he stood alert to see,
That Little Red Book he was forced to read.
Miles across borders he left as a dutiful young man.
Some forty-odd years passed before he returned.
Felt mocked as a stranger to trespass the shore.

I remember through my father's eyes,
Startled cries from the people as they ran through fields.
'What took you so long to return to your homeland?'
'Alone years ago, I left by slow seas.'

But now I return via the lightning sky.'
Nothing has changed. Everything's the same as it was.
But through all things transmuted, a mammoth has changed.

I have sensed through my father's eyes,
The path carved out by his fathers before him,
To seek out a new life by crossing oceans and seas,
But the forebears returned, bearing gifts from the past.
Forced by starvation and evil despots that war,
Fire, brimstone and burning with upheaval running amok.

And so, Kwong Chun Ji tried desperately to see the new China through his father's eyes. But whichever way he turned, it was still anathema to him. Abject despair overwhelmed him, and there was very little he could do about it.

Chapter 37

STARK REALITY

A T THE WESTERN END of the village, as the dying sun began to set behind the mountain range, lending it a golden glow, the whole of the Kwong family, with the brothers, their wives and their many children, crammed inside Chun Yee's house for a celebratory meal. It was supposed to be a joyous occasion, with their oldest brother coming home at last. It was something that they had been waiting years for. But the atmosphere was soured by what had just happened outside their father's house.

Chun Tin said that, in other, less austere times, on such a momentous occasion as this, Chun Ji, as head of the family clan, would traditionally be expected to pay for the whole village to celebrate with a feast. Rose and Sam rolled their eyes in horror after hearing how much their father had already sacrificed to pay for this trip, and all the money he had sent home over the years.

Frantically, Chun Ji shook his head. 'This isn't the time to *even* consider such a thing, with all these changes going on!'

'I have to tell you that everything in the towns and villages has changed out of all recognition over the years. You wouldn't believe what has happened,' offered Chun Yee. He picked at his rice bowl, chewing thoughtfully. 'The new generation aren't as loyal as they were in the olden days when the respected elders ruled the families. Today, *no one* dares to talk about the past for fear of reprisals and of being reported to the authorities.'

Out of the corner of his mouth, Chun Tui dropped his voice to a whisper. 'We must tell you that, earlier this year, even our own brother was accused of deserting the peasants for the intellectual classes.'

Chun Tin shifted uncomfortably in his seat, reddening as the family directed their gaze across the table.

His wife tapped a warning finger across her ear. 'Careful. The very air around us has ears! Spies are everywhere. *You could be betrayed for a single grain of rice!*' Under her breath, she hissed, 'Even you, brother Chun Ji, a proletarian once, now turned bourgeois, could be arrested at any time for saying something fairly innocuous, or if it was discovered that you are at heart a Western capitalist. I mean; just look at you – openly wearing European-style clothes and flaunting a gold Swiss watch!'

Open-mouthed, like fish gulping for air, Sam and his sister stared blankly at their aunt and trembled. Their father merely plucked at his shirt in defiance, shrugging helplessly.

In the streets throughout the village, Radio Peking could still be heard. Unnervingly, it was as though the ears and eyes of the government were permanently alert, their all-pervading propaganda refusing to abate for one single moment.

There was a moment's hesitation.

'At the start of the Cultural Revolution earlier this year,' whispered Chun Tui, 'there was a sudden madness that affected everyone. Schools and colleges were forced to close on government directives. Teachers, school administrators, writers, artists, musicians and in fact anyone considered to be intellectuals or Revisionists were targeted, humiliated and beaten. Prominent individuals in the community were betrayed. Many were even murdered, for no other reason than that they had been born into a different stratum to others. The elderly were attacked because of their intransigent and traditional views. Pupil turned against teacher; neighbour against neighbour. Even members of families turned on one another. Our own brother, Chun Tin, was along with many others taken away by the Red Guards during the night, and then paraded through the city of Taishan to be mocked, vilified and then punished by the people. It was relentless!'

The other brother, Chun Yee, joined in. 'He was forced to wear a large, pointed dunce's hat, and a placard was hung around his neck, denouncing him! Roped by the ankle to the midriff, he was pushed along the street, jostled, kicked and spat at by a jeering mob. The crowds screamed at him, baying for blood. At the top of their voices, his faults, now laid bare, were repeatedly criticised, forcing him to renounce his past and to beg on his knees to be re-educated.'

Lost in thought, Chun Tin could only stare at the floor, looking disconsolate, shaking uncontrollably.

His wife cried, 'It was terrible. He was betrayed by a neighbour and put on the list!

'*What?! Do you mean by one of our kinsmen here?*'

They all shook their heads helplessly.

Sam started to shuffle uncomfortably in his chair. He could not believe the treachery... and all because his uncle happened to be a schoolteacher – teaching history as part of the curriculum!

Chun Tin's wife started to tremble, whispering from the side of her mouth. 'The influence of the Denunciation Committees has infiltrated everywhere, like cancerous tentacles that can suck the very life out of you. We, as a family must be extremely careful with the money you have sent us from the West. Some jealous members of the village would report us for accepting tainted bourgeois money! Some even want a secret share of it – the vile hypocrites!' – her self-righteousness rapidly turning to outright indignation.

'But wait a minute,' protested Chun Ji vehemently. '*If I hadn't sent you money over the years, you all would've starved to death!*'

Reluctantly, his brothers nodded sheepishly.

'And *another* thing,' said Chun Ji. 'What happened to the several acres of rice fields our father left us? And the square of land behind the village, which we used for grazing and for growing vegetables?'

For a minute or so, he was met with a stony silence.

Chun Tin looked wearily at his older brother. Lowering his gaze, he slowly ambled around the room, deep in thought. 'Ten years ago, the Land Reform Committee colluded with the Party Peasants Committee and forced us to agree to divide the land amongst the villagers. From that day onwards, we were reviled and labelled as parasitic landowners!'

'*Shush! Lower your voice!*' warned Chun Tui. He covered his mouth with his hand. 'All of us, including some of our cousins, were herded into the village square. We were slapped and beaten, and we were forced to confess our sins for owning more land and houses than some of our neighbours! Two of the elders were shot dead for refusing to give up their plots of land. Another was smashed to death by a shovel. It wasn't as if we were unscrupulous, *rich* landlords, like those in our ancestors' time. But nevertheless, it was still a terrifying ordeal!'

The wives suppressed an agonised cry, remembering what they had endured. Chun Tin and Chun Yee added that they were glad that their eldest sons, Kat Moon and Yau Chin, had already left China to join Chun Ji's business in the West, as indeed had their youngest brother, Chun Tileng, many years before.

After their meal, and after much conversation had been exchanged about the families, nightfall loomed, and Sam and his father retired to the ancestral home. Rose stayed with one of the aunts and the rest of the womenfolk. They had a restless night as the government broadcasts continued at full blast during the early hours, making sleep virtually impossible.

Early the following morning, shortly after sunrise, Chun Ji gathered his son and daughter together and they were taken to the family tombs some ten miles away to the west. It was still misty, but damp and humid with a sheet of drizzle which began to fall in earnest by the time their driver arrived to collect them.

Climbing the mountain, escorted by his three brothers, proved no small task for Chun Ji, bearing in mind their senior ages, but determination to reach the peak spurred him on.

'Our parents are near the top with our forefathers,' said Chun Yee confidently. He pointed sharply upwards to encourage Rose and Sam, who looked dismayed at the hostile terrain facing them.

If their father was concerned, he did not show it. Tackling the path which zigzagged along the crude terraces that had been hacked out of the side of the mountain by families and visitors over the years, Chun Ji forged enthusiastically ahead at a pace which belied his age. His steps didn't appear to falter. It seemed like a lifetime ago when, as a young boy, he had been taken by his parents to pay his respects to their forebears in the ancestral graves. Over centuries, the hungry silence of the highest peak of the mountain had claimed their dead. They were buried with their feet pointing down to earth so that their heads were higher than their bodies and they would be closer to heaven in the afterlife.

Returning now as an old man, he was desperate to see the resting place of his parents, whom he last saw alive when they waved him off from the village nearly half a century ago. He clambered over the terrain at speed, with total disregard for his own safety. Over jagged, lichen-covered rocks and rampant, dense vegetation that snapped and snagged relentlessly at his ankles he went. But he didn't seem to notice or even care.

The others followed in his wake, breathing hard in the increasingly rarefied air. At a small grassy knoll, beside the roots of an old, gnarled tree, they stopped to gather their breath. Apart from the crunch of their footfalls and the intermittent swishing of the branches they pushed aside with knives and sticks, the silence was profound and overbearing. Rose had remarked to Sam that, strangely, there was not even a bird singing or an insect rustling in the undergrowth, until a slimy grass snake happened to slither soundlessly over her brother's foot.

'Hurry up, you slowcoaches!' shouted Sam, as he scrambled sure-footedly a few paces behind his father. Just then, a bleak patch of watery sunshine broke through, casting long shadows across their paths. They hurried on.

Chun Ji was the first to reach the family burial ground. As if by instinct, he found his father's grave, next to his mother's. Immediately, he fell to his knees, staring silently at the burnt orange earth beneath the mossy coating clinging to the side of the headstone. Solemnly, he caressed the raw earth, pinching a morsel of it between his fingers to raise it affectionately to his lips. He tried to imagine that part of his parents' earthly remains had integrated as carbon dust, now indivisible with the soil. This was the closest he would get to touching them. There was an eerie silence as a sombre dark cloud suddenly passed by, giving a sudden coldness to the air around him.

Without a word, his left hand gripped the top of the headstone, as if for support. Then, reverently, he slowly traced the inscription of his father's name with the fingers of his right hand.

Kwong Loong Cheung Ham. Born 25th day of the 7th month 1875 in the year of Yuet Hoi Nin, in the reign of Emperor Kwong Shui, and died on the 16th day of the 12th month 1923 in the year of Kwai Hoi Nin.[90]

Chun Yee signalled, with a cautionary wave of a hand behind his back, for the others not to follow just yet so as to allow Chun Ji time to himself at the graveside.

A few paces to his right, Chun Ji shuffled on his knees to his mother's grave and solicitously carried out the same ritual. He traced his mother's inscription on the gravestone.

Fung[91] Ting Sei, born 28th day of the 9th month 1878 in the year Mow Yun Nin in the reign of Emperor Kwong Shui, and died on the 27th day of the 1st month 1947.

Then, as if a foggy mist had suddenly descended in a curtain in front of his eyes, it all came back to him. His mother's final letter in December 1946:

---

90   *Nin* = year.
91   *Fung* = maiden name.

"I have grown weak over the days, so I fear that there is not much time left. A quarter of a century has passed since you left your home in Taishan. Each year we waited patiently for news that you would return to visit us, before I grew too old. Now I fear it will be too late...

I ask from you, my son, these last requests. When you do return, please attend your father's and my grave at the ancestral burial ground on the mountain, light joss sticks and pay your respects to us and to your ancestors, in the hope that you will meet us again one day..."

Try as he might, he could not stem the tears that fell from his eyes. Openly, he wept. Deliberately, he then turned his back on his family so that they could not witness this escape of emotion. But he failed to hide it from his daughter, who had already seen this outpouring of grief that had been suppressed for all those years. Racked with guilt that he had failed to return home earlier to see his parents alive, he was inconsolable. Feeling for her father, she was overwhelmed with a desperate and sympathetic sadness. Giving a nervous cough, she cleared her throat and tactfully averted her eyes.

From a bag handed to him by his brothers, Chun Ji carefully placed offerings of food and wine at his parents' graves. Then, lighting joss sticks clenched flat in the palms of his hands, he kowtowed low three times to each of his parents in turn, offering a silent prayer and an apology for being too late to see them in this earthly life but promising them that he would meet them again in the afterlife. His son and daughter followed suit. Then it was the turn of the three brothers to pay their respects to their parents.

After a pause, which seemed like an eternity, Chun Tin led them to a spot nearby. It was hidden by a dense thicket of shrubs that had overgrown over the years where the thickening bamboo had multiplied out of control. The air smelled heavy, dank and cloying. Abruptly, Chun Tin stopped in his tracks, appearing agitated and evasive. For some reason there was a distinct reluctance to show his elder brother where the rest of the ancestors were entombed.

A quizzical look crossed Chun Ji's face. Due to the overgrowth and overhang, it was difficult to see the graves of their paternal grandfather and great-grandfather – until he lost his footing and stumbled. Looking down at his feet, he noticed pieces of old headstone which appeared to have been broken and scattered, half buried, across the surface of the earth. Thinking that it was due to natural decay through the passage of years, he bent down and carefully picked up two of the fragments that had become entangled in the undergrowth.

To get a better look, he held up one of the pieces to the shaft of light that shimmered reluctantly through the branches overhead. The stone was heavy in the palm of his hand. It was damp and porous, and the surface was covered in differing shades of brown and khaki. Though encrusted with verdant spots of lichen and clinging moss, he turned it over and, with the tip of his finger, traced some letters that were covered in mustard-yellow algae. Then with some difficulty he managed to make out the letters 'B' and 'S', but the rest of the word had been snapped off from the jagged stone edge. He scratched his head, puzzled, until his brother snatched the other piece from his hand and showed him some residual fragments of numbers: *18 – 3*. It then struck him that he was standing at the foot of the grave of his grandfather Biu Shu, who had been born in 1843, the Year of the Hare.

'*What's happened here?*' he demanded.

His brothers caught him up and surrounded him protectively. 'Look. It's better if you don't look too closely,' they said solemnly in an attempt to spare his feelings. They began to choke on their words, not daring to look him in the eye. 'Our ancestors' graves have been dug up and desecrated by some of the young Guards. Anything of value has been stolen by grave robbers. Even some remnants of old skeletons have been crushed and scattered.'

'*But why?!*'

'It's an instruction from the party: that the old, the ancient should all be destroyed as they remind them and the Chinese people of the country's wilful and decadent past!'

As his eyes swept around him, Chun Ji noticed that the headstones had been attacked – kicked over, or uprooted at the base, slogans daubed in paint all over them, with cynical references to the past. The stone marking his great-grandfather Wah Oi's grave had been smashed into small fragments. The only reference left was that he had been born in 1821, the Year of the Snake.

Riven with anger, Chun Ji started to shake. He couldn't help it. Then he doubled over and fell onto his front, his face inches from an open grave with its churned-up soil. 'But why?' he wailed. 'Why on earth was this allowed to happen?' He started to beat the side of his head with his bunched-up fist.

His brothers stared at the sky, averting their eyes, gesturing helplessly.

'And what has happened to the graves of one of our greatest, great-grandfather Yip Gee Doo, and his father before him, our most revered ancestor, Ming Jid Doo, whose tomb was laid here in 1709?' asked Chun Ji, increasingly distraught. 'Why is this vandalism going on unchecked in our homeland today? And why such venomous hatred for the very thread that connects us to our ancestors, whose past shaped our lives and moulded us in the present? *Can't they see that if we obliterate the past, we'd have no future?!* If our father knew what was happening, he would be screaming in his grave!'

Seething with outrage, he already knew why it was happening, but not the logic or reason behind it. But what could he – a lone voice do – but to rage impotently against it? Since returning home, he had already witnessed wholesale, irreversible changes in this new China. Certain landmarks from his boyhood had already been flattened. He felt that he could, with copious persuasion, cope with that in the name of progress. But before he set off from England to visit his ancestral home, he had not expected to see such radical upheaval in *every* aspect of Chinese life.

The wise would have cautioned him not to expect too much; but to embrace and to accept that the hurried and dispassionate passing of almost half a century would not have left life unchanged since he had left. Try as he might, he could *never* recreate the past, or return to it, for whatever sentimental reasons were running through his mind. Moreover, he questioned whether it would have made any difference to his attitude today if he had never left all those years ago. Would he, like his siblings, have been more immune to the seismic changes around him? Countless travellers before him would have had to confront the shock of fundamental changes that had taken place in their absence from their childhood home; especially after such a long time away, and furthermore, having been living on a completely different continent and with a totally different culture.

His brothers, especially the younger ones such as Chun Tui, who had grown up under Mao's revolution, questioned whether it was *all that idyllic,* having been born and grown up during the dynasty of the Manchu Emperors. Under the Imperial Rule, with its unbridled wealth and privilege dictated from the Dragon Throne in the Forbidden City, their father and their forefathers before him would have suffered the burden of heavy taxes meted out on the peasant population. Constantly, they lived in fear under the oppression by unscrupulous landowners, who owned and treated them like worthless chattels, with wives and daughters forcibly taken in lieu of rent arrears and sold into slavery. Their womenfolk would have had no rights whatsoever; not even allowed to utter a single word in their defence. Then there was the constant threat of starvation, the lawlessness, homelessness, rampant disease, lack of medical help, premature death and so on. Moreover, due to the weak and corrupt Imperial Court, they were under continual danger from armed insurrection among the warlords and renegade militia, as well as being subject to the controls and dictates from the foreign powers which had colonised their major cities and ports, such as Peking, Canton, Nanking, Shanghai and Hong Kong.

But Chun Ji felt like a minute creature swimming hopelessly against a roaring tide. Fight as hard as he might, he was drowning slowly in a sea change that was out of control. He was tempted to spit on the soil in protest but did not dare out of respect for the dead.

And so, with heavy hearts, the brothers gathered the family together and started to make the descent. Once at the foot of the mountain, reluctantly, Chun Ji looked upwards towards the peak for the last time. Then, impatiently, he ushered his children and his brothers into the minivan and their driver quickly drove them away from the site, refusing to look back.

I have cried through my father's eyes,
What once stirred a proud nation now destroying itself;
Ancient texts, art, history, even culture, all burnt to the ground.
Individual clothing now banished, mass uniform enforced.
Poisonous gossip betraying family – even a father and son.
It's an edict that's unshakeable, that came from the rule.

I have wished through my father's eyes,
That things could have worked out differently, history to change.
Yet death and starved strife were always part of this land.
Separate nations developed through vast mountains and valleys.
Impregnable passes formed barriers to a language unborn.
Scared of all that was foreign, became abhorrent to them.

I have hoped through my father's eyes,
The frank fear in their faces will eventually erase.
The Guards in their madness will come to their senses.
That wilful destruction, like a disease, would burn itself out.
He had hoped that it would be a passage – fluid in time.
He warned, 'Be patient and be tolerant.' But for him it was too late.

Chapter 38

HONG KONG – DOORWAY TO THE DECADENT WEST

18th August 1966

IT WAS CHUN JI's original intention to spend thirty days or so in his ancestral village with his siblings. But after ten days, he felt that he had seen enough. The taste of nostalgia and visiting the past had brought disappointment and sadness in equal measure. The precious image he had retained of his childhood, terse and imperfect though it had been in reality had been shattered. The innocence and happiness of his memories of growing up in old China had been destroyed within days of returning to his homeland. To him, the new China felt like another world, hostile and alien. Disillusionment having set in, he and his children had rapidly grown restive. They longed to return to the simple comforts they were used to in Europe. Hong Kong was the welcoming and nearby doorway to the so-called 'decadent West'. But Chun Ji didn't dare to share these thoughts in so many words as he bid his brothers goodbye at the exit from the village. Hovering self-consciously under the archway, they shuffled awkwardly, wondering what to say.

'*Dai Lo. Sun nin, wah jek, nee fan yuk kee mah?*' ('Senior brother. Perhaps you'll return home to visit us next year?')

'I really can't say when I will be able to return. Try to understand that I've been away far too long. Circumstances have changed. *Even I have changed,*' he admitted in a moment of weakness. He tried not to hurt their feelings. But how could they possibly understand the gulf of cultural, social and economic enormity that stood between their lives and that of their eldest brother? What he had previously had in common with them seemed a lifetime away. In truth, they were complete strangers. Nothing much was left: only the bond of blood and the ancestral thread that held their family name remained. It was tenuous at most. Was it enough to keep him bound to them forever, until he or they died?

On feeling their disquiet, the driver, without a word, collected them as arranged to drive them back to the port of Macao. Quickly and gratefully, the Kwong Chun Ji family slid in across the seats of the van. This time, without the bicycles and bedding they had brought with them, they had little luggage compared to when they had first arrived in China. Apart from the clothes on their backs, they had left virtually everything with their relatives. Chun Ji insisted that his brothers needed these things more than they did, and that clothes, toiletries, writing paper, pens and so on could be quickly replaced once back in Hong Kong. As they drove away from Dai Dune Chun for the last time, the air grew heavy and oppressive under a blanket of stagnant cloud. The humidity had returned with a vengeance. It was similar, to that which had plagued them when they first arrived. Beads of perspiration broke out on the old man's brow. Apart from the weather, relief and anxiety must have played a part in that.

The driver said that he would take them directly to the border at Zhuhai from where they had entered ten days ago. He would leave them at the same place by the roadside next to the semi-rural smallholdings where they had previously made their rendezvous. From there they could walk to the border which they could see in the distance.

As dusk began to fall, the air started to cool rapidly, and the family pulled their jackets up around their necks for some extra warmth.

Not long afterwards, the enormous, grey, corrugated iron shed, now so familiar to them, loomed across their path like a vast obstacle to the West. It felt impregnable. The stark interview space inside the claustrophobic shed was just the same as when they first came to China, except they had to enter via a door at the back of the shed. It was savagely kicked open by a uniformed immigration official and a member of the PLA, who nodded expressionless towards an interview table with a jerk of the head. At the table, their papers were painstakingly scrutinised page by page, which added to their anxiety. With nervous humour, Sam mouthed to his sister, *'They'd better let us out of here; otherwise, I'll yell for the Brits!'*

Shortly afterwards, their father was handed a copy of Mao's Little Red Book. In a trembling voice, he read out excerpts from selected quotations from the thoughts of Mao Zedong, under the censorious eye of the Chinese officials:

"The Revolution and the recognition of class struggle are necessary for peasants of the Chinese people to overcome both domestic and foreign enemy elements... Socialism must be developed in China... it is important to unite with the middle mass of peasants and to educate them on the failings of capitalism..."

How convincingly he carried it out was hard to say, for the inscrutable stare of the officials barely penetrated the impassive look on his face.

Then it was the turn of his son and daughter to read their version in English. Holding his breath, their father hoped that they would not recite the same chapter, **On Class Struggle,** facetiously; otherwise, they could all be thrown into prison for insulting Chairman Mao.

Abruptly, with a curt wave of the hand, they were then summarily dismissed and shown through a door next to the front entrance.

There was an audible gasp of relief when they eventually left this section of the Chinese mainland. They exited through the barrier gate of no man's land and entered Portas do Cerco to reach the ferry on the Portuguese side. 'The East is Red', from Radio Peking, faded in the distance as they hurried across the bridge that connected the two countries. Never before had they been so overjoyed to see the Portuguese flag fluttering over the port buildings a short way ahead of them. They just managed to catch the overnight ferry to Hong Kong. Overcome with fatigue, they dozed restlessly in their seats.

When they reached her apartment, Aunt Chun Rei was relieved and happy to see them. Over breakfast, she wanted to catch up on all the news of the family left in Dai Dune Chun. And had her brother, whom she thought had aged visibly since his visit, manage to pay his respects to their parents and their ancestors? And furthermore, what...?

Wearily, Chun Ji slumped down in his chair. He gripped the edge of the table distractedly, his normally irascible manner completely deflated. A sad and haunted look fell across his face.

'There's such a lot to say. Really, I don't know how to start. But you wouldn't recognise our homeland anymore. I must tell you that *everything* has changed out of all recognition since we left. And, what's more, the people and...'

Part VII

1967 – 1970

Chapter 39

THE SUMMER OF LOVE (A CHINESE WEDDING, HONG KONG, 13TH MAY)

1967

O N THE 27TH JANUARY 1967, the UK, the Soviet Union and the United States signed a historic Outer Space Treaty setting out the protocols for the non-military exploration of space. Ten days later, the Soviet Premier Alexei Kosygin arrived in Britain for an eight-day State visit, during which he met the Queen. Was this a sign that the Cold War between the Eastern and Western Blocs was at last beginning to thaw?

In May, the first British-designed satellite, *Ariel 3*, was successfully launched into space. Not long afterwards, in the Middle East, the fragile peace collapsed after President Nasser of Egypt expelled the United Nations peacekeeping force (UNEF) from the Sinai Peninsula which bordered onto Israel. He then closed the Straits of Tiran, the entrance to the Gulf of Aqaba to Israeli shipping. On the 5th June, Israel went to war against Egypt, who had an alliance with Jordan, Syria and Iraq. This became known as the Six-Day War, in which Egypt and its Arab Alliance suffered an ignominious and heavy defeat. Israel captured the Gaza Strip and the Sinai Desert from Egypt, the Golan Heights from Syria, and the West Bank and East Jerusalem from Jordan. Fearing another explosive conflagration in the Middle East that would involve the superpowers, the international community held its breath.

Then, on the 17ᵗʰ June, China rocked the world by exploding its first hydrogen bomb.

It was against this turbulent backdrop of world events that dominated the year of '67; so therefore, could that year, be rightfully called the legendary 'Summer of Love?'[92] Was this wishful thinking? We shall have to wait and see.

As luck would have it, towards the end of April, I had found a small mews house in Paddington which I felt I could afford to buy on mortgage. Emboldened, and in a state of excitement over an evening meal at an Italian restaurant which opened out over a tiny Juliet balcony onto the Fulham Road, I proposed to Caroline. As luck would have it, a lone guitarist serenaded us at our table with an off-key rendition of 'That's Amore'. In the circumstances, with the eyes of the other bemused diners bearing down on us, Caroline could hardly turn me down!

We immediately telephoned her parents in Godmanchester for permission to marry. Sadly, her father Charles had been ill for some time, so he was unable to come to the phone; but two days later, I received a letter from Mary, her mother, saying how extremely happy they were, and that Charles had given us his blessing. I was over the moon. Then, suddenly, a dreadful thought crossed my mind. How was I going to broach the subject with my father? Pushing the problem to the back of my mind, I intended to cross that bridge later, when I needed to. I consoled myself with the fact that he and the family were preoccupied with the events in Hong Kong, where Rose would soon be getting married in an enormous traditional celebration that would

---

92 Coined after a social phenomenon whereby, in the summer of 1967, up to one hundred thousand people – mainly the young – converged on San Francisco's Haight-Ashbury district, sporting hippy fashions in psychedelic patterns and colours, and wearing their long hair beatnik style. They espoused love and peace, and railed against the establishment and convention, whilst protesting against the escalating Vietnam War. Drugs such as hash and LSD were common currency. Rock bands such as Jefferson Airplane and The Byrds, and artists like Jimi Hendrix and Janis Joplin, entertained the masses. The flower-power hippy movement, with its 'be in and drop out' message, spread across the USA, Canada and Europe.

last for days. Because of what was happening on both sides of the world, there was going to be an awful lot of explaining to do to both sets of family.

It was well into March when my mother received the family's formal wedding invitation from Hong Kong. Mailed in a large red envelope together with a lucky cake, and decorated with gold 'double happiness' characters, like those inscribed on the traditional Hongbao (red packet) in which money is gifted during weddings, birthdays, Chinese New Year, etc., the card formally announced that Rose was to be married to Daniel Lam. In keeping with tradition, a dowry list had been prepared by the bride's family.

Most of us couldn't attend, but Eileen was determined to fly out to support her sister. I read Sam's letter all about it with jaw-dropping incredulity.

Lai Chi Kok Road
Kowloon
Hong Kong
20th May 1967

Dear family,
   You may or may not know that Rose was married to Daniel Lam on Friday the 13th May (believe it or not, this day is considered lucky in the Chinese calendar). We were fortunate in having Uncle Kit Siang (Mother's brother) and his wife flying in from Borneo to join us. They managed to bring Mother's aged mother, Moy Gwut Kwai – a tiny old lady in her mid eighties, who wobbled about like a large owl; especially with her oversized horn-rimmed glasses over her birdlike frame. It was the first time that Father had met Mother's family, the Chows, so it was a little awkward to say the least. We must remember that Mother left the Chow family home over thirty years ago as a teenager to marry Father by proxy during her stay with the Kwong family in their ancestral village.

Eileen also managed to arrive from England in time. Luckily, there was enough room to put her up in the flat that Father had bought in the Lai Chi Kok Road shortly after returning from China. It was here, in the dusty, old-fashioned offices of the government registry, full of mahogany and worn leather seats, that the blood families assembled for the declaration of vows and to 'tie the knot'. It was a small wedding party, with Aunt Chun Rei (who actually introduced Daniel to Rose via relatives in the first place!) and one of Daniel's brothers, before he decided to move to the States to join his mother and the rest of their family.

I know that all of you would have wished upon wish that you could have been at our sister's side to witness our first family wedding which had been welcomed with open arms and tacitly sanctioned by our parents, but unfortunately, circumstances and logistics didn't allow it. I assume that invitations were sent to Father's family in China, but of course they are prevented from travelling, even if they had the financial means to do so. A cousin – Ah-Ming, who is a daughter of Father's second brother, Chun Yee (who is still living in China) – managed to turn up with her husband as they live in Hong Kong, working as pharmacists. Luckily, Uncle Chun Tileng, Father's youngest brother, and his wife flew in from Merseyside to attend the wedding, which made Father a bit happier.

You would have been fascinated by the celebration that followed. The banquet was full of extravagant rituals – the setting – off, of firecrackers, exotic tea ceremonies and the playing of Mah-jong – for the entertainment of the guests, which went on and on for days. God knows how much it cost Father. Everyone I meet here thinks that he is filthy rich!

In keeping with Chinese tradition, on the morning of the first day of the wedding banquet, Daniel, the groom, had to travel to Father's family home (our flat in Hong Kong), escorted by his groomsmen, to collect Rose, his bride. The door was barred, so he had to shout, then rattle and bang on it to gain entry to claim her. Tasks to demonstrate their determined endeavour were set for the groom and groomsmen, such as transferring black seaweed from mouth to mouth, and eating spoons full of raw green beans. It was a hilarious sight. Blocking his way were Rose's bridesmaid Eileen and two female friends who demanded bribes of red envelopes of money!

Only then, after bowing formally to Father and Aunt Chun Rei, did Rose agree to accompany her new husband to the banquet, which was held in a gigantic restaurant in the centre of Hong Kong. In a private room, away from the guests, both families were formally introduced during the tea ceremony, wherein bride and groom crossed arms and drank Tsao Chun – a traditional tea. They also paid respects to the elders, burning joss sticks and bowing obsequiously to them. Having exchanged rings, the bride and groom then received Lai See (Hongbao), a lucky red envelope filled with money and gold jewellery, from the families.

For the lavish feast, you will be startled to hear that over 150 guests turned up, filling fifteen tables of ten. This was despite the riots and curfews in Hong Kong following the unrest in China. Where they all came from, Heaven only knows ! Rose thinks that the word went round, and even the most tenuously connected of relatives and friends of friends managed, by some fair means or foul, to obtain an invitation, and turned up knowing that the majority of the Kwong family remained stuck in the UK or in China! But at least they all gave packets of lucky money to Rose and Daniel. I must tell you that Rose turned up dressed stunningly from top to toe in a traditional red dress called a Qipao, with her face covered by a red veil. She had to change her dress after each course of the incredible and lengthy meal.

But, true to Chinese culture, both sets of parents had to have separate wedding feasts. And blow me; incredibly, we were feasting again the very next day. I have never eaten so much in my life! Daniel, our new brother-in-law, again had to go around each table to toast the guests with shots of baijiu – a strong spirit. Then it was Rose's turn to circulate, but she toasted them with tea as she didn't drink.

And you won't believe this, but the celebration went on into a third day! Daniel had to bring Rose from his home to visit Father. By now she was no longer considered a part of the Kwong family but was welcomed as a guest. Daniel then presented a roast suckling pig and joined in a family meal with the rest of the Kwongs.

At the end of this gastronomic extravaganza, I was thoroughly exhausted. Heavens knows what Rose and Daniel must have felt. By the way, Francis, you ought to be warned. The relatives are searching for a Chinese bride for you at Father's behest. They tried it on me, but I swore that I was too young! I'm afraid that I landed you in it, as I protested that the older brothers should be married first. Therefore, you had a lucky escape when you didn't travel to Hong Kong to be at this wedding.

You know, quite often, I really miss the quiet, sedate life in England. But I still haven't got over our extraordinary visit to China last year: the cauldron of the Cultural Revolution; the hundreds of marauding Red Guards; Father's old ancestral home that stood with its ancient ghosts over all those years; the ancestral tombs in the mountains; the hordes of Kwong/ Gong relatives looking to Father for help; and the incredible and conflicting sights and smells of the old and the new China in juxtaposition… It still doesn't seem altogether real.

Finally, during this wedding business, I saw for the first time how Father's face, although understandably harassed and tired, changed dramatically when he suddenly beamed with dutiful pride as he presided over one of his children's marriage, that he actually approved of and was instrumental in influencing. I wondered then if it had sunk in that there might be eight more of us to go!

Sam

Giving a wry smile, I finally folded the letter away and tucked it beside my bedside reading lamp to read again at another time. There was so much to absorb. But I was really pleased that Rose had finally got married after all the unsuitable suitors who had courted her in England over the past few years. It at least cleared the way for me to marry later in August, on a date to be finalised by Caroline.

Chapter 40

SCOTLAND THE BRAVE

June 1967

HOWEVER, BEFORE MY WEDDING could take place, there was a host of work commitments to fulfil. A tour of the major stores in Scotland had been planned for months. Darlings of Edinburgh in Princes Street was an important stockist of Carolyne Stuart leisurewear, and ICI expected Caroline to feature personally in a prominent sales drive using their fabrics. Copland and Lye, an old, established store in Sauchiehall Street, Glasgow, carried a full range of day and evening dresses in Tricel – a new and versatile fabric from British Celanese – and would be mounting a Carolyne Stuart Week to coincide with her visit.

But as with many other industries around the country, sales and manufacturing had slowed down dramatically due to the struggling economy. Everyone (not least Caroline and I) was nervous of what might happen. Unemployment was rising, the national debt was getting out of hand, and international creditors, such as the IMF and the European Central Bank, were pressing for repayments. Interest rates were hiked to record levels. Costs of imports and exports were escalating with the Suez Canal closed following the Six-Day War. There was a downturn in the global market. Governments were jittery. For months now, speculation and rumours of an impending devaluation of sterling had wreaked havoc on the economy. Confidence amongst ordinary citizens was shaken. The knock-on effect was spreading out of control.

After the initial euphoria and optimism at the start of the swinging '60s, the mood of the British people was changing rapidly.

I should have sensed that something ominous was on the horizon. On the 16th May, Caroline's father suddenly died. He had been suffering from cancer, but, rightly or wrongly, her mother Mary had stoically tried to shield her children from his accelerating and serious decline so as not to worry Caroline and her young brother more than necessary. Immediately, I said to Caroline that we should cancel the Scottish sales tour. Like a professional trouper, she would not hear of it as she didn't want to let anyone down. Mary concurred, saying that work would be a sensible distraction. And thus, in the face of Caroline's grief and sorrow, and with heavy hearts, we drove up to Scotland shortly after the funeral in torrential rain amidst a violent thunderstorm on the motorway. The black and rumbling skies with their hostile sheets of lightning mirrored our mood as they escorted us through the border country and into Scotland.

The next day, the unfriendly skies had dried up sufficiently to reveal breaks of limp, diluted sunshine that would enable photo shoots to take place using outfits in the new season's designs from Darlings' store. Under the ancient grey walls of Edinburgh Castle, two local girls were photographed for the evening paper wearing the clothes. Without a murmur, Caroline fulfilled her obligation to feature in the media to help the store's sales drive.

The work at Copland and Lye in Glasgow was more intense and demanding. The *Glasgow Herald* wanted photos of Caroline posing on the rooftops and in the main windows of the store. Crowds of curious shoppers gathered excitedly in Sauchiehall Street to stop and stare.

In other interviews, much was made of her Scottish name, Stuart. How she carried it off under the circumstances with a brave and meaningful smile for the public, I shall never know. But, back at the hotel in the evenings, it was inevitable that she would burst into tears as a veritable dam had been held back since her father died. Feeling completely inadequate, I tried my best to console her.

As soon as the campaign had finished, I suggested we return home to London to be amongst our friends and family. We decided to cancel the many social engagements that were choking up our calendar. But Caroline wanted to see a little more of Scotland, since we had travelled hundreds of miles to be there. And so we made our way through the Lowlands, with their undulating landscape of winding valleys and gentle mountains, and headed towards the vast expanse of the lochs. As we stood silently, staring through the mist at the deep, dark waters of Loch Ness, hoping for a glimpse of the legendary monster, we wondered whether the loch – being the largest and deepest lake in Britain had an unknown and undiscovered network of underground caves and tunnels that led to the sea at the Moray Firth. Many rumours had proliferated since the VIth century, when St Columba stated that he saw a monster-like creature rising from the deep. Some speculated that it might have been a giant, prehistoric aquatic animal that had evolved in the deep waters unexplored by man. Through the years, many sightings had been exposed as hoaxes; from a series of rubber tyres strung in a line, to a dinosaur-like creature emerging from the water with a long neck and a relatively small head, but a body the size of an elephant.

Soon afterwards, we drove quickly north-westwards, chasing the tail of the elusive sun towards Oban and Loch Lomond, and from there on to the Highlands. Our stale city senses were abundantly refreshed and our anxieties soothed by the sights and smells of the rolling vista with its unbroken banks of heather in vibrant purples and delicate pinks. Alternating with the bright rape-yellows of the prickly gorse, it seemed to go on forever towards the horizon with its jagged margins meeting the sky. In the echoing silence of the untainted and purified air of these vast and majestic mountains, hardly any other human being could be seen for miles on end.

It seemed like another world and ages ago since we had left Glasgow, with some of its shameful slums, such as the notorious Gorbals[93] hidden not far from the city centre, when Glencoe's fresh, dense forests of virgin-green pines were spotted in the distance. After meandering leisurely through the tortuous and steep inclines of the Highlands, I suddenly realised that we had to gather some speed in order to reach the inn we had booked at Fort William – a further ten miles north of Glencoe before it grew dark. Dusk was falling rapidly as we skirted around the foot of Ben Nevis.[94] I pushed the accelerator on our little MG as much as I dared, bearing in mind the abrupt twists and turns in the undulating landscape, which in places was hazardously devoid of help from the luminous 'cat's eyes' embedded in the road for safety.

As we reached the valley of Glencoe and passed its historical stone monument, the decline of the evening light made the ghosts of Glencoe surround us like an oppressive shroud. You need not possess an overactive imagination to feel its bloody past floating thickly in the air. It was here, in 1692, that the MacDonald Clan was mercilessly slaughtered in their sleep by Archibald Campbell and his government troops who had recently arrived to billet with the MacDonalds to a hospitable welcome. Trembling, Caroline gripped my arm and urged me to get out of the valley as soon as possible. She said that the atmosphere was too oppressive to linger, and she shivered as if she was suddenly cold.

Several miles onwards, just before midnight, we managed to get to our B&B; a quaint old inn overlooking the water's edge at Fort William. The snow-capped peaks of Ben Nevis loomed like a colossus behind the picturesque town which was situated at the foot of Loch Linnhe. Although arriving extremely late, we were made welcome after being excused as typical foreign tourists – notorious for getting

---

93   A large slum area, a legacy from the Victorian era, situated on the south bank of the River Clyde not far from the centre of Glasgow. Hundreds of archaic, soot-blackened tenement blocks housed several families in a single damp, rat-infested room without electricity or running water. Some thirty-odd tenants had to share a single outside lavatory. For decades, disease and child mortality were rife.

94   At 1,345 metres, the highest peak in the UK.

lost. A stooped, craggy-bearded innkeeper shuffled jovially towards us in a threadbare old sweater and a baggy pair of trousers of a worn and indistinct tartan. He made a fuss of us and insisted on giving us a taste of his best single malt whisky. The next morning, his rotund and cheerful wife served a breakfast of oatcakes and porridge, with freshly laid eggs from their own hens. We tasted Scottish rural hospitality at its best.

After taking in the prominent sights, we decided to hug the coast and try to reach our last stop, Mallaig. It was fifty more miles of gobbling up the breathtaking views of the Western Highlands, with their ever-rising mountain peaks shadowing us on the right as we carefully negotiated the wicked blind bends of the narrowing roads that were poised dangerously high up, with the sea to our left. The disaster of falling off the edge of the precipice into the sea far below was only averted by the rugged cliff formations and a stout row of trees that acted like barriers formed long ago by the helpful forces of nature.

By the time we reached the outskirts of Mallaig, the sun was sinking low over the Atlantic in the distance, bathing the rooftops of the town in a deep orange glow. Made up of a collection of pretty cottages and stone-built houses scattered about the rugged shoreline, Mallaig was a bustling fishing port and was also a strategic route to the Scottish Isles. No one spoke English, but the friendly natives, speaking only in Gaelic, managed to direct us to a guesthouse run by a welcoming family whose relatives came from the Isles of Eigg and Rhum, whose outline could be seen across the sea to the west on a clear day.

After three more carefree days strolling along a deserted beach in the clean white sands and dipping our toes into the murky waters of Loch Morar, it was time, we felt, to return south. Soaked in sea mist and sudden flurries of Scottish rain falling off the mountains, we meandered our way home. Tracks from *Sgt Pepper's Lonely Hearts Club Band* were playing on the car radio for most of the journey. The Beatles' newly released album would soon be considered one of the most acclaimed and influential records in rock music's history.

Suddenly, we were brutally shaken out of our relaxed and happy state of mind by a newsflash on the radio that on the 25th May, British diplomats had been attacked by an angry mob of Chinese Red Guards at Shanghai Airport. Ray Whitney, the First Secretary at the British Consulate in Peking, had been flown in after a violent demonstration by Red Guards at the British compound's gate in protest of British suppression of Maoist demonstrators in Hong Kong. Peter Hewitt, the outgoing British Consul, was also attacked. Even though Hong Kong seemed under control, it appeared that the riots and unrest had boiled over with the turmoil of the Cultural Revolution continuing relentlessly in mainland China.

The Sino-British relationship was at a breaking point.

Naturally alarmed, we were concerned as to how some individuals from the British community as well as the Chinese, who did not really know us, would treat us if the troubles in the Far East continued to worsen. Fearfully aware that racial prejudice from some quarters could rear its ugly head sooner or later, we continued our journey in thoughtful and anxious silence.

Eventually, ten tiring hours later, London and its polluted smoke greeted us like a long-lost friend. We were back in the rat race, lost and anonymous amongst the melting pot of millions of cosmopolitan Londoners. Soon, we were immersed once more in the frantic pace of city life. We knew that, being brainwashed long-term urban dwellers, the fresh magic of the Highlands of Scotland would soon become a distant memory.

Chapter 41

A QUINTESSENTIAL
ENGLISH WEDDING

Godmanchester, England, 18th August 1967

IT WAS HARDLY SURPRISING that Caroline, with all her business commitments, was having difficulty finding time to organise her wedding. But at least she had a date. The 18th August was put in the diary at her family's local parish church, St Mary the Virgin, which was situated just behind the garden at Hatton House, the family home in Godmanchester. The foundations of St Mary's Church dated back to the thirteenth century, about the time when Godmanchester (founded on an old Roman settlement) received its charter from King John in 1213. The little stone church with its long history made a deep impression on me. I must admit that I could not wait to get married there, and to stay once more in Godmanchester, where I had spent many happy hours with the Stuart family, indulging in a typically quiet English village way of life.

Hatton House was situated in Post Street, opposite a tributary of the River Great Ouse. At the western end of Post Street, set back from a small green, was The Black Bull, a prosperous inn and traditional English pub. At the eastern end of the street, abutting a large lake where swans and geese had made their home, was an old, white-painted bridge carved in wood and fine latticework. Spanning the junction of the lake where it spilled into a millstream of the Ouse via a waterfall, this old bridge, built in 1827, was known to the locals as the Chinese Bridge due to its remarkable likeness to those in ancient China.[95]

Whilst back in London, it was rather difficult for Caroline to work in secret on her wedding dress or her bridesmaid's outfit in her flat in Fulham which she shared with three other girls, as our mews house in Paddington wasn't quite habitable, with builders doing alterations. All she would say was that the dress would be a surprise. Then, adding to everyone's delight, Rosemary, a childhood friend accepted Caroline's invitation to be her bridesmaid.

The clock was ticking disconcertingly down towards the big day when, on the 15th July, I received an official-looking letter from the Board of Trade. With trepidation, I ripped open the ubiquitous manila envelope, thinking that it would be about a dispute over the customs duties involved in our recent foray into exporting dresses to H. A. & E. Smith, a store in Bermuda together with some sample designs to Saks Fifth Avenue, New York.

Dear sirs,

We have had an enquiry from the Naples Italian Tourist Office – Ente Provinciale del Turismo – for a recommendation for a young and enterprising new fashion designer from Britain who is willing to participate in an exhibition and mount a fashion show to promote British fashion during a forthcoming film festival to be held in Sorrento on the 24th September to the 1st October 1967 to celebrate the premier of major British and Italian films. The event is to mark the collaboration of the British and Italian film industries under the aegis of Unitalia Film.

Carolyne Stuart's name has been shortlisted at the British National Export Council (BNEC). If you are interested, please

---

95 The white lattice timber work was typical of the Chinese Chippendale style made popular in the early Victorian period, when the influence of the Orient (particularly China), in decor, design, furniture and artefacts, was fashionable.

arrange to discuss the matter further with the undersigned as
soon as conveniently possible, as time is of essence.
Yours faithfully…

My immediate reaction was that the letter was a hoax, so I screwed it up ready to throw it in the bin so as not to worry Caroline. Hoaxes and crank letters inviting her to a party or to attend some obscure assignation were a common occurrence. Then there were the unpalatable and sometimes sinister telephone calls asking for a 'Lady Caroline', and if she designed lace lingerie in black, and what, if anything, she wore during the night…

Three days later, one dreary, damp morning after a welcome thunderstorm during the night to break up the humidity of the long, hot summer, I answered the telephone to a Miss Vivienne Hall. At first, I thought it was the bank chasing the tardy progress of repayments of our overdraft, but it was the Board of Trade asking if we had received the above letter. Miss Hall mentioned that Sorrento had been planned as the venue for a new and enterprising film festival, to follow on from the Venice International Film Festival in September. She explained that the Ente Provinciale del Turismo was keen to promote the unique setting of Sorrento on the beautiful Amalfi coast, with Positano, Capri and the bay of Naples with Vesuvius and Pompeii as its backdrop. She went on to say that British fashion and pop music epitomised the present period of the swinging '60s, and it was important to represent them in the films due to be launched.

Naturally curious, I asked why we had been chosen. She said that she was sorry that she couldn't give a specific answer. All she would say was that Carolyne Stuart's name had been proposed as one of the up-and-coming designers, and it may have been the work she had been doing as part of the group of new young designers working with Courtaulds, ICI and other major companies that alerted them.

Unfortunately, she added, the organisers could not actually pay us for our week's appearance in Sorrento. However, all expenses, flights, accommodation, and press coverage would be paid for all members of our company, professional models and attendant staff. More details would follow when a representative from Unitalia Film in Rome contacted us to see if Caroline was interested. I thought that it would be a chance of a lifetime to visit Italy, and a wonderful opportunity to break into the Italian market. I made the decision on Caroline's behalf.

Owing to our full diary, I decided to put the proposal on ice until after the wedding. Furthermore, I was still rushing back up the motorway to Birmingham at weekends whenever I could in order to support my brother-in-law who was running the family business. It was a promise that I had made to my father. The restaurant business was changing fast, and it needed fresh ideas to fight off increasing competition from Italian, Indian and Thai restaurants. What's more, the building was getting dated after all these years, and so a modernisation programme was under way to update the kitchens and to modify the rear of the building in Hinckley Street where my father owned an old shop, and thereby to expand the restaurant facilities and bar. Thinking back, it was probably not a particularly good time to do this. Costs were escalating and the business was shrinking. The state of the economy and the rising interest rates dented people's ability to dine out. I dreaded facing my father to tell him about the business situation when he returned from the Far East, but something radical had to be done, for if we had stood still, we would have been swallowed up in the rising tide of competition.

To add to these worries, my attempts to successfully compartmentalise my private double life had been difficult enough, in the course of which I had honed considerable skills, but now to hide my intended marriage from my father was a dilemma of indescribable proportions. My only hope was that he would not return to England until the new year, and that, by that time, I would find the courage to tell him.

Two days before the wedding, the builders finally finished their work at the mews house. My good friend and best man Robert together with Caroline's former flatmates, helped us to frantically clean up the place. The next day, we locked the front door and, in a mad rush of panic, hit the road to Godmanchester.

The night before the wedding, Robert and I stayed in the cottage attached to Hatton House. Sleep was disturbed due to the excitement of the next day. When morning arrived, it was with overwhelming relief that the overnight rain had gradually eased and the clouds had disappeared to reveal pockets of bright sunshine that had broken through.

Following breakfast, with the freshness of the morning dew in her hair, Rosemary arrived early to help Mary next door as she got the bride ready. Caroline was to be given away by Richard Tipping, her surrogate godfather and old family friend from the BBC. Promptly at half past eleven, Robert and I went to meet our friends outside the church and to greet Ian, my future brother-in-law, and my brother Alan, who would act as ushers.

The only other member of my family to attend apart from Alan was my youngest sister Ester, who arrived with a friend. There was little time or opportunity to dwell on the glaring absence of my parents and the rest of the family. With Caroline's friends and family friends in considerable numbers, my anxiety about explaining to strangers about my family not being there was assuaged somewhat in the excitement of the moment. Suffice to say that I had already made my explanations and apologies to Mary, albeit in a tactful and roundabout way, for my father's old-fashioned attitude and predicted resistance to my impending marriage, emphasising that it was not aimed personally at her lovely and wonderful daughter, and that neither I nor anyone else could change, in a mere few months, what had been ingrained in him since birth.

Soon after adjusting our eyes to the dimness in the old church, helped only by the vivid splashes of colour and slits of light that radiated from the beautiful stained glass high above the altar, amidst the familiar smells of beeswax and mustiness from old mahogany and burning candles, Robert and I took our places in the ancient wooden pews. Following some polite conversation and nodded greetings to the many guests, we briefly studied the order of service after shaking hands with the minister, the Reverend Harry Russell.

It was an anxious five minutes or so after the appointed hour of twelve when the bridal party of Caroline on the arm of Richard, followed by Rosemary, arrived to the organ strains of the 'Trumpet Voluntary'. The rousing music gave a resounding echo that bounced off the blackened beams high up in the roof and drowned out any sign of nerves.

The congregation, numbering about fifty guests, did their best not to make it obvious by twisting their heads in curiosity to stare at the bride and bridesmaid as they walked down the aisle towards me. There was an audible gasp of surprise as the congregation had their first glimpse of the bridal dress. Tempting though it was, I did not dare to steal a look before I was allowed to, so I forced myself to look directly ahead. As Richard formally handed Caroline's hand to me, he took a short step back, acknowledging me with a reassuring smile.

I suppressed my delight as I sneaked a side glance at Caroline's stunning dress. I had assumed that it would be a traditional white dress and veil, but it was nothing of the sort. It was long and closely fitted from neck to ankle in a pale aquamarine silk. Gathered around the neck was a ruff in stiff white lace which matched the cuffs – a throwback to the Elizabethan era with a nod to the setting of Caroline's home in Post Street, with its Elizabethan architecture. No wonder the congregation had gasped in surprise. Rosemary's dress echoed the design of Caroline's, but in the palest blue and ending at the knee.

Most people would swear that their wedding day would be just a blur and that they would forget what went on. Naturally, I wanted to drink in every moment of this quintessentially English wedding, so I focused my mind to remember, so that one day I could tell our grandchildren.

After welcoming the congregation following the opening hymn, 'The King of Love', the Reverend Mr Russell started his address, which echoed in the silence that fell.

'Dearly beloved, we have come together to witness the marriage of...'

Whilst this was going on, a sudden thought of the extravagant rituals of my sister Rose's wedding in Hong Kong flashed through my mind. Try as I might to block it out, it was difficult not to compare this simple, elegant English ceremony to my sister's long, drawn-out and complex Chinese one.

Fortunately, I was rapidly shaken out of my reverie by the minister asking if anyone in the congregation knew of any reason why the marriage should not proceed. There was an awkward silence, with the odd surreptitious glance around as the minister's eyes swept challengingly across the church.

The service continued with due solemnity and the appropriate decorous speed following our vocal assent and declarations. In a clear and uncompromising voice, the minister then delivered his sermon based on the sanctity of marriage, kindness and unselfishness with its highs and its lows.

No sooner had he finished than we had to make our vows, so there was little time to dwell on any extraneous thoughts with the declaration…

'…for better, for worse; for richer, for poorer; in sickness and in health, till death do us part…'

As these words were repeated after the minister, there was a sudden crash of thunder high above the church spire. Torrential rain began to fall from the heavens. Caroline and I looked at one another with dismay. There was some anxious whispering from the congregation.

The Reverend Harry Russell nervously adjusted his glasses and briefly looked upwards. He closed his eyes as if in fervent prayer that the recent and expensive roof repairs would not leak in the sudden downpour. Then, with his composure recovered, he quickly carried on with the service.

Slowly, the minister turned to face the congregation. Peering over his glasses to scrutinise the expressions on their faces, with his booming voice resonating to the rafters he announced;

'…have made their marriage vows to each other. I therefore proclaim that they are husband and wife. Those whom God has joined together, let no one put asunder…'

There was a sudden and audible silence, until a sharp burst of thunder and lightning rolled by. Anxiously, we looked upwards, high above the altar, and crossed our fingers in silent prayer.

It was fortuitous that an address by Mary's cousin, James, arrived at just the right juncture to provide an interlude. Caroline's Uncle Jim, a retired Methodist preacher, lavished considerable praise on Caroline and how she had grown up from a restless child that he used to bounce on his knee to the beautiful girl who was determined to become a fashion designer.

Then, with a disarming smile and a cautionary gesture of the hand, he turned to me and said, 'Mary has reminded me to tell you that you *must* find time in your busy lives for Caroline to spend some time alone; to quietly read a book or simply to allow her to do absolutely nothing! She has done this since she was a little girl. *So, dear boy, ignore this advice at your peril!'*

I swallowed a deep gulp. I suddenly thought that I had probably inveigled this petite and delicate girl, with her natural English reserve, into facing reporters and press photographers. Perhaps it was too much to ask her to model clothes for the public, to be stared at, to appear on television or to face intrusive interviews ad nauseum in a whirlwind of publicity... and all in the quest for fame and fortune. If the truth be known, I had been trying to live vicariously through Caroline's life in the limelight. A momentary pang of guilt crossed my mind, although, I confess, it didn't last long. She had carried out her public engagements with professional detachment and without a murmur, as any good actress would.

Immediately after the blessing of the marriage, with 'Ave Maria' playing quietly in the background, the wedding party followed the minister into a side chapel to sign the register. Shortly after the concluding prayers and a closing hymn, there was the formal dismissal which brought the ceremony to a joyful and thankful close.

Accompanied by a virtuoso rendering of Widor's 'Toccata', with smiles of relief we made our way back up the aisle. Our friends and guests greeted us with fulsome congratulations and applause as the bells of St Mary's rang out with such vigour that the pigeons that were hovering over the porch scattered as if shot at by a blunderbuss. In answer to our prayers, by the time we had reached the church door the rain had stopped. The sun beamed down upon us in all its magnificence, to warm us and to encourage us. Handfuls of confetti and rice were thrown high over our heads and rained down all around us like a protective cloak. Caroline threw her bouquet high over her shoulder, but in the melee she forgot to find out who caught it.

As soon as the photographs had finished, we led the way, followed by everyone else in a long crocodile of anticipation, as we strolled leisurely and carelessly through the church grounds. Passing the old gravestones, we weaved our way into a welcoming field of wild summer flowers, towards The Black Bull not far in the distance. It was here that the reception was waiting patiently, umbrellas at the ready in case there was a resumption of rain. But the gods shone down on us with brilliant rays of sunshine on our grateful heads.

The pub had arranged with Mary a quite magnificent wedding breakfast, and the Elizabethan rooms were heady with the overwhelming scent of flowers. A roaring log fire in the old inglenook lent the soot-covered beams a rosy and welcome glow. The best man's speech was witty, apt, and did not embarrass the groom. Standing with my back to the fire, I spoke with nervous emotion, if somewhat tremulously. It briefly crossed my mind to joke about the symbolism of the Chinese Bridge just down the road – and the story of the Willow Pattern, in which the irate father chased the eloping couple who ran away across the bridge to marry against his wishes. But on reflection, I decided against it, for it was too close for comfort. Cautionary words of wisdom from my sister and brother had warned me off. Anyway, keeping my own counsel, I was extremely relieved that Caroline wouldn't have to go through the three-day extravaganza that my sister Rose had had to endure earlier in the year.

Some hours later, it was time that Caroline returned to Hatton House to change in readiness to leave. There was an air of expectancy and debate about what her going-away outfit would look like.

Congregating outside in Post Street, our friends, family and guests did not have long to wait.

A shriek of delight went up from her flatmates when Caroline emerged out of the front door of Hatton House in a whirl of vivid colour. Dressed in a trouser suit, with wide flared bottoms and a matching cape in a startling pattern of psychedelic flowers in dazzling crimson and yellow, she spun around at the behest of the photographer and her friends without protest.

Not long afterwards, my brother brought around our little MG, which had been hidden, filled with our bags, in the barn at the back of the house. My jaw dropped, as it had been decorated with *Just Married* daubed with fresh cream in large letters on the bonnet and windscreen. Tin cans had been attached to the rear bumper and a bunch of bright balloons strung to the aerial. After many fond farewells and some goodbyes, we climbed in amidst the rice that had been strewn over the seats. The car roared away down Post Street, the cans rattling on the surface of the road as we headed back to our house in Paddington.

With the reflection on the car of the sun sinking low over the edge of the village, we soon reached the London Road. It turned out to be a balmy summer's evening despite the earlier storms. Facing the deepening pink streaks in the fading dusk through a lazy cloud of midges, I wound down the window to take in the warm breeze. Over the roof of our car, swallows and swifts came out in their numbers. Stretching their wings, they swooped and soared effortlessly, high above us into a clear, welcoming sky. Perhaps an extended Indian summer of wonder was in the offing. Perhaps it was an omen that we were about to embark on something just as unusual, and perhaps just as unpredictable, in our new journey together. In defiance of my father, I was determined to make a success of our lives as the new Mr and Mrs K. But this was not the time to dwell on such matters. I had to focus on the present, if not the future.

But as the age-old saying goes, we would have to see what was around the corner.

Chapter 42

FOREIGN FIELDS

France, 1967

W E WOKE UP EARLY in a flush of great anticipation. Drawing back a makeshift curtain, dawn was just breaking over the rooftops opposite. After a hasty breakfast, we collected our bags and loaded up the car. There would be just enough time to make the 11.30 ferry crossing from Dover to Ostend for the start of our long-awaited honeymoon overseas. We couldn't quite believe it – nearly two whole weeks away from work to tour Belgium and France away from the rat race of London life.

I had never travelled abroad before, let alone on a ferry across the Channel. Just like my father before me when he took his first trip on the open seas over half a century ago from Canton, I suffered a bout of seasickness. 'Wait till you sail across a vast expanse of a really rough ocean!' laughed Caroline.

Soon we reached the port of Ostend and gratefully disembarked. We meandered at leisure along the picturesque Meuse Valley, where we were made welcome at a tiny old auberge, whose proprietors just booked us in as 'Le GB'. Due to the currency restrictions imposed by the Wilson government on UK citizens touring abroad, fifty pounds in sterling was the maximum each person could take overseas. With one hundred pounds between us Caroline and I would have to manage on that; but luckily, we had the foresight to purchase some foreign currency well in advance, blissfully ignorant as to whether that was legal or otherwise.

On the outskirts of Brussels, at the edge of the royal estate we came across a pagoda and an ornately decorated Chinese pavilion, which had been transported and rebuilt in the most unlikely of places by a past King of Belgium, Leopold II, at the turn of the century. Ensconced next to an isolated green field in a lonely part of Europe, it seemed inexplicably incongruous.

Travelling through the ancient city of Reims, stopping briefly to visit its historic cathedral, marvel at its stained-glass window by Chagall and take in where the Kings of France were crowned, we soon reached Paris. Against all odds, we managed to park at the edge of the Place de la Concorde, where we found a small family hotel whose owner was delighted to give us a room with a tiny bath right under the eaves of the attic. From there we decamped to gather our breath. I travelled around almost in a daze, pinching myself as, at long last, I was seeing the foreign sights that I had once dreamed of. Not surprisingly, I immediately fell under the spell of the Louvre with its *Mona Lisa*, marvelled at the scale of the engineering of the Eiffel Tower, and mingled, open-mouthed, with the masses that crowded into the Gothic cathedral of Notre Dame with its sculptured facade and flying buttresses.

The Parisian sun shone benignly as we climbed the hill to the atmospheric square in Montmartre, where we dined al fresco as the amber sun set over Sacré-Cœur. Surrounded by modern-day artists plying their trade and the sweet, pungent smell of oil paint, it wasn't hard to imagine the ghosts of Van Gogh and Modigliani who had once frequented this artist colony, where they and other Post-Impressionist painters gathered at the turn of the century. Caroline reflected ruefully that they had led such tragic lives of poverty and frustration without reaping the rewards or gaining the recognition they richly deserved until after they were dead.

Sadness overcame us when we had to say goodbye to this beautiful city of Paris, whose long, straight boulevards flanked by imposing buildings and formally styled parks had been planned and laid out so attractively in the mid 1800s by Baron Haussmann, a revolutionary urban planner appointed by Prince Louis Philippe Bonaparte, the first President of the second republic, recently returned from exile. But we promised that one day we would return. Before leaving, we sent a postcard home to Mary in Godmanchester. I decided to let my mother know that I was travelling abroad, without saying with whom; knowing that the news would eventually filter back to my father in Hong Kong. At the very least, I owed him that.

Driving south via the gateway of Versailles, with its mammoth-sized palace of Louis XIV (known as the Sun King) in all its opulent splendour, we headed westwards, following the River Loire. Further on, hugging the wide Loire Valley, we stopped in the tiny village of Amboise. To our surprise, we happened to stumble across a small, faded sign for the tomb of Leonardo da Vinci. It was so low-key that it was easy to miss. We clambered up a small hill through the outer perimeter of the village, and there it was, the great man's final resting place, buried in a small chapel in the gardens of the Château d'Amboise. Not many tourists happen to know of this, for they expect his final resting place to be in Rome with Michelangelo and Raphael, the other famous sons of the Italian Renaissance. But Da Vinci spent the last three years of his life in Amboise under the patronage of Francis I, the new King of France. Having left Rome in 1516, he crossed the Alps by donkey, carrying the *Mona Lisa* with him.

Several chateaux later, we travelled languidly west, tracing the large river, which guided us. Soon we reached the estuary at the Loire-Atlantique, where Saint-Pierre-Quiberon, a tiny fishing village, stuck out into the Atlantic like a plump finger. I suffered an acute bout of self-inflicted gastritis after overindulging in local wine and seafood.

Once recovered, our plan was to follow the coast road north towards Calais. Dover's white cliffs soon beckoned and, sadly, we knew that our holiday would soon be over as the sultry, sunny month of August came to a rapid close.

On reaching London, we heard with dismay the news that there had been violent clashes between demonstrators, police and journalists with members of staff and soldiers from the PLA, outside the Chinese Embassy in Portland Place. Journalists reported that they had been attacked with iron poles, bottles, and even an axe was wielded. This outbreak of extreme violence was a reaction to the invasion a week earlier on the 22nd August, when the British Embassy in Peking was torched by a horde of Red Guards, and Donald Hobson, the British Chargé d'Affaires, had been threatened with his life as he confronted the mob. Over the last month, the riots and demonstrations in Hong Kong had escalated out of hand, with the British authorities closing several Communist newspapers and putting Chinese newsmen on trial on sedition charges in an effort to quell the unrest. Skirmishes along the Kowloon border with mainland China, involving the British police and the PLA, continued to inflame the situation.

Shaken to the core, Caroline and I could only hope that this dangerous international situation would eventually settle down, for everyone's sake, and not least ours. It was at times like this that I was starkly reminded of my father's warnings about the dangerous and hostile bigotry that could play havoc on an interracial marriage. Banishing the thought to the back of my mind, I hoped that my father's words would not come back to haunt me.

Chapter 43

THE ITALIAN JOB

24th September 1967

OVER THE ENSUING WEEKS, the events in the Far East appeared to quieten down. The preparations for the film festival in Sorrento now dominated our time. A representative from Unitalia Film contacted us to work out the details of how the fashion show would feature on stage. In Italian mythology, where the Gulf of Naples abuts the peninsula of Sorrento, ancient mariners were lured to their death by beautiful mermaids. Therefore, it was agreed that a symbol of these mythical creatures ought to be present to impress our Neapolitan hosts from the Ente Provinciale del Turismo. Mara, a good friend who from time to time helped us out for little or no reward, remembered that once we had seen a production at the Old Vic using a mermaid as a prop. She immediately contacted them. As soon as they heard about the festival – the Incontri Festival del Cinema, without hesitation the company loaned us a glittering mermaid costume covered in sequins.

'Now, you realise who is going to pose inside that costume as the siren?' I said, grinning from ear to ear.

Mara blushed and blustered, 'Oh no!' But being a striking, tall and slim girl with model looks and long blonde hair, the costume fitted her like a glove.

Our planned trip to the festival now began to take shape like a well-oiled theatre production. Through friends, Mara recruited an enterprising young photographer called Mike Teasley to join the team. To fit in with the theatrical theme of swinging London, he photographed the giant clock face of Big Ben and ingeniously mounted it on a full-sized cardboard prop which featured a Union Jack. Not only that, but he diligently recorded the chimes of Big Ben on a portable tape recorder.

Pam Tiller, a loyal and skilful dressmaker who had been helping Caroline since the company's inception, managed through contacts to persuade an inventive, up-and-coming Mayfair hair stylist named Barry Noble to accompany the team and style the models' hair. Shortly afterwards, six professional fashion models were chosen through agencies. Vicky, Tess, Jo, Shona, Lisa Marie and Sandie fitted the look of the show and had the personality to go with it.

The next day we were put in touch with Jim Harrington, who ran Blaises, a well-known music club in Central London. Their resident band was a professional group called The Majority. It was suggested that, since they were planning to attend the festival to represent British bands and to launch EMI's latest new singer, they could supply the music for Caroline's fashion show.

Including Pam, who was acting as our PA, we now had our full team to take up the air ticket allocation from Alitalia and the hotel reservations in Sorrento for the 24th September. It was impressed upon us that all the men had to take dinner jackets for attending presentation events and screenings, as film stars, other dignitaries and the British consular representative would be present. Similarly, the girls would take something that would glitter and be elegant for the evenings. There was little time to rehearse, with Caroline and Pam working furiously to get the clothes ready for the show. We were advised that, in order to make an impact on the Italian media, the more outrageous and eye-catching the clothes were, the better.

As there was an export drive in the UK – the 'I'm Backing Britain' campaign – hospitality was extended to us by Pimm's, who offered to throw cocktail parties for the British contingent, which included our team, for the duration of the festival. Against all expectation, and not without a great deal of anxiety, everything seemed to fall into place.

Just two days before we were due to fly out, Alitalia requested a press launch with the girls wearing some of the outfits planned for Sorrento. Though short of time, how could we refuse? At the airline's showrooms in Piccadilly, the photographers insisted that the girls modelled with one of their Boeing airliners as a backdrop. The girls paraded like the true professionals they were and enjoyed their moment of fame in front of the cameras. This was something that they would have to get used to, I warned, in the week ahead; though to be honest I didn't really know what we were about to face.

On the 23rd September, the team flew out from Heathrow on the same flight as Jim Harrington and The Majority. It was a night flight, changing at Rome for Naples in the early hours. Startled curiosity and amazement greeted us during transit. Caroline and the girls, having changed during the flight, were outrageously dressed in colourful outfits, ready for being collected at Naples Airport, when we almost lost her and some of the girls among admiring Italians who grabbed and surrounded them in the ensuing melee.

However, nothing had prepared us for the landing at Naples Airport. We had been told that a team from Unitalia would meet us. However, we were not warned that the Italians were famous for revelling in anything unusual and would send out the paparazzi in their numbers. Also, little did we know that the Italians were notorious for creating celebrities out of nothing overnight. And so, as we disembarked in the blinding sunshine and the dry Mediterranean heat of late morning, dishevelled, short of sleep and disorientated, Caroline emerged at the top of the steps carrying a now-tired bouquet. Immediately, we were surrounded by a crowd of journalists from Rome and Naples (we later discovered, from *Il Tempo*, *Corriere Della Sera* and the *London Evening News, Daily Mirror, etc.*)

Although completely exhausted, we had to hand it to the girls, for they did not complain when the press insisted on photographing them posing precariously on the wing of the plane we had just flown in on. Heaven knows how much the pilot and the mechanics cringed at the potential damage, not only to their precious airliner, but to the people balancing precariously in stiletto heels on their aircraft.

Thankfully, our reception team hurried us through passport control and customs and accompanied us onto the coach that would take us to our hotel in Sorrento. After a rest and a dip in the swimming pool, we were all refreshed as we sat down to the magnificent lunch the chef had prepared for us. For the rest of the day, everyone was allowed free time to explore the town and the coast, and to orientate themselves to prepare for a week of unprecedented madness.

The next day, it was back to business after an early breakfast on the sunlit pool terrace, with the heady scents of bougainvillaea and oleander thick in the air.

'*Buon giorno*, Signor Franco and Signora Carolina!' called out the cheerful hotel manager. 'You have a visitor in reception who wants to meet you.'

Then striding purposefully towards us was a tall, handsome Italian, immaculately dressed in a well-tailored cream linen suit. 'Signor and Signora' He beamed with his hand outstretched, as I stood up to shake it. 'My name is Carlo Marguilo, and it is my honour to show you around Sorrento and Naples.'

Carlo Marguilo was a well-known lawyer from Naples. It was said that everyone knew him, from the Mafiosi to the Consul. He had been assigned as our guide and 'minder'. After breakfast, he insisted on taking us out on his magnificent motorboat for a trip around the bay to see the colourful buildings and the gilded cupolas of the churches perched on the cliffs of Positano and Amalfi. Powering across the bay with the spray of the aquamarine sea in our hair, we stopped at one of his favourite tavernas in Capri, where the owner fussed over us like old friends.

Returning to Sorrento, Carlo remarked, with an expansive sweep of the hand, 'If you look at Naples from the sea it has the shape of a sensuous mermaid, with Vesuvius as her head, the curve of the gulf as her glittering body, and Sorrento as her tail.'

Against the dazzling light that bounced off the shoreline linking Naples to Sorrento, with the volcano of Vesuvius rising majestically in the background, it was not hard to visualise this magical image as the crystal-clear blue ocean rippled invitingly in waves towards our boat.

'Legend has it that, on these sun-kissed western shores, seductive mermaids known as sirens tried to lure Odysseus to his death. He tied himself to the mast of his ship and told his companions to plug their ears, and so escaped this watery fate. Spurned, the aquatic creatures perished. Local myth claims that Naples rose from the body of a beautiful, dying mermaid goddess called Parthenope, who gave the city and its people her name,' added Carlo proudly.

The press soon turned up at the hotel to interview Caroline and to photograph her and a couple of the girls in contrasting black-and-white tops and voluminous skirts – the latter of which could convert into trousers by detaching a front panel held by Velcro. The journalists found this novel, if not revolutionary. They also insisted on photographing Mara the mermaid outstretched in the sun on a diving board next to the pool, much to the amusement of a crowd of onlookers who had gathered.

That evening we were all invited to attend the screening of Sean Connery's *You Only Live Twice* with some of the cast and film crew. The rest of the week was filled with British and Italian films, with many of their stars, directors and producers flying in. The schedule was, as expected, planned to the last detail and occupied our time from noon to night, as our diary showed:

Day 2: Carolyne Stuart party invited to a reception at the Hotel Excelsior in honour of Claudia Cardinale, one of the prominent guests of the festival, presently filming with

Henry Fonda and James Coburn in an Italian Western by Sergio Leone.

Day 3: Carolyne Stuart group presented on stage to the film festival audience by Trevor Howard (*Brief Encounter,* '45: *The Long Duel* with Charlotte Rampling and Yul Brynner, '67) and his distinguished actress wife, Helen Cherry.

Afterwards, the girls were invited to a late-night party by the rich young men whose fathers owned most of Sorrento. Driven up to the hills at midnight in their Alfas and Ferraris, it turned out they were not having a party but planning to abduct some of the girls. Francis threatened to call Carlo Marguilo. Fearful of the consequences, they immediately drove the girls back to their hotel.

Day 4, am: RAI TV interviewed Caroline about 'Swinging London'.

pm: Fashion show before a packed audience of press, public and dignitaries, introduced and compèred by Nigel Davenport (*A Man for All Seasons* with Paul Scofield) choreographed to rock music by The Majority. At the strike of Big Ben booming through the PA system with our mermaid languishing next to it, the girls burst out of the model of Big Ben through the Union flag, dancing. Yashmaks and dramatic masks accompanied flowing dresses heavily influenced by the *Arabian Nights*; capes draped over catsuits in shiny black leather-like ciré; headgear doubling as cloaks with only the models' heads peeping through; micro-miniskirts, trouser suits and hot pants in vivid orange-and-yellow psychedelic patterns, and so on. Finally, serenely, to an upbeat version of the 'Wedding March', Caroline's own wedding dress and Rosemary's bridesmaid's outfit finished the show, which was met with wild applause. Royal Shakespeare Company's Richard Johnson *(Deadlier Than the Male, etc.)* amongst others, came to offer his congratulations.

But there were also some muted responses from the older members of the audience, and a shaking of puzzled heads. Representatives of the British Consul came to congratulate us. However, the British National Export Council (BNEC) thought that the revolutionary swinging '60s look from King's Road and Carnaby Street might have been too outré or too gimmicky for the young Italians to digest. We protested that we had been advised to mount a show whose clothes would be 'way out', if not outrageous, in order to create a stir. And so, the images, took off via the papers and TV. The show was followed with a crowded reception hosted by Pimm's until 2am.

Day 5: After a screening of *The Whisperers* with Edith Evans, we attended a reception with a party to honour British actors and actresses.

Under a large harvest moon and basking in the humidity of a sultry Neapolitan evening and trailing in the wake of glamorous screen icons, Susan Hampshire *(The Forsyte Saga)* and Viviane Ventura *(The Saint: The Persuaders)* we joined the parade through the festooned streets of Sorrento with The Majority, mingling with a gathering crowd of Italian and British festival celebrities.

Day 6, pm: Hotel Excelsior threw a last-night party in their stunning gardens at the edge of the sea against a moonlit bay facing Vesuvius. Our group was invited to dance for the filming for TV of this spontaneous 'Happening', and Francis was invited to announce the frenetic event for the cameras. On our return to our hotel, he (in his dinner jacket) and then Pam was thrown into the pool by an exuberant Jo, full of high spirits.

Day 7, am: Jim Harrington drove Francis at breakneck speed in a tiny Fiat along the coast to the British Consulate to get signatures to settle our expenses for the festival. It was not an appropriate moment, because there was an ambassadorial reception in full flow on the well-manicured lawn amongst the palm trees. Then preparations were made to leave Sorrento and catch the night flight back to London via Milan. Vicky, Jo and her boyfriend (who had flown out with us) decided to stay on for an extended holiday.

We were thoroughly worn out, but we finally made it back to London. Gallingly, not a single Italian buyer contacted us. Not unexpectedly, we did not sell a single stitch of clothing to the Italians, but we were told that *at least* we had made an indelible impression on them. In hindsight, perhaps we should have stuck to a collection of more conservative and sophisticated clothes. As a pioneering designer, Caroline disagreed. But our main consolation was that we had nevertheless had a whale of a time; an unusual experience on the warm, sun-drenched shores in a most enchanting part of Italy. It was something that we were unlikely to ever forget, and something we would never be invited to do again.

Like countless others in Britain, as we counted the costs of the trip, our financial reality began to bite. Around the country, strikes at the docks and on the railways added to the nation's economic woes and started to strangle its imports and exports. After months of rumours, with gold and foreign reserves depleting to an all-time low, the government devalued sterling by a substantial fourteen per cent, making the pound fall against the dollar from \$2.80 to \$2.40. James Callaghan, the Chancellor of the Exchequer, was immediately replaced by Roy Jenkins from the Home Office. The uncertainty of sterling was met with glee by currency speculators and profiteers. Harold Wilson defended his decision on radio and television, saying that, due to the continuing strikes, coupled with the hostilities in the Middle East and the continuing closure of the Suez Canal, he had been forced to take action to protect the economy. Superciliously, and with a straight face, he announced, "It does not mean the pound here in Britain, in your pocket or purse or in your bank, has been devalued!" Scathingly, many commentators were waiting for a pound note to be conjured out of his pocket in an extravagant flourish, like a hapless rabbit out of a hat.

Adding to our anguish, Caroline and I had heard that, during our absence abroad, there had been several more incidents involving confrontation – albeit verbal to begin with, but nonetheless potentially explosive – between Chinese restaurant staff and customers around the country in the aftermath of the clashes at the Chinese Embassy in August. I wondered how my aged parents and the rest of the family were coping in this febrile atmosphere. Naturally, I was worried about their safety. Although, due to my duplicity over my clandestine marriage, like a coward I felt that I couldn't pick up the phone to see how they were. Feeling utterly ashamed, I felt completely powerless to help them. Together with this, coupled with the depressing economic news and a letter from our bank chasing repayment of our overdraft, we came down to earth after the incredible highs of Italy with an almighty and resounding crash.

Chapter 44

EXPORT OR DIE

1968

O N ONE BITTER JANUARY morning, as the frosty winter turned to snow, we stood at the frozen window and stared in despair at the sombre and thickening skies. Feverishly, we began to work out what the next chapter in our lives would be. Time was already flying by like a veritable whirlwind. It had become apparent that for the company to survive, like many other fledgling businesses we needed to sell to other countries around the globe rather than just relying on domestic sales. Accordingly, we began to make plans. But wherever we looked, depressingly world-shaking events still dominated the headlines.

In Czechoslovakia, at the start of 1968 Alexander Dubček came to power by defeating the hard-line Stalinist candidate Novotný, bringing in a brief period of liberalisation and reform, dubbed the Prague Spring. It was not to last, as a few months later Soviet armed forces invaded and occupied the country and reinstalled a Soviet hardliner. The Cold War between the Soviet Bloc and the West continued to chill. Meanwhile, balanced delicately and precipitously, relations between China and Britain rumbled on.

However, this was not a propitious time to return to England, but shortly after Easter, my father flew into Heathrow. Aunt Chun Rei also returned in order to live with us, and from time to time, help with the Uncle Chun Tileng's family as she had done some years earlier when her brother's children were young.

In April '68 the Civil Rights leader Martin Luther King was assassinated as he attended a rally in Memphis, Tennessee. Shock waves reverberated around the world.

Back home in Birmingham, in the same month, a political storm erupted following a controversial speech by Enoch Powell, a Member of Parliament for Wolverhampton, savaging the Race Relations Bill. In his 'Rivers of Blood' speech, Powell advocated an immediate halt to immigration from the Commonwealth and the repatriation of immigrants, particularly those from the West Indies and Africa. As race relations in Britain were already poised precariously on a knife edge, moderating voices cautioned that his words could only inflame the situation. Very few politicians dared to stick their heads above the parapet to remind the country that, in 1948, Commonwealth citizens from the West Indies were shipped in numbers (starting with the initial voyage of the HMS *Empire Windrush* on the 22nd June that year) to help to rebuild Britain after the devastation of war. There was a dire shortage of manpower on the docks, railways, buses, roads, as well as in factories, housebuilding and office construction. It was also forgotten that, during the war, Britain had drafted in workers from the colonies, including India, Ceylon and Hong Kong, to man the Merchant Fleet to protect supplies and armaments. It was from these early seeds that the first non-white immigrant communities grew.

In the fallout from the speech, gangs of mindless youths began to provoke trouble amongst the black community, crying, "One knock for Enoch!" Edward Heath sacked Powell from the Shadow Cabinet.

Not surprisingly, tensions were rising in the Midlands, and with the continuing erosion of the restaurant business due to multifarious factors, Father and I were on a collision course trying to work out how to get the business back on track. I suggested altering the menu radically and changing the decor to attract new customers, but he refused to even consider the idea. Since his return to England, I had noticed that he had aged considerably during his time away in the Far East. His energy and enthusiasm for business had dwindled noticeably. Our mother reminded us that he was not getting any younger; in fact, I didn't want to face the truth that he was now seventy years old. It is a common fault in most human beings that we fail to admit that our parents are growing old in front of our eyes. From childhood, we think that they are evergreen and indestructible. But at this pensionable age, most men would have retired. My suggestion to that effect was met with exasperation and derision.

'And what do you expect us, and the ones in China, to live on, then – *THIN air?* The business is all we have got left. *It's our livelihood* – your lifeblood! And who do you think will carry it on?'

He snapped his fingers in front of my face accusingly.

'And just look at you! At your age, you haven't even married or demonstrated that you have made a success of your so-called business! And what's more, over the years I can't remember the countless number of times when respectable Cantonese families called on us with their eligible daughters to choose from, and you rudely ignored them and then disappeared with some lame excuse or other.'

He prowled around me like a tiger waiting to pounce, his face contorted in anger and disappointment. I couldn't look him in the eye, knowing that I had already deceived him. Deep down, I wanted to blurt out the truth. But like a coward, I held my tongue and turned away to mask my guilty secret.

'Apart from the two eldest, the rest of your brothers and sisters are still unmarried or haven't yet found their feet. And *another* thing – in the time I was away, the capital I had left in the bank all but disappeared on the worthless "building improvements" *YOU* sanctioned!'

'But I… I…' My voice trailed away. I pushed my fingers through my hair in frustration. I tried to explain that the kitchens and toilet facilities had to be modernised radically due to pressure from the local authorities, and that we were under obligation under the terms of the lease from the landlords for renovations at the rear of the premises to be done. The new bar and extra dining room created there would provide for dinner dances and for large groups of diners celebrating birthdays, anniversaries and so on, once a licence was applied for.

'That was a stupid waste of money!' he countered angrily. *'If I had been here, I would have sold the whole damn place as it stood for a decent price!'* He berated me as if I was a recalcitrant child.

I tried to reason with him that the lease was short and decreasing by the minute. Having an old-fashioned restaurant in aged premises that needed work, with falling customer numbers and competition from the new restaurants that were opening daily around us and offering fresh ideas, it would be virtually impossible to find a buyer in the current climate.

But the dismissive look of anger on my father's face mirrored exactly what he thought of me. It didn't require any further words from him.

For as before, our difficult relationship was always steeped in truculence that soured all our conversations even since childhood. Because I was convinced that my father was holding something back which coloured his judgement of me, and everything that I did. Our present row did not allow me to dig deeper; but one day, before it's too late, I was determined to find out the reasons that had been constantly eating at him. But, at that moment, my throat and my will had both run dry in trying to argue with him.

So, like immovable objects, with backs to the wall we faced each other – both of us implacable in our stubbornness. As always throughout the history of our turbulent relationship, I could never win the argument. Aggrieved, I had to walk away, fearing an escalation of our differences would lead to a permanent rift that would never heal. With a heavy heart, defeated, I retreated to the haven and tranquillity of my London home and to my long-suffering wife, and buried myself in work. It would be a matter of years or so before I dared to return to face my father. But I was determined to make a success of my life to prove him wrong.

In the States and in Europe, protests continued to swell against the Vietnam War. Student unrest was simmering like a angry undercurrent waiting to explode. Demonstrations were happening in Paris at the Sorbonne. In June, Senator Robert Kennedy, the former US Attorney General was assassinated by a lone gunman in Los Angeles. The country was again in turmoil. Meanwhile in the Far East, violence continued unabated in Hong Kong. And so in early September, Sam returned to England, followed by Rose with her husband and their young son because of the volatile situation and the uncertain future in the colony.

Gradually, fashion-wise, the North American market was waking up to British fashion. The doyen of modern designers and the pioneer of the miniskirt, Mary Quant, had already made inroads into the major cities there. Our thoughts turned across the Atlantic. As it happened, Caroline had a childhood friend named Andrew Fordham who had emigrated to Canada some years ago and established himself as the sales manager of an enterprising fashion jewellery and accessories company based in Toronto, with factories and offices in New Jersey and Costa Rica. On one of his visits to the UK, they got talking. It was agreed that he would test the market with the Carolyne Stuart range of clothes, starting with the stores in Toronto. We had now come to the reluctant but inescapable conclusion that it was export or die.

Now talking of dying; on a foggy November, with its bleak grey skies looming on the horizon, I felt that, after a long, wet English summer, a break in the sun would be welcome to lift our spirits. By coincidence, a friend of ours happened to borrow a couple of summer dresses from the collection to be photographed on the Spanish island of Majorca for an advertising brochure for an overseas tour operator who specialised in package holidays in the sun. We had no real knowledge of Majorca, only that it was somewhere in the Mediterranean. The tour company was offering a two-week holiday by a sunny beach, all inclusive with hotel and flights, for a princely sum of fifty-nine pounds per person. We could hardly turn it down.

It was a new resort, with just two newly built hotels on a wide bay, fringed on both sides by rocky promontories not far from Formentor, which was on the north-east corner of the island. Arriving late morning, we were greeted with a clear azure sky and a sweeping beach of golden sand with several holidaymakers lazing about under straw parasols. Tempted by the empty, shimmering sea lapping the beach with a gentle wash of pure white foam that sparkled in the sunlight, we rushed into the seductive warm water.

At noon, as the sun reached its zenith, I swam ahead of Caroline and soon I was out of my depth. Then it hit me. I felt the tug of a vicious undercurrent pulling me quickly away from the shoreline. Suddenly, powerful waves that seemed to come from nowhere came crashing down on my head as I tried to swim back towards the shore. Straight away, I knew I was in difficulty. The waves kept knocking me down under the water as I struggled to keep afloat. Each time I emerged to glimpse the welcoming sky, I saw the sun blazing down directly above me. *What a time to die*, I thought. *What will happen to my poor wife?* This was the second time in my life that I was staring death in the face! Dare I cry out for help and look a fool in front of those tourists on the beach?

As I went under again, swallowing water, I thought of the life insurance policy I had just taken out for ten thousand pounds. That would solve our financial worries in a flash... Then, as the survival part of my brain kicked in, a hidden voice said;

'*NO – forget that stupid idea! There's some unfinished business, especially with your father... swallow that foolish pride and scream loudly for help if you want to live!*'

Coming up to gulp some air for the third time, I waved frantically and shouted for help. At first Caroline thought I was merely waving to her in jest. Then when I disappeared under the waves again, she realised that something was seriously wrong. Being a good swimmer, she quickly reached me. Unfortunately, we then both got caught in the undercurrents which were pulling us out to sea. Suddenly, a man who was standing on the rocks nearby dived in and quickly reached us and hauled us one by one onto the safety of the rocky outcrop. He was a young, athletic German, and a strong swimmer. He helped us back to the safety of the beach, and, as I gratefully spewed out what seemed like gallons of seawater, I looked around to thank the young man, who had promptly disappeared.

That evening at dinner, our fellow guests told us that there were dangerous currents in certain parts of the bay. There had been reports of several people drowning earlier in the season, but the authorities refused to put up a warning sign, employ lifeguards or even fly a red flag in case it put people off the new resort, which was still in the throes of early development. After dinner, we went to the adjoining German hotel to try to find the young man who had rescued us; but he was nowhere to be found. I wrote a large thank-you note and pinned it on the reception noticeboard:

> *"To the young chap who heroically saved my life today: my wife and I would like to thank you properly. Please contact me in Room... at the adjoining hotel. Yours gratefully..."*

Whether it was because he was shy or modest, he never did contact us. From that day onwards, having faced my own mortality, I vowed that I would respect the sea, and also improve my swimming, which I did over the years, for I had to remind myself that I was not yet ready to meet my maker.

Chapter 45

SWANSONG

USA and Canada, 1969–1970

On the 13th January 1969, Richard M. Nixon succeeded Lyndon B. Johnson as President of the United States. It was some time later when peace talks between the US and North Vietnam were mooted to reconvene in Paris. Insurmountable differences and mistrust plagued any meaningful progress. This led to inevitable suspension, with the talks stuttering on without any real achievement. In France, President Charles de Gaulle resigned following a defeat over a host of government reforms.

At the beginning of April, Andrew Fordham reported back to us that two major Toronto stores had expressed an interest in sampling a range of Caroline's clothes. Meanwhile, the first UK-built Concorde made its successful inaugural flight from Bristol to Gloucestershire. It was a landmark for civil aviation.

On the 20th July 1969, America's *Apollo 11* propelled Neil Armstrong and Buzz Aldrin into space to successfully land on the moon. After a historic walk on its surface, they returned safely the next day. Space exploration would never be the same again.

Whilst back here, it appeared that there were some teething

problems with North American sizing that needed to be sorted out. Furthermore, the dress buyers were cautious about the revolutionary fashion from England, saying that their customers were perhaps not quite ready for the new look. Thereupon, Andrew insisted that a visit to Canada and the States was essential to see the market at first hand and to promote the design label. He was also aware that we were hampered financially and suggested that, in order to make a decent financial return, an expansion of the company would have to take place in order to increase sales and production exponentially. That meant fresh injection of capital investment… but from where?

In September, financed with a loan from Andrew's company to cover the cost of the flights and hotels, we flew to Toronto in the midst of the fall with the maple trees turning a golden hue. Almost immediately, we went to work. To stimulate interest in the next season's new range of clothes, a carefully crafted publicity drive was mounted. CBC filmed Caroline in one of main thoroughfares, Bloor Street, sketching one of the fashion models trying on one of her new outfits from one of the major department stores. The next day, in the crisp, cold air and the autumn sunshine that managed to squeeze between the skyscrapers, British Leyland Motors lent us two pristine new E-Type Jaguar sports cars for a television shot of Caroline with two girls showing off her designs. A curious crowd soon gathered, causing a traffic jam, until the Canadian Mounted Police cleared the highway. To round off the campaign, the BNEC exhibited the collection in its downtown showrooms, followed by a Pimm's drinks reception. Newspaper interviews appeared in the *Toronto Star* and others. Three days later, skirting the perimeter of the great Lake Michigan, we drove to Montreal to exhibit at the BNEC and to visit the stores.

The following week, we flew to New York. Caroline visited an old friend and former flatmate who was working as a shoe designer in the Empire State Building, and I met up with Robert's brother, who was working for the *New York Times*. Some of the buyers came to visit us at the Sheraton on 7th Avenue. We were encouraged when preliminary orders were placed by two of the major department stores, B. Altman and Saks Fifth Avenue: it was the breakthrough we wanted. Towards the end of the trip, which took in the sights of the Big Apple, we scrambled up the Statue of Liberty, battling vertigo and walked under Niagara Falls and got thoroughly drenched.

Caroline sent a postcard of the Statue of Liberty back home to her mother and brother. I posted copies to my parents and siblings. Later, I heard that my father's only wry comment was that at least I had managed to get across the Atlantic to America, when in 1921 he had failed to do so in order to follow in the footsteps of his great-grandfather.

The next day, we were invited to dinner to meet Andrew's bosses to discuss possible investment. Collected by a gold-coloured Cadillac, we were driven through an imposing set of wrought-iron gates to a large estate just outside New Jersey to meet the four brothers who owned the jewellery company. Flanked by ornamental cypress trees and weeping willows, and rolling, pristine lawns that surrounded a lake, we reached the top of a small hill, on which stood an imposing mansion constructed in white stone in a Neo-Palladian style. A solicitous footman with a doleful expression opened the door to us, and, as we swept in, Caroline grabbed my arm and whispered that the paintings in the giant entrance hall looked as if they were from the hand of the Russian maestro Chagall.

Just then a petite, slim lady of an indeterminate age, dressed in black silk that reached her ankles, came to greet us. She wore a single row of pearls that shimmered in the light and complimented her silvery grey hair that was swept up in an elegant chignon held securely by a tiny, ornate comb in mother-of-pearl.

'Welcome, my dears,' said our host, Madame Stanislov, in a soft drawl with a hint of an Eastern European accent. 'I was at school with Marc… Marc Chagall. He gave me many of his early works, long before he came to be well known. Now, please come and take a seat in the drawing room. William will bring us tea.' She nodded to her butler, who, with a slight bow, glided quietly out of the room as if on roller skates.

We perched at the end of a silk-covered chaise longue redolent of the style of Louis XIV, with Andrew sitting calmly between us making polite conversation.

Later, in the car as we were leaving, it was explained that the Stanislovs had escaped from St Petersburg just before the revolution in 1917. Miriam's late husband, a jeweller and an expert in precious stones, promised his young wife that one day he would buy this park, where they now lived, if, and when their fortunes changed. During the Depression that gripped America in 1929, he managed to buy the park estate at a knock-down price after the owner threw himself from the nineteenth floor of a building in Wall Street after losing all his stock in the market crash. The Stanislovs managed to raise four successful sons, Nathaniel, Jacob, Abraham and Ruben, who each built a house on one of the four corners of the estate. It emerged that only the first two brothers continued to run the present business. The other two were academics and had other interests.

Not long afterwards, we were joined for dinner by Nathaniel and Jacob. Although we got on extremely well despite our being relative strangers, the aspirations that we had did not accord to theirs, for production in volume and the weakening of the design label for the mass market in cheaper clothes did not appeal to us. Perhaps we were naive, but they insisted that their expansive plan was the only way to make 'big bucks', as the Americans say.

An hour before midnight, we proffered our grateful thanks and numerous apologies for keeping the family up so late. Back at the hotel, we sent Madame a bouquet of orange and yellow roses to thank her for her gracious hospitality.

Soon, we were to leave New York and, via Kennedy Airport, return home to England. It was somewhat of a relief. There was much to mull over concerning the future direction of our lives.

Over the winter, work progressed routinely. Not even a fun job supplying clothes for a television film on the BBC, designing costumes for an obscure horror movie in Germany, or even a substantial contract from Avon Cosmetics to help design and supply brightly coloured rings to match their lipsticks, could lift our mood or allay our anxieties about the future.

It seems that momentous decisions are made with the start of a new decade. The beginning of the '70s was no different. The voting age in the UK had been lowered from twenty-one to eighteen, following a Representation of the People Act passed in Parliament the previous year. In the US, Nixon sanctioned the covert bombing of Cambodia, followed by ground troops in an effort to disrupt the supply routes to North Vietnam. A further escalation of protests against the war inevitably followed.

In April, the Beatles announced that the band had finally broken up, leading to heartache and tears among their legions of fans throughout the world. Oil was discovered in the North Sea and Britain thought that this would bring untold wealth to the country. Sensible voices from industry and government cautioned that the nation should wait and see.

It was well into Easter, following a holiday to North Africa, and after much soul-searching, that Caroline and I decided that to take the discussions much further with the tentative offer of investment from the Americans would not be in our own interest in the long run. We would in effect lose control of the business and the label, and would be bound by contract to a large overseas corporation for over ten years. And where would that leave us, if we wanted time off to start a family? Crucially, we recognised that fashion was a young person's business, with the need and capacity for endless energy, promotion, networking, travel and so on. I knew, deep down, that I wanted something different to fulfil me as I grew older – something, perhaps, that involved my earlier scientific training.

And Caroline desperately wanted a break from having to think season after season into the future, trying to forecast trends a year in advance, which in effect lopped off years before we even had the chance to live them. *Because living in the future, and not in the present made us feel older before our time.* She had fulfilled a large part of her design dream and had done her bit, well in excess of what was expected of her, in the five years of our business partnership and the three of our marriage. Now we felt that Caroline had nothing else to prove. Looking back, as a twosome, we had covered a lot of ground from scratch.

Earlier in the spring, an architect friend and our next-door neighbour in the mews, named Jeffrey Sorenson, had persuaded us to buy his magnificent large house, which was treble the size of our property and had been completely modernised, winning many design awards. Ahead of its time, it had a teak and stainless steel fitted kitchen with a waste disposal unit and hob, a bathroom with a sunken bath and bidet, underfloor heating, quarry tiles, bleached wood, bifold double-glazed doors from a design studio that opened into the mews, and even a spacious roof terrace with a fitted barbecue. Having sold our house to a director of a merchant bank who wanted a pied-à-terre in town, we realised that, if needed, the new house could easily be divided into two units, each with its own bathroom, living space, bedrooms and kitchen, so that one flat could be let for income and to mitigate the large mortgage.

It was not long after the General Election in June, when the Tory leader Edward Heath defeated Harold Wilson, that we saw Andrew on his visit to the UK, told him of our decision and repaid his company's loan with interest. He asked us to reconsider; but it was all in vain. Our minds had been made up.

After a sustained period of good, sunny weather, with clouds of leaf blossom flying through the air prolonging the hay fever season, three major events happened that changed our lives forever.

Firstly; we brought the curtain down on our fashion business at the Carlton Tower Hotel, where two Carolyne Stuart dresses were chosen, with others, to feature on stage in the Woolmark Quality Awards. I thought there and then, with quiet satisfaction, that this was probably Caroline's swansong.

As things stood, we had come to terms with abandoning our search for fame – that elusive commodity that we, like so many when young and hungry, had craved when starting out. In retrospect, it can be said that Caroline had tiptoed onto the first rung of its slippery ladder. In doing so, we had flirted on the periphery of a world inhabited by some of the rich and famous – but, more often the struggling and the not-so-famous. Forsaking that dream that had once gripped us, we were now perfectly happy to retire to the relative oblivion of peaceful obscurity and to find another part of ourselves. But in seeking the flip side of the coin – the twin part of fame, called fortune – well, as my father cryptically once said;

'Like sipping the rarest nectar from the golden tree, or ascending the highest peak in the world, you never miss what you have never tasted.'

But would we miss the adventures, the parties, the creative gatherings and the interesting people of the last five years? There had been many. Amongst them, one stuck in my mind. Earlier in the year, we had been invited to a house-warming party at Wimpole Mews, in the former flat of the late society osteopath Stephen Ward, who seven years earlier had taken his own life during a trial at the Old Bailey following the highly charged political sex scandal concerning John Profumo and Christine Keeler. The flat was rented by a sophisticated, amusing girl called Dolly Bird (perhaps a sobriquet?) who worked for an American textile company. Transiently, like many others at the time, we became short-term friends. Over coffee one day, she remarked pointedly to me that I wasn't really cut out for sales, nor ruthless enough to pursue the high altar of Mammon in the rag trade. And she suggested that, in her humble opinion, due to my supposedly empathetic nature I was more suited to work somewhere in the medical field, rather than the rat race of making money. I dismissed it out of hand as idle chatter. But we will never forget that famous party, during which some of her guests, high on something more than champagne, set the curtains on fire. Just before the police and fire brigade arrived to investigate, we were advised to escape by climbing out of the bathroom window. We never saw Dolly again.

Secondly; my brother Alan called on us and announced that he had won a scholarship to Harvard Business School and was soon to be married to a delightful girl named Jean, prior to taking up his place in Boston. We were thrilled for him, and extremely proud of his achievement. I must admit that there was a tiny pang of envy for his being in a position to radically change direction and his life. I would have to bide my time to see if, and when my opportunity would come along. In the meantime, there would be a bit of a dilemma, as Alan had held the fort with our brother-in-law Daniel, the acting manager of the restaurant, after my falling-out with my father. He asked if I could go back to Birmingham to help sort out the lease and the business, which was now practically collapsing and causing strife between our ageing parents. I was in a quandary; a most invidious position. To return to Birmingham, I felt, would be a retrograde step.

Thirdly; the decision was then taken out of my hands when a call came from the police in Liverpool. My father had crashed his car on a dual carriageway on the way to visit his brother, Chun Tileng, on Merseyside. He was in a confused and agitated state. It had apparently happened after a family row and his walking out on the business. The staff had been agitated by the falling trade. Bills and threatening letters kept piling up one after another. All his life, he had never been in debt, and furthermore, he had never been in a position of not being able to pay his creditors. According to the police, my father had taken with him the last of his cash savings from the safe, stuffed the notes into his pockets and vowed that he would never return home to Birmingham. Feeling sorry for a frail old man who was plainly distraught, the police were sympathetic and drove him to my uncle's after calling out a garage to take away his crashed Wolseley.

Uncle called me on the telephone and said that Father was bruised, shaken and extremely distressed. He put him on to speak to me. It was the first time we had spoken for over two years. I didn't recognise his voice. It was weak and hoarse and kept breaking up.

'*Look, I'm coming to Liverpool to get you!*' I said immediately.

What I had just said, didn't seem to register.

'Your mother,' he mumbled with a plaintive cry, 'kept on about the children and failing to get you and the rest of the family married off. There were arguments… And what would happen to the family and to the business? She *just* doesn't understand! *It's a damn mess,* and the staff… the suppliers… the bank… the landlords…'

'Don't worry, *ah Ba*,'[96] I offered, trying to calm and reassure him. From the top of my head, without really thinking how it would work and without having the chance to discuss it with Caroline beforehand, I blurted out…

'*Look, I'm coming home. I'm going to take over the business, get the lease renewed, sort out the problems with the bank and the creditors, and then sell it for you so that you can retire!*'

'*WH – YOU WHAT?!*' he said in disbelief.

I repeated what I had just said. This time, I was unsure whether I really meant it or not.

The next morning, after telling my wife what had happened, and before she could dissuade me, I caught the late Saturday morning train to Lime Street. Father was waiting for me. I hardly recognised him. He was a shadow of the man he had been when we had last set eyes on each other; frail and unsure of himself. I wanted to take his arm, but, in typical Chinese fashion, unused to physical contact, we did not embrace or even shake hands. I hailed a taxi, and without a further word we travelled to Uncle's house in resigned silence. This time, I could not refuse to help him in his hour of desperate need.

---

96   Familiar address for 'Father'.

Part VIII

1970 – 1974

Chapter 46

THE MOMENT OF TRUTH

Wallasey, Merseyside, England, 1970

T HE TAXI JOURNEY TO Uncle's house in Wallasey seemed to take
an age because of the long, drawn-out silence. As we approached
the house, increasingly I dreaded facing Uncle, his wife Fong, and
Aunt Chun Rei. But I needn't have worried unduly as they opened the
door to me with a relieved expression, added to which, a determined
smile.

'*Shui Lun… a Lun… Dai doi.*' ('Shui Lun… Francis… Son.')
Solicitously, Aunt Chun Rei ushered me through the front door.
'*Ngyam-ngyam fai sik fan!*'[97] ('Just in time to eat dinner!')

Uncle and Father quietly followed us into the dining room, and
my four young cousins tumbled downstairs to greet me as we all sat
down to a family meal. Winnie, the oldest of my cousins, a gregarious
young teenager, told me to tuck into the fried noodles and stuffed
mushrooms. 'What brings you to Merseyside, cousin?' she asked with
her mouth full.

'Oh, just passing by… thought it was about time to visit you,
having not seen you since your sister Lisa was a little baby.' I faltered,
lying through my teeth.

---

97   *Sik fan*: literally, to 'eat rice'. A colloquialism for eating a meal.

Uncle stared in my direction, hoping that there would be no more searching questions. Quickly, using her chopsticks Aunt Fong speared off a piece of steaming fish covered in black beans into my rice bowl. '*Fai sik fan! Yee ho fie doong!*' she commanded, defusing the situation. ('Quickly, eat up! It'll soon get cold!')

After the meal, we convened in the sitting room and the children returned to watch television in their sisters' room. Aunt Fong indicated that I could sleep on the sofa for the night, pointing to an untidy stack of blankets already there. I apologised for putting them out, but Uncle just waved me away and raised the matter of my returning to Birmingham to tackle the lease and business for my father. Not daring to look him in the eye, I nodded assiduously.

There was a pregnant pause. Everyone wondered what was going to happen next. The moment's silence dragged on. Slowly, Father got up out of his chair. He pushed it backwards with a squeal of the feet and went to stand in front of the window with his back to us. Gazing out into the street as if gathering his thoughts, he said, slowly and with a shake of the head,

'*Shui Lun... A lun. Gnor, hung nee lo moo, hee-mung nee fai go yun. Nee yee gar samsut sui. Chun Rei sieng gai suei a ho jung gwok nui!*' ('Shui Lun... Francis. We and your mother want you to get married soon. You are now thirty years old. Your Aunt Chun Rei will introduce a nice Chinese girl to you!')

Straight away, I had to blurt out in English, half-hoping that they could not fully grasp what I was about to say...

'But – but, um – *ah Ba*... Father. I am *already* married. *I have been for the last three years!*'

You could have heard a pin drop. It was followed by an awkward silence – a deathly long silence. Uncle looked askance at his wife. Aunt Chun Rei stared at me with astonished but sympathetic eyes.

Then my father spun around on his heels to face me, his weary face reddening as his jaw gripped in a savage grimace. 'You WHAT?! Pardon?! *What* did you say?'

'*I-I have been ma-married since 1967,*' I stammered. 'You were in

Hong Kong for Rose's wedding. You had just returned from China with Sam and her. You know… I got married near Cambridge, in August three years ago,' I reiterated, to emphasise the fact.

Stupefied, he stared at me in silence. He then slumped back into his chair and pulled out a handkerchief to dab at his forehead, his face ashen. He opened his mouth to say something, but nothing came out. Tactfully, to ease the tension, Aunt Fong got up and rushed into the kitchen to make some tea.

'Do you remember that petite European girl, smartly dressed, whom I brought to the restaurant – the one you met at Chinese New Year five years ago?'

I could see that my father's brain was racing furiously, trying to recall the meeting. His blank eyes suddenly blinked as the penny dropped with the image of shaking hands with Caroline, whom I had introduced as a journalist from London. Knowing that, without daring to admit it, he secretly admired attractive women who had style, whatever their origin, I now took the chance to reveal parts of my clandestine life to him. The situation was like it had been many years ago in Wrexham in 1952, when he was at his lowest ebb on hunger strike, just as vulnerable as he was now. I felt I could say anything to him at this moment, for I had the upper hand, just as I had then.

'But… but she was… um… *lo fan nui* – an *English* girl!' His voice, already disjointed, crumbled as both languages became confused in his distress.

'I have to tell you that my wife, Caroline, is an educated graduate. Her mother is a deputy head teacher, and her late father was a headmaster and a distinguished British Army major during the war. We have worked successfully together in the clothing business over the last five years. We have bought a house in Central London, with good neighbours and friends.'

Desperately, I looked towards Uncle and my aunts for support. Gently, Uncle nodded approvingly but did not dare to say a word. Bound by filial tradition as the youngest, he kept palpably silent – wrestling with his conscience.

Just at that critical moment, Aunt Chun Rei came to the rescue.

'*Um gun-yiu! Yee gar a Lun… yee jung yee… ho sek lo fan nui… um… wah jek, jung gwok nui. Um gun-yiu.*' ('It doesn't matter, young Francis! If you love an English girl or a Chinese girl. Doesn't matter.')

She spread out her hands in a resigned gesture. '*Gee gun-yiu – quoi ho yun. Hung moi tan bak. Um dai hok. Gee gun-yui fun a sik!*' ('Most important is that she's a good person, honest, educated. And that together, you find a good living!')

Somewhat encouraged, I thought I had better strike while the going was good. I then told Father that sister Milly had also got married last year in the same village in Godmanchester as I did, through the kindness of my mother-in-law, Mary Stuart. I explained that Milly's husband was an English graduate, a former Oxford tutor and now a top manager in an international company.

But when I mentioned that Alan was planning to get married to a local girl, a schoolteacher, and then take his place at Harvard in a matter of months, Father's face, already swollen with pain, collapsed. He was absolutely, distraught at his favourite son leaving for the States. I could swear that I detected his eyes welling up, which he did his utmost to conceal. Immediately, I felt guilty for suddenly burdening him with this trio of revelations at such a vulnerable time, considering his rift with my mother and the turmoil and crises in the business. It was a cowardly time to do it, but I felt that there was no other way. Furthermore, I quickly realised that it would probably kill him if I sprung more surprises on him; namely that the two younger sisters, Brenda and Ester, were planning to marry after Alan – and to English men whom they'd met at college. And so I buried the news for now.

It had been bad enough when, ten years ago, his eldest, Eileen, had run away to marry against his wishes. The fallout in the family had been indescribable. To see him defeated and so exposed gave me no pleasure. The image of his tiger-like control over us that, frankly, had once scared me when I was growing up no longer held true. For the moment, he had shrunk into a quiet shell of what he had once been. It was a hollow victory, and evoked my guilt and remorse.

Inevitably, sleep that night for all concerned was a nightmare. But fortunately, the following morning at breakfast, there was no further mention of the clandestine marriages. I think my father, my uncle and my aunts were still shell-shocked at the sudden bombshell of the day before.

Father agreed, albeit reluctantly, to return home to Birmingham the next day. For the second time in our lives, there would be a reversal of roles, with the son protecting and escorting the father, now weakened and vulnerable, back home, and not the other way around. I could see that he was nervous and still troubled, but from time to time on the journey, I chatted selectively about my plans for the restaurant business to get him out of the firing line. It seemed to calm him down.

By the time we got to Portland Road, it was early evening. Mother said hardly a word, but there was obvious relief in her eyes that I had turned up after such a long time away. She sat us down to dinner, with just Rose with her baby son sitting on her lap. After some persuasion, Father sat reluctantly at the opposite end of the table, eating very little. No one spoke as we stared numbly down at the dishes of food, which were quickly getting cold. Like the food, the atmosphere rapidly chilled.

As soon as Father went upstairs to his room, I told my mother what I had told him about my being married since 1967, as well as Milly marrying last year. Remarkably, she took it well in her stride, after initially blowing her top in exasperation at my duplicity. After a barrage of tears, she asked if I had a photograph of my wife. I showed her a wedding photograph which I kept in my wallet. Tears started to flow again. I wasn't too sure whether they were for me or for her, bearing in mind the yoke of unhappiness she had carried for all those years since, as a young girl, she had been made to leave home in an arranged marriage in which she had no say. But she had stayed in her turbulent marriage through thick and thin, because it was her duty, and because it was expected of her.

The following morning, I told my parents separately that I had to return to London to sort things out. I planned to return as soon as I feasibly could. Sacrificing my life in London and the compromise of status by running a difficult restaurant in Birmingham were essential if I was to save the family and heal the rift between my parents. My promise to my father would be carried out, regardless of the obstacles that faced me.

Chapter 47

THE FREEZE BEFORE THE THAW

Birmingham, England, 1970

A WEEK HAD FLOWN by in a flash by the time my affairs in London were in some semblance of order. We managed to let out the upper part of the house to an extremely pleasant engineer named Anthony, who took a tenancy for six months as he was in the process of starting a new job in Brussels, having sold his house in Yorkshire following his divorce. Over the following months he would spend a considerable amount of time travelling, which suited us both. In the meantime, I managed to rent a small flat in a residential part of Birmingham called Moseley Village, and after packing a few clothes, drove there to settle in. When I told my parents of my plans, they quite naturally did not believe it until it had really happened.

Immediately, my brother-in-law Daniel and I set about trying to sort out the restaurant's problems. This allowed Alan to return to London to finalise his move to the States and organise his imminent wedding before he left. It was a chaotic time. The task appeared daunting, for it was magnified under the impossibly strained atmosphere of my parents not speaking to each other. Getting two intransigent and old-fashioned Chinese people to break their deathly silence when they had never had to learn the art of verbal communication was tantamount to impossible, because all their lives, my father had just issued orders to my mother on the assumption of her obedience. In old China, this was the traditional norm. But if her years living in Britain had taught Mother anything at all, it was that wives had the right to an opinion and the facility to answer back. Not surprisingly, this had contributed to their almighty row.

For a start, the apartment Father had bought in Hong Kong three years ago was lying fallow. It would be empty for months on end, used only occasionally by his relatives passing through. Realising that his savings were shrinking, and declaring that we, the children, had no intention of living there, he had instructed one of the cousins to sell it. Instead of the proceeds returning to England, however, the money was sent back to China to be shared amongst his brothers. My mother had protested vehemently that my father should have considered his own family first, if not his own needs.

Taking over my father's business was not as easy as I first thought. The problems appeared insurmountable. High on my list of priorities was shielding my father from creditors and possible bailiffs, which proved no easy task. They would just blunder through the door, demanding to see the owner. After a little while, I could recognise them as soon as they approached the premises. They came in all shapes and guises, some more threatening than others.

A well-spoken man came twice, asking for 'Mr Kwong Chun Ji'. Alarm bells rang, as to me he looked like a lawyer, perhaps with a summons. To protect my father, my standard reply, and what I had instructed the staff to say, was, *'The old man has retired and has nothing more to do with the business. What's more, there was no forwarding address.'*

The man asked if I was his son. Vehemently, I denied that I was. I said that I was *just* an employee. But, as soon as I said that, I had a momentary flash of guilt and wondered if Peter, who once denied his reverend master, felt the same – *(although the two examples cannot be considered even remotely, comparable).*

Apart from trying to stabilise the dwindling business with a range of new ideas – a fresh menu, decorating the restaurant floor and making the dining room more intimate by altering the lighting – I set about prioritising paying off the suppliers who had outstanding invoices beyond the forty-day period. Many of them were old, loyal firms whom I had engaged over twelve years ago when I set the place up with my father. The linen hire company, the fruit-and-vegetable suppliers, the market butchers, and the suppliers of frozen seafood were relatively happy, if not surprised, that I had returned in my father's place. Like the landlords, they were quite prepared to give me a chance to sort things out. But I was warned that there would be a time limit for my endeavours. Supporting Daniel, together with the history of my previous relationship with the suppliers and the bank and so on, bought us time to try to improve the turnover. But that would count for nothing if I failed to deliver.

Next, on my list of priorities, it was vital that I introduced Caroline to my father, who, despite the prevailing circumstances, was quite welcoming. Frankly, he was still stunned by the events that had overtaken him over the past few months, so, in a state of shock, he couldn't have been more polite. Moreover, it reassured him that bringing my wife to stay with me in Birmingham and letting out part of my house at least demonstrated the seriousness of my intent regarding the business.

Rolling up my sleeves, it was hands on in the dining room to welcome the customers, and that helped to lift the morale of the Chinese waiting staff. Unfortunately, but not unexpectedly, lacking fluent English and the nuances of good, cheerful service, they gave the impression of a dour and impersonal attitude that would never enhance the flavour and experience of a meal, however good the cooking. *That had to change!* In the kitchen, the head chef was still the amiable Mr Yip – a rotund, smiling Cantonese who had cooked at the Chinese New Year dinner dance in 1965. We got on like old friends; for he at least was on my side and willing to help to turn things around.

But how to mend our broken family and revitalise an empty nest that had grown increasingly cold after the children had left home presented the biggest challenge I had faced for a long time. The task seemed insuperable. Eileen and her husband had opened a successful business of their own on the outskirts of Birmingham for they also had their own house, not far away, where they were bringing up a fine young son as well as their daughter Juliet. It was now left up to Rose and me to think of a ruse to get two immovable statues – our implacable parents – to thaw. It was easier said than done.

It is often said that, as we humans grow older, however much we try to slow down the passage of time, it is nigh impossible. Alan's wedding arrived before we had the chance to gather our breath or sort out our parents. It took place in Warwick, the home of the bride. Remarkably, Mother and all my siblings agreed to turn up, as we knew that it would be some time before we would see our brother again, once he left for the States. The sun shone magnificently on that windless, cloud-free day, but it couldn't overcome the rancorous atmosphere that overshadowed it.

As we congregated outside the church, outwardly Mother did not seem fazed on meeting Caroline for the very first time. Language proved difficult, but tactile gestures, emollient smiles and the holding of hands transcend most barriers, however awkward or alien it felt to either of them. Similarly, she seemed to take meeting Milly's new husband in her stride, followed by the respective fiancés of my two younger sisters. If she was anxious, then she did not show it. I thought that it must have been a terrifying revelation and an awful surprise enough for her to meet two new English daughters-in-law, Caroline and Jean – *ALL in one day*. And now, being forced to absorb all these strangers into her family in one fell swoop, without any preparatory warning or preliminary contact, was asking a lot of her. Having been sheltered all her life in a different society, cut off and not speaking English, I think shock carried her through that day. Thinking back on it, it was particularly unfair to someone who wasn't used to meeting people, never mind those from another country. To outsiders, this seemed a cruel way to do it. I tried to justify the situation by saying that the circumstances dictated the events, but it still did not alleviate my feelings of guilt about the way that it unfolded.

Above all, Father was distraught at not being able to be present at his son's wedding. It was soul-shattering to observe his reaction. Alan and I tried to persuade him to attend. *'How could I possibly, in the circumstances?'* he cried. Overcome with grief, he retreated to his room and slammed the door.

He had, of course, been invited, but felt that due to the family rift, he just, couldn't attend. This added anguish was heaped onto an old man whose one fault was that all his life as a father, he had tried his level best to earn a living to protect his children from the vagaries of life across racial and social barriers, and to look after his siblings in China. ***All because of duty.*** And now, this fallout, because of his intransigence – rooted in his background, his isolation from the family, seemed grossly callous. He had already taken immeasurable blows over the past few months, if not decades, with his children growing away from him and all that he had fought for. It was something no man, however seemingly indestructible, could be expected to continue to take before ultimately breaking.

Whilst my brother and his new wife were away on their honeymoon in France, my sister and I worked on the side lines in an effort to erode the icy atmosphere that had infected the family. We tried to normalise the situation by talking to both Father and Mother about the different members of the family, and especially the newcomers – who they were, and what they were all doing – in the hope that they would eventually seem more familiar and less like foreign interlopers.

At Heathrow, six weeks later, Caroline and I saw Alan and Jean off to the States. It was a sad and emotional moment, and a turning point in our lives.

Refusing to dwell on this, I diverted my attention to trying to save the business. It struck me that I was hopelessly out of touch with the massive rise in competition in Birmingham catering over the past few years, with the mass development and changes in the city centre. The mushrooming competition came not only from Greek, Indian and Italian restaurants, but revitalised pubs and wine bars that now offered cooked food. Meanwhile, the number of people eating out was remaining noticeably static, if not shrinking. Several new, modern Chinese restaurants had also sprung up, as well as a plethora of Chinese takeaways, kebab shops, hamburger bars and pizza places. The days of Liang Nam having a monopoly were patently over.

New ideas to spruce up the family restaurant, coupled with some publicity in the local papers, stimulated some interest in the short term. A photograph of the head chef, Mr Yip, in his chef's hat and uniform, beaming from ear to ear and brandishing a boar's head on a silver platter brimming with lychees and longans (translucent white fruit that look like dragon's eyes) appeared in the evening paper. A cooking demonstration in which honey-glazed duck was prepared on TV for a party of diners drew a surge in bookings. And the hanging of oil paintings loaned by Tamara Tipping (who was an accomplished artist, having exhibited in various London galleries) to embellish the walls attracted the attention of the papers and gave us some respite with a spike in new customer numbers. But deep down, I knew that in the longer term something radical had to be done; for catering to the public at large, I realised from dining out, was an extremely fickle business as any seasoned restaurateur will testify. Customers drift restlessly from one new venue to another in their insatiable curiosity to try out new things.

Meanwhile, with the tail end of autumn fast approaching, Caroline and I did our best to return to our house and friends in London every two weeks or so. It was extremely hard for her to make a life and new friends in a new city, especially with the unsociable hours of the catering business, which added to her isolation and sense of herself as an outsider, having suddenly been thrust into an alien society, which was predominantly Chinese, because of me. The irony now was that *she*, like my mother, was cut off due to language and cultural barriers. We had to admit that it put an early strain on our marriage.

Nevertheless, my sister and I continued in our quest to bring our parents together. We were aware that, for some considerable time prior to their monumental row, they had speculated about selling the rambling old house in Portland Road since all their children had left home. The house needed updating, and buying a smaller, more modern place that needed less maintenance and which had gas central heating and a new built-in kitchen seemed sensible. Father had also talked of having a garage adjoining the house.

Therefore, working on that premise, we hinted broadly to them both (separately) that we, as a family, ought to look at modern houses outside of the city say, in Staffordshire, perhaps ready for the future. After much resistance and innumerable objections, we finally managed to get them into the same car and take them to see several properties around Burntwood and Lichfield, about fifteen to twenty miles away. It was an achievement to get them into the same place at the same time. This provided them with a natural opportunity to spontaneously voice comments or offer criticism about different aspects of the properties – the layout, for instance; or the suitability or not of the location; and so on. It provided a diversionary tactic to focus on a third object or situation. Such a galvanising ploy is often employed when warring factions (say, in government) unite against a third party – such as a common enemy. Without trivialising the serious nature of how certain parties operate in a make-or-break crisis *(our situation was hardly comparable)*, the strategy usually works.

Above all else, it was refreshing to take them out of the frigid atmosphere of Portland Road to see new places and towns that they didn't really know. It gave them (and us) something to talk about instead of dwelling on the perennial problems of family or business. Moreover, it was fortuitous that Father insisted on bringing young Juliet with him, as she was the glue that had previously kept our parents together. Their interaction could not fail to be provoked, because, intermittently, they would lavish their love and attention on their favourite and firstborn grandchild. This youngster, through her uninhibited laughter and singing managed to coax a few short, civilised words from her grandparents, individually at first, then gradually in unison, without their realising it initially. By the time they noticed, it was too late for them to retract or to retreat into their self-imposed shells.

At the house, gradually, with a little subterfuge, we managed to get our parents to increase their cooperation; say, in preparing a meal, which necessitated some discussion – albeit with the minimum number of words – using my sister and me as conduits. Words fail to describe adequately the feeling of relief that washed over us. We felt that there had been a breakthrough.

Then, with the atmosphere in the house thawing despite the temperatures falling rapidly outside, I promised that, in the spring of next year, Caroline and I would take them and some of the family to Venice. They had never been on holiday since they came to Britain – Father fifty years ago and Mother some thirty-five years likewise. In fact, even when we were small, we had never experienced a family holiday with our parents. It would be a first. Encouraged by their receptive reaction, we gave them travel brochures to look at. We detected a frisson of anticipation. As family foils, we would take Juliet and my brother, Tom, on this trip of reconciliation. How Caroline would feel about going on holiday with a Chinese family, one that was laborious and difficult to get to know, was another matter. And this time, she would stick out like the ubiquitous sore thumb. Courageously, she said that she did not mind.

Now that the family was getting on again, it was right and proper that Mary, Caroline's mother, should visit and meet my parents, which she did. We also discovered that, unknown to the family, Father had surreptitiously taken Juliet in his car and visited Jean's parents before Alan and Jean had left for the States. No one knew about this until we found a photograph of them all together outside Jean's family house.

In keeping with tradition, Father felt that it was important that he should meet his sons' in-laws at least once, regardless of the difficult circumstances that prevailed.

But for now, our business worries had eased somewhat, with Daniel having stabilised the situation, though we knew that with each month that passed there would be new problems. Therefore, I put that to the back of my mind; but only for the time being. I felt that, with things at Portland Road and at the business gradually improving, Caroline and I could return home to London for a few days. At least my parents were talking again. My siblings gave a massive sigh of relief. Suppressing jubilation, I wrote to Alan and Jean with the good news.

With the weather changing rapidly, as late October gave way to its fellow month of fog and frosty interludes, Caroline returned to London ahead of me to open up the house as Anthony, our lodger, was returning from a business trip. We planned to go out to dinner in order to catch up. The underfloor heating under the quarry tiles on the ground floor needed switching on for the winter, and the coke-burning, Pither stove needed to be fired up. We were confident that this would warm the two upper floors through its steel flue.

It was a freezing Sunday morning, with condensation still hanging like a spray of white emulsion on to the windowpanes, when I was rudely awoken by the telephone ringing from the hallway in the flat. Looking at the clock beside my bed, it was still only 6.30 in the morning. The telephone persisted in its shrill ring. Cursing, I climbed out of bed and quickly put on my dressing gown, as it was cold, damp and dark outside. The flat had no central heating, just an ancient two-bar electric fire which seldom worked.

It was Anthony, ringing from London. 'Francis, dear chap, are you sitting down?'

'What do you mean?' I replied as I stifled a yawn.

'Look, Caroline is here. Sorry, old chap... but I have to tell you that your house burnt down last night as we lit the stove!'

There was an audible silence. This time, I did sit down on the nearest chair that I could grab. My teeth started to rattle; a quiver spread to my whole body.

'Wha... *what in hell do you mean?* Is this your idea of a joke?' I snapped back aggressively.

'Yesterday evening, your wife asked me to help her fire the stove. After a while, we got it alight. At first it was stubborn, not having been used since last winter, so we had to use extra firelighters. Eventually, it was warming up. Then, as we added more fuel, it suddenly became red hot. I went back to my rooms to unpack and, whoosh, before I knew it, the place was full of smoke!'

Caroline came on the phone. I could barely hear her voice through her tears. Distressed and still in shock, she said that, luckily, Anthony had rushed downstairs and dragged her out and our next-door neighbour Chris had telephoned the fire brigade. Apparently two fire crews quickly arrived, followed by the London Salvage Corps. She said that at first it seemed like an eternity, but after ten minutes or so, the fire was under control. It appeared that the flue from the stove had split going through the joists between the ceiling and floor of the first and second floors, before emerging via the terrace on the roof.

'*Our poor, lovely new house has been destroyed!*' Caroline cried like a wounded banshee as the painful cadence in her speech petered out.

'*Please, please, my love, don't worry too much. I'll sort it out... as long as YOU are safe and all right; the damn house doesn't really matter one bit. It's only bricks and mortar... As long as you are unhurt. That's the main thing!*'

Although as soon as I said it, I felt a bit of a hypocrite. I didn't dare to voice what I *really* felt at the sudden loss of our beautiful dream home, into which we had sunk our last penny and that of our parents. Losing our London base, our sole refuge from the alien and stressful life in Birmingham and the symbol of our only remaining anchor of continuity with our friends and our former life, was devastating. My heart, already out of control, exploded loudly in my chest

'*Nothing really matters as long as you are not injured! Tell Anthony that I'll get there as soon as I can.*'

My trembling voice, now hoarse, trailed away. In the circumstances, not only did reassurances seem inadequate, but the words sounded quite hollow coming from me. I felt totally useless and helpless, being stuck 130 miles away.

Prue, our good and kindly neighbour who lived opposite us in the mews, and Chris next door had put Caroline and Anthony up the previous night. They were safe. The house, however, was badly damaged and full of rancid smoke, with parts of it having been charred to cinders.

I quickly changed and told my parents and brother-in-law what had happened. Without waiting for their reaction, I jumped into my car and drove at speed, shaking all the way to London and worrying about whether I had paid the house insurance with our not inconsiderable mortgage.

Chapter 48

RESTORATION

March, 1971

ON A DEPRESSING, CLOUDY afternoon, as I stood outside the house with Caroline shivering beside me, staring at the front of the building, there wasn't a hint on its exterior as to the extent of the damage inside. Outwardly, it appeared as if nothing of consequence had happened the night before. But as soon as we opened the front door, the sight of the blackened, charred remains of the front room where the Pither stove stood hit me with its full force. It was like I imagined the aftermath of a tornado would look. It was the choking smell of the pungent smoke, which had lingered, trapped within the house, that was the biggest shock and made us gag. A cloying smell of burnt wood and plaster seeped throughout the building, seeking out every tiny crevice. It clung to every single thing that remained there – whether they were soft furnishings or furniture in the other rooms of the house that had miraculously escaped damage, clothing, or other personal effects that we had thought would be immune. Even the crockery hidden in the kitchen cupboards was covered in a thick film of carbon dust or smeared in a brown, glue-like substance. Nothing had escaped the ravages of the fire, which must have devoured everything in its path.

Our neighbours, seeing our discomfort and misery, persuaded us to have some tea at their house next door, where we were joined by a mournful but remarkably stoical Anthony, who tried to lift the sombre atmosphere with a joke about not wanting anything remotely barbecued or even toasted. We were too bewildered to argue or to make light of it.

In times of crisis, it is an unassailable fact that you can always count on real friends and good neighbours. And so, it turned out. Jeffrey, our architect friend, the previous owner of the house, had rushed over from his place in the country to offer his support and professional help. Straight away, he offered to help to deal with the insurance company, which of course we immediately accepted as we were too numb and still floundering around trying to work out what to do next. True to his word, he got in contact with the insurers the following day. Expertly, he cut through the red tape of bureaucratic negotiations. Two days later, a professional cleaning company was instructed to fumigate and swab down the interior of the house to enable suitable conditions for us to enter the building to sort out our belongings. All the remaining furniture and possessions that had escaped the fire were moved into a lock-up garage at the end of the mews.

Within five weeks, a financial settlement was secured that would allow restoration works to take place. The charred remains were stripped out by a family firm of builders. The offending stove was removed for salvage. Renovation and rebuilding proceeded with due haste. Towards the end of March 1971, our dream home, against all expectations and devastation, rose out of the ashes like a phoenix reborn. Not long afterwards, to celebrate we threw a raucous party to exorcise the ghost of the fire that had nearly destroyed us, even though poor Caroline continued to have nightmares for some time to come. But in the end, it made us appreciate the true and lasting value of the priorities of life – good health, being alive, unconditional love, kindness, and friendships with good neighbours and friends which meant so much more than mere material possessions that had proved so fragile and flammable.

In May, with early summer hovering on the cusp of the Whitsun bank holiday, we took my parents, Juliet and Tom on a ten-day holiday to Venice. We stayed at a large, modern hotel with its own secluded beach on the Lido di Jesolo, which enabled us to cross by a short ferry ride from a pier conveniently located at the bottom of the road to the island of Venice. A delightful English family from Norfolk befriended us during mealtimes at the hotel. Juliet palled up with their young daughter, who was the same age as she was.

Contrary to what Caroline had expected, after a nervous start, she enjoyed the trip as much as the rest of the family did. Like me, she was pleased to see my parents relaxed and happy; surprisingly, they even waded together into the calm blue sea, which was remarkably warm for the time of year. The Venetian sun shone down in all its benevolence and banished the clouds each morning to prevent the dampening of our spirits. The locals made us welcome, as did the pleasant heat from the Adriatic breeze that surrounded us each day like a friendly cocoon. It was just the tonic that everyone needed after the traumatic and dramatic past six months, and we savoured every single moment of it, wishing, unrealistically, that it would last forever.

On alternate days, we took excursions to see the astonishing sights of Venice. Armed with a guidebook, Caroline pointed out with relish the Gothic grandeur of the Doge's Palace, the imperious bell tower and the striated golden domes on the flamboyant Byzantine basilica in St Mark's Square. With an excited sweep of the arm, she showed us the ornate Rialto Bridge in the distance, with its glittering jewellery boutiques and market stalls gracefully straddling the Grand Canal. Our eyes followed the magical stretch of water with its bubbles of sunlight bouncing effervescently from the wash of the lagoon, churned up by the pretty painted gondolas weaving their way along the canal. We were told that this was the main thoroughfare and lifeblood of the city, and that we could travel the length of it via water bus, which we eventually did.

Languidly gazing along the canal, grand palazzos and elegant churches too numerous to mention filled the vista with a blaze of colour that hinted of their treasures, some of which were hidden away from mortal sight with their richness of art, culture and wealth. Caroline said that we could virtually taste and feel Venice's proud and arrogant past through the paintings by the maestro Canaletto from the XVIII century.

On other days, we took trips around the islands of Burano and Torcello, and observed the ancient skill of glass-blowing on the island of Murano. Not surprisingly, my parents enjoyed these excursions most of all. Dragging them around the grand churches, and cathedrals such as the Basilica of Santa Maria della Salute, so that Caroline could show me a Titian or a Carpaccio masterpiece in all its sacred magnificence, was more meaningful to my artistic wife than them. And why shouldn't it be?

But above all, my parents were made to feel at home when the family from Norfolk mentioned the famous exploits of Marco Polo, who, in the latter part of the thirteenth century, travelled east, eventually reaching China and the court of the Emperor. It was well known that the common denominator between Italian and Chinese cuisines was the love and use of rice and noodles, influenced somewhat by this intrepid explorer. So, during our mealtimes, the chef at our hotel relished the opportunity to serve risotto and pasta to our parents and family, given that we were the only Chinese staying there.

Like all good things, the holiday came to an end. I promised Caroline that one day I would bring her back to this magical place in its ancient lagoon. From Gatwick Airport we took the express train to Victoria Station, where we took a taxi to our newly renovated house in the mews. We hadn't replaced all the furniture that had been destroyed but managed to cope as the bedrooms had new beds and bedding. My father, somewhat overwhelmed, didn't say much, but after I had described the fire to him, he nodded his approval of the house and its restoration. Then with mixed feelings, we caught our train from Euston back to Birmingham the following morning.

The remainder of the year flew by now that the family was at relative peace with one another, and the memory of the catastrophic falling-out was consigned to the past. As the leaves began to fall from the trees, early one morning I went to visit my parents at Portland Road to bring them up to date on the progress of the business. Feeling rather satisfied that there were no foreseeable disasters on the horizon, I breezed in with a smile to greet my mother.

But my mood quickly changed when I noticed that my father was paler than usual, his lips clenched and blanched. Not only that, but as I sat down, I saw that he was sweating a little, even though it was cold in the house. I pushed open the curtains in the lounge where we were sitting. He was slumped in an armchair and found it difficult to shuffle forwards to take a drink of tea from a cup on the small table directly in front of him. The cup rattled unnervingly on the saucer as his hand shook.

'Ah Ba... Nee ho ma? Mo see gwun?' I enquired. ('Father... How are you? Nothing wrong, I hope?')

He kept dabbing his face with his handkerchief, as though it was unbearably hot.

'Er... Um gun yiu... Gnor ho gwoi.' ('Er... Not to worry... I'm just a bit tired.') His voice trembled disconcertingly, as though he was having difficulty catching his breath.

I reached over and felt the pulse on his wrist, which was resting, lifeless, on his lap. It was racing, and I noticed that he kept clutching his chest. Immediately, I called for Mother, and gave him a sip of water with a tablet of aspirin and loosened his collar and jacket.

Without delay, I went into the hallway, dialled 999 and asked for an ambulance urgently. *'I think my father is having a heart attack. Please hurry!'* I pleaded.

I covered the phone, hoping that my father wouldn't overhear. 'Father don't worry; I'm sure it can be sorted out. You've been overdoing it a bit. I've called for the doctors, just to make sure.'

He waved his arm, trying to dissuade me. I reassured him that everything would be fine if he could just relax. As soon as I opened my mouth, my attempt to soothe him felt totally inadequate. But at least, it made me feel better that I was doing *something*, and rightly or wrongly, reassured my anxious mother.

Barely a few minutes had passed when the paramedics arrived, having called ahead to the local hospital, which, fortunately, was not far away on the main road. I accompanied my father in the ambulance and was relieved to see that a cardiac team was already on alert at the hospital entrance. I was told by the attending doctor that the symptoms indicated that my father had suffered a cardiac arrest, and without further ado he was rushed into the hospital's specialist unit.

In the cold starkness of the hospital waiting room with its empty, pale green walls, I reflected on how it was possible that one moment I could be standing on the highest peak of a mountain, luxuriating in the warmth of the sun and so very pleased with myself; and then, the next minute, be abruptly plunged into a dark ravine of despair. The roller coaster of events that our family had endured since my childhood seemed never-ending. My mother had often wondered whether the curse from some misdemeanour in our ancestral past was still seeking retribution.

Dismissing this as foolish folklore from old-fashioned Chinese parents who were highly superstitious, I still bemoaned the unutterable fact that, having just healed our differences, and now I was getting on quite well with my father, he was now facing the possibility of death. I felt so helpless and so alone.

Chapter 49

RECUPERATION

December 1971 – January 1972

A FTER WHAT SEEMED LIKE an interminable wait of three hours or so, a tall, slim man in his late forties approached me from a nearby corridor, gripping a folder. He offered his hand. 'Ah, you must be the son who accompanied the patient.'

Nervously, I stood up to shake his hand. 'How bad is he, Doctor?' I asked, barely whispering, dreading bad news.

The consultant pushed back the bridge of his horn-rimmed glasses, which had slid forward as he leant towards me. 'Well, young man. Your father's not brilliant, but he's tough, and a fighter. It's lucky we saw him when we did. Initial tests appear to show that the blood vessels in his heart are rather furred up with plaque deposits, particularly the main coronary artery – hence it affected his central and peripheral circulation, and, consequently his breathing.'

'Will… will he… er… *live?*' I stammered, breaking out in a sweat.

'We will have to keep him here under observation for a few days or so and see how we get on. My team has started him on blood thinners, and drugs to widen his blood vessels. To regulate his heartbeat and blood pressure, he has been put on a type of drug called a beta blocker.'

'Tha… thank you, Doctor. Thank you for taking care of him. My father has never been overweight. Although, like a lot of Chinese, he enjoys a bit of fatty gristle from time to time, he has a varied diet of fish and vegetables,' I continued in his defence. 'He stopped smoking years ago and rarely drinks. He is, I must admit, a rather stressed sort of person, and he has been through a lot of family problems recently.'

The consultant cardiologist arched his eyebrow for a second or so but, tactfully, did not comment on what I had just volunteered. 'Look, you can see your father for just a few minutes before you go; the nurse will direct you to the ward. Please rest assured that he will be in good hands.'

No sooner had he said that, the consultant spun on his heels and left through a pair of swing doors.

I was directed to a ward on the ground floor. I must confess that my heart was in my mouth, not knowing what to expect. However, Father was sitting propped up in bed, not far from the door. He had regained some colour in his cheeks and looked less like he was at death's door than he had a few hours ago at Portland Road. But he was noticeably tired from all the exertion and panic. Haltingly, I explained what the consultant had told me. I reassured him that he would be all right but said that he needed to rest quietly at the hospital for a few days so that he could be monitored by the specialist team and to enable the medication to stabilise his condition.

Circling proprietorially beside an adjacent bed, the nurse told me that my mother and I could visit the next day, and that I had better not overtire my father any more than I had to. I took the hint, and my visit came to an abrupt close. Never having touched my father in my life (apart from taking his pulse in a fit of unthinking panic), involuntarily, my hand strayed out to touch his arm briefly. It felt alien, as if a sudden electric shock surged up my arm at the unfamiliar contact. Blushing, not knowing what else to say, having never had to face him in a situation that necessitated small talk, I muttered that I would see him tomorrow and quickly turned and left his bedside.

Members of the family visited Father each day, bringing my mother, who, with the hospital's permission, brought him some rice with a stir-fry of vegetables and pork. He didn't eat much, although he managed the home-made soup and the steamed fish, which were more digestible. He said that the tablets left a metallic taste in his mouth and ruined his appetite. Two weeks later he was able to come home, with strict instructions from the nursing team regarding taking his medication and walking and gently stretching in gradual spurts. The consultant warned of the dangers of getting stressed and the importance of avoiding undue excitement. Out of the earshot of my parents, I agreed with my sisters that another row within the family would kill him.

But what could we do? It was impossible to patrol these adults every minute of every day.

Whilst the country was shivering in the ice and snow, on the 9th January the coal miners went on strike over pay, demanding an increase in excess of forty-three per cent, compared to the seven per cent the Heath government was offering. It was the first time in over forty-five years that there had been a national shutdown in the mines, and the people of the country were made to suffer. But, as February made its entrance after a long, drawn-out winter that had appeared as if it would never end, crocuses and early jasmine began to flower early in the hedgerows and gardens around the city. Spring was around the corner, and the family, if not the whole of the population, should be at ease with itself after the depressing events of the winter.

During a short break at our house in Paddington, Caroline, I noticed, appeared to be more relaxed and happier than usual. She always was when we returned to our life in London; and who could blame her? However, that day I thought it was because of our brisk walk around the Italian fountains in Kensington Gardens under a clear, crisp sky, or feeding the screaming swans who squabbled with the neurotic geese on the Serpentine.

To escape the wind, we sat down on a bench in Queen Anne's Alcove near the Lancaster Gate park entrance, and gazed lazily across the stretch of Hyde Park beyond the first stone bridge in the distance. The oak-panelled enclosure, like a gigantic seashell ensconced in a womb-like stone casing, had been built by the celebrated architect Sir Christopher Wren in 1705, and was a favourite resting place of ours. Caroline pulled down the collar of my coat, and whispered in my ear that she had some news to tell me. Thinking that it might be the earth-shattering announcement that President Nixon would be visiting China on the 21st February 1972, seeking to improve Sino-US relations by meeting Chairman Mao (which would have ramifications for the whole of the West); or, more down to earth, that she had bought some exclusive tickets to a play in the West End for my birthday in March, I didn't pay much attention, for I was distracted by some children fighting over an ice cream from a refrigerated van parked nearby.

'Darling, I think I might be pregnant,' she whispered conspiratorially.

I nearly fell off the bench in shock. I wanted to grab hold of her, jump up and down and do a little jig, but because of foolish convention, and with a sea of tourists milling around us, I didn't dare. Stunned for a moment, I just said, 'Wha… what, my love?! *Are you sure?*' I stared in disbelief at the latent glow in her face.

'I will be certain in a week or so. I have an appointment to see the doctor next week.'

Gently, I raised her up carefully to her feet, as if she was suddenly fragile.

'Now, don't be silly. I'm not going to suddenly break like a piece of old china!' she laughed, wagging a finger. She ticked me off without realising the pun.

Then, with me covetously guarding her as though she was made of eggshell, we walked slowly back to the house in a state of shock and joyful surprise.

Chapter 50

WARLEY WOODS

April 1972

I T WAS PATENTLY OBVIOUS that we couldn't continue to live in the tiny flat that we had rented. Within two months, we found a small house north of where my parents lived in a place called Warley. It was a solidly built '30s house, semi-detached with an adjoining garage and a large, well-stocked garden back and front sheltering a mature laburnum tree. On the slope of a hill, it faced the woods of a hilly park called Warley Woods. An old couple had lived there since they were married, and, although the building was in excellent structural order, it was extremely old-fashioned, and that was reflected in the asking price. The kitchen and the bathroom had not been touched since the house was built. Knocking through the wall between the lounge and dining room, our builders advised, would offer a double aspect to let more natural light in. It was essential to provide some form of heating, and the electrician, who did some work at the restaurant arranged for electric night storage heaters to be installed, as the three bedrooms seemed icy even in the increasing warmth of the spring because the house was susceptible to northerly winds, being exposed on a hill.

As the pregnancy was confirmed, I plucked up courage to tell our respective parents. Mine just nodded with cautious approval, whereas

Mary, Caroline's mother, was over the moon. Arrangements were made for our child to be delivered at St Mary's Hospital, Paddington, as we were still medically registered at our main home in London. The date anticipated was early October.

My father, having survived his heart attack, shortly afterwards asked me to arrange with our solicitors for my mother and him to be naturalised and to take British citizenship for the remainder of their lives. I didn't question his decision in the face of his recent health scare. There must have been a seismic change of heart regarding his former homeland; reinforced, after his visit there. I started the ball rolling. Three months later, he and my mother applied for new British passports, surrendering gladly their old brown-covered travel documents which had considerable restrictions on them. Plans were made to visit our brother in the States in the summer, which pleased the family.

Alarmingly, despite our hard work, the restaurant's turnover was shrinking again as a further two new Chinese restaurants had opened in the city centre. Costs were still escalating, and the staff was agitating for a pay rise. It then happened that we were approached by a small Chinese social club, whose premises near the wholesale vegetable market were being demolished. We were asked if we were prepared to rent out the spare rooms above the restaurant and storeroom, with an entrance/exit via Hinckley Street at the rear. The proposal was that this would allow the club's members to assemble there regularly to play Mah-jong and Chinese dominoes, to meet friends and to catch up on the news via Chinese TV and newspapers and so on. Apart from the rent, which would help ease our financial pressures, their members, families and friends would arrange to eat at the restaurant. In the circumstances, it seemed to make economic sense.

It was about the same time that I decided that a radical change in the look and style of the main restaurant was urgently needed, and that we should combine this with the introduction of Cantonese and regional cooking, with a dim sum menu in order to keep up with the competition. This new venture needed a considerable injection of capital of about twenty-five thousand pounds. I decided to approach Eileen's husband, Will, who was doing extremely well with his takeaway catering business, and suggested that we could buy into the restaurant business in Station Street, together with Daniel, my other brother-in-law. For my share I would raise ten thousand pounds, using our London property as collateral. A limited company would be formed and my father could finally retire and get out of the firing line of business.

Our builders soon started work and the design and decor of the dining rooms were changed dramatically to a more modern look, with a new bar and seating area for drinks. Two new chefs were hired, and five-spiced aromatic duck, lobster, fresh crab, snapper, eels and a vast variety of dim sum was offered on the new menu.

It proved an immediate success with the local population. On Sundays the restaurant was fully booked, with a mass of Chinese visitors pouring in for dim sum, lotus sticky rice with barbecued pork, coriander beef, prawn har kow, siu mei, steamed dumplings in bamboo baskets, a variety of noodles, steamed pork and chicken buns, and so on. Members of the Chinese club dined regularly and seemed to fit in seamlessly with the new look and ethnic diversity that the place appeared to attract.

It was also well known that, on Sundays and Mondays the vast majority of Chinese staff working in restaurants, takeaways and supermarkets had their day off. Enterprising cinemas, including the News Cinema next door to us in Station Street, started to screen, at eleven o'clock at night, kung fu films and other Chinese epics that were popular in Hong Kong given the increasing fame of a celebrated martial artist by the name of Bruce Lee. After the cinemas had emptied at 1am, the audience would seek out a quick meal in any Chinese restaurants that stayed open. Not wishing to miss out on this captive and good source of business, our restaurant was forced to follow suit. At first, I was reluctant to agree to this suggestion, but, faced with the mammoth interest payments on the capital raised against our London property I caved in.

Inspired and intrigued by these action films and the increasing popularity of martial arts, I decided to take lessons in kung fu. Private lessons in the afternoon, from a keen young man of considerable skill called Lee, who was introduced to me by a member of the staff, improved my fitness and agility. Thirsty for knowledge, I coordinated a class in a nearby church hall, which gradually, based on reputation, attracted more and more students, and soon I was teaching martial arts exercises to beginners. After work, quite often I would jog around Warley Woods Park to increase my cardiovascular output, which made my wife smile with knowing indulgence. She knew full well that the business I was in, with its complexity of problems, was proving increasingly stressful, and that this was a good distraction from work that I didn't particularly enjoy but was obliged to do because of my father. Day by day, my early promise to my long-suffering wife that I would ease myself out of the business and return with her to London kept being postponed, as the accumulating commitments in Birmingham sucked me into a bottomless quagmire whenever I raised a hand to extricate myself.

A visiting martial artist from Hong Kong befriended me, as my instructor Lee was a former pupil of his. This older man, who was well known in some quarters, sometimes supervised some of the classes. He went by the title of Master Ho Lung Deng, and made a considerable impression upon me, my being a novice. We often talked about Chinese history and the importance of the ancestral thread that bound the Chinese clans together in perpetuity with the filial obligations attached thereto.

It was a scorching hot summer's morning towards the end of August, and the air outside in Warley Woods remained static and dry. The roses were in full bloom and the bright yellow laburnum was blossoming in the middle of the lawn, when Caroline woke up early and said nervously that the baby was kicking like mad and a sixth sense was warning her that she might give birth early. The due date of the 8th October seemed like a lifetime away, so it seemed impossible that anything would happen so soon.

Confused and in a panic, I had a dreadful and stupid thought that St Mary's Hospital in Paddington would be too far away. We were in the wrong place at the wrong time. I immediately telephoned for an ambulance, and, picking up Caroline's overnight bag, which we had kept on standby in the hall, I followed the ambulance by car to the nearest hospital in Smethwick, just fifteen minutes away.

Completely at a loss as to what to do in this situation of which I had no prior experience, I asked the doctors what to expect next. I was told that they did not think that the birth was imminent, and that I should go home for the moment while Caroline was kept in for observation.

I was at work when a call came from the hospital to tell me that my wife had suddenly given birth to a baby girl, five weeks premature and three and a half pounds in weight. I was reassured that mother and daughter were doing well, but our baby daughter was being kept for the moment in an incubator in the neonatal unit. Stunned out of my mind, I immediately abandoned everything I was doing and rushed to the hospital to see my poor and no doubt frightened wife, to reassure and comfort her.

Chapter 51

TANYA CHARLOTTE MAYLING YING

Birmingham, England, 31st August 1972

I COULD TELL THAT Caroline was still traumatised. In the completely different surroundings of an old-fashioned hospital, and in a place where she hadn't expected to be, having given birth to a child who had not been expected for at least five weeks, without me by her side at the crucial moment, she was stunned and disorientated.

I did my best to be upbeat, but failed miserably as I was just as at sea as she was. Being separated from our newborn child from the outset and her being kept in an incubator in another part of the hospital was harsh in the extreme, but it seemed that there was no alternative.

The next day I returned, accompanied by my mother, who had just returned from Boston after visiting my brother. She at least was optimistic about the outcome.

'Look, son,' she said, pointing to the tiny creature wriggling under the light of the incubator. 'Your little daughter is *perfectly* formed. And look at the way her limbs are moving about. She is a fighter, extremely strong, and will be all right.'

Coming from someone who had borne ten children – most of them at home and with the minimum amount of help – I had to accept that she spoke from experience. The neonatal team at the hospital was exceptional in their care. We were reassured that our daughter was fine, but she needed to be kept in to gain some weight before she could be discharged.

A week later, feeling completely alone, Caroline was able to come home. Our daughter was given the name of Tanya Charlotte Mayling (meaning 'Beautiful Rose'), and we made plans to take her to Godmanchester one day to be baptised in the church where we were married. Mary, on her visit to her first grandchild, was delighted that we wanted to do that. Four weeks later after she had gained another one and a half pounds in weight, we brought our daughter home, and, after extensive reading of Dr Spock's evergreen manual on infant care, embarked on the intricacies and complexities of our lives as new parents.

Sleepless nights, the perennial nightmare of new parenthood, continued for months on end and in fact lasted for the next three years, as young Tanya did not get into the pattern of sleeping through the night until she started nursery school. Endless searches for a cure for childhood insomnia didn't bear fruit. Sundry experts blamed her premature birth – the hospital staff waking her up every two hours or so to feed her, and the separation of mother from newborn in those early weeks, had contributed to the problem. A myriad of solutions was suggested, some more lethal than others, including whisky in her milk, the dangerous administration of phenobarbitone, and even behavioural psychotherapy for us as parents. What made her sleep was driving her about in the car; but as soon as it stopped, Tanya would wake up, wide-eyed. Despite this, our exhaustion was compensated by the natural joy she brought us.

Christmas arrived, with the relief of having a break away from Birmingham, and Hatton House in Godmanchester once again proved a haven for Caroline. Not long afterwards, we managed to visit our friends and neighbours in the mews, who all rushed out of their houses, impatient to greet our new child. Returning to the Midlands, we were soon snowed in as snow fell heavily throughout January and

February. The park over the road, with an exaggerated degree of rose-tinted euphemism, looked like a scene from the slopes of Switzerland with the boughs of the conifers lining the hillside weighed down by the virgin snow. But even when romanticising the vista in our fertile imaginations, we knew in reality that it was just a dull urban sight on the outskirts of a stark industrial city – a place where I had reluctantly brought my wife to live because of a promise to my father. But with the fresh fall of snow that settled overnight, we managed to take young Tanya out, snugly wrapped in a bundle, on a sledge which we had found in the garage. We hoped that the fresh, brisk wintry air would make her sleep better; but that too was to no avail.

On the 1st January 1973, whilst the country was struggling under a blanket of snow and ice, Prime Minister Edward Heath announced that Britain had finally been accepted as a member of the European Common Market with the signing of the Treaty of Rome. Retaining its sovereignty, the country was hopeful that it would eventually flourish with its new trading partners in Europe. Business and industry across the country had high hopes for future prosperity. Basking in the plaudits for attaining a successful diplomatic outcome the previous year, when Heath had managed to ratify a resumption of full diplomatic relations between China and the UK,[98] the recent treaty with the European Common Market was considered another triumph by the Tory-led government on the international stage. And yet, Britain held its breath as matters on the domestic and overseas fronts started to take a turn for the worse.

During the remainder of 1973, the restaurant business in Birmingham rumbled on with boring routine. As autumn beckoned, following our daughter's reaching her first birthday on the 31st August, I happened to

---

98 Full diplomatic relations were ratified in 1972. Edward Heath had for many years had a good relationship with the leaders of China, including Chairman Mao Zedong, Premier Zhou Enlai (also written as Chou Enlai) and, on the death of Mao in 1976, Deng Xiaoping. In 1974, following a visit to Beijing, he was presented with a pair of giant pandas (Chia-Chia, a male, and Ching-Ching, a female) as a goodwill gesture to the UK.

call on the Chinese social club at the back of the premises in order to collect the rent. Pushing past me, I thought I recognised a couple of the visitors amongst the milling crowd playing Mah-jong. One, I thought, was Man Lok, one of the first waiters my father had hired in 1958 when the restaurant was opened. I know it was an awfully long time ago, but I have quite a good memory for faces. He and his younger brother had worked for us for some months, until my father, I believe, sacked the latter due to his persistence in flirting with my sister Eileen, apparently at the expense of his work. A gaunt Man Lok, now greying extensively at the temples, had accumulated a clutch of lines on his face, but he looked as though he had done rather well for himself over the years, as he was wearing a sharp mohair suit and smoking small Dutch cigars with a swagger. He gave me a dismissive, contemptuous look across the gambling table, as if he remembered me.

The other person who brushed past me, I could have sworn was one of the former cooks – a surly man called Wang Fieng, who had led a walkout of staff against my father some ten years ago, having left under a dark cloud following a fight with my cousin. He had gained a bit of weight since I'd last seen him, but still looked as scruffy as he did all those years ago, with an unruly moustache over his narrow lips which enclosed tobacco-stained teeth. When I mentioned them to my brothers-in-law, Will remembered the latter, but not the former as Man Lok was before his time. Daniel, who had only arrived in the UK in 1968, didn't have any recollection of either of these men. I mentioned that, separately, they had threatened my father on different occasions. But Will said that it was such a long time ago and they were probably idle gestures made in the heat of the moment. And in any case, we could not bar either of them from visiting the social club, over which we had no jurisdiction – particularly since they had not committed any crime. Nevertheless, my overactive imagination went into overdrive, thinking of all the people in the past who had threatened to kill my father.

When I mentioned these encounters to my father, an anxious look crossed his face. *'Be careful, son!*. I don't particularly like the idea of this kind of people returning to the premises, like proverbial rats skulking back to their former nest. It's possible that they could be up to something sinister. *Who knows?* But, on the other hand, it could be entirely innocent – a simple coincidence!'

He gave a half-hearted shrug, arching his eyebrows, and glowered, which worried me. 'And where else could they go to socialise? You know, many Chinese workers, once they are sacked from a business which used to provide them with the security of food, money and accommodation, wander around, rootless. Lots of them become completely unemployable.' He shook his head for emphasis, his eyes ablaze. 'They just drift in and out of gambling dens and other haunts with time on their hands, getting up to no good!'

I didn't think that my father was all that convinced by that explanation, try as hard as he might to believe his own words. Deep down, I was extremely worried that it had all the elements of a dangerous vendetta waiting to happen.

The 6th October 1973 was globally significant. It was the start of a conflict known as the Yom Kippur War, in which a coalition of Arab states, led by Egypt and Syria, attacked Israel. True to form, the Soviet Union and the USA backed opposing sides. As in 1970, at the beginning of the oil crisis which led to soaring oil prices and the stock market crash, it brought the oil crisis to the fore again in an effort to strangle the West. The Organization of the Petroleum Exporting Countries (OPEC) proclaimed an oil embargo, the repercussions of which were about to unfold. During the next six months, the price of oil quadrupled. Petrol rationing was on the cards in the UK. The days of my thirsty Jaguar and MG sports cars were over.

As the days got shorter and darker, with the chill of late October shrivelling the autumn leaves, a strange and frightening thing happened. I had just arrived at the restaurant at five o'clock to greet Daniel, and, as I was taking off my jacket, a group of burly men barged their way in. Dressed in dark clothes, there were seven or eight of them. One hurried to the front door, turned the notice around to

'Closed' and slipped the catch to lock the door. Another rushed to the rear entrance and did the same. It was terrifying. The leader barked out orders for the staff to sit down with their hands exposed on the tables. The kitchen staff was told to do the same. I was ordered to come out of the office behind the bar and sit down. Two of the intruders ran up to the social club and delivered the same instructions, even though only the manager and two other visitors were milling around up there. At first, I thought it was a robbery, but I found it strange as there was hardly any money on the premises, it being far too early. What seemed odd, was that they ignored the cash in the safe, which my brother-in-law was forced to open for inspection.

On asking what was going on, I was completely ignored. A thorough search went on throughout the premises. Who or what they were looking for, I didn't have a clue. They examined every shelf, nook and cranny in an organised manner, which informed me that they had been trained professionally. Files and our books were scrutinised skilfully and thoroughly. And then a fleeting thought crossed my mind that they might be the Inland Revenue; but again, I knew that we were up to date with our tax affairs thanks to our extremely efficient accountants.

A request by me to phone my wife and Will was met with a savage blank look, as they had taken the phone – which was in a covered yard just outside the door to the still room – off the hook. My abiding concerns were for my dear wife and child, whom I would normally telephone at about this time before they went to bed.

One and a half hours later, the raid suddenly ended as rapidly as it had begun, and the group abruptly left. Rushing out via the front entrance, they jumped into unmarked vans and drove off without a single word of explanation. No sooner had that happened than the phone started to ring. Will and Eileen reported that the same thing had happened to them at their place of business at 5pm. Will said that as far as he was aware, based on contacting a friend in the CID (as he acted in court for the police as an interpreter), it was a coordinated drug raid following a tip-off. Then Rose phoned in a state of distress, saying that their house in Lichfield had likewise been raided. On contacting Caroline in Warley, she was crying for she had also experienced a raid by a similar gang, who had burst through the front door. I told Daniel I was rushing back home to see my wife and young child and that I was not going to return to the business that evening.

I was met by Caroline, who was at the end of her tether, in a flood of tears. The raiders had turned the house upside down searching for something; and again, we were not given any indication as to what they were looking for. Caroline said that even when she went into the kitchen to heat up some food for baby Tanya, who was hungry and crying, an officious-looking woman stood over her and searched the containers of baby food, even turning out the milk powder onto a tray to have a sniff at it. Undeterred, she also felt inside the baby's nappy, but hastily retracted her fingers due to the soiling there. Having strangers going through our house and our personal possessions without explanation or even a search warrant, we felt defiled and brutalised. The invasion of our privacy had not only frightened my poor helpless wife out of her wits, but also my baby daughter. And when you are totally innocent of any wrongdoing, it makes the outrage that much greater. Furiously, I stomped about, my hand fluttering with anger under my chin.

'Well, that's it! I've had my fill of Birmingham and the damn Chinese community right up to here!'

My duty to the family had been fulfilled at a considerable cost to my marriage. At the earliest opportunity, I promised Caroline and her mother, we would be going back to the sanity and sanctity of our home in London.

The covert operation by the clandestine authorities did not stop there. Our home telephones were tapped for several weeks thereafter, and I could have sworn that on many occasions we were being tailed. *It was not paranoia.* On speaking to my father, he was horrified. He wondered whether the curses and vendettas of his old enemies had passed to me as his son, through the malevolent thread, now that he was no longer the target. It was something that I could not prove. But from that time onwards, I couldn't help but worry about the sins of the father... and perhaps even the ancestors.

Will, again through his police connections, had discovered that calls had been made from the restaurant phone by persons unknown regarding the dealing of drugs. It appeared that a heroin ring that trailed from Hong Kong via Holland and the US had infiltrated certain businesses and used them as a cover. Many of the criminal Tong gangs, some of them connected to the Triads, then imposed protection rackets in order to silence the business owners through blackmail. This did not appear to be the case with our restaurant; however, certain unsavoury elements from the Midlands who frequented the Chinese social club had used the place to meet, and, by using the restaurant phone, had hoped to disguise their tracks. We immediately revoked the tenancy of the social club and closed it down. In time, we heard that they had latched on to another Chinese eatery, which, thankfully, was none of our concern.

Six months later, we heard that Interpol had arrested Man Lok in Amsterdam in connection with drug trafficking. It appeared that he and several others had been on their radar for some time. Authorities in several countries had been covertly following members of this criminal network for months, if not years. Wang Fieng had gone on the run, but five others in the ring, including a Mr Big and someone called the Fish, had been rounded up. My brothers-in-law and I were exonerated. We had unknowingly hired out premises to a club which had, also unwittingly, allowed criminal degenerates to meet and to dine at the restaurant. It is common knowledge that no proprietor, however vigilant, can effectively control who does or does not dine in his restaurant when it is open to the public.

We never did get an apology from the relevant authorities for the invasion of our privacy and the ransacking of our homes that had brought so much terror to our families. It left a bad taste in our mouths, even though we had to accept that they had a difficult job to do against the rising tide of this corrupt and evil business. Thinking back, it reminded me of the destruction of one of my ancestors during the Opium Wars in China in the mid 1800s. The open sale and availability of opium throughout the country, promoted by a foreign power (mainly the British at that time) to contain and stupefy the indigenous population in order to protect the lucrative tea and opium trades, was undeniably wrong. Some historians have even argued that it was reprehensibly immoral. The drug continued to be pedalled by pernicious dealers and local Chinese gangs to feather their nests, and nearly brought the country to its knees.

Sadly, today we face an uphill battle against the spread of a similar poison which infiltrates all corners of society, and the fight against it is as relevant now as it was then. In our selective ignorance, we fail to acknowledge its seriousness until it hits us head-on, as it did us. But by then, a display of helpless handwringing seems embarrassingly self-indulgent and utterly futile.

Chapter 52

THE THREE-DAY WEEK

February 1974

JUST AS THE BUSINESS was getting back on its feet again, on the 9th February 1974, the National Union of Mineworkers (NUM) called miners throughout the country out on strike. All power stations – electric, gas and oil were picketed, as well as steelworks, ports and coal depots, in order to strangle the country's supplies of fuel. This was a concerted, cynical effort to highlight the oil crisis still affecting the country. Without coal and oil, the electricity generation stations could not operate. Without electricity, homes, businesses, offices, industry, hospitals, schools and the infrastructure of communication, railways and airports, all had to shut down.

The Heath government declared a state of emergency, and all businesses were forced to close and to ration their working days to three days a week. One day the restaurant would be open and functioning, with customers sitting at the tables, and then suddenly there would be a power cut that would last for the rest of the day. Candles for lighting, though romantic, could not replace gas for cooking. Other electrical equipment, such as heating for water and the radiators, the electric food lift from the basement kitchen, and the refrigerators, ceased to function. The shutdown led to the wholesale destruction of food. It was a disaster on an unprecedented scale no one had experienced before, except during the bombing of the Second World War.

Forced into a corner, Edward Heath called a General Election on the 28th February. Harold Wilson was returned to power at the head of a minority Labour government. The miners were offered a pay rise of thirty-five per cent. They called off their industrial action and coal production resumed on the 11th March. By then, the damage to the already weakened economy was terminal.

As a business, we couldn't suddenly sack the whole staff, as we did not know when the knock-on effects of the fuel crisis would finally end. Bankruptcy loomed. In fact, many businesses in Britain had collapsed by the time the fuel strike and the oil crisis came to an end in March. Our business had suffered irreparable harm and accrued debt into the thousands. It tied me more tightly to the business, even though I wanted to walk away.

Because of the unpredictability of the heating and power, Caroline and Tanya took the opportunity to stay safely in Godmanchester with Mary, with my encouragement and blessing. To regain some equilibrium in my life, and to retain my sanity, I intensified my martial arts training. Following a number of injuries and a case of back strain, a recommendation took me to visit the student clinic at the British School of Osteopathy[99] (BSO) at Buckingham Gate whenever I returned to London. The clinical care in this professional setting was an eye-opener. It sparked an interest which could be considered by some, the closest thing to my conversion on 'the road to Damascus'. When thinking back, it probably was at that instance, a type of epiphany. It was *certainly* a pivotal moment in my life, although, it did not register at the time.

In my leisure time, I began to avidly read up on human biology and anatomy, using manuals which had not been available to me at school

---

99 The British School of Osteopathy (BSO), now called University College of Osteopathy is the oldest teaching and training establishment for the profession in Britain. Founded in 1917 by Dr J. Martin Littlejohn, an Edinburgh practitioner, it became the flagship of osteopathy in the UK. Its practitioners are governed by a professional council and register to regulate the standard of their education and to enforce ethics for the protection of the public. Motto: *Pro Natura et Veritate* (Nature and the Truth).

as a teenager, and which had captured my attention. Already I would often attempt to manually remedy dislocated knee and shoulder joints in my martial arts students in emergencies, and with remarkable success. Therapeutic massage of strained and bruised muscles and joints, using '*Ah Dew*', a pungent Chinese herbal remedy steeped in alcohol, from an aged formulation from my parents, achieved encouraging results. At a local level, like the barefoot practitioners of ancient China, my reputation gradually spread; although it was considered debatable by some opposing cynics.

The subject of anatomy brought back with a jolt that, many years ago, prior to entering university to study science, schools in the late '50s, even at sixth-form level, had been rather prudish, if not backward. Animal biology was restricted to the study of the rat or the dogfish. Any mention of the intimate structure of the human being was avoided like the plague, and the merest hint of mentioning sexual reproduction in humans was taboo. In our school in Liverpool, the rabbit was used as a prime example of mammalian reproduction, and dissection and study of its anatomy was contrasted with that of the rat. From there, as pupils, we were expected to deduct parallels with the human form. Caroline said that this practice was part of the national curriculum throughout the country. No wonder then, with that type of school syllabus being skewed and airbrushed for teenage consumption, many youngsters assumed that babies were delivered by the stork or found under a mulberry bush!

It was during one of my enlightening and inspiring visits to the BSO, I found myself convinced that I had taken a wrong turn in my career. However, one must remember with caution the old adage that… *the grass always seems greener on the other…*

In the summer months meanwhile, the restaurant business stabilised, but the devastation of the fuel crisis had eroded into our capital. Combined with a depleted income, it affected the repayments to the banks, whose interest rates were penal following the international oil crisis and the change of government.

However, we were just about meeting our financial obligations when, on the 21st November, I happened to be working in the premises when I heard an almighty explosion not far away that shook the windows of the restaurant. Another explosion quickly followed. For one brief moment, it took me back to the air raids in Liverpool as a child. But this was different. A strange, ghostly silence followed for a few minutes or so as staff and customers ran to the front door to stare across at the Bull Ring shopping mall. Then suddenly, a cacophony of wailing sirens from ambulances, police cars and fire engines screamed through the streets, heading towards the centre. A customer yelled that some pubs had been attacked by the IRA (Provisional Irish Republican Army). Straight away, we bolted our doors for security as people raced across the street and from the nearby railway station in the confusion. Not far in the distance, smoke rose from the Rotunda in the city centre. Someone screamed that the pubs, The Mulberry Bush and The Tavern in the Town had been bombed to smithereens.

My heart in my mouth, I told Daniel that I must get back to Caroline and Tanya as they had just returned to Warley by public transport. I was concerned for their safety. I jumped into my car and drove out of the city centre like a maniac. I tried three times to get through by the usual route, but it was blocked. There were police barriers and emergency services everywhere. Another plume of black smoke wafted into the sky. The cordite stink of high explosives choked the throat and filled the nostrils. In a state of sheer terror, people were running blindly out into the streets. They took taxis; jumped onto buses – anything just to get out of the city centre. Pandemonium filled the air.

Taking a diversionary route, going south first, then skirting the city from the west, I managed eventually to head north to Edgbaston, Bearwood village and then Warley. On the car radio, I heard the news that dozens had been killed and hundreds injured. My heart sank at hearing of this latest outrage in the death and destruction of innocent people just having a fun night out.

To my enormous relief, my family was safe. Later, on television, it was reported that a total of twenty-one people had died and 182 had been seriously injured. The emergency services were doing their best to cope. Hospitals were overflowing with casualties. The devastation amidst the rubble of the pubs and surrounding buildings was indescribable. It was like a war zone. There had been a similar picture of utter carnage with the pub bombings in Guildford earlier in October, in which four soldiers and one civilian were killed.

This outrage in the centre of Birmingham, in which I and others just happened to be helpless passers-by, was the final straw. At the beginning of January 1975, I told Caroline that Birmingham had beaten me. On the 30th April we made our move. The date was unforgettable, because on that day we had heard on the world news that it signalled the end of the Vietnam War, as the last of the Americans,[100] together with others, had fled for their lives. From the roof of a smoke-filled building, a military helicopter had begun to airlift them out of Saigon as the city fell to the Communist forces.

We were returning to London to try to rebuild our lives once more. The mews house would be sold to pay off the mortgage and the bank loans. We would cut our losses and try to begin again. The house in Warley would also be sold and, again, the banks paid off. I told my parents of my plans. Father nodded silently, knowing full well the many times that he had had to start again to protect his family against all the odds. Daniel and Will understood. They knew in their hearts that I had never fully adjusted to living in the Midlands and wished me well. Through our accountants, who thought I was a coward for jumping ship, I sold my forty per cent stake in shares for a nominal one pound to my brothers-in-law, who would try to rebuild the business and then sell it off.

However, the joy of returning to London was dampened somewhat by what I wanted to do in the future at a point in what I considered to be the prime of one's life. I had to start again before it was too late.

---

100 On the 9th August 1974, Gerald Ford had become the thirty-eighth President of the USA, taking over from the disgraced Richard Nixon, who resigned over the Watergate Affair.

My father had achieved it without a second thought, and much later in life than me, and that spurred me on. If I had learnt anything from my father, it was the art of survival. I had a remarkable, loyal wife and a vulnerable young child to support, and deep down I knew that the future would hold no fear for me. The challenge of success was staring me in the face, if only I had the nerve to grasp it.

Part IX

1975 – 1979

Chapter 53

ANOTHER DOOR OPENS

London, England, 1975

'M R KWONG, YOU WOULD need a minimum of five GCEs in order to apply for study at the British School of Osteopathy. A minimum of two A Levels, preferably chemistry and biology. Maths and English are required at O Level,' stated the school secretary over the phone.

Buried somewhere in my archives, I had eleven GCEs, which included biology, chemistry and physics at A Level, although they had been acquired a generation ago.

'Furthermore,' she continued, 'you will have to undertake an assessment as to your suitability to train for the profession by a Regional Careers Officer at one of the practices. You will also be invited for an interview with the principal and members of the faculty following a written statement from you on your reasons for wanting to train for this vocation.'

I was pleasantly surprised when she stated that mature students were equally welcome, as a third of each intake happened to be older students who, having worked previously, had life experience and were often considered an asset to the profession. But the crunch came when she said that it was a four-year course, full time, the last three years of which involved studying and practising at the school's outpatients' clinic. A prospectus, she said, was in the post with a summary of tuition fees and so on.

On reflection, four years seemed like a lifetime at my or at any age. But there again, as one of my professional referees declared, once qualified, I could be in practice for a further thirty-odd years if I remained fit and well. What attracted me most of all was the opportunity to work with people whilst applying manual skills that were immersed in practical science, anatomy, and health, treating the vast range of muscular and skeletal complaints that plague us in modern life, and the associated stress that went with it.

'Hopefully, the studies will be so absorbing that the years will fly past!' Mary said. But deep down, I knew she was naturally worried because I had a wife and growing daughter to provide for. Tactfully however, she remained positive and encouraging.

Possessively clutching a BSO prospectus to my chest, I explained all these implications to Caroline. Nervously, I waited for a response. A broad smile of encouragement crossed my wife's face, which said everything that I wanted to hear. I reaffirmed that osteopathy was the type of physical medicine (albeit one considered alternative or fringe) I wished I had come across years ago, but which, I could not have put a name to at the time, or even described what it entailed having no prior contact with the practice. The only osteopath I had heard of in those days was the ill-fated society osteopath Stephen Ward, who in the early '60s had come to grief when his foolish head was turned when he dealt exclusively with the rich and famous.

Immediately, I set about arranging finance for my intended studies, even though there was a faint possibility of a local authority educational award, which could at least contribute towards the tuition fees, if nothing else.

Our mews house was put on the market. We were warned that there was still an economic crisis haunting the country and that the property market was sluggish, with prices nationally, never mind in Central London, having tumbled.

On the 5th June, in a national referendum, the majority of voters supported the UK's continuing membership of the European Common Market hoping for an economic miracle.

The summer months of blazing sun and endless cloudless skies, though welcome, did little to encourage property viewings by would-be buyers. People opted to spend time lazing by the sea or in the country rather than struggle in the stifling, polluted heat of the city. And so Caroline and Tanya spent much of the summer in Godmanchester at Hatton House.

Eventually, however, an offer was made by a director of a merchant bank who wanted to buy the house for his daughter as a wedding present. He struck a hard bargain. Working it out, after clearing our mortgage and paying off the crippling secured loans which had been raised for the restaurant business, we were left with a mean sum of thirteen thousand pounds with which to start again. The house in Warley was also sold, but there was little left in its equity after paying off our debts.

Completion of the sale of the mews house was required by September. The panicked search was on to find a property to live in which could be purchased with the shrinking remnants of our savings. After much searching, I found a wreck of a house not far away in W2 on the fringes of an area called Notting Hill. It was a three-storey Victorian property built in 1845, in a tree-lined road directly opposite a popular Roman Catholic church, St Mary of the Angels, and a historic parish house built in stone that wouldn't look amiss in rural France.

But it was in an appalling state and uninhabitable, having suffered some damage during the last war from the bombing in the streets nearby. Full of damp and dry rot, poorly maintained with sloping walls, ceilings and floors, it stank of condensation and decay. It had been on the market for three years or more. Looking at the state of it, it was no wonder there had not been any interest. Furthermore, a tramp had made his home under the hedge in the front garden. Potential buyers had not been able to secure a mortgage from a building society due to its condition, and neither could we. The sale price was excessive for what it was. But on entering the hall, a surge of optimism overcame me, for it had a friendly, welcoming air, and one could fantasise that a benign spirit was at work therein. As there was not much on the market within our price bracket, I felt I had to try to buy it in order to provide a roof over our heads. There was no other option. As the saying goes, beggars can't be choosers.

Then the difficult part was how to purchase it. I worked out that, if I could obtain a private mortgage of forty per cent of the asking price for one year from the vendor, together with our deposit of the remaining sixty per cent, and offer higher than the market rate of interest in our monthly repayments, it would be achievable. Based on a legal agreement, we would restore the structure to acceptable building society standards; replacing the roof, eradicating the damp and rot, installing a bathroom and kitchen, repairing the windows and ceilings, and so on. Once all that had been done, we would re-mortgage it via a building society in order to repay the vendor. Luckily, he agreed to our proposal.

I have to say, Caroline was appalled by the state of the house compared to where we used to live. However, she was persuaded of its ultimate potential, and that it would eventually make a fine family home. Gradually, with time and money, we could extend upwards and provide a roof terrace with a design studio from which she could work. And one day, it could also provide a base from which I could start my practice once I had completed my training. Anyway, overcome with a surfeit of optimism (probably misplaced), we daydreamed of the future with its end result; otherwise we would never have had the courage to take that leap of faith and to take on such an onerous commitment.

The property's saving graces were its large, south-facing walled garden, and its generously proportioned rooms with their ornate cornices and period marble fireplaces. It needed work and a bottomless reservoir of money to restore it. It was a challenge.

Our architect friend, Jeffrey, after initially trying to dissuade me, capitulated. He agreed to do the basic drawings and to give advice on how to restore the fundamental needs of the property in order to make it at least habitable. Straight away, he provided a roofer, who retiled the roof and repaired the gutters. At least that stopped the rain coming in. Next, through my work in martial arts, I happened to befriend and engage an enterprising and versatile young builder from Luton. He was a former student of mine who was prepared to be paid solely for his labour, providing I bought the building materials and helped as a labourer. Separate tradesmen were engaged, such as an electrician to rewire the house and a skilled jobbing plasterer for the walls and ceilings. A local plumber and central heating engineer would install a new heating and plumbing system.

Inspired by much hope and considerable naivety, we started ripping the place apart to get rid of the rotten woodwork, ceilings, floors, and so on, using a succession of skips. As soon as the building work started, the tramp left in a huff, threatening violence.

The road had been badly run-down since the war and contained an eclectic mix of private dwellings, and council and housing association flats. The neighbourhood remained ominously quiet and badly neglected, as if something surprising or shocking was about to happen. Nevertheless, it retained with pride a rare and cherished spirit of community, now often lost. Being on the fringes of the location of the historic Notting Hill race riots of the late '50s, and once encroaching on the territory of the notorious slum landlord Peter Rachman,[101] with his appalling bedsits and flats whose rents were reported to be enforced by his terrifying henchmen, the area wasn't very popular amongst the middle classes. Indeed, the celebrated Notting Hill Carnival gradually crept towards the adjoining streets,

---

101 In the '50s and early '60s, Peter (Perec) Rachman owned swathes of slum properties around the Portobello Road, Westbourne Park and Powis Square vicinity in an undesirable area in West London called Notting Hill. Allegedly involved in vice, drugs and extortion, he supposedly used 'heavies' and dogs to evict tenants. Friends with Mandy Rice-Davies, Christine Keeler and Stephen Ward.

where en route, the carnival floats and steel bands swayed along, cheered on by the dancing crowds. Soon, Carnival Mass became an annual event at St Mary of the Angels, with visiting priests from the Caribbean.

The rebuilding rapidly absorbed our capital like a sponge. Fortunately, parents came to our aid, particularly Mary. Looking at photographs, my father was appalled at the state of the place, saying that it reminded him of some of the houses that were devastated in the Blitz in Liverpool. That was hardly an encouraging endorsement of our hard work, hopes and aspirations.

I happened to be working in the garden when, at the end of another balmy day in September, I got a call from my mother. She was extremely distressed, having just heard that Aunt Chun Rei, had tragically drowned off the coast of New Brighton whilst visiting Uncle's family. The coroner on Merseyside pronounced that it was death by misadventure. After the initial shock, I knew deep down that this may or may not have been strictly true. Aunt had been widowed for many years since the civil wars in China in the '30s, and losing her only child at birth. She had felt that she had no more to achieve in life by staying in England, but returning to China on her own was not a feasible option. Not wanting to be a burden on any of us in her old age, she decided that she wanted to be reunited with her late husband and parents in the afterlife.

In old Chinese thinking, this tragedy was not unusual, or that dishonourable. Still, Mother was inconsolable, as it reminded her of what had happened to members of *her* family, the Chows, in tragic circumstances in China in the late 1800's/early 1900's. Such deaths had of course, occurred for different reasons; but primarily, fateful decisions had been taken in order to save the family from having another mouth to feed during the conflict of war and in the face of starvation. I told my mother that no one, least of all Uncle's family with whom Aunt had been staying, should feel guilty about what had happened. No one was to blame, tragic though it was.

It was another scorching day in March 1976 when Harold Wilson, at the age of sixty, decided to retire from holding the reins of power in Britain. James Callaghan replaced him in Downing Street. As head of the Labour government, he grappled with the continuing financial crisis gripping the country. An application to the IMF for a loan of four hundred million dollars did not augur well. The country continued to struggle in a severe economic recession as inflation escalated to over twenty per cent.

By Easter, at the beginning of another blazing hot summer, as the repetition of a drought from the previous year gripped the country in a sweltering vice, Caroline and Tanya returned to live in the house after spending most of the time away in Godmanchester. There were no carpets or floor coverings. We faced bare walls and ceilings, but it was warm and safe. The garden flourished under Caroline's green fingers. The previous owners had planted beds of magnificent roses and clematis, whose perfume wafted through the open French doors that our builder had installed opening out onto a balcony. Access to the garden from the basement was restricted and hazardous, particularly for our active young child. We couldn't use any of the rooms there: firstly; we could not afford to repair the basement as yet, and secondly; because it was acting as storage for all the building materials and tools that we needed for the continuing works.

Meanwhile, the suffocating dry months of '76 seemed to go on forever. Temperatures nudged forty degrees. Water was rationed due to the devastating drought. Reservoirs dried up. Even the tarmac in the roads melted. Vegetation, grass and trees wilted and died. A hosepipe ban was in place. In many areas of the country, standpipes were installed in streets. Bathwater was used to water the garden, and the washing of cars and driveways was forbidden.

The drought brought on by the extraordinary weather echoed the drought in the economy. Like most people, we were longing for rain to quench the thirst of the parched grass and the withered trees throughout the gardens and parks, when one day I received a letter through the post. I opened it with trepidation.

British School of Osteopathy
16 Buckingham Gate
London
SW1
Date as postmark

Dear sir,

Further to your application for enrolment at the British School of Osteopathy, I am pleased to inform you that, following your interview and the report from the Kensington Regional Careers Officer who assessed you, we would like to offer you a place in Year One this September.

As there is competition for places due to the restricted intake, we would be grateful if you would respond as soon as possible.

Yours faithfully...

Immediately, I showed the letter to Caroline with a flourish. I was over the moon with anticipatory excitement.

However, unexpected challenges can suddenly crop up for which you weren't prepared. For instance, common sense should have told us that it was the wrong time to take on another mouth to feed. But a neighbour asked us to look after a kitten – a long-haired tabby with a sad, doleful expression. He was looking for a permanent home, having been shunted from place to place. Tanya implored us to keep him. Because of what I regarded as our impoverished circumstances we were hesitant. My parents discouraged the idea based on cost. 'He will eat you out of house and home,' my mother warned. Despite everything, the cat stayed. Although we stocked up with cases of tinned cat food, he persistently pestered us for bits of our meals. Bizarrely, he had a penchant for Italian olives and macaroni. Tanya called him Mog, after a cat from one of her favourite books. Then, not long afterwards, a new family moved into the house next door but one. They were from Holland. Tanya and their daughter, who was just two years younger, instantly hit it off. They became firm friends, and spent most of their time playing in each other's houses.

Thanks to the costs of the renovations, holidays, presents and new clothes were out of the question. Caroline made clothes for Tanya, much admired by fellow parents and their children. Home-made wine and simple food, using low-cost ingredients, kept us fed and healthy. To be honest, such material deprivations could not be described as real hardships by any stretch of the imagination, compared to what millions of people in the world have to endure. I consoled myself that this would have been the norm for my parents when, in the early days, they were forced by circumstances to raise their children in abject poverty, especially during the dark days of the war in Liverpool. Certain deprivations during childhood hadn't harmed my siblings or me one iota. Now I would have to make sacrifices if I wanted to achieve my goal and to be able to devote my future to my new vocation; one which had grabbed my imagination. Again, I hoped that my new career would turn out to be all I had imagined it to be.

Then reality struck home. On my first day at the school in Buckingham Gate, there happened to be an intake of sixteen students in the first year, of which six were considered mature students. With such a small group, tuition would be intimate and personal – the ratio of students to lecturers would be almost four to one. I couldn't wait to get started. Confident though I was, I must confess that nerves consumed me from the outset. Despite sharing my first-day nerves with two friends who were returning to college at the same time as me to study as mature students (one being the wife of a dentist friend who started to retrain as a clinical psychologist, and another as a schoolteacher), the prelude to my new life was still daunting, however much I pretended to my wife and friends with much bravado that it wasn't.

Another door had been fortuitously opened. But at my time of life, it had to be the final opening, and I had to make the most of it. Failure or falling by the wayside was not an option. In order to succeed this time around, I realised, there would be no second chances.

Chapter 54

METAMORPHOSIS

1976–1979

THE INTRODUCTORY FRESHERS' WEEK, with its customary ball that included the whole of the school of eighty students or so, with a faculty of twenty-odd, held little attraction for me at my age. But my fellow students, who proved to be an interesting coterie of men and women ranging from age eighteen to thirty, twisted my arm to join in.

Anatomy and the practice of medicine were taught by medical doctors and surgeons; physiology, pathology, X-ray diagnosis, nutrition etc. by physiologists and pathologists. From the beginning, osteopathic technique was taught and demonstrated by experienced osteopaths in practice. It was a comprehensive and progressive modern course.

The conflicting reactions I got from friends, when they heard that I was retraining at this juncture of life, were quite a revelation. However, a good friend who had qualified as a surgical anaesthetist was surprisingly supportive. As she was leaving for the US to marry one of our former tenants (and a good friend) from the mews, she wanted me to have some of her medical books she had finished with, as well as selling me her little Renault at a bargain price to replace our old car which threatened to break down, having transported all the heavy building materials for the past year or so.

Another friend, who was the godson of Richard Tipping, having recently entered medical school as a mature student, donated a set of bones from a skeleton which he had used in his first year. The exchange took place in a coffee shop in Soho one day, to the horror of the customers and staff, when the human skull, affectionately dubbed Horatio, was delicately handed over and placed onto the table in a paper bag which unfortunately burst at the wrong moment.

The first year of studies was extremely difficult and demanding, as I still had to work on the house in the little spare time that I had. Caroline was a revelation. She managed to hang wallpaper and paint the bedrooms to make the place more like home. Similarly, the lounge and dining room captured her attention, with the stripping of the lead paint off the woodwork and fireplaces which caused her a severe allergic reaction that required medical attention.

My father telephoned me to say that Mao Tse-tung had died on the 9th September 1976 at the age of eighty-two.[102] It was reported that he had died from complications from Parkinson's disease. From the tenor of my father's voice, I got the impression that he was no longer affected by such headline news from the country of his birth. China as a country no longer drew him back. Mao held little meaning for him. He had accepted for some time that he would die in England, now that he was a British citizen – notwithstanding all the years that he and my mother had been regarded as stateless. Now that he was retired and unable to continue supporting his family back in Taishan, contact with his siblings had dwindled and the begging letters had long since ceased.

---

102 After Mao died, the 'Gang of Four', including his wife, Jiang Qing, jockeyed for power, but were arrested and convicted for crimes against the state. From 1977, Deng Xiaoping, following the rapid demise of Premier Zhou Enlai on the 8th January 1976, emerged as the dominant figure amongst pragmatists in the leadership. Under him, China undertook far-reaching economic reforms advocating individualism and incentives – tenets redolent of leanings towards capitalism and other ideas that were once considered subversive, and for which he had previously been censored, and then banished during the Cultural Revolution.

After reluctantly accepting the fact that I had returned to college to retrain, the closest my parents got to understanding what I was studying was thinking that it was a type of bone-setting (which was far off the mark). Because in some isolated rural areas of Britain and certain places abroad, bonesetters still practised. In Chinese, my father called it '*Gwut Fore*'. Remembering our volatile history, I dared not argue with him.

Although I had little time to see my parents, there would soon be an opportunity for a reunion, for my brother, Sam, was about to get married to a delightful girl from Merseyside who came from a good Chinese family, having been introduced through our uncle and friends. The large wedding took place in Liverpool in the spring of 1977. It was a two-day affair, though not quite on the scale of Rose's wedding ten years earlier in Hong Kong, which Sam had witnessed. I had never seen Father so animated. As he approached the couple, who were circulating around the tables of guests, he pressed a large Hongbao (*Lai See*) of lucky money into my brother's hands and said, with undisguised pride, '*You have been a good son! Be a good husband and, hopefully, one day, a good father.*'

There were tears of emotion in Father's eyes, for in his long, hard life, it would sadly turn out that, out of his ten children, he would have the opportunity to attend *only* two of their weddings – Rose's and now Sam's. I can say with certainty that these two alone were the ones that he fully approved of, having partly influenced both unions in the traditional Chinese way. *Two* out of *ten* was by any calculation a poor return in odds. I only wished that he could have been favoured with a little more luck from the large array of sons and daughters he produced to bring him the happiness that he craved. But, in reality, that was how it all worked out in the end, for him and for us. It is an unalterable fact that none of us could change the sequence of events. In the end, all of us chose the partners we wanted through our own free will. At least his status as head of the Kwong – Gong Clan and wider family had been restored and enhanced in the eyes of the Chinese community with the blessing of one of his sons' marriages that he openly approved of.

Exams and projects at school progressed slowly because of the tardiness of my rusty brain. The viva voce exams, I must say, were extremely arduous. Practical studies, such as the manual skills in technique, came to me much more easily. At first, I tried to hide my interest in martial arts, fearing professional disapproval, until I discovered that two of my lecturers were highly qualified and skilled martial artists. The first, was the renowned osteopath Professor Hartley, who was a first dan in karate. The second was Mr Papadopoulis, a judo expert. Like all true devotees, they were the gentlest and most quietly confident men I had come across. I soon discovered that certain osteopathic techniques called HVTS (high-velocity thrusts) to free up, say, for example, a seized-up joint in the spine or a peripheral articulation, required the tiniest of movements with a minimum amount of force to achieve the maximum result. Quite a lot of movement in martial arts is like that, which could partially explain why I relished this type of work so much, and particularly when came so naturally to me. Enthused with practising, I was determined to refine and then master such techniques.

By the summer of 1977, with dedicated help from Rose, our parents moved out of Birmingham with the sale of Portland Road, which became part of a residential old people's care home. They found a large bungalow in a place called Burntwood in Staffordshire. On the ground floor there was a bedroom with an en-suite bathroom. A further two bedrooms were situated upstairs. There was a large garden, which they did not expect or really want. However, the bungalow had a modernised kitchen/diner, gas central heating, and an attached garage and forecourt. It was perfect, I thought, for my parents' retirement. Climbing stairs had become an increasing problem for my father, because as he grew older, he exhibited some breathlessness due to his heart condition, and his joints were stiffening up with arthritic changes.

In November 1977, as the daylight shrank and the dark evenings returned, the Fire Brigade Union called for its first national strike asking for an increase of thirty per cent from the Callaghan government. Given the continuing state of the economy, their demands were not met. Over the winter, Army troops were hastily recruited to man the ancient, slow Green Goddess trucks to fight fires. Without access to modern breathing apparatus and equipment, over one hundred people tragically died due to fires, including four children. The strike lasted until after Christmas 1978. It was an untrammelled disaster of a magnitude never previously witnessed in Britain, particularly for a situation that could have been avoided in the first place.

Other public sector unions flexed their power, presenting pay claims that the government could not afford to settle. Cleaners and hospital workers came out on strike throughout the UK. Laundry couldn't be washed or replaced Hospital infections reached dangerous levels. Food could not be provided for the inpatients. Cemetery employees had joined the national unrest. Bodies were piling up and couldn't be buried. The strikes spread like wildfire to other local authority workers. Refuse collectors, street cleaners and so on joined in. Rat-infested rubbish began to pile high in the streets. Even Leicester Square in London was used as a dump for mountains of rubbish. In history, the winter of '78–'79 became known as the notorious 'Winter of Discontent'. Callaghan's government could not cope. Inflation rose to double figures again. The British economy became an international joke. To many foreign observers, the paralysis in the country with its industrial woes turned the UK into a laughing stock. The situation became intolerable. In Parliament, a vote of no confidence was passed. A General Election was called and, on the 4th May 1979, a Conservative-led government came to power with Margaret Thatcher as Prime Minister.

Friends who were sceptical in the beginning when I returned to my studies, suddenly began to say that, due to the current turbulence and uncertainty prevailing in the job market, it was a fortuitous time to retrain.

As much as I could, I took the time to take my family to visit my father. Despite his getting tired, he was always pleased to see our daughter Tanya, whom he called, '*Hoi lieng soi nui*' ('a good, pretty little girl'). She in turn called him '*Goong-goong*' ('Gramp-pa-pa'), though not necessarily to his face, as to her, he was still an imposing figure, particularly due to the language barrier.

On one or two occasions during the college holidays, I drove to see him on my own as Caroline and Tanya went to stay with Mary. Using my new-found skills at carpentry, I managed to repair and enlarge a garden shed for him. I thought that he might have been impressed by my newly acquired building skills, but, typically, he didn't say much – he just grumbled to my mother that he hoped that the roofing felt I had brought with me from London would keep out the rain. With good grace, I put it down to his being a typical curmudgeon, like many others in their old age.

Over the years, I had got used to never receiving compliments from my father. As an adult, it wasn't so important or relevant to my life as it had once been. There had been a time, growing up, when I had been desperate for his approval. Repeatedly clashing with my father over the years, I had often questioned why. On many occasions, Uncle had intimated that it was probably to do with our personalities or egos, that many a time mirrored each other. He felt that we shared an ebullience and an obstinacy (even pig-headedness) that came to the fore when we were in the same room, like two lions in a pride trying to get their own way. It was fine, said Uncle, for that trait to have existed in our ancestors as it could aid survival during conflict and famine, but when it spilled over into modern family life it could cause trouble and strife. But at least I felt fortunate that I had also inherited some empathetic qualities, I assumed, from some distant forebears. I took pride in having a sympathetic understanding of the underdog and the vulnerable. This quality, I was told by close confidants, proved in the end to be my abiding and saving grace.

Often, I tried to understand my father's overbearing dominance and strictness in the way he had treated us over the years – particularly me as the eldest son, when I also did so much for him. As I have said from the beginning, it was an unanswered question as to why he behaved as he did. Was there some secret reason for it? His austere nature I could reconcile with his upbringing in old China, but his dismissal of me as a child was mystifying, if not cruel. Fortunately, I had the resilience to cope, and if anything, it made me more determined to not let it define me. I had to use the experience constructively to improve my tolerance and understanding of my fellow man. Accepting and applying this had often circumvented the flashpoint moments over the years whenever my father and I met.

Owing to the demands and intensity of my course, I didn't manage to visit my parents as much as I wanted to. We kept in touch by telephone as often as I could, though my Cantonese was getting quite rusty, no longer having much contact with the family or the Chinese community. By then, we as students had for the past two years been firmly established in clinical practice in the school clinic with our own list of patients, albeit under supervision; but with the latter decreasing as our experience matured.

When I did eventually manage to see Father, I noticed that his health was declining as he aged. Now that there was no family business to discuss like in the old days, there was little meaningful conversation between us. To break the long, difficult silence, I took the opportunity to ask him a bit about his old life in China. I had to be extremely diplomatic, as the history of our previous clashes did not make for easy conversation especially at a personal level. I had to be aware that it was a delicate subject – one that had caused so much strife between my mother and him. Nevertheless, I thought that he would enjoy some light nostalgia, reminiscing about the past. Apart from this, on occasions I would try to satisfy my curiosity about his former life, which he had revealed so little about. In hindsight, I wish that I had asked about it a lot more; but there again, our volatile relationship did not allow it. Like many others, we would leave these questions to the last moment – left in abeyance. But by then, all too commonly, it was too late.

It was at times like this that I noticed with increasing sadness that Father would slump into a melancholic silence, and I knew instinctively that his thoughts were drifting to my brother Alan in the States. As a family, we often wondered when we would see him again. It had been almost ten years since he had left to start a new life across the Atlantic. Letters now and then told us that he was frenetically busy working for a worldwide computer company. After Harvard, he had forged a successful career in IT, with financial responsibilities that took him across the southern hemisphere – at the expense of his marriage. We were hoping that one day soon he would get a posting in Europe, before it was too late for Father, who, like the rest of us, longed to see him.

Again, the weeks flew past. Soon the next year would be upon us, and my finals were looming. I drove up to see my parents. It was a fine, sunny day with just a few wisps of cloud scudding high across an otherwise unblemished sky, which made the drive that much more tolerable in my sluggish little Renault.

I met my mother at the door. She was looking a little tired and anxious, and promptly ushered me in to see Father, who was sitting in an armchair in his room on the ground floor. The television was on, but barely audible, and he was half-dozing rather than paying much attention to the screen, or to the fact that I had just come through the door.

'*Ah Shui Lun, dai doi gnam, gnam yee gar fan yuk kee!*' ('It's Francis, Shui Lun – your son has just come home!')

Gently, my mother tapped him on the arm in order to wake him.

I stood beside him and quietly said, '*A Shui Lun... Ah Ba. Nee ho ma?*' ('It's me... Father, are you, all right?')

He managed to open his eyes and stir. I noticed that he was rather pale, especially his lips. He mumbled something, which was hard to hear, as his voice was weak and quavering. I recognised the signs from when he had suffered his heart attack in Portland Road some years ago. I drew up a chair to be a bit closer so that he didn't have to strain his voice.

'*Shui Lun... Mah mah dee,*' he croaked with a supreme effort, waving me away. ('Francis... I'm not too bad.')

Instinctively, I rearranged the cushions behind his shoulders and pulled up the rug around his lap. I offered him some tea, which had grown stone cold beside him on the coffee table.

'Father, have you taken your tablets?' I asked solicitously.

From the doorway, Mother shook her head vigorously. Then Father said that he hated his tablets as they left a dry, sour taste of iron in his mouth, and food didn't taste the same. I was about to tell him off, but felt that it wouldn't achieve anything in the circumstances, for it would only make him feel worse than he already did.

I persuaded him that he ought to be resting in bed. After dismissing the suggestion that he was all right, I managed to help him get out of the armchair and guide him carefully into bed, then prop him up with pillows.

From the dining room, out of my father's earshot, I telephoned his GP, who, to his credit, came around to visit him immediately after surgery hours. Meanwhile, in the interim I was given advice on how to administer my father's different heart medications, which apparently he and my mother had got confused about. The frequency of taking the different capsules and tablets in their different doses was confusing even for me, never mind an old person struggling with a language barrier. Therefore, not surprisingly, the drugs had been taken erratically or, more often than not, abandoned.

The GP said he would call again tomorrow and the next day, and if there was no improvement he would prefer my father to be moved to the local hospital to stabilise his condition under supervision.

So that I wouldn't worry my father unduly, I tactfully told him what the doctor had suggested. At first he protested, saying that he didn't want a fuss, and that once he went into hospital he would never come out. But I said that it would help to make him better. Gently and firmly, I emphasised the positives to reassure him and told him that I would be staying for a little while to keep an eye on him. Mollified, he gave a conciliatory grimace and shrugged, defeated.

I telephoned Caroline to tell her what was happening. She fully understood. Next, I put in a call to Alan in Boston, and then informed the rest of the family. I stressed that they must not rush back to visit all at once, because that would add to our father's anxiety, and probably hasten his demise by overstressing his heart. I assured them that he would be well looked after while we were waiting for a hospital bed to become available.

Over the next few days, without thinking I switched over into my professional mode. I checked his blood pressure and heart rate, which were understandably erratic. Bilaterally, I checked his pulses from the wrist, to his groin, to the back of his knee and ankle. There was a diminishing blood flow to his extremities. After twenty-four hours, with some coaxing, I persuaded him to take his medications, spaced over the day as prescribed. I managed to get some food down him after advising Mother to cut the meat and vegetables into smaller pieces and even liquidise some of it into a savoury gruel with rice.

For the first time in his life, he allowed me to massage his hands and arms, as well as his neck and shoulders. The stiffness in his knees and ankles needed some gentle movement to stimulate the circulation. The embarrassment we both felt, quickly dissipated, as I reassured him that it was part of my professional training. He began to relax.

I just kept my fingers crossed that I was doing the right thing, and hoped that I wouldn't have to call on my CPR training or other clinical methods in an emergency. In this situation, I would have preferred to bow to higher medical expertise, but, left on my own, silently and repetitively, I made myself repeat like a mantra one of the oaths I took whilst training, dedicated to the patients at the school: *Fac Primum Non Nocere*, which means 'First, Do No Harm'.

Repeating this over and over again whilst I was treating him would reinforce my professionalism, and act as a brake, reminding me that Father was just another patient. Forcing myself to remain clinically detached and to regard him strictly as a patient, as much as I could, made the task a little easier. But this was extremely difficult; for in all my life, I had never been in such close and intimate contact with my father. I don't think that we had ever shared even a handshake in adult life, never mind an embrace when I was a child. This might prove one of the most challenging hurdles of my life, but I had to carry on looking after him, hands on, as my father needed me now as he never had before.

Chapter 55

REVELATION AND REDEMPTION

Burntwood, England, 11ᵗʰ June 1979

A s I walked onto the ward, he was standing solicitously over the hospital bed where Father was lying. His back was to me. Taller and broader than me, he abruptly turned away and, calmly and nonchalantly, strode out of the ward. He gave me a cursory glance and nodded politely.

In that transient moment there was something familiar about him that stirred my memory. Perhaps I was wrong. He must have been aged about mid forties or so. Clean-shaven, with dark hair swept back. Some women would regard him as handsome in a dark sort of way. I shook my head. I must have been mistaken. Foolishly, I hadn't been wearing my glasses, blaming the burst of rain that I had been caught in on my journey here. Quickly, I checked that my father was safe and breathing. He was in a deep sleep, snoring sonorously with his mouth slightly agape.

I went to find a nurse who was on duty. 'Nurse,' I said anxiously, thinking of the worst, 'there was a man, a tall stranger in a dark blue jacket, standing over my father in his room. He's just left.'

'Oh, he's been here a couple of times before; usually in the early evening, about this time. I thought that he was from the local church. They often call here.'

Having given that explanation, which did little to reassure me, the nurse hurried away to attend to other patients.

Father stirred as I returned to his beside. Bleary-eyed, he murmured something I couldn't quite grasp. I asked him if he was all right and if he needed anything. He shook his head plaintively, swallowing hard. He said that he was tired, having been awoken during the night to check his blood pressure and temperature. I nodded. Regardless of the many questions that were on the tip of my tongue, I decided that this was not the time to have a meaningful conversation. After plumping up his pillows and smoothing out his blankets, more as a mollifying gesture rather than because of necessity, I stayed until he fell into a peaceful sleep.

The next afternoon, as I walked purposefully along the corridor towards my father's room, which was in a side ward just off the main wing, I happened to catch the back of the stranger at the other end of the corridor where there was another exit which led to the car park. I was convinced that he was the same man who had been in my father's room the day before. I quickened my step, short of breaking-out into a run to chase after him, because I did not want to attract unwanted attention from the security from whom there would be awkward questions that I couldn't answer. Just then, a crowd of chattering visitors struggling with someone in a wheelchair blocked my way in front of the exit stairs. I had no option but to slow down and make a detour. By the time I reached the exit to the car park, the stranger was nowhere to be seen. Out of breath, and furious with myself for arriving twenty minutes late due to public transport delays, I might have overlapped with the mysterious visitor. I kicked myself in frustration.

Before reaching my father's room, I went to the nurses' station and asked if my father had just had any visitors, particularly a tall, well-groomed stranger, whom I tried to describe. I was told that my sister Rose and her husband had called earlier during the lunch hour, and the nurse on duty said that she thought that a pastor had called from a Chinese church in the city. But again, she was unsure of the facts as she had been extremely busy, having a couple of emergencies to deal with. And, she intimated with due respect, unfortunately, all Orientals looked the same to her!

None the wiser, I entered my father's room with trepidation. Pale though he looked, he seemed somewhat brighter. After a few pleasantries, I was about to ask him some searching questions, when suddenly my sister Eileen arrived with my mother to bring Father his evening meal. As he was being fed, I fiddled with the clipboard at the end of his bed. As far as I could interpret the medical notes – the observations and chronology of the patient's progress – it appeared that his vital signs were within normal range for his age and condition. Visiting hours came quickly to a close, and Father understandably became tired. I promised him that I would visit him again the next day, and this time, I decided, I would ensure that I arrived earlier in the afternoon with enough time to spare so that I could talk to him while he was properly lucid.

Having rehearsed in my head, over and over again what I planned to say to him, it immediately went out of the window when I saw him again. Unfettered, I just blurted out, 'Father, there's a tall man – a stranger – who has been visiting you over the last few days. *Who on earth is he?'*

There was a long silence as he turned to face the window with a glazed look. I knew that he wasn't really focusing on anything in particular, even though he was wearing his glasses. A rasping cough followed, and he asked for a sip of water, which I gave him from a jug on his bedside table.

I asked him again. 'I bumped into the back of him as he was leaving the other day. *Who is he?'* I persisted.

Evading my gaze, he mumbled into the bedclothes. Tears began to well up in his eyes, then streamed down his face. I felt awful having to press him when he was weak and frail, but I simply had to know.

'Er… that… that ma-man – that visitor – I think is my son… *my oldest child!* The one I thought was dead!' His voice faltered, choking between the tears.

Of all the things in life I have had to cope with, this must rank as one of the most bizarre and unbelievable. The room fell silent as a grave. It grew icy, and just as macabre. His words suddenly struck me like a thunderbolt in the pit of my stomach.

'Par... *Pardon?!*' Incredulous, I doubled up with shock. I felt a bit faint, so I sank quickly into the chair beside the bed and grabbed a glass of water from the table. 'Are... are you su-sure?' I mumbled hoarsely, not daring to look him in the eye. I repeated my question, just in case I had misheard him; really hoping that I had.

Another pregnant silence followed. Eventually, he nodded. 'It was a very long time ago. Years before I married your mother.'

Holding back tears, it was one of those moments of revelation that I really did not want to hear, but felt compelled to listen to in order to satisfy my curiosity. It seemed that a dam had finally burst. He had been harbouring this secret for all these years. I was speechless. But now he wanted desperately to tell me – *anyone*, as it happened, who cared to listen – about what he had lived with all this time. If only he had been able to confide in someone years ago; a close friend, anyone. Although it would have been very unlikely due to his religious views, he could have sought help from the church in confession with a priest... it would have helped. The guilt he must have felt all these years would have been assuaged to some extent, and not festered in his heart like a poison for which there was no antidote.

He told me the story of how he had met Ruby, a pretty, dark-haired Liverpool girl, in 1933. He was thirty-five at the time, ten years older than her, and they had lived together. But after two years, as soon as he received a letter from the elders of his family in Taishan, telling him that he was to be married by proxy to a Chinese girl half his age from the Chow village, he had no choice but to get rid of Ruby and their baby son. As the eldest son, it was his duty to obey the family. The dowry had already been paid to the Kwong family in Taishan. The bride-to-be had already been escorted by the marriage broker to his ancestral home. It was a transaction – a loveless contract in which he had no say. The marriage ceremony would take place in Dai Dune Chun using a proxy, although not another human being, as it would be regarded as bigamy.

'In those days, I would have been regarded as soiled goods if the Kwong and Chow families back in Taishan had heard about my life here in England. And so it had to remain a dark secret.'

Astounded, my mouth still open, I allowed him to gather his breath.

'But, Father, wasn't she – your friend – er... a... *European... an English girl?*' I tendered curiously, my self-righteousness rising.

A sheepish black look in return silenced me, and the incendiary word 'hypocrisy' began to cross my mind as I recalled all the times he had preached his disapproval of consorting with European girls, in no uncertain terms – particularly to me.

He then told me that the letter of September 1935 from his family in China about this arranged marriage was kept, along with all their other letters, hidden in a dented biscuit tin buried in an old suitcase. The latter was in the boiler cupboard behind the upstairs bedrooms at home.

'Amongst the papers, you will find the gold signet ring bearing the clan name. It has been kept for the er, ***eld...est*** son...'

No sooner had he said that, than he abruptly stopped in his tracks as a profound dilemma struck him. The confusion that suddenly dawned on his face was nothing compared to the consternation that it caused me.

After a moment's hesitation, although visibly shaken, Father continued intensely, as though he had given the following considerable thought. 'Erm... now that you have *finally* decided to return home, there are serious considerations and plans you have to make on my behalf, for time is running out. And there is another important thing. I've been thinking hard about it. The role of the eldest, I think, has got to be earned, rather than simply given as a birthright. You see, you have *no* sons; only a daughter – your firstborn. So, probably, the family thread now needs to be re... wov...'

Another pause followed as he lost his train of thought. I wish now that I had persisted in asking what he had started to say about the ancestral line.

'In the tin, you will find a scroll bearing all the names of the children and when they were born, according to tradition. The family tree – which goes back to 1679, starting with my ancestor Ming Jid Doo's father Ging Sun Doo – I have asked to be buried with me. If, and when you, or any other member of the Kwong-Gong Clan, trace further back over the centuries through finding more of the clan records in the Ancient Ancestral Hall,[103] then I want you to burn any newly discovered documents at my graveside in a brief ceremony, so that the ashes can be subsequently buried in the soil beside me. And you must keep your promise to your late Aunt Chun Rei that you will visit our ancestral home in China before it is too late. I want you to visit the ancestral tombs on the mountainside and scatter a handful of soil from my grave here in England, so that I can be united with my parents one day.'

His voice, already weakened, trailed away. More tears fell and soaked the pillow, which I rapidly changed.

'In spring 1936, your mother arrived in England. Shortly afterwards, your sisters Eileen and Rose were born, just as the country went to war with Germany in the autumn of '39. It was a terrible, terrifying time. We struggled to feed ourselves in a laundry in a poor part of Liverpool. Ruby and the little boy moved in just opposite us, I thought at first to taunt us, but on reflection it was probably to be near me. I didn't dare tell your mother. Shortly after you were born, during the Blitz, Ruby's building took a direct hit. I ran across with the fire wardens to do what I could. It was a blazing inferno. It was futile – hopeless. I was told everyone in the building would have perished in the fireball.'

---

103 Discovered in the northern part of Guangdung Province, in a place preserved for posterity as Zhuji Ancient Lane. Many clan records of different families and their ancestral shrines can be found there. The Kwong-Gong Clan records are held there, although incomplete, and those that were saved from the Cultural Revolution and collated from ancestral village records probably predating Ming Jid Doo's birth in 1709. Of late, his earlier ancestor, Ging Sun Doo's birth records in 1679 were discovered there.

Increasingly agitated, he began to wail as if he was in sudden, intractable pain. Concerned, the nurse on duty rushed into the room. I explained that my father was distraught at recalling some bad news from the past. She shook her head, glared at me disapprovingly and insisted on giving him a sedative to soothe him.

I held up my palm, saying that we mustn't talk anymore, as it was tearing him apart, which was not only distressing for him, but for me. But he insisted on continuing his story, which had been simmering within him for years, waiting to boil over.

'I thought that the boy had also been killed in the air raid. But apparently, he had been staying with Ruby's mother on the other side of the city and therefore escaped with his life. All these years I couldn't get rid of my guilt for the part I played in Ruby's death. Even more, I thought about the death of the innocent young boy – *my FIRST son*. The nightmares have haunted me ever since.'

By now, Father's voice was a breaking rasp, almost unintelligible. It suddenly occurred to me that he might have genuinely loved Ruby and their son. Dismissing that notion out of hand, I made him take a sip of water as he was shaking with emotion.

'Then unbeknown to me, in a shocking surprise, this grown man turned up at the hospital a few days ago. He had traced my whereabouts through some persistent detective work from his London office. He told me that, before the end of the war in 1945, his grandmother suddenly died of a stroke. Left alone in the house, he had to fend for himself, until his teacher at school alerted the local authorities, and he was taken into care. Eventually, he was adopted by a Chinese family called the Yeohs, who were childless. To give him a fresh start, they renamed him Raymond, which was his middle name. Shortly after the war ended with the atomic bombing of Japan, they emigrated to California to start a new life.'

Father then fell silent, thinking about what might have been.

'Years later, they became immensely successful, owning chains of supermarkets in San Francisco's Chinatown as well as some other cities in the US. The boy grew up, studied at Stanford University and became a lawyer. Raymond Yeoh is now working for a large American bank. He is married and has two children, a boy and a girl. He wants to meet you. He travels to Europe every few years or so for meetings.'

I gestured with a wave to slow him down. Although clearly agitated, having started, he still wanted to get it all off his chest.

'But, Father, I don't understand. What does he *want* from you, if not money?'

A long sigh of exasperation escaped from Father's lips. This time, pushing down with his arms, he raised his body pointedly out of the bed and stared directly at me to emphasise his point.

'Don't you know by now, son, that everybody, particularly the Chinese, needs to know their ancestors; where they came from; who they were? Possessing this knowledge is more precious than gold or money. All his life, this man has been searching for his ancestral thread. He has wanted to trace his birth father, since his adoptive father died ten years ago. He now wants acknowledgement from me that he is *my* son! He wants *MY NAME*, so that one day he can pass it down to his son!'

Hysterically and in pitiful gasps, his voice rose to fever pitch. 'But I am too old to help him now. *It is too late!* A lifetime has passed. Too much has happened. How can I atone for the past? I can't undo the last forty-five years for him. But at least I can tell him the truth about his mother.'

By now, I could see in my father's face that he was completely wiped out by the revelations. A whole host of septic worries had been shed. It was a cathartic moment – *a pivotal turning point.*

'Look, Father, I think it's better if we continue this conversation another time.'

I made a promise to him that I would not tell my mother. The secret would go with me to the grave. I also agreed to meet this Raymond – the newly discovered eldest son – in the afternoon of the following day. I made my father comfortable and stayed until he fell into a deep, tired sleep. After the earth-shattering confession, it was not surprising that physical and mental exhaustion had completely devastated him.

I couldn't sleep very well that night. The unburdening of my father's secret had at least taken a weight off his mind, but it had now been offloaded onto my shoulders. It was a cross that I would have to bear. In the light of these revelations, looking back, I have tried to reconcile his autocratic behaviour towards me for all those years; as a child growing up, and as an adult. Generously, I have also tried to justify his ambivalence towards me, which may have occurred largely because of his guilt over Ruby and their son... and now the existence of this person – Raymond – as a grown-up.

Suddenly, it *dawned* on me. It was one of those light-bulb moments. *This man had from the beginning been the missing piece in our jigsaw.* It was both a merciful relief that I finally knew, and equally, a damning curse to hear that he even existed. It sunk in that he had been the spectre haunting us, and which had always stood between my father and me. It all fell into place. Clearly, I could see that now.

However, it didn't fully explain the clashes we had continued to have over the years. Part of me has got to accept that the austere manner in which Father treated not only me, but my siblings, was steeped in the way he was brought up by his parents in ancient China. To be cold and unemotional was, I now understand, a protective mechanism for survival that would kick-in in the face of threats and danger, as it had in his father's time before him. But for me, it was extremely difficult to share moments of intimacy for fear of embarrassment or rejection. However, what I can say for certain that, after what my father had just revealed to me, he was no longer the ogre he had been in my eyes, now that the nemesis that had troubled me all my life had been slain.

The following day, I steeled myself to face this stranger. Brimming with fortitude – full of self-righteousness that I was the legitimate son in the pecking order and determined not to buckle – I went to meet him. Thinking back, it would probably have been better if I had taken a stiff drink instead. As I climbed the stairs towards the hospital ward, Raymond Yeoh was already there. Proprietorially, he had taken up the armchair next to Father's bed and appeared to be fussing around him in a one-way conversation. He quickly jumped up as if he had been shot and held out his hand to me in greeting.

'You must be Francis. I've heard a lot about you.'

Warily, we stared at each other, trying to size each other up, but at the same time attempting to be civil to one another.

Then it dawned on me. We had met once, or even twice before. The revelation hit him at exactly, the same time in the same way.

'Haven't we… met before?' he asked, his face contorted animatedly.

Fortunately, Father was slumbering away; or if he wasn't, then he put up a good act.

'I came to the restaurant in Birmingham, nine years ago, when I was working in London.'

Slightly unnerved that I had been found out, I replied lamely, 'I do remember now. You asked for Mr Kwong or a Mr Gong Chun Ji. Thinking that you were one of the creditors, or a solicitor who was about to serve a summons for a debt, I had to say that the old man no longer worked there.'

'But when I asked if you were his son, you openly denied it and said that you were one of the staff!'

I blustered indignantly, going slightly red in the face. 'I did it to protect him from all the people chasing him for money!'

Just then, Father stirred with a short cough. It caught our attention momentarily, and we immediately leant over his bed, both trying to show our concern. His eyes were still closed.

'Look,' Raymond said quietly, 'he's quite frail and extremely tired. It's probably better if we discuss family matters somewhere else. I'm staying at the hotel down the road for the moment. Here is my number, and my home and office address in Los Angeles. I hope that you and your family will visit us.'

His concern for my father's welfare jarred, producing a pang of jealousy. Try as I might, I still couldn't come to terms with the fact that this tall stranger, in the prime of life – having on the face of it, everything going for him: health, looks, education, status, a good job, seemingly a devoted wife and children, and apparently not short of money – didn't want anything from Father. To seek just his name seemed to me to be seeking some sort of obsessive and perverse benediction that was too late to be reversed. I shook my head, still puzzled and confused, then took the card and put it into my back pocket. I explained that I had to return home to London for the weekend, as my brother Alan was flying in from Boston; so I agreed that Raymond and I would meet when I got back. He told me not to worry, as he would still visit Father each day and keep an eye on him.

I collected Alan from Heathrow in the early hours of the morning. It had been nine long years since he had left to start a new life in the States. It was wonderful to see him again. There was so much to talk about. So much water had passed under the bridge, as Caroline cryptically said. After allowing my brother to catch up on sleep, I drove him up to see our father.

On the motorway journey to the Midlands, I felt I *had* to tell Alan about the other son, Raymond. Like me, he couldn't quite believe it. Frankly, he was gobsmacked, as I had been – to use a phrase in the common vernacular. For a stranger to turn up out of the blue, after all this time in an attempt to claim his birthright, Alan wondered if there was an ulterior motive – although for the life of us we couldn't think of one. Meanwhile, Raymond had left a message with Caroline in London to say that he had been called back to his London office for a few days but would be in touch. I felt that it was just as well to allow Alan an uninterrupted couple of days to be with Father.

Mother and my brothers and sisters were over the moon at Alan's return. We managed to see Father in one of his lucid moments, because he had been muttering to the family that he had seen a clutch of evil-winged funeral spirits, hissing and waiting for him at the foot of his bed; and that he had chased them off by hurling his pillow at them, and shouting that he wasn't ready to follow them. When I mentioned this to his doctors, they just shrugged knowingly, and explained that older patients with erratic blood pressure and under certain drugs commonly hallucinate.

Although there was so much to ask about the missing years, surprisingly, Father didn't say that much to Alan. However, the quiet acceptance that his good, favourite son had returned to visit him was better than nothing in the circumstances and gave that much-needed tonic that no medicine could provide. The following day, Alan and my sisters spent some extra precious time with him.

Again, there was so much to catch up on in such a short time before Father got too tired to respond. I noticed that he had developed a persistent cough that he hadn't had before. I thought that it was due to his having to talk so much. Drawing the doctor's attention to it, I was told that he had been given a mild course of antibiotics as a precaution in case the upper respiratory tract infection spread to his chest. Noticing that he was increasingly pale and disorientated, we were advised to allow him to sleep a bit more in order to regain his strength. The flood of visitors over the last few days, including one from the past turning up, must have overwhelmed him.

I told Father that I would visit him again the next day. How much he understood, it was difficult to say. The shadows under his eyes had etched deeply with all the efforts that he had made to talk to me (and others) over the past week or so. Despite that, I couldn't deny the momentary glow that lit up his face as soon as my brother had walked through the door.

I was just falling asleep at our parents' house at a quarter past eleven at night, when Eileen telephoned me to say that she had heard from the hospital that Father's breathing was getting shallower and more rasping due to the bronchial pneumonia that had spread to his lungs, and that we had better visit him as soon as possible if we wanted to see him.

Quickly getting dressed, I told my mother and brother that we needed to go to the hospital straight away. By the time we got there, it was already way past midnight. Entering his room, I noticed that the bed was empty. A stupid thought suddenly occurred to me that he must have got up and gone for a walk around the ward. The bedclothes had been folded back tidily.

428

The duty nurse came in and said quietly that she was really sorry, but Father had died from a sudden cardiac arrest thirty minutes ago. My brother asked her where our father was. She pointed the way to the Chapel of Rest, saying that my sisters were already there. Alan calmly escorted my mother and followed the nurse to the chapel which smelled vaguely of disinfectant and some obscure air freshener that had gone rancid.

Stunned, and left alone in the room, I could not keep a flood of tears from rushing down my face. I knelt over Father's empty bed and dried my face on the bedclothes. I cursed myself for arriving too late. There were so many things that I wanted to ask him; to tell him. I wanted to apologise for what had happened between us all those years ago. I wanted to thank him for making me who I am; for teaching me how to survive in the face of adversity. There were so many things unsaid that needed to be explained. I wanted to show him that I could forgive, and that I understood. And perhaps most of all, I wanted to say to him that **evocative word** that through embarrassment during our lives, we had so often avoided expressing that simple, emotive entity, called… **'Love'** to one another, until it was too late. I realised now that it didn't matter one jot if my love for him was never reciprocated. It had taken me nearly all my life before I had even dared to utter the word to him. How foolish we are, that we as humans often cannot express such intimate emotions to our parents face to face, until that opportunity passes us by for good. Perhaps, in the end, all I wanted was to seek some sort of redemption.

Joining the others beside my father's body lying in the dim, soft light of the chapel, I, like the rest of us, felt like an outside observer, detached and useless. We could not communicate with our father's body or even each other. The awkward silence was overbearing. All the platitudes and words of encouragement that we had said to Father over the last few days – that he was getting better – now felt hollow. We could have been accused of giving him false hope, when deep down, we knew that he had just been hovering in the waiting room, waiting his turn for the last call; to the last stop – this, *his final destination.*

His time had now come. Collective guilt and a conflict of emotions are common when this happens. It is a natural phenomenon when an aged loved one dies, particularly the first time one faces the death of a parent, because you have no prior experience of how to deal with such things. It savagely reminds us of our own mortality, with a warning that life is so transient, and as such, could be snatched away from us in a blink of an eye.

It also suddenly occurred to me: how would my mother cope, living on her own? All her married life, since she came to England forty-odd years ago, my father had done *everything* for her. She was unable to read or write letters without his help. And even worse, how would she cope, since she was so lacking in English, with dealing with the mundane, everyday routine of household bills, money matters and so on? In ancient China, she would not be on her own, as tradition would ensure that several generations would continue to live with her under one roof. But this was not China.

In the shallow, warm light, instinctively, I leant over my father's body and gently placed a kiss on his forehead. It was already cold. Rigor had already started to set in. Out of the corner of my eye, I noticed that my mother was startled at what I had just done. It was the first and last time that I had ever had the courage to demonstrate such intimate tenderness towards my father; for only now he was dead was I able to be brave enough. Numbness took over. Over time, grief would also have to be played out. I reassured Mother and the family that at least Father had held out to see Alan again. Silently, I wondered if Raymond had been in touch with the hospital.

We returned to our beds like zombies, in a state of shock and, if I may dare say it, with a degree of relief that it was all over. Perhaps Father's death would bring us a kind of closure and peaceful redemption. And there again, perhaps it would not.

Chapter 56

KWONG (GONG) CHUN JI (1898–1979): REQUIEM

Stafford, England, 25 th June 1979

I am the restless wind that blows,
The breeze that lifts you on a summer's day,
East and west and back again.
I am the rain that will soothe your brow.
The snow that comes to chill your winter.
I am the ray of sun that brings you comfort.
A star at night, that blinks and fades.
I am the soil beneath your feet,
To weave a path where others might follow.

IT WAS ONE OF those sunny days of midsummer in England, and the sky was an unblemished canvas of clear turquoise blue without a cloud in sight. The breeze was so light that it carried a faint scent of wildflowers and new-mown grass to infuse the senses. The sort of day when all you wanted to do was to laze in the garden and allow the gentle warmth to wash over you.

However, it was two weeks since my father had died, and the carefree sunshine felt incongruous and at odds with the dark bleakness we felt. And today, the day of his funeral, there was so much to do and to contemplate. In keeping with Chinese tradition, the cortège bearing my father's coffin, which was covered in white lilies and white chrysanthemums, had crawled its way from the Chapel of Rest at the funeral directors to stop briefly outside our parents' home in Burntwood in an acknowledgement that my father had come home for the last time. Brimming with curiosity, his neighbours came out and stood in silence to pay their respects with bowed heads and dutiful expressions. I was in the second car with my wife and daughter, Alan, Tom, Sam and their respective spouses. My sisters Eileen and Rose, with their husbands and children, accompanied Mother in the first limousine. And, fittingly, Father's surviving brother, Uncle Chun Tileng and his family, as well as two nephews, were escorted in the following car.

The rest of our siblings and their families made up the cortège and followed the hearse. At a slow and respectful pace, the cortège then wound its way to Father's final resting place in the cemetery in Stafford. Along the journey, we threw money out of the open windows of the cars. It was a symbolic gesture to ensure that he wouldn't be short of money on the next part of his journey to the other world. Astonished passers-by rushed surreptitiously to the roadside and grabbed the coins as the cars swept by. In parts of ancient China, a band of mourners dressed all in white (the traditional colour of mourning) would play a haunting, wailing dirge to accompany the deceased, weaving their way to the graveside with as much grandeur as possible, as befitting a prominent head of a clan; but that would be impossible to arrange in the fair, green pastures of England.

On arrival at the cemetery, a further group of mourners – friends and former restaurant staff – were waiting patiently in the bright sunshine. My father could not have chosen a better day. Inside the non-denominational chapel, the acting priest delivered a short and suitable reading from a generic set of texts.

Will, being the most senior of my brothers-in-law, was invited by the family to deliver the eulogy to my father. He draped a pure white cloth over the coffin, on which he had inscribed, in beautiful calligraphy, the name of my father intertwined with those of his parents. His voice breaking with emotion, Will addressed a large photograph of Father and began to read out from the beginning the Kwong (Gong) Clan's ancestral line.

'*Firstly, Kwong Chun Ji's, greatest great-grandfather, Ming Jid Doo (son of Ging Sun Doo, 1679-1739) born on the sixth day of the tenth month of 1709, the Year of the Ox. Died on the seventeenth day of the third month of 1781, in the reign of Emperor Qin Long.*

Secondly, his next greatest great-grandfather, Yip Gee Doo, born on the eighth day of the fourth month of 1745; died on the eighth day of the eleventh month of 1814, aged sixty-nine, in the Year of the Dog.

Thirdly, his great-great-...'

And so, it went on… the roll call continued in a monotonic droll, until it came to my father's father.

'*Kwong Loong Cheung Ham, born on the twenty-fifth day of the seventh month of 1875 in the Year of the Boar, under the reign of Emperor Kwong Shui. Died on the sixteenth day of the twelfth month of 1923, aged forty-eight.'*

Several times, Will's voice broke down due to raw emotion, forcing him to take a pause. He cleared his throat and carried on.

'Kwong Chun Ji was born on the twenty-seventh day of the tenth month of 1898, the Year of the Dog; the eldest son of Kwong Loong Cheung Ham and Fung Ting Sei. Born, like his father and grandfathers before him, in the village of Dai Dune Chun near to Taishan, China. On the 10th January 1921, at the age of twenty-two, he left his village to make some money in the West in order to save his family. Due to wars and revolution, they were on the verge of starvation. All alone, he arrived in Liverpool on the 2nd April 1921, after a terrifying journey by sea during which nearly half the passengers died from murder, disease and starvation. Penniless, he immediately set to work, seven days a week in appalling conditions. It was back-breaking manual work in a laundry, which in those days the Chinese were restricted to doing. Married to Chow Mou Lan in 1936, they set up a hand-laundry business in Liverpool. Eileen, Shui Dee, was born in 1937; followed by Rose, Shui Mein, in 1938; Francis, Shui Lun, in 1940...'

In a tremulous voice, Will then went on to describe the births of the rest of the ten children, five boys and five girls. He described the hardships of war and the Blitz, and Father moving the family to Wrexham in 1946. Then, on returning to Liverpool in 1953, the opening of the café – his first foray into catering. He mentioned that, in 1958, Father opened a successful restaurant in the centre of Birmingham. He was one of the first to pioneer Chinese cooking in the Midlands at that time. It was there that Will had first met Kwong Chun Ji, who later became his father-in-law. He admitted that, despite their initial differences, they grew to respect and to depend on each other. Finally, he said that, in 1966, Father had returned to China after forty-five years away to visit his brothers and sisters at the ancestral home in Taishan. Disconcertingly, it was at the height of the troubles in the middle of the Cultural Revolution. Four years later, he retired due to ill health and increasing old age, which, typically, he refused to accept.

By now, my brother-in-law was trembling like a jelly. His eyes were swamped with tears which he couldn't suppress. Reaching for a handkerchief, he blew his nose noisily as the coffin was closed.

Marshalling his thoughts, Will then went on to say,

'On the death of his father in 1923, Kwong Chun Ji became head of the Kwong-Gong family. He took on the combined obligation of looking after his family in Taishan, as well as his own ten children here in England, until his last days. It was considered his duty as the eldest son, which he did not question. He devoted his life to the family and would die for the family.

That epitaph should be proudly etched on his gravestone!

'And so, Dai Gong Sing Bak,[104] we as a family – your children and your grandchildren – now pay our heartfelt tributes to you for

---

104 *Dai Sing Bak*: an affectionate term of seniority and respect, equivalent to 'Grand/ Venerable Uncle'.

all that you have done for us. Regardless of the trials and difficulties that you faced in your long, hard life, you still triumphed against the odds. We only wish that the journey had been made easier for you. Unfortunately, real life, with all its vicissitudes and booby traps, is not like that. We thank you for your hard work, your sacrifices, your unerring loyalty to us, your family, and your courage in protecting the family through all the challenges and the early prejudices and disappointments that you came across.

'You demonstrated the ability to overcome grief and setbacks and gave us hope and love when all seemed lost. You showed us the way to battle on despite wars and across the racial and social divide. It has been an honour as well as a privilege to be part of your family. Finally, Dai Gong Sing Bak, we can say that no pain or suffering can touch you now. We hope that your passing has been smooth and peaceful, and that you will soon meet your father, your mother and your siblings once again.'

At the graveside, under a young cherry tree where there was a visible slope,[105] the vicar offered a short prayer and then, quietly and diplomatically, departed.

I was asked to make the final tribute:

I am the bough that gives you shelter;
The anchor in earth in the teeth of the storm.
You are the branch that reaches the sky.
For I am the root from which you will grow,
I am the cord and you are the thread,
And the search for it, that will never cease.
For who you are, and what I am, or for what I was,
Then look no further than to stare in the mirror,
For the river of life will go on and flow.

Then burning joss sticks, we shed our final tears and bowed in homage, each of us in turn, to our father. At the same time, we burnt ghost paper

---

105 According to Chinese tradition, the deceased was buried on an incline with his head higher than his feet, so that his body would be nearer to access the heavenly afterlife.

money to ensure that he would have enough in the afterlife and threw the ashes into the grave. Then, nervous and overwrought, Mother stepped forwards and placed a tray of food and tea beside the coffin for Father's remaining journey. I threw a glass paperweight – which came from China – containing a white rose into the grave. Falling soundlessly on top of the white roses that my siblings had thrown onto the coffin, I hoped that it, like Father's spirit, would survive forever. Shortly afterwards, my sisters distributed a small packet to each of the mourners. Inside was a small silver ten-pence piece for enduring good luck, and a boiled sweet to take away the bitterness of the day.

As we made our way out of the cemetery to the hotel for light refreshments, our car followed the stream of vehicles leaving the car park. In front of us was a dark blue BMW. As I was driving, Alan suddenly pointed, gesticulating wildly at the car in front of us. *'My God! Heh, look at that!'*

'What are you talking about?' I grumbled, not thinking properly, as my mind had drifted back to the people at the cemetery.

'That. *That car in front!* The number plate's got **KWONG 35G** inscribed on it. *Can't believe it!'*

Then, as I accelerated to catch up, after a brief wobble of the wheel, I realised that it was Raymond driving. I elbowed my brother to tell him so.

'Well, that's as close as he will **ever** get to Father's legacy!' offered Alan scornfully.

I just shrugged indifferently. I had other things on my mind.

At the hotel, there were strict instructions that red wine was not to be served, as it was a symbol of blood. As expected, there was a quiet and sober acceptance pervading the atmosphere.

Father's former accountant and his wife came up to me and offered their condolences. His solicitor, who had dealt with our parents' naturalisation papers, did the same. A few minutes later, Raymond sought me out and shook my hand whilst extending his sympathies. I thought at first, that he was just politely going through the motions;

but in hindsight, I may have misjudged him. Cupping his hand to my ear, he whispered that he wished that he had had more time with our father. He then reminded me that I was to contact him, for there was much to resolve.

Not long afterwards, Mother came up to me and asked who that man was. To save further probing, I had to lie and say that I thought that he was from the Chinese church. She nodded, saying, 'Oh, I thought that I had seen someone like him at the hospital a couple of times. He was attempting to convert your father before he died.'

Just before we left to assemble at the house, Uncle accosted me and said that, as I was now the eldest son and head of the Kwong-Gong family, there were certain obligations and responsibilities that came with the territory. He suggested that, when we met next, he would spell them out to me – especially regarding the remaining family back in China. Immediately, I craned my neck to sweep around the room, desperately looking for Raymond in order to grab him, and get *him* to take the responsibility. Fortunately for him, and unfortunately for me, he was nowhere to be seen. I was told he had left earlier, seemingly in a hurry.

It was in a moment of conspiratorial confession that I admitted to my brother Alan that, the night before the funeral, I had been awoken, I thought, by someone standing at the foot of my bed. I'd switched on the bedside lamp, my heart thumping uncontrollably, thinking that I had seen a ghost. Later, when I spoke to Rose, she said the same thing had happened to her. She swore that it was Father's restless spirit moving about before flying away to China. It is often said that, in times of being overcome with emotion, your mind can play tricks on you. You can often see what you wish for. I have to say that I wasn't in a fit state at that time to test the theory, one way or the other.

Moreover, as I said to my brother, there were so many unbelievable events that had happened recently. There was so much to mull over and to assimilate. Knowing that there exists a fine line between reality and illusion, I had to make certain that it had all taken place and that it wasn't a dream. And so, during that night, I put on my dressing gown, got up and went to look for the card that Raymond had given to me. I thought that I had put it for safekeeping into the back pocket of one of my pairs of trousers. Rummaging through them, it wasn't there. In vain, I searched high and low and everywhere, even in jacket pockets where I thought I might have put it by mistake. But, like phantoms, the card and its giver had disappeared from the face of the earth.

And so when I next had the chance, I vowed that I would try to trace Raymond's whereabouts in the States by contacting the International Directory, and confront him in a sort of truce. But perhaps, in reality I didn't *want* to face the truth. Therefore to this day, to my eternal shame, I never did get around to contacting him.

During the rest of the night, to pass the time away, something came to me spontaneously in my subconscious as I was half-dozing. It suddenly occurred to me that my father's restlessness that had troubled him all his life might continue to do so for a long time yet, even in death; and that his rootless spirit would continue to haunt me with impunity as there was some unfinished business between us.

After much soul-searching, I began to understand why he had spent his life railing against things and situations I didn't understand when I was growing up. Thinking back, I think that he had always felt that any ambition he'd once had, had been killed off, owing to family ties. Sadly, he felt that he had spent his lifetime underachieving, which fuelled his frustration. He had missed out on education and the freedom of opportunities that others had. Perhaps, if he had managed to achieve *just a sliver* of those *opportunities* which we in the West take for granted, the gulf between us might not have been that wide.

Tragically, he must have felt a failure as a father, being head of a family of ten children here in England, but having only *one* son and *one* daughter for whom he could openly and proudly claim that he had had an approving hand in their choice of spouse. And however hard he tried over the years to hold back the relentless tide of change, he was unable to protect and preserve the Chinese culture and family way of life here in England. An iron wedge had been driven between him and his children, gradually alienating them from him because of their being steeped in the English way of life. But any objective observer would just accept that it would be impossible to prevent this happening, given their Western birth and the titanic clash of cultures between East and West, which are so diametrically opposed to one another. Such a conflict was bound to present a dilemma of monumental proportions that millions of immigrant families, like ours, would have to face sometime, sooner or later in life.

However, regardless of these drawbacks, he never once questioned his obligations. He had sacrificed everything for his family back in China because of duty for it was expected of him from the day he was born.

Throughout his life, he accepted his fate, and he carried out that duty so that they might have a chance to live.

It was quite ironic that he died following the Winter of Discontent. But I have now come to terms with the inevitable. His umbilical cord has been cut. He has been set free. But it begs the question: have I, likewise, now been set free?

Many times, over the years, in the still of the night, as I thrashed around due to habitual insomnia, I have tried desperately to go over my father's last words to find a meaning to his life and how it impacted on mine in order to reconcile both.

'Shui Lun, you are the last of the Kwong-Gong male line from me, the eldest. But you must never forget where you came from. You must always be proud of your family and of your beginnings. Whatever you become in life you must never be ashamed of our humble peasant roots!'

Remarkably, his initial angst faded as soon as he mentioned the rebirth of his old country. 'Like the mass of people in China today, it was from this peasant class that dominated China a hundred years ago that the country was able to emerge from the shackles of its Imperial past.

Because without us, the peasants, the revolution for an independent republic in 1912 and 1949 would never have succeeded. And without us, and without the force and strength of the clan families working together, the modern China you see today would not have happened.[106]

I tell you now, that old grandfather Biu Shu would be dancing in his grave, knowing that his dearest wish has come to pass and the sleeping dragon has finally awoken.'

As soon as he said that I realised that, even though my father was resigned and grateful to end his days as a citizen of Britain, having been rudderless and stateless for most of his adult life, deep down he remained proudly Chinese. As with so many others in his situation, it was something you cannot alter in the Chinese psyche which was ingrained in his DNA. Paradoxically, despite the many irreconcilable and seismic changes in his former country under the Communists, he still revelled in the re-emergence of China after so many years in the wilderness. Crucially, I hadn't truly realised that he still cared so much for his motherland. He, like so many of his fellow countrymen divorced from the land of their birth, would have spent a lifetime searching for that elusive utopian dream...even though it was more in hope, cloaked in fantasy, rather than in actual reality.

'But returning to the matter of the family: I remind you that when I die, like it or not, you will become the head of the family; not only here, but also in the States and in China! Your role as the eldest, I think, has now been earned, although it is regrettable that you have no sons; only a daughter. Therefore when the time comes, the family thread needs to be rewoven.'

Although this would fly in the face of my father's male line, in the end, I think he was trying to tell me that it was time to rethink – to change the family order. It could only be altered with his sanction as the head

---

106 China's economic and industrial expansion owes a debt to its overseas families' traditional financial obligations, as well as the cohesive strength and enduring industry of their clans due to their blood ties. Although overall credit must be given to Deng Xiaoping's rule in 1977 after the death of Mao, which kick-started the economic reforms using 'capitalist ideas' of incentives and individualism that transformed China into a global power.

of the clan in a sort of secular absolution. I think he kept this back to the last moment until I returned and proved my worth as we made our peace, and I *again* became his son.

It had taken nearly a decade before he finally accepted that I had married differently to his hopes. Though reconciliation came through my daughter. Before he died, my father acceded, although with some reluctance to the inevitable, and gave his blessing that, through the succession of my daughter and eventually her children, the ancestral thread would not die. And so, under her mantle, it would continue – albeit somewhat differently.

However, after he said that, it suddenly occurred to me what would happen to the other family clans of China in the years to come, if the male line one day became defunct through not producing male progeny and having *only daughters* left to continue the line? *How would the thread survive?* Would this filial obsession which was predominantly male-orientated that had united the Chinese people in China in the past, and which had moulded them into the cohesive nation they are today eventually die out? It was a question that I foolishly failed to ask my father in the last weeks of his life.

But then it also occurred to me that, knowing the angst-ridden type of person my father was in life, I quickly came to realise that the family ties of blood that drove him all his life would be just as pervading after his death, as it was when he was alive. Its tentacles would never let me go. And this I feared, would be his enduring legacy for me.

And again on reflection, I have to say, that despite my being utterly convinced that my father before he died, had *never* come to terms with his position in life after spending sixty odd years away from his homeland through living in the West, he at least knew his role as head of the family and that of the wider clan. It was that, and the responsibility thereto that kept him motivated and alive. However, the conflict he must have felt about feeling a foreigner in this country all his life in spite of his swearing allegiance to the Crown when he was naturalised, must have been assuaged by his continuing contact with China, even though he was passionately at odds with its current politics and its authoritarian society.

When coming to the end of his life and embarking on the autumn of mine, I began to rationalise my position in Western society, which as a child growing up Britain, once caused me some confusion, and more often than not, episodic despondency. Also, by not being truly accepted in Chinese society when often mocked as akin to a "banana" (white inside, but yellow on the outside!), and having previously been ignored and frequently, rejected by English society, I had often felt that I had fallen between two worlds with the inevitable conflict in the quest for identity. At the time, it was of no consolation to me to realise that millions of others in a similar situation must have suffered the same.

Nonetheless it was long ago, that when asked by others to which country would my loyalties lie if it came down to the wire; the answer then – as now, was quite simple. Because right from the outset, I felt that I would lay down my life for Britain, being the country of my birth and one that had reared and educated me, and one which had provided a refuge as well as succour and opportunities for my father and his family.

As an adult, now seamlessly integrated with an English family and with English friends, my role in society has now been defined. I have to admit that my life and my obligations are to the West. It was the one which has given me its values as well as its cultural and ethical ideals. But however, it was my father who had instilled in me discipline, family duty and the art of survival and a work ethic. Between the two cultures, regardless of their empirical differences, I am grateful that it has put many things into proper perspective and has given me my place in the world.

But then, on returning to my father's final warning about the family thread during which his eyes widened as if suddenly reborn, he reminded me that the thread came at a price.

'It is saddled with obligation, both financial and filial.[107] *It is an everlasting duty to the family clan that is irreversible.* For you must always continue to send money back home to China, like millions of other Overseas Chinese families, to enable the blood family to rise again. The belly of the hungry dragon must always be fed!'

No sooner had he uttered this, I swallowed hard, thinking that his former homeland – with the few remaining relatives had little actual or practical relevance to me. And what is more, I didn't think for one single moment that if I, and millions like me stopped sending money back to China, their economy (which in my father's time had benefited from such overseas largesse) would *suddenly* collapse like a pack of cards. And furthermore, there was a crucial question that remained unanswered; what would happen if the Chinese dragon, now having woken up, got out of control? What were the dangers? Then inevitably, others like me will reasonably ask, can the flame of the dragon be tamed? Who will curb the excesses of the behemoth once the lid of Pandora's box is finally opened?

These are the burning questions that must sit on many peoples' lips; not least on mine.

Nevertheless, I nodded gently to my father, just to mollify him in the last moments of his life.

'You must never forget that this family obligation is the glue that has kept the generations together from the beginning of time. But, my son, if nothing else, it will revere your *past,* it can define your *present,* and, more than that, shape your *future!'*

As that gradually sank in, for a long time afterwards, I often wondered if Raymond had heard about what had happened and all that it implied for him and his family. Perhaps his ancestral quest continues to this very day. There again, perhaps one day he, or even his son, will turn

---

107 Filial obligation, an integral part of which is that the eldest son of the surviving male line not only continues to support his remaining siblings in China, but also to maintain the family home financially; ultimately boosting the country's coffers and sustaining the nation.

up to challenge the thread. If that time comes, there will be little my daughter, I, or anyone else for that matter, could do about it. We will just have to patiently wait and see.

And furthermore, I began to realise that with the death of my father everything in our lives had come full circle. Nevertheless, for me there were still so many questions during my father's lifetime that remain unanswered: because right from the start, the quest for who I am, what I am and what he made me into, has focused my life and those of the future generation under the scrutiny of the microscope. Moreover, it will enable all of us one day to reassess our position, not only in the context of the family, but also in the wider society.[108]

The quest goes on...

---

108 On the 29th January, 1979, full diplomatic relations were re-established between China and the US. Jimmy Carter – the thirty-ninth President of the United States, signed a new and historic accord with Chairman Deng Xiaoping recognising The People's Republic of China. The Chinese Government imposed a one-child policy in order to curb population growth. This inadvertently led to the wholesale rejection and abandonment of baby daughters. On the 11th February 1979, the Iranian Revolution toppled the monarchy leading to the establishment of an Islamic Republic.

EPILOGUE

O NCE THE LID OF China's Pandora's box had been prised open, the behemoth of the country's industrial might and political clout was unleashed upon the world. The speed of its transformation in just a few decades, from a semi-feudal state to a highly industrialised economy with implications for the rest of the industrialised nations, was truly remarkable. Not unexpectedly, many international commentators cautioned about the political and socio-economic ramifications if the country or its ruling C.C.P (Chinese Communist Party) allowed its tentacles of influence to spread unchecked throughout the world.

Demographically in 1918, the population of China stood at four hundred million. Within one hundred years it grew by a further one billion, despite revolution, wars, social upheaval, famine, disease, the death of millions of its indigenous population, and the country's one-child policy of 1979.

It is well recognised that millions of Overseas Chinese individuals, such as Kwong Chun Ji and others, have sent money back to China over the decades to sustain their families. Arguably, these substantial funds of foreign aid have contributed in part to the growth of the Chinese economy, supplementing and underpinning China's remarkable economic revolution of today. This is not to deny that the bedrock of the Chinese nation has always been the constancy, strength and unity of the family clans, on which the foundation of their success has been built. But the role played and the sacrifices made by the Overseas Chinese families such as Kwong Chun Ji's should not be understated or ignored. History will eventually be the best judge of that.

1980

Completing over two thousand hours of independent clinical practice, Francis passed his finals at the BSO. He only wished that his father had been alive to see it. Joining the ranks of professions inhabited by his siblings, nephews and nieces in the fields of legal, medical, scientific and education, as well as in design, technology, local government and business etc., he wondered if his father would have been proud of the family's achievements, but failed to say so before he died.

Registered with the GCRO (General Council and Register of Osteopaths), Francis acted as a locum and associate in established practices in Epping and Hertfordshire, as well as starting his own practice in West London. Becoming known as the first Chinese osteopath in Britain was a mixed blessing. He was sometimes expected to perform miracles. Some patients asked him to treat their pet animals. Others even requested consultation and treatment over the phone for a third party.

His broad patient list encompassed those from council estates, students, members of government, world-renowned music artists, and performers from stage and screen from Pinewood to Hollywood, as well as royalty et al. He worked to remain grounded and avoid neglecting the average person in the street in order to help all patients across the different racial, social and religious spectra of society (*Omnes Aequales*, or 'All Equal'); remembering all too well the cautionary tale of Stephen Ward, the society osteopath of the '60s who fell from grace with tragic consequences.

Alarming incidents tested his professionalism; for example when armed bodyguards swept through his premises in Bayswater before an Arab Princess was allowed to enter. Or when he had to calmly deal with a murder suspect, or an alleged rapist on remand, as the police waited patiently outside. Or the runaway heiress, or a notorious arms dealer hunted by the press. His patients – famous, infamous or otherwise – and other bizarre episodes belong to the past, and to another story that will never be told.

In September, Francis and his family visited Sicily. Francis and Caroline's daughter Tanya caused a stir. The locals thought that they had adopted one of their own. With her sculptured face, her light olive complexion and her dark brown hair and large, oval eyes, they called her '*Bella Italiana*'. They couldn't see much Chinese in her. It was often wondered what his parents or even his ancestors would have made of it.

1981

Former Hollywood actor and Governor of California Ronald Reagan became the fortieth President of the United States. Relations between the US and UK blossomed.

Gwut Kwai Moy (born the 7th July 1883), mother of Choi Lin Kwong, died in Brunei aged ninety-eight.

1982

The ten-week Falklands War took place between the 2nd April and the 14th June. The British dependent territories of the Falkland Islands and South Georgia were invaded by Argentina, whereupon the Prime Minister Margaret Thatcher mobilised a task force from the UK to expel the invaders.

1983

No sooner had the restoration of Francis's family home been completed than disaster struck. The whole terrace cracked and subsided because of the previous long, dry summers drying out the underlying clay on which it was built with the oak and lime trees in the adjoining gardens sucking up the moisture, and with the Victorian foundations being extremely shallow. After years of wrangling with insurance, in 1988 the house was restored using new, deep, concrete foundations.

1984

Mikhail Gorbachev, a rising and moderate member of the USSR's Politburo, met UK Prime Minister Margaret Thatcher, who famously declared that they could do business together. He was credited with bringing about the end of the Cold War.

On the 19th December, Mrs Thatcher visited Beijing to meet Premier Zhao Ziyang and Chairman Deng Xiaoping. A historic Joint Declaration was signed to agree the transfer of the sovereignty of Hong Kong and its surrounding territories back to China.

1989

On the 15th April, Hu Yaobang, the ousted former General Secretary of the Chinese Communist Party, died aged seventy-three. The next day, thousands of students gathered in Tiananmen Square, Beijing to mourn him, as he had become the figurehead of reform. A week later, thousands more civilians joined in the occupation. On the 19th May, Premier Li Peng imposed martial law. Wholesale protest escalated. On the 4th June, troops with tanks and armed vehicles fired on the protesters, resulting in a death toll of hundreds, if not thousands. Thousands were arrested and dozens executed for their part in the demonstration.

On the tenth anniversary of his father's death, Francis attended his father's grave to 'sweep the headstone' according to tradition. At his uncle's behest, he was persuaded to taste the ripe, blood-red cherries growing next to his father's grave. "Nephew, it will give you strength and longevity, as your father's ashes will have fed that tree." Horrified at the idea at first, Francis reconciled this with the carbon-and-nitrogen cycle of nature from his days in the biology lessons at school.

1990

Mikhail Gorbachev, as President of the Soviet Union, promised Perestroika and Glasnost – a period of change and "openness".

On the 11th February, President F. W. de Klerk of South Africa released Nelson Mandela from prison after twenty-seven years of incarceration.

In August, the Gulf War began. President George H. W. Bush's Operation Desert Shield saw a US-Arab allied invasion of Iraq to drive out Saddam Hussein's forces from Kuwait.

In October, Germany unified after the fall of the Berlin Wall in 1989, triggering the collapse of communism in other Eastern European regimes such as Poland, Yugoslavia, Czechoslovakia, Hungary, Romania and Albania.

In November, In Britain, John Major replaced Margaret Thatcher as leader of the Conservative Party and Prime Minister.

1991

In May, Jiang Qing (Madame Mao) died in Beijing, having committed suicide by hanging following years of incarceration for treason.

In June, Mary Stuart, after laying the foundation stone marking the Performance Centre and Mary Stuart Hall in Hinchingbrooke, suddenly died of a stroke at the age of eighty-six, following the summer ball. At the memorial service, hundreds including family, friends, former pupils, colleagues and members of the Montagu family came to honour this unique and modest lady. Her ashes were laid in the rose garden of Hinchingbrooke, one of her favourite places of retreat when she lived there with the family.

In December 1991, Gorbachev resigned as leader of Soviet Russia, but remained a vocal critic of his successors, Boris Yeltsin, and later Vladimir Putin.

1992

The Chinese leader, Chairman Deng Xiaoping, retired. He had held the reins of power since 1978 following the deaths of Mao and Zhou Enlai in '76.

Between 1992 and 1995, international armed conflict took place in Bosnia and Herzegovina involving Bosnians, Serbs and Croats. The USA and European Economic Community formally recognised the Republic of Bosnia and Herzegovina.

1992–1994

Francis was co-opted to serve on a multidisciplinary education team at his old alma mater, the BSO, to fundraise at the new school in Trafalgar Square, assist with student recruitment, give talks to GPs and schools, appear on local radio, etc. Helping to modify the degree qualification and the extended pathway of study, he also acted as a Regional Careers Officer for prospective students and mentored new graduates in practice. In 1993, the Osteopaths Act was passed in Parliament, cementing the legal status of osteopathy alongside orthodox medical therapies such as physiotherapy, dentistry etc.

1994

Nelson Mandela was elected as the first black President of South Africa, abolishing apartheid and social injustice. He served until 1999 and died in December 2013.

1995

Francis's mother, Choi Lin Kwong (formerly Chow Mou Lan), was taken by his brother and sister to visit her homeland in China.

For I will return, and return I must,
To be recalled by fresh seasons when born again.

It was sixty-odd years since, as a young girl, she had left her ancestral village of Shek Tsui Chun near Taishan to marry Kwong Chun Ji by proxy in his family home across the mountains in Dai Dune Chun. Her family home in the Chow village was falling into disrepair, but her surviving sister, Chow Choi Ping, three years younger than her, had remained. In 1937, due to increasing blindness, she hadn't been able to flee with their mother and younger brother Chow Kit Siang to Borneo to escape the Japanese invasion.

When Choi Lin was reunited with her blind sister, they couldn't recognise each other. Choi Ping placed her hands over her sister's face to try to remember, but simply could not. When they had last met as teenagers in 1935, Choi Ping was just fifteen and Choi Lin was eighteen. A lifetime had passed since then. Choi Lin had (after initial hardship) grown up in relative comfort in a different culture in a different country, whereas her sister had remained in relative poverty in ancient rural China. The sisters felt that they had nothing in common now as old women. They met as strangers and parted as strangers. Choi Lin left Choi Ping some money for her son and daughter, for she never saw her sister again.

Weep no more for me, you sheltering willows,
For no telltale signs have been left of childhood there...

1997

On the 19th February, Deng Xiaoping died. His legacy of individualism and incentives had made their mark in the socio-economic revolution of China.

On the 1st July, the historic handover of the colony of Hong Kong back to Chinese sovereignty took place in the presence of the UK's Labour Prime Minister Tony Blair and Prince Charles. The returned territories, comprising Hong Kong Island and the Kowloon Peninsula, had been ceded to Britain in 1842 and 1860 respectively following the Opium Wars, along with the New Territories, which were leased for ninety-nine years from 1898.

Francis's great-grandfather Biu Shu, having mourned China's ignominious defeat in the Opium Wars and the ceding of the territories of Hong Kong, would now be celebrating in his grave. After many centuries, the slumbering dragon of China had suddenly woken up with a vengeance, marching on inexorably to exert its growing economic power and political influence on the world.

Choi Lin died on the 27th October following duodenal cancer. She was laid to rest in the same cemetery as her husband, in a simple ceremony. On her deathbed, she instructed her ten children to stick together after she had gone. She chose her own outfit and shoes she wanted to be buried in. Keeping a promise, her family brought her body home to keep vigil before the burial.

1998–1999

Civil war was waged in Kosovo due to ethnic unrest between Albanians, Serbians and the forces of the Federal Republic of Yugoslavia, previously kept under control by Tito in the former Communist State of Yugoslavia. NATO bombing of Serbia brought an end to the war.

1998

After a succession of high profile and outrageous attacks on the British Mainland and in Northern Ireland with a tragic loss of life, on the 10th April, the historic Good Friday Agreement was struck between the British and Irish governments and major political parties of Northern Ireland regarding how the latter should be governed. This led to a ceasefire between the Provisional IRA and the Unionist paramilitary.

1999

Uncle Kwong Chun Tileng's wife, Fong, tragically died of motor neurone disease. The family was devastated.

2001

In January 2001, the Republican George W. Bush took over the US Presidency from the Democrat Bill Clinton and declared a War on Terror.

On the 11th September, a terror attack by al-Qaeda involving hijacked airliners targeted and destroyed the Twin Towers of the World Trade Centre in New York.

A joint US-British invasion of Afghanistan was mounted to dismantle al-Qaeda and remove the Taliban from power started with US-led bombing in October. (From 1979 to 1992, Soviet troops had previously invaded Afghanistan to prop up the Communist government.)

Francis visited his uncle on Merseyside. He was asked to keep the Kwong-Gong name alive, and to keep in touch with his uncle's children. He was reminded of a promise he had made in 1970 that he would visit the ancestral home and pay his respects to his grandparents and ancestors. Visiting Liverpool, he tried to locate where the family had once lived. He also tried to find out where Ruby had lived close to where his parents had first set up home in 1936. Due to the bombing and then the rebuilding, there were no traces left of the property or the street. His childhood memories had disappeared, like the buildings which had gone before, disintegrating into the ether of the past in a puff of smoke.

2002

Francis's daughter Tanya, having earned her PGCE and qualified as a schoolteacher following a degree at art school, was offered a good job at an excellent primary school in Teddington, and moved to live in Hampton. Dedicated and popular, she mounted art exhibitions each year and also helped to bring Art Funding to the school.

2003

Uncle Chun Tileng died. He had been Kwong Chun Ji's last surviving brother. The siblings who had remained in Taishan, and their husbands and wives, had all long since died. The children had left the village and scattered far and wide, mainly to the States, to seek a better life.

US President George W. Bush, supported by British Prime Minister Tony Blair, led forces from the US, the UK, Australia and Poland in a combined invasion of Iraq – the War on Terror. Saddam Hussein was captured and subsequently executed on the 30th December 2006, having been sentenced to death by the Iraqi court for the 1982 mass killing of Iraqi Shi'as.

Will Chen died of complications from diabetes, followed shortly by Francis's sister Eileen, who died of cancer having nursed her husband for over a year. It is believed that stress had much to do with Eileen's demise. The family was bereft.

2005

On the 6th August, Tanya married Simon Young in a large family wedding at Hinchingbrooke. Caroline made her wedding dress, which was much admired. Francis proudly gave his daughter away.

In November, Angela Merkel elected Chancellor of Germany.

2009

Barack Obama, leader of the Democrats, was elected as the forty-fourth President of the USA. He ended the Iraq War and was credited with the elimination of Osama Bin Laden.

2010

David Cameron, leader of the Conservatives, formed a coalition UK government with Nick Clegg of the Liberal Democrats.

In November, China was admitted into the G20 group of industrialised world economies.

2011

After thirty-odd years, Francis retired from practice, selling the business premises and the house in Notting Hill. The practice was absorbed into a large, established practice in Notting Hill Gate, where his associate also practised part time. It was an end to an era. Having managed the practice for many years with the help of part-time receptionists, Caroline was now able to retire, and dedicate herself to her new passion: designing and making jewellery.

In January, Francis made a momentous journey to China with his brother Alan. They visited their father's old home and paid their respects at the shrine therein. When they tried to climb the Mountain of Ancient Spirits to reach the ancestral tombs, they failed to reach their grandparents' graves at the top due to the overgrowth of the bamboo and undergrowth. Gutted and disappointed, they paid their respects from halfway up and bowed to the peak from a distance.

Across the valley, they visited their mother's old house, where she was born. Now becoming derelict, it had for years been looked after by a caretaker in the village and used for storing herbs and straw from the summer harvest. The caretaker was paid for by their mother's younger brother, Kit Siang in Borneo, but on his death, his children, who had emigrated to Canada, began to lose interest in the house, which was kept as a monument – but to them, an unnecessary and expensive white elephant.

Slogans daubed on the front wall of the house during the Cultural Revolution were still visible. When Francis and Alan asked the few remaining Chows what they meant, they were rather evasive and embarrassed. It appeared that Choi Lin's father (the village gambler, the late Chow Yuk Yiu, born there in 1882), having died years ago, had left the house to one of his daughters, Choi Ping. The remaining villagers rather resented this, as it was one of the largest properties facing the open paddy fields to the south. Choi Ping had left to live with her husband in his village nearby, leaving the family house empty for years to serve as a shrine. Contrary to common perception, after all this time, resentment still ran deep if one family was better off than another. This situation intensified after the Communist Revolution of 1949.

In October, Colonel Muammar Gaddafi, deposed leader of Libya, was captured and killed.

2012

Xi Jinping emerged to become a major power in China. Deng Xiaoping's collective leadership of the country was abandoned on Xi's becoming Chinese President in March 2013. China's political and economic influence on the international stage continues to spread.

2014

On the 3rd February, a cold, sunny winter's day, Francis's twin granddaughters were born. Saskia Jessie Sui-Lan Young, fair and green-eyed, was born first; Alexia Sasha Mei-Ling Young, with dark hair and hazel eyes, second. Life for their parents and grandparents changed forever. Helping to bring them up from the day they were born, was an exhausting though undeniable joy. Francis had often said to his daughter Tanya that he believed that she had waited for her parents to retire before having children in order to secure their help. Since then, he admitted to growing greyer, older and certainly poorer! 'Just wait until they get older,' warned their good friends and neighbours the Jurens, from considerable experience.

2015

Tamara Tipping, Caroline's surrogate godmother, died at the age of nearly 102, but was able to see and hold the young twins first, stating with pride that there were one hundred years between them and her.

2016

The UK's Conservative government called a referendum on the country's membership of the European Union. The country voted to leave by a majority of fifty-two per cent to forty-eight. David Cameron resigned, to be replaced by Theresa May as Prime Minister.

2017

The Republican, Donald J. Trump was elected the forty-fifth President of the USA.

Emmanuel Macron elected President of France.

2018

On one sun-filled summer day, as Francis was playing with his grandchildren in the garden, Alexia Mei-Ling ('Beautiful Tinkling

Bell'), dimple-faced like a china doll, suddenly asked in a serious voice, 'Grampy, did *you* have a daddy? *Did you have a grampy? Where did they come from?* Where is this place called China? Is it on the other side of the moon?'

Then her fair-headed sister, Sassy Sui-Lan ('Delicate/Daring Flower'), wide-eyed and beaming, joined in. Puzzled, she asked, 'Grampy… are they dead? *Were they Chinese, like you? But why isn't Granny?'*

Now, it is sometimes said that out of the mouths of babes, wisdom often flows… or something along those lines. You see, on many occasions, before bedtime Francis had regaled the twins with stories of his Chinese childhood and of the past. They especially loved the stories about his early days, particularly Christmas. And, with his family being so poor and having so many children, he told them that there were no toys, just a tangerine and a sweet in his Christmas stocking.

So what could he say in reply to their probing questions?

'One day, my dear children, when you grow older you will read about what happened to your grandpa, as well as your great-grandpa many years ago. And then perhaps you will gradually understand about everything that took place, not only here, but in China, and how it affected the lives of each, and every one of us – whether for better or for worse.'

ACKNOWLEDGEMENTS

I AM INDEBTED TO the following, for not only their critical input for making this book work, but also for their comradeship along the journey. The list is rather onerous: but however, here goes. Firstly, my wife Caroline, my first and sternest critic, who kept the faith; Judith and Robin Anderson, Sylvia and Bohdan Juren, as well as the Hon Alix Lawrence, Audrey German, Edna Crone, Ian Stuart and Judy Wilkinson for wading through the various drafts with an enthusiastic smile. As well as to Peter Riding, MBE for suggesting rejuggling of the foreword etc., and for generously registering the title at webserve.co.uk. To Simon Holder, fellow scribe and TV director for his perceptive suggestions regarding the historical backstory in Ancient China. My thanks to the late Rayne Kruger, erudite author, historian and bon viveur for sharing with me when we met many moons ago, about the definitive history of China which he subsequently published by Wiley. To Benjamin and Mia Gong for their recollections of the Cultural Revolution in 1966 and to Mike Jackman for his stunning images of China. And to the Tams, James Gong, Gong Yiu Gnai (Chicago) for their research on the Gong/Kwong Ancestry from 1679. Thanks to Kat Chow (San Francisco) for his research on the Chow Ancestry.

To W. Eric for teaching me the computer. And to complete the "Ying Yang" circle, to Anna Siulen Green granddaughter of Kwong Chun Ji for the cover design and for her invaluable input.

Furthermore, to Mao Wen Biao, international artist supreme and expert on antiquities from the Han dynasty to the Ming. As well as to Denis Buckingham for his professional advice to a debut novice such as me. My immense thanks to the magnificent and professional editorial and marketing team at The Book Guild; Jeremy Thompson FRSA, Lauren Bailey, Philippa Iliffe, Rosie Lowe, Hayley Russell and Jack Wedgbury et al., for their expertise and enduring faith in my work. A huge debt of gratitude to Jane Conway-Gordon, eminent literary agent, for her unselfish help and unstinting encouragement to get the book to see the light of day, even though she was unable to represent me.

Finally, to all those protagonists – alive or deceased, be they part of the eponymous clan of the Kwong/Gong or not, whose ghosts and spirits – whether benign or malevolent – still haunt the pages of this book when allowing me to tell their story...and without whom, it would never have been written.

Francis G. Kwong

1. Map of locality of Kwong (Gong) Ancestral Village, Dai Dune Chun (Deep Waters Village) NE of Duanfen Town – 15 miles south of Taishan City and 75 miles from Canton in Guangdong province. Also, image of the last Emperor of China, Hsiang-t'ung, the Boy Emperor, P'u-i.
2. Painting of the signing of The Treaty of Nanking, 29th August 1842 ending the 1st Opium War between Britain and China on HMS Cornwallis with Queen Victoria's envoy Sir Henry Pottinger and representatives, Qiying and Yilibu of the Daoguang Emperor from the Qing Court. Image of painting reproduced with kind permission of the renowned artist, Mao Wenbiao (and colleague

Yang Keshan). Displayed in The Sea Battle Museum, Humen, Guangdung. Author's gt-gt-gt grandfather, Wah Oi (1821-1878) whilst in Canton, witnessed the battles on the Pearl River from 1839 onwards.

3. Dai Dune Chun, Taishan, Guangdung. Author's late father, Kwong Chun Ji's ancestral home, where his forebears were born, lived, and died. All the immediate Kwong (Gong) family dwellings line the waterfront.
4. Ancestral Shrine in Kwong Chun Ji's ancestral home – latter empty for decades.
5. Fung Ting Sei (1878-1947) mother of Kwong Chun Ji. Photo, circa 1930's.
6. Kwong Chun Ji, 1898-1979 (Author's father) aged 23, Liverpool, England.
7. Bust of Gong Yuk Fong – prosperous kinsman, died in USA, dedicated in the Kwong-Gong Clan Shrine where the Ancestral clan records are held in the hall of the Ancient Zhuji Lane Museum, Guangdung.
8. Kwong Chun Ji's set of traditional, travel-implements for his journey from Taishan, and thence onwards to Canton and Hong Kong on 10th January 1921. Knives and silver-tipped chopsticks for hunting and for self-protection from bandits.
9. Abacus belonging to Kwong Chun Ji, displayed with his remaining banknote in Chinese Yuan, which shows image of Dr Sun Yat-sen; the founder of the first Chinese Republic in 1912. Also shown is Kwong Chun Ji's registration certificate at the Aliens Registration Office on arrival in Liverpool, 2nd April 1921.
10. Moy Gwut Kwai (1883-1981) mother of Chow Mou Lan – author's mother, (later called Kwong Choi Lin, when married). Photo Taishan, 1935.
11. Kwong Choi Lin, 1916-1997. Formerly Chow Mou Lan, aged 18. Photo Taishan, 1934.
12. Shek Tsui Chun (Beak Slate Village) Taishan. Chow Ancestral home and birthplace of Chow Mou Lan.

13. Ancient Watch Tower at entrance to Shek Tsui Chun. Used in the past as lookout for bandits from the mountains and pirates from the sea nearby.

14. Gravestone of unknown kinsman on roadside adjacent to the Watch Tower in Shek Tsui Chun. Inscription: "May the Spirits – Immortals, guard over here."

15. Chow Mou Lan's (aged 18) document with permission from consulate in Canton 1935 to travel to join her husband in UK. Permission also from the Bureau of Public Safety, Taishan. Image showing her last five yuan from the Bank of China with her remaining possessions and some medicine for her sea journey.

16. (a) Kong Ying's (aka Kwong Chun Ji) Certificate of Registration issued by The Republic of China Bureau, Liverpool 26/1/1937. (b) Ying Toy Ling Wong (aka Choi Lin Kwong) registered at Aliens Registration Office, Liverpool, 12th May 1936. Issued with National Registration Identity card – surrendering Chinese Passport – issued Canton 8/5/1935. (Wong=Gong. Kwangtung=Guangdung. Toi-Shan=Taishan)

17. Chow Mou Lan's father's younger brother Chow See Ngen. Circa 1929, Sarawak, Malaya. Has Chow facial features.

18. Low Jin Chien, wife of Chow See Ngen (Chow Mou Lan's uncle) Malaya 1929.

19. Duanfen: 5 miles SW of Dai Dune Chun (Kwong-Gong village). Once a prosperous market town in the '20's & '30's where the Kwong families and others traded in the square. Sai Mee (Author's cousin) lived here with family during the Civil War between Chiang Kai-shek's Nationalist forces and Mao Tse-tung. Sai Mee fled to Canton after the earthquake in 1936. Town now deserted and used for film locations.

20. Post wedding photo of Kwong family – siblings in Taishan 1936, following Chow Mou Lan's marriage in Taishan to Kwong Chun Ji (in Liverpool) by proxy. Top row standing, UK photo inserted of the groom, 2nd from right. Bride, seated 2nd right next to Kwong mother-in-law, Fung Ting Sei.

21. Invasion of China by Japan 1937. Author's Chow grandmother, Moy Gwut Kwai then fled with her son Kit Siang and her brother-in-law to Malaya. Painting – "Battle of Lugou Bridge" (Marco Polo) by kind permission of the artist Mao Wenbiao and team. The wall mural is displayed at the Sino/Japanese War Museum in Beijing.

22. Author's parents and their first born: Liverpool 1937.

23. Author as a toddler, flanked by older sisters, Liverpool 1942-43.

24. Ancestral Mountain of Ancient Spirits – burial ground of Kwong-Gong ancestors.

25. Chow Choi Ping (1912-1999) sister of Chow Choi Lin (Author's mother) with family, Taishan 1944.

26. Chow Choi Ching (1898-1989) older sister of Chow Choi Lin with impoverished family, Taishan 1948 during the defeat of Chiang Kai-shek forces by Mao Tse-tung. In 1949, Mao declared "The People's Republic of China".

27. Image of the Dragon from the Dragon Dance at Chinese New Year, February 1965 at author's family restaurant, Birmingham. Photo reproduced by kind permission of Sunday Mercury.

28. Author and Caroline (Stuart) at Chinese New Year's dinner dance.

29. Author's cousin: Taishan paddy fields, 1966.

30. August 1966 during height of The Cultural Revolution: Taishan. Author's father, Kwong Chun Ji visiting his siblings and spouses in his ancestral home after forty-five years away – accompanied by daughter Rose and son Sam.

31. "Swinging London in the Sixties". Carolyne Stuart Fashion Group invited to hold a fashion show – presented on stage to audience of international stars of film, stage, producers, directors, consular representatives, press etc., at Incontri Festival del Cinema during the British/Italian Film Festival held in Sorrento, Italy, September 1967. Caroline on extreme right.

32. Author's daughter, Tanya Mayling aged two with her grandfather, "Goong-Goong" in family home, Edgbaston, Birmingham, 1974, bringing about a reconciliation between author and father.

33. Author's father's three brothers and wives in Dai Dune Chun, Taishan, circa 1977.

34. An offering of food and wine with eulogies at the grave of Kwong Chun Yee's wife (author's aunt) to provide for her journey to the afterlife to meet her ancestors. Laid to rest on the mountain of Ancestral Spirits.

35. Dai Dune Chun – traditional ancestral village feast hosted by author's cousin on his visit to author's father's homeland circa 1990.

36. Kwong Choi Lin, formerly Chow Mou Lan meeting her younger sister Chow Choi Ping (1912-1999) at ancestral home Shek Tsui Chun, Taishan in 1995 for the first time after leaving China sixty years previously.

37. Lake of Tranquillity in Taishan. (photos of this and others from Taishan by courtesy of Mike Jackman).

38. Stone Rubbing from gravestone of author's late mother (1916-1997) stating that she was married to a member of the Kwong-Gong clan. (photo and stone rubbing courtesy of Edna Crone)

ABOUT THE AUTHOR

After thirty years in osteopathic practice in Bayswater, Francis G. Kwong retired to devote time to his other passion – writing. Living in london, married to a fashion designer with their young granddaughters not too faraway – who constantly keep him on his toes with so many probing questions about the mysterious circumstances hitherto of his family background and the complicated ways of the world!